ADOPTING AGILE ACROSS BORDERS

A GUIDE TO NAVIGATING CULTURAL COMPLEXITY IN AGILE TEAMS AND ORGANIZATIONS

Glaudia Califano
David Spinks

Apress®

Adopting Agile Across Borders: A Guide to Navigating Cultural Complexity in Agile Teams and Organizations

Glaudia Califano
Milton Keynes, UK

David Spinks
Milton Keynes, UK

ISBN-13 (pbk): 978-1-4842-6947-3
https://doi.org/10.1007/978-1-4842-6948-0

ISBN-13 (electronic): 978-1-4842-6948-0

Copyright © 2021 by Glaudia Califano, David Spinks

This work is subject to copyright. All rights are reserved by the Publisher, whether the whole or part of the material is concerned, specifically the rights of translation, reprinting, reuse of illustrations, recitation, broadcasting, reproduction on microfilms or in any other physical way, and transmission or information storage and retrieval, electronic adaptation, computer software, or by similar or dissimilar methodology now known or hereafter developed.

Trademarked names, logos, and images may appear in this book. Rather than use a trademark symbol with every occurrence of a trademarked name, logo, or image we use the names, logos, and images only in an editorial fashion and to the benefit of the trademark owner, with no intention of infringement of the trademark.

The use in this publication of trade names, trademarks, service marks, and similar terms, even if they are not identified as such, is not to be taken as an expression of opinion as to whether or not they are subject to proprietary rights.

While the advice and information in this book are believed to be true and accurate at the date of publication, neither the authors nor the editors nor the publisher can accept any legal responsibility for any errors or omissions that may be made. The publisher makes no warranty, express or implied, with respect to the material contained herein.

Managing Director, Apress Media LLC: Welmoed Spahr
Acquisitions Editor: Shiva Ramachandran
Development Editor: Matthew Moodie
Coordinating Editor: Nancy Chen

Cover designed by eStudioCalamar

Distributed to the book trade worldwide by Springer Science+Business Media New York, 1 New York Plaza, New York, NY 100043. Phone 1-800-SPRINGER, fax (201) 348-4505, e-mail orders-ny@springer-sbm.com, or visit www.springeronline.com. Apress Media, LLC is a California LLC and the sole member (owner) is Springer Science + Business Media Finance Inc (SSBM Finance Inc). SSBM Finance Inc is a **Delaware** corporation.

For information on translations, please e-mail booktranslations@springernature.com; for reprint, paperback, or audio rights, please e-mail bookpermissions@springernature.com.

Apress titles may be purchased in bulk for academic, corporate, or promotional use. eBook versions and licenses are also available for most titles. For more information, reference our Print and eBook Bulk Sales web page at http://www.apress.com/bulk-sales.

Any source code or other supplementary material referenced by the author in this book is available to readers on GitHub via the book's product page, located at www.apress.com/9781484269473. For more detailed information, please visit http://www.apress.com/source-code.

Printed on acid-free paper

For everyone who helped us on our journey

Contents

About the Authors vii

Forewords ix

Acknowledgments xiii

Introduction xv

Part I: Getting Started 1

Chapter 1: Welcome to the World 3

Part II: South America 23

Chapter 2: Argentina 25

Chapter 3: Chile 41

Chapter 4: Colombia 57

Chapter 5: Uruguay 79

Part III: Asia 97

Chapter 6: India 99

Chapter 7: Indonesia 121

Chapter 8: Japan 141

Chapter 9: The Philippines 169

Chapter 10: Singapore 183

Chapter 11: United Arab Emirates (Dubai) 217

Part IV: Europe 223

Chapter 12: Germany 225

Chapter 13: The Netherlands 249

Chapter 14: Poland 267

Chapter 15: United Kingdom 283

Contents

Part V: Africa. 303

Chapter 16: South Africa 305

Chapter 17: West Africa 319

Part VI: Survival Guide. 333

Chapter 18: The State of the World. 335

Chapter 19: Unite and Move Forward. 363

Index 395

About the Authors

Glaudia Califano and **David Spinks** are Agile practitioners, coaches, and trainers at Red Tangerine.

Glaudia Califano was aware of cultural differences from an early age, growing up in the Netherlands with a Dutch mother and Italian father. She moved to the United Kingdom in 2005 and started working with Agile teams. Her experience has spanned roles in testing, business analysis, Product Ownership, Scrum Master, and Agile and Lean coaching.

David Spinks has been in the IT industry since 2001, starting in software development and team leadership roles. In 2012 his journey into Agile started when he became a Scrum Master, and he has worked with dozens of Agile teams since then.

Together, Glaudia and David have experience that spans the fields of ecommerce, higher education, finance, insurance, and social housing. They are active members of the Agile community, regularly attending meetups and speaking at conferences around the world. They are active bloggers on their company website at www.redtangerine.org/blog.

Glaudia and David are both Scrum.org Professional Scrum Trainers (PST), Accredited Kanban Trainers (AKT) with Kanban University, and ICAgile Authorized Instructors.

Glaudia is also a trainer of the Cross Cultural Competence course which was developed based on the work of Richard D. Lewis. She is also a facilitator of Lego® Serious Play®.

About the Authors

David enjoys the outdoors and spending quality time with his guitar. Glaudia enjoys karaoke and ice-cream. They are both keen travelers and enjoy taking part in volunteering projects.

For more information, visit `www.redtangerine.org`.

Or find us on:

Twitter at @RedTangerineOrg

Instagram at `www.instagram.com/redtangerineorg/`

Facebook at `www.facebook.com/RedTangerineOrg/`

Forewords

I'm writing the foreword for this book in times when travel has been restricted and countries face great uncertainty due to the COVID-19 outbreak. It is hard to imagine now how fortunate Glaudia and David were to travel the world when it was safer, and I trust that one day in the future, when you read their book, all this sorrow will be gone for good.

Glaudia and David embarked on a quest that took them from continent to continent to prove that culture matters when we talk about Agile teams. I've found their book immensely valuable because, as a product of different cultures myself, I have always thought that culture plays an essential role in Agile.

I'm a South American, and I'm very fortunate to have met some of the people whose stories are being told in this book. I haven't yet met Eugenio – the Chilean accountant-turned-developer – whose story is personal, moving, and full of encouragement.

The 10Pines' story, about a company with no managers, is living proof that there is such a thing that we all, as agilists, can look to as an exemplar of an Agile company. I am fortunate to be friends with Federico Zuppa, and I visited 10Pines on multiple occasions, so I can say it is true that this happy place does exist.

This book presents a very accurate description of differences and commonalities in South American cultures. I had never looked at it this way before, and thanks to Glaudia and David, I now have a better appreciation of what I've intuitively learned from my interaction with people from my neighboring countries.

This book is making another great contribution to the Agile community at large: it proves that Agile does exist in all corners of the world. In cognitive science there's a bias for only trusting the things that we see. Well, Glaudia and David are our eyes, and through them we can see now that Agile has expanded, and has taken different forms as local cultures mold it.

I missed the opportunity to meet Glaudia and David in person. We were supposed to meet in Buenos Aires where I was also supposed to participate in the event that the Agile Alliance co-organized. Back then, I was an Agile Alliance Board Member, and a very distracted one too – I missed my plane for the first time in my career all because I was at the wrong gate: a demonstration of cultural behavior, as we Bolivians don't normally read monitors.

| x | *Forewords*

Marco Polo explored the Silk Road several centuries ago and mankind benefited from his discoveries that opened the doors for trading and knowledge transfer. I'm anticipating that Glaudia and David's book will similarly help to create bridges among Agile practitioners globally.

—Juan Banda, Agile trainer, speaker, coach, and Community Developer for Latam at Agile Alliance (April 2020)

Many of the readers of this book know Japan as an eastern country and are familiar with its unique cultures/subcultures like Zen, Tea ceremonies, Manga, Karaoke, Sushi, and other fun parts. People who visit Japan become fans of Japanese culture … but don't know deeply about our psychological dynamics.

Glaudia and David visited our company in Fukui city (a four-hour train-ride from Tokyo) in addition to other companies in Tokyo (from small software firms to large enterprises), and also attended conferences to gather insights and actually feel the high-context psychological dynamics of the Japanese people. With their affable personalities, they met, talked with, and got to know many people described in this book. This is the secret of this book; their experience makes it so vivid, lively, and full of wonders, and it comes from their curiosity not only for theory but also for people.

—Kenji Hiranabe, Agile software development practitioner, book writer/translator, and winner of the 2008 Gordon Pask Award Recipient for contributions to Agile practice (May 2020)

Agile adoption isn't just about organizational transformation. It's a cultural change; and cultures tend to be disposed to change – or not – in unusual ways.

Many organizations will create grand statements around their values and how they would like to work, but here we can read about organizations which truly live them, like the Argentinian companies putting the well-being of their people above short-term profit; the Columbian retailer prepared to abandon traditional hierarchy; the Indonesians using phrases like, "The higher up you go, the more you serve"; the Scrum Teams of Singapore demonstrating true respect through listening, patience, and gentle but forthright language.

Agile transformations are assisted or constrained by a multitude of aspects: existing systems and processes, organizational structure, commitments both internal and external, and above all the culture. David and Glaudia have combed the world, bringing us not only authentic stories from around the globe, but also a portfolio of ways of looking at the problem differently and of things we might try – things that those of us in Western countries with our focus on individual excellence might not have considered. Even when aspects of culture provide a poor match for Agile, the stories invite us to reflect on whether our own organizations might be similarly suffering.

Forewords | xi

The stories also contain the patterns that all Agile transformations have in common: the need for change, the difficulty of communication and dependence on each other, the surprise and delight or despair of discovery. In the detail of the stories I found a rich treasure trove of practices, many of which were new to me: the result of human beings everywhere trying to solve the same problems as the clients I work with here at home.

Dave Snowden, creator of the Cynefin framework, once described humans to me. "We're not *Homo Sapiens*," he said. "We're *Homo Narrans*. We're storytelling apes."

The stories are told well and worth reading.

—Liz Keogh, Independant consultant,
Lean/Agile coach and trainer (Nov 2020)

Acknowledgments

We owe a tremendous debt of gratitude to all of those people that contributed to this book, not only for the time spent writing contributions (in almost all cases in a second language) but also for the hospitality shown in agreeing to meet and discuss Agile with two people contacting them out of the blue.

So an enormous thanks goes out to the community that shaped this book and the shared learning behind it.

Thank you to all of those that contributed their stories to this book: Gonzalo Barbitta, Pawel Brodzinski, Kiran Divakaran, Nono Donsa, Mercy George-Igbafe, Rez Hardityia, Daniel Hauck, Martin Hinshelwood, Sander Hoogendoorn, Liliana Zuluaga Hoyos, Elroy Jumpertz, Ilona Kędracka, David Leach, Donna Marie Lee, Eugenio Lopez, Yves Lin, Pranshu Mahajan, Sylvain Mahe, Antony Marsh, Hugo Messer, Khwezi Mputa, Futhi Mthupha, Resmi Murali, Renato Otaiza, Andrés Peñailillo, Sebastián Pérez Jiménez, Jon Pheasey, Juan Rucks, Ziryan Salayi, Suwilo Simwanza, Boris Steiner, Sarah Toogood, Rhea-Luz R. Valbuena, Claudia Liliana Toscano Vargas, Jean-Baptiste Vasseur, Danny F. Wuysang, Federico Zuppa.

Thanks to those that encouraged all of the writers above. A special shout-out to Alfredo Feibig and Liliana Reyes of Continuum; Emilio Gutter and Jorge Silva of 10Pines; Chandra Setiadji, Joanna Zhan, and Jean Ho Min of Titansoft; Regiane Folter, Gustavo Clemente, and Waldemar Lopez of UrulT.

Thanks to those whom we spoke to that inspired many of the stories and discussions in this book: Ernesto "Boogie" C. Boydon, Kenji Hiranabe, Satomi Joba, Martin Kearns, Mirko Kleiner, Dominic Krimmer, Yoshinobu Okazawa, Avi Schneier, Tushar Somaiya, Leo Soto, JJ Sutherland, Keisuke Wada, Ferdinan Wirawan. We also owe a tremendous debt of gratitude to the many more people that we met on our journey that helped to shape our perception of their cultures and Agile in their part of the world.

Thanks to all of those who reviewed and shared their feedback: Lavaneesh Gautam, Kenji Hiranabe, Liz Keogh, Antony Marsh, Satomi Joba, Edo Suryo Pamungkas, Boris Steiner.

Many thanks to Tasia Graham and Haroon Khalil for creating some truly beautiful illustrations for the book.

Acknowledgments

Thanks to Michael Gates for reviewing the book and helping to ensure we did justice to presenting the great work of Richard D. Lewis. Thank you to Ric Lewis and Blaga Mileva for reviewing our descriptions of the CultureActive platform.

Thank you to Dr. Douglas Robinson of Université Paris-Est Marne-la-Vallée (LISIS) and University College London (UCL) for guiding us as we carried out the research for the book.

An extra special thanks to Edith Wortley for helping us to properly organize and arrange the content of the book. We may never have finished it without you.

Thank you to the team at Apress – Shiva Ramachandran, Matthew Moodie, Nancy Chen, and Rita Fernando – for their support, patience, and guidance. You helped us to create a better book and make it a reality.

And a massive thank you to Juan Banda, Kenji Hiranabe, and Liz Keogh for writing the forewords to the book.

We really were – and continue to be – blown away by the courage, commitment, focus, openness, and respect shown by the global Agile community.

Introduction

Let us start by what this book *is not*. This is not a text on any of the Agile frameworks. There are many great resources out there to gain an understanding on the basics, such as the Scrum Guide (`https://scrumguides.org/`) and the Agile Alliance (`www.agilealliance.org/`) website.

This is not a guidebook to tell you how to be Agile. We would be suspicious of any book that claimed this! While Agile methods are beautifully simple, their adoption and implementation are anything but easy.

While we used cultural models to hypothesize behaviors of Agile teams in different parts of the world, this book is not presented as a scientific study of cultural impact on Agile adoption.

Instead, this book is intended as a source of inspiration for team members, Agile Coaches, Scrum Masters, Product Owners, stakeholders, managers in Agile organizations, or anybody working in an Agile setting. This book includes a collection of contributions from people across the world. Our aim is to share real-world tips and techniques that other people are using in the global community. We hope it will give you valuable insights into the opportunities and challenges Agile ways of working can bring within and across different cultures.

Perhaps one of the stories resonates with you. Perhaps someone from another part of the world has faced similar challenges that you are facing and their story will inspire you. Maybe your team spans the globe, contains many different first languages, values, and cultural behaviors, and you are curious to learn how to avoid team misunderstandings. Our hope is that this book will encourage the global community to share experiences for greater continuous improvement in all of us.

As with everything we do in life, with any decision we take, any choice that we make, context is king. We believe that no two people, no two teams, and no two organizations are alike. There are always going to be differences in our core values and behaviors as people, be it due to our upbringing, nationality, political beliefs, socioeconomic background, or any combination of the many other factors that make up our culture. Understanding the impact that these differences have on Agile adoption was the inspiration that took us on the journey that led to this book.

Introduction

While we present some of our observations and thoughts on Agile adoption around the world, this book is not about us. The community of writers that have contributed to the book are who should be center stage. This book is our thank you to all of the people that we met, the individuals and organizations that took the time to meet with us to discuss and demonstrate their adoptions of Agile. The global community generously shared their Agile stories with us; now we want to share these experiences with the rest of the world.

—Glaudia Califano and David Spinks

Using the Book

Part 1 of this book serves as an introduction where we discuss culture and why we think its impact on Agile adoption warrants attention. We explore cultural models and explain their basis for the research that led to this book.

In parts 2, 3, 4, and 5 we focus on countries in the continents of South America, Asia, Europe, and Africa in turn. In each chapter by country, we include the following sections:

History: A brief history on the country with events relevant to Agile adoption today

Insights: Our main discoveries about Agile and teams in the country

Getting On and Around: Our tips if working in, or with people from, the country

Each chapter is interspersed with stories, case studies, and tips from Agile practitioners.

In part 6, we conclude with discussions on the culture shift needed to adopt Agile, the motivation for adopting Agile, and dealing with diversity in our teams and organizations.

Takeaway In these sections, we share general takeaways discovered during our journey that we have added to our own toolbox as Agile practitioners. We hope that you can add some of these takeaways to your own toolbox.

This book includes numerous contributions from Agile practitioners around the world. The following demonstrates the format of such contributions:

> Contributions in the forms of stories, case studies, and tips from Agile practitioners around the world are presented as text blocks like this.

PART I

Getting Started

There is more that unites us than divides us.

—Mauricio Macri, President of Argentina from 2015 to 2019

CHAPTER 1

Welcome to the World

Thousands of teams from all around the world have been building products using iterative and incremental methods since the 1990s, with traces of the techniques going back as far as 1957.[1] A number of lightweight frameworks such as RAD, DSDM, XP, and Scrum subsequently emerged, and in 2001, 17 pioneering figures in the field of software development met at a resort in Snowbird, Utah, to discuss these development methods. Out of this historical meeting, this group published the *Manifesto for Agile Software Development*:[2]

> Individuals and interactions over processes and tools
>
> Working software over comprehensive documentation
>
> Customer collaboration over contract negotiation
>
> Responding to change over following a plan

---

[1] Weinberg, G as quoted in Larman & Basili. (2003). www.semanticscholar.org/paper/Iterative-and-incremental-developments.-a-brief-Larman-Basili/058f712a7dd173dd0eb6ece7388bd9cdd6f77d67 (pp. 47–56 *"We were doing incremental development as early as 1957, in Los Angeles, under the direction of Bernie Dimsdale at IBM's Service Bureau Corporation"*)

[2] Beck et al. (2001). *Manifesto for Agile Software Development.* https://agilemanifesto.org/

© Glaudia Califano, David Spinks 2021
G. Califano and D. Spinks, *Adopting Agile Across Borders,*
https://doi.org/10.1007/978-1-4842-6948-0_1

Chapter 1 | Welcome to the World

Seldom can a group of statements have had such a profound impact on the way we work and tackle problems as those of the Agile Manifesto. The pace of change in recent years has increased exponentially, and innovation spans just about every industry. The way we communicate, how we shop, the means of doing business, when, how, and where we work have all changed and continue to evolve. We are in the midst of a revolution, and Agile is at the core of it. And the revolution is global.

As visualized in Figure 1-1, the 4 values of the Agile Manifesto, together with the accompanying 12 Agile Principles[3] are embodied in what seems like an unlimited number of practices, tools, and processes. Without the mindset at the core though, the tools and practices achieve little.

---

[3]Beck et al. (2001). *Principles behind the Agile Manifesto.* https://agilemanifesto.org/principles.html

Adopting Agile Across Borders

Figure 1-1. The Agile Mindset is described and defined by the Manifesto for Agile Software Development and implemented by an almost unlimited number of practices (image courtesy of Haroon Khalil)

Adopting Agile then requires a shift in mindset. But what impact do national, organizational, and people's own values have on their interpretation of the values and principles of the Agile Manifesto? And how does this affect attempts at the implementation of Agile practices?

Chapter I | Welcome to the World

Given the range of circumstances in politics, economics, and history across the world, can it really be true that ideas emanating from Japan and developed in the United States can find acceptance and be effective in all cultures of the world? National cultures have evolved over hundreds of years with different values, behaviors, and belief systems. How and why has Agile gained such popularity in such a relatively short space of time? Are some cultures naturally more suited to adopting an Agile mindset than others? What impact do national cultural behaviors have on the adoption of Scrum and Agile methods as they have spread across the world? Is there such a thing as an "Agile culture" that results from adopting Agile ways of working? Or will aspects of national cultural behaviors prevail?

These are the questions that prompted us to begin the journey that led to this book.

Top Ten Experiences

The Heart of Agile Teams at 10Pines (Page 32)

10Pines, a software development services company in Buenos Aires, Argentina, is also known as "la empresas sin jefes" (translated as "the company without managers"). But how does this work in reality? In this story, 10Pines partner, Federico Zuppa, discusses how 10Pines has a focus on creating great teams by putting people at the heart of everything they do.

Glad, Mad, Sad in Japan (Page 157)

Agile Coach Donna Marie Lee, originally from the Philippines, tells a story that demonstrates that techniques that work in one culture will not necessarily work well in another culture, as she recounts her first use of the Glad, Mad, Sad retrospective technique while working with a team in Japan.

Building Trust, Learning, and Understanding: An Agile Approach to Project Discovery (Page 81)

There is much uncertainty at the start of a project, and the Agile mindset of emphasizing discovery and learning can be disconcerting to those of a more traditional mindset that seek the comfort of defined budget, scope, and timelines upfront. Juan Rucks, Senior UX-UI Designer at UruIT, a software development company in Uruguay, explains the Agile approach to project discovery from his and UruIT's own experience.

Agile Organizations Set the Stage for Emergent Leaders (Page 252)

Elroy Jumpertz is a professional software engineer who started his career in his home country of the Netherlands. Elroy discusses his experience of working in companies that support individual's development, and he shares what he believes are the traits of organizations and leaders that enable leadership to emerge naturally.

Finding My Voice (Page 308)

Courage is one of the Scrum values and a core behavior for any Agile adoption. What courage means is going to be context specific. In her story, Khwezi Mputa, a Certified Scrum Master/Agile PM Practitioner in South Africa, talks about the courage needed to stand up and speak out.

Trust: The Basic Building Block of Agile Teams (Page 115)

While building trust is fundamental to any Agile team, in some cultures it takes on extra significance. In his story, Pranshu Mahajan, a Scrum Master with many years of experience working in a number of different roles in India, shares his experience of trust as the basic building block of Agile teams in India.

Forced Fun (Page 278)

Knowledge work requires people to work collaboratively, thus the need to build trust and understanding. But every team is different and some team-building activities or meeting formats that work for one team may backfire when used with other teams. Ilona Kędracka, based in Poland and Product Owner/Blogger at Poczatkujaca.pl, shares her own experiences and examples that she has encountered when teams become frustrated or uncomfortable with activities designed to be "fun," but have questionable practical value.

Accelerating the Supply Chain of Goods and Services (Page 62)

Agile ways of working are not just for software development. Claudia Liliana Toscano Vargas, Agile Coach at EPM, tells the story of the approach she used to help non-IT teams implement Agile ways of working. Claudia shows us how

Chapter 1 | Welcome to the World

she presented the adoption of Agile as an experiment to be tried with hypotheses on expected improvements that could be tested. Taking this approach, she gained buy-in from the teams involved and was able to work with them to achieve success.

Retrospectives at Every Level (Page 51)

Change should be embraced across the whole of an organization. The retrospective is an effective tool to instigate change, yet many organizations see retrospectives as something that is done at the team level. Renato Otaiza, Agile Practitioner and Coach at Scotiabank, shares his experiences on the importance and effectiveness of running retrospectives at every level of an organization.

Learntor: On a Mission to Create a Level Playing Field for Africa (Page 325)

Mercy George-Igbafe has the mantra, "True greatness is not in being great but in the ability to make others great." She shares her personal story where, despite a life of adversity, she achieved a university education and went on to found Learntor, a digital consultancy and training company based in Nigeria that is on a mission to create a level playing field for women and youths in Africa.

Understanding Culture

As the world becomes more globalized, with increases in mobility and migration, finding tools to help us to understand each other is becoming evermore important. This is as relevant in the field of software development as in any other industry, where many teams have members distributed across different geographical locations and are made up of people from a number of different nationalities.

When Cultures Collide

Our nationality, region, language, religion, generation, political persuasion, economic status, gender, profession, and many other factors feed into what makes up our culture as an individual. Some of these various factors are illustrated in Figure 1-2.

Figure 1-2. Some of the many layers of culture (image courtesy of Haroon Khalil)

Many of the misunderstandings that we have with others arise when we have a clash of culture. One of the greatest sources of frustration is as a result of us being unable to relate to one another culturally. We know that good collaboration is a critical part of the success of Agile teams. If we are to have highly performing teams and organizations, the ability for individuals to

Chapter 1 | Welcome to the World

interact successfully is essential. Awareness of each other culturally is key to this, both within teams and across our organizations as a whole.

The different components of culture also make up the layers that influence a corporate culture. After all, companies are made up of individuals. However, often companies have, over time, built up a unique identity and their own corporate culture, diluting the influence of some of the layers of individuals' own cultural aspects. This may not always be the case though. For example, there are significantly different perceptions of organizational wrongdoing, such as sharing passwords or piracy of software, depending on where you come from.

A study focusing on South Korea[4] found that different cultures may have differing influences on the occurrence of misuse, and differing perceptions on the seriousness of it. In the United States, organizational rules are communicated, with IT security and HR departments "laying down the law" of what is permissible. However, the opinion of people in someone's social network has a higher influence in South Korea. Here, embarrassment and the loss of face caused by the discovery of misuse is of greater concern than any organizational policy. At the same time, in a South Korean organization, someone seeing others committing an offence and getting away with it is far more likely to commit the same offence. In this example, the importance of harmony in South Korea is so important that actions that appear unethical to people in the United States are fully justified to people in South Korea if they prevent conflict and discord.

It is these alternative perspectives that are based on individual values and may be at odds with one another that lead to tensions, arguments, disengagement, apathy, and many other negative behaviors to the detriment of collaboration. We would argue that clashes of culture are at the very heart of most of what holds teams and organizations from fulfilling their potential.

At the Risk of Stereotyping

German people are efficient. The Swiss are always on time. Dutch people are direct. Americans are loud. Japanese are shy and quiet. Italians are always late.

These are sweeping, stereotypical statements. Surely we should not group people in this way because not all people categorized into groups based on nationality are going to behave in the same way. We need to be careful with our generalizations about culture. As we have discussed, culture consists of so many layers and we as humans are all complex individuals.

---

[4]Hovav, A. (2017). *How Espoused Culture Influences Misuse Intention: A Micro-Institutional Theory Perspective* https://scholarspace.manoa.hawaii.edu/handle/10125/41891

Adopting Agile Across Borders

When we began our research into the topic of Agile adoption in different countries, we found a number of generic statements from often frustrated Agile practitioners who expressed doubts that the society they worked in would be able to adapt to more Agile ways of working. Commentary came up such as if Agile would ever really be embraced in a country where traditional hierarchical structures and the behavior of top down control are embedded. Or where the cultural preference is for keeping harmony above having transparency.

When we started our journey to find out how culture impacts Agile adoption around the world, we quickly found ourselves treading a minefield. There were the dangers of stereotyping by national cultural categorizations and having biased opinions. Identifying groups based on data can be a useful starting point though. When developing a product, be it software or some other product, using archetypes or personas is a common way for designers to build empathy with the potential users of their product. Empathizing with our customers is an essential aspect of Design Thinking.[5] However, this is just a starting point. Our knowledge and understanding of user behavior develops over time, allowing adaptation to their needs as we learn more about them.

Just like designers looking for a starting point to build empathy with their users, models can be part of the starting point to build empathy with people from other cultures.

Such a model would help us for the purpose of social study, something that would give us a cultural reference point and allow us to form hypotheses on how Agile may be used in different contexts. This could then form a basis for analysis and testing of our hypotheses to validate or invalidate the assumptions we and our fellow Agile practitioners make.

Categorizing Behaviors

Given the number of factors that could feed into a definition of culture, any attempt at categorization could result in the creation of dozens, if not hundreds of different groups. The dilemma is clear: for a cultural model to be useful, it needs to provide a level of succinctness while also taking into account the complexity involved. There have been many attempts by sociologists in creating cultural models. We give a brief introduction and overview of two such models that have emerged: the Hofstede Model and the Lewis Model.

---

[5]*What is Design Thinking?* Interaction Design Foundation. www.interaction-design. org/literature/article/what-is-design-thinking-and-why-is-it-so-popular

The Hofstede Model

The Hofstede Model[6] is one of the best-known models of national cultural behavior in the workplace. It is based on the extensive research carried out by Professor Geert Hofstede, Gert Jan Hofstede, Michael Minkov, and their research teams. The research was carried out between 1967 and 1973 and was based on data returned from some 116,000 questionnaires from more than 70 countries.

The model consists of six "dimensions," each dimension representing a preference for one state of being over another. Countries are given a quantitative score indicating the degree to which their culture exhibits these preferences.

The six dimensions consist of:

- Power distance index

  The power distance index is a measure of how less powerful people in society accept and expect power to be distributed unevenly. High power distance index scores indicate a higher acceptance of hierarchical structures.

- Individualism vs. collectivism

  Individualism refers to loosely knit societies where individuals look after themselves. Collectivism refers to societies where groups will unquestioningly look after each other.

- Masculinity vs. femininity

  Masculine societies display characteristics such as rewarding achievement, heroism, and assertiveness, whereas feminine societies show characteristics such as cooperation, modesty, and valuing a good quality of life.

- Uncertainty avoidance

  Uncertainty avoidance is a measure of how much a society is comfortable with uncertainty and ambiguity. It includes the extent to which the society believes in trying to control the future.

---

[6]Hofstede, G. (2001). *Culture's consequences: Comparing values, behaviors, institutions, and organizations across nations.* Thousand Oaks, CA: Sage Publications. ISBN-13: 978-0803973244

Adopting Agile Across Borders

- Long-term avoidance vs. short-term normative orientation

    This category refers to a societal preference to established, long-term traditions as opposed to its willingness and pragmatism toward change. Low scores indicate a preference to adhere to traditions and a suspicion of change, while high scores indicate societies that take a pragmatic approach to prepare well for the future.

- Indulgence vs. restraint

    This is a measure of the level of restraint that a society shows in gratifying their needs and desires.

There is an online tool at www.hofstede-insights.com/product/compare-countries/ where different countries can be compared according to the Hofstede dimensions. For example, Figure 1-3 shows comparison between Argentina, Japan, and the United Kingdom.

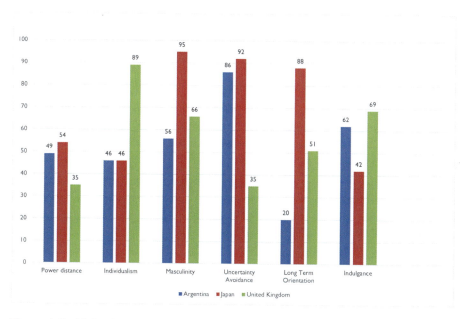

Figure 1-3. Hofstede six-dimensions comparison between Argentina, Japan, and the United Kingdom

Chapter 1 | Welcome to the World

According to the Hofstede Model, we can see that the United Kingdom has a much more individualistic culture compared to those of Argentina and Japan. The United Kingdom scores much lower in the category of uncertainty avoidance, meaning people are comfortable with ambiguity and relaxed with the fact that the future can never be known. Japanese culture is very long-term oriented, while Argentina's is at the other end of the scale, with the United Kingdom in the middle. Japanese culture stands out as being very masculine yet significantly less indulgent in nature by the Hofstede Model's dimensions definitions, when compared to the other two countries.

The Hofstede Model has been used across the world for a multitude of purposes. It has been used in industry for management and leadership strategies. It has been applied as a basis for further research and study. We found that there has been some study of the effect of culture on Agile adoption using the Hofstede Model as a guide. These include those by Bas Vodde,[7] co-creator of the LeSS framework, and Jaakko Palokangas[8] for his MSc thesis at the University of Tampere.

The Lewis Model

The Lewis Model was developed by Richard D. Lewis who published his work in the book *When Cultures Collide: Leading Across Cultures.*[9] This book has now sold more than 1 million copies worldwide and it has been published in 15 different languages.

Lewis formed his cultural categorizations from data gathered during visits to 135 countries. He spent significant time working in more than 20 of these countries. Data gathered from 50,000 leaders and executives on residential courses and 150,000 online questionnaires across 68 countries provided the basis for the Lewis Model.

Lewis considered other cross-cultural experts were at risk of creating confusion due to the number and types of categorizations that were being produced. Lewis wanted to go beyond academic thinking and supply business leaders with a simple model to avoid this confusion, provide succinctness, and something for use in the real world.

---

[7]Vodde, B. (2012). *Scrum doesn't work in China.* www.odd-e.com/material/2012/10_scrum_barcelona/culture.pdf

[8]Palokangas, J. (2013). *Agile Around the World – How Agile Values Are Interpreted in National Cultures?* https://trepo.tuni.fi/bitstream/handle/10024/94766/gradu07165.pdf

[9]Lewis, R.D. (2006). *When Cultures Collide: Leading Across Cultures* (Third Edition). First published in hardback by Nicholas Brealey Publishing in 1996. ISBN-13: 978-1-904838-02-9

Adopting Agile Across Borders

The model created by Lewis is based not on nationality, but on observations of human *behavior*. Lewis came to the conclusion that humans can be divided into three clearly distinct categories. This was an extension of established expert opinion at the time which included the definitions of "monochronic" and "polychronic" of the Northern and Southern hemispheres that had not recognized a very different set of behaviors in Asia. Lewis named his three categories as *Linear-active*, *Multi-active*, and *Reactive*. Lewis identifies a common set of behaviors for each of his three categories. These can be seen in Table 1-1.

Table 1-1. Common behaviors of Linear-active, Multi-active, and Reactive categories (copyright Richard D. Lewis)

Linear-active	Multi-active	Reactive
Talks half the time	Talks most of the time	Listens most of the time
Does one thing at a time	Does several things at once	Reacts to partner's action
Plans ahead step by step	Plans grand outline only	Looks at general principles
Polite but direct	Emotional	Polite, indirect
Partly conceals feelings	Displays feelings	Conceals feelings
Confronts with logic	Confronts emotionally	Never confronts
Dislikes losing face	Has good excuses	Must not lose face
Rarely interrupts	Often interrupts	Doesn't interrupt
Job-orientated	People-orientated	Very people-orientated
Uses mainly facts	Feelings before facts	Statements are promises
Truth before diplomacy	Flexible truth	Diplomacy over truth
Sometimes impatient	Impatient	Patient
Limited body language	Unlimited body language	Subtle body language
Respects officialdom	Seeks out key person	Uses connections
Separates the social and professional	Interweaves the social and professional	Connects the social and professional

The Linear-active category contains behaviors that include a tendency for logical thinking and argument. Linear-active behavior consists of making detailed, step-by-step plans. It includes respect for job-titles, officialdom, and hierarchy. Social and professional lives are largely kept separate.

The Multi-active category includes traits of being highly verbally communicative, showing a comfort, and often even a preference, for multitasking. Openly displaying feelings and emotions is evident in confrontations.

Chapter 1 | Welcome to the World

In the Reactive category, behaviors include attentive listening, politeness, and the tendency not to display feelings and emotions in public. It is very important to avoid both confrontation and losing face.

While each category is distinct, it is important to note that no one set of behaviors will apply in its entirety to a particular individual or group. While one category's behaviors may dominate in an individual or group, there will always be elements of behaviors from the other two categories present. It is a question of which behaviors are dominant and by how much.

The behaviors in each of the categories should not be judged as either positive or negative. Making such a judgment is an indication of our own cultural bias. An individual that exhibits the behavior of being flexible with the truth may be doing so because they value diplomacy over candor given the context of their situation and environment they are in.

Based on his research, Lewis created a visualization of his three categories, plotting nations onto the model depending on how strongly the behaviors of each category are exhibited. This is shown in Figure 1-4.

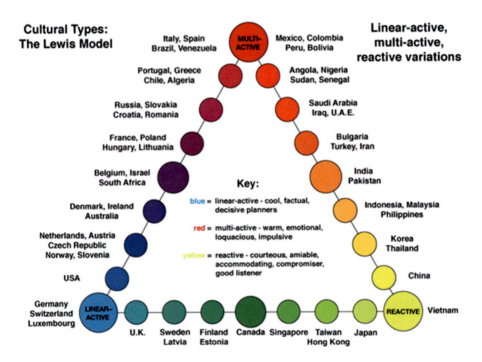

Figure 1-4. The Lewis Model Triangle (copyright Richard D. Lewis www.crossculture.com/)

**Adopting Agile Across Borders** | 17

The model is relative. There is no intention of giving an impression of scale along the triangle's axis. It is important to understand that countries may be at similar points on the triangle but not necessarily for the same reasons — there could be different behaviors from a category that are more evident in each case. Within each country, we would expect variation in behavior. For example, some people in Reactive Vietnam may well have more Multi-active traits relative to other Vietnamese people; however, in comparison to other parts of the world, they still remain relatively more Reactive.

Lewis found that there is a link between individuals' behaviors and their area of study and profession. Examples of this from those that were surveyed are as follows: engineers and accountants — whose professions require attention to detail for example — have more Linear-active traits; teachers, sales people, and those in people-centered professions demonstrate more Multi-active behaviors; while lawyers and doctors who we expect to be good listeners, for example, are inclined to be more Reactive. Those that are in a profession that is a poor fit with their culture as an individual are likely to be unhappy and poorly performing.

Lewis's research shows that a high proportion of Linear-active behavior is seen in Northern Europe such as in the United Kingdom, Germany, Switzerland, as well as in North America. Scandinavian countries exhibit some Reactive traits along with Linear-active ones. Multi-active behavior is encountered more in the Latino nations in South America such as Argentina, Chile, and Colombia. Parts of Africa and Arab countries also display Multi-active tendencies. Societies dominated by Reactive behaviors are in countries that are mainly in Asia such as Vietnam, Japan, China, Indonesia, and the Philippines, for example. The model is periodically updated and positions are not fixed — countries can move on the scale as time passes and events affect societal behavior.

The model is not intended to stereotype nations, it is rather just a starting point to explore how we can develop our intercultural sensitivity.

The CultureActive platform tests according to the LMR Model, based on the Linear-active, Multi-active, and Reactive categories originally derived from Lewis' writing. Through the completion of a self-assessment, it can be determined where on the scale an individual's personal cultural profile would fit. The results then enable groups of people to compare their results and to start building cultural awareness and understanding of one another.

Oftentimes, we are compelled to hire people who are similar to us, those that share the same values, mindset, and behaviors. However, and especially in Agile teams, a greater diversity of people will bring with it a wider spectrum of backgrounds, ideas, thinking styles, and perspectives, enabling wider creativity and greater innovation. A team of people that are mostly Linear-active in their behaviors are likely to be working efficiently but could also be

Chapter 1 | Welcome to the World

held back by a lack of innovation and problem solving. A team of people who are mostly Multi-active in their behaviors may generate lots of ideas but could lack focus. A group of people who display mostly Reactive behaviors may have harmonious teams, but struggle to come to a decision. So in order to have highly performing teams, a conscious effort can be made to build a team with a mix of styles and behaviors using the Lewis Model and the LMR test.

Having a team with a wide range of diversity is likely to cause conflicts. However, by understanding cultural behaviors, making them transparent to all, and coming up with strategies to integrate and leverage those differences, teams can reach higher levels of performance and innovation.

A Basis for Study: Cultural Behaviors and the Agile Values

The Lewis Model in particular gives us a good basis for forming hypotheses of behavior for Agile teams in different parts of the world. In Lewis' work, we could see that some of the main aspects of his research focused on areas such as communication, values, behaviors, leadership styles, negotiation techniques, and team dynamics. These are certainly areas of interest when it comes to forming highly performing Agile teams.

We felt that the simplicity, the focus on workplace behaviors, and the purely qualitative nature of the Lewis Model would be a better guide for us in studying Agile teams than other models, including the Hofstede Model. We also believed that no studies had taken place using the Lewis Model as a reference to the way Agile teams and organizations work in practice.

Lewis' discussions on behaviors could help us to understand what was behind our observations and anecdotal evidence from the field. Given many of the behaviors as described in each of the cultural categories in the Lewis Model could be seen to work well or impede Agile ways of working, our intention was to test the hypothesis that culture impacts how Agile is adopted. Our method was to gather qualitative evidence directly from Agile practitioners around the world.

With this hypothesis in mind, we began our journey.

On the Road

Driven by our passion for Agile and understanding culture, we began travelling the world in January 2018, talking to Agile teams and visiting organizations adopting Agile methods to see how Agile was being used in different parts of the world. We wanted to talk with people using Agile in their day-to-day working lives and observe teams in action. The aim was to understand how

Adopting Agile Across Borders

culture impacts Agile adoption around the world by looking beyond the mechanics of any particular Agile method. Figure 1-5 is an illustration that captures a flavor of our journey and just some of the countries that we visited.

Figure 1-5. A flavor of our journey and some of the countries that we visited (image courtesy of Tasia Graham)

We gathered qualitative data of Agile teams in their workplaces, with a mixture of direct observation and anecdotal evidence provided by expert Agile practitioners working locally in the field. The intention was never to restrict our observations to teams and organizations that were using any particular Agile method. Rather, we were interested in meeting teams and Agile practitioners with experience with the implementation of any Agile method such as Scrum, XP, Kanban, or any hybrid approach.

Chapter 1 | Welcome to the World

Given the breadth of the undertaking, we focused our attention on visiting countries at different extremes of the Lewis Model triangle, though took advantage of opportunities to go to companies and talk to practitioners when they arose. This was often through referrals as the Agile community supported our journey. No restriction was made regarding the size or type of company that we visited, though we acknowledge the large part that the size, structure, and corporate culture of a company has on the workplace culture. However, it could be argued that our collective individual cultures and national culture influences company culture, and that the company culture is a reflection of the culture of the people within it.

From our own experiences as Agile practitioners and countless anecdotes of the difficulty that many organizations have in adopting Agile methods, especially those transitioning from traditional ways of working, we narrowed our observations to organizations that had been practicing some form of Agile for at least one year. This was to ensure that there was some level of understanding and experience of Agile in those that we were speaking to.

Regardless of experience or specific practice, it was more important to us that we saw certain fundamental characteristics in the ways of working to consider teams or organizations "Agile."

Incremental and iterative. Instead of a "big bang" single release of a completed product, Agile methods evolve products in iterations, releasing successive working product increments regularly.

Self-organization. The people doing the work are the most suited to decide how the work should be carried out and are trusted to do so. No one tells those doing the work how to perform the work.

Collaboration. Silos of knowledge and specializations are broken down. People on the team help and support each other. Collaboration reaches out beyond the people doing the work, with regular communication between the delivery team and stakeholders, fostering a sense of collective responsibility for success or failure.

Sustainable. Environments are such that people are motivated, and have been given the tools and support to be able to carry out their work to the best of their abilities.

Continuous improvement. Teams and organizations strive to get better at what they do through regular reflection and experimentation.

Transparency. Problems impeding progress are surfaced so that they can be eliminated. Knowledge is shared, a common language is used and the current state of work items are visible.

Inspection. Frequent inspection of various artifacts are performed for understanding of progress toward the fulfillment of goals.

Adaptation. Direction is based on feedback, understanding changing customer needs, market and environmental conditions.

Empirical. Empirical processes operate under the assumption that the future is unknowable. Progress is made through forming hypotheses and validating them through the scientific method. Empiricism is founded on transparency, inspection, and adaptation.

We travelled across South America, Asia, and Europe. Along the way, we met many people working in a country that they had moved to, and so were able to provide a unique perspective as a foreigner. We had numerous conference calls with people in parts of the world that were not on our itinerary. This includes calls with people in Africa, which we were unable to travel to due to the coronavirus pandemic.

Though the Agile movement originated from the software development industry, Agile methods can suitably be applied anywhere. We found instances of Agile practices being applied in a retail company, in marketing departments, in the registration and student administration processes of a university, and many other places outside of software development.

This book is not intended to be a presentation of a scientific study. Instead, we wanted to produce something that was accessible. We have presented the four values of the Manifesto for Agile Software Development together with the categories and behaviors of the Lewis Model to encourage you to think about the underlying influences of both people's culture as well as the Agile mindset that may be affecting the practices, techniques, and stories shared by the community with us in the sections that follow.

As we shall see, we both learned so much during our study; we learned many new Agile tools and techniques that we would come to apply in our own work as Agile practitioners. But above all else, we heard many great stories of Agile in action.

What follows includes stories, case studies, tips, tricks, and the best of the experiences from those we met on our journey.

PART

II

South America

Curiosity, courage, and compassion. Resilience, resourcefulness, and respect. These and other cultural traits that we saw in South America would seem to be well aligned with the values of the Agile Manifesto.

With nearshoring being an attractive alternative to offshoring, South America has seen a rise in software development teams in the last decade. This in turn has given rise to the widespread adoption of Agile software development.

The very first Latin-American conference on Agile development – Ágiles Latinoamérica – took place in 2008 in Argentina, with 900 Agile enthusiasts attending. Since then Ágiles Latinoamérica has been a recurring event, and interest has been steadily growing across South and Central America. Local meetups are popular places to share, collaborate, and learn. A sense of community is strong.

Agile techniques could be the factor to unlock the continent's full potential. An ability for generating grand ideas in spades and a focus on building relationships – whether with colleague or customer – ahead of the formality of contracts and plans may appear chaotic to those from Europe or the United States. But if the South Americans can meet their partners halfway, if those same partners can loosen their ties a little and collaborate through conversation, then great things could happen for both sides.

If they can shrug off the decades of political and economic uncertainty, perhaps, in the age of Agile, South America will become the next big thing.

Agile Community Events and Meetups

- Ágiles Latinoamérica: www.agiles.org/
- Agile Women: https://agile-women.org/

CHAPTER

2

Argentina

The streets of Buenos Aires hint at a people that are stylish, courageous, and cool. Warm and welcoming, fun and friendly, gregarious, passionate, and proud. The Argentine socially oriented psyche, where empathy for people, intolerance for wasteful activities, and an innate willingness to experiment would seem to be a perfect cultural fit for Agile.

Our visits and conversations in the Agile community in Argentina revealed some of the most experimental and forward-thinking Agile people anywhere in the world. Self-organization and people-orientation, both in the teams we met and in the consideration for the end customer above all else was central to the Argentine mindset.

Perhaps it is only the country's complicated political backstory and economic volatility that is holding Buenos Aires back from being the Silicon Valley of the South Americas.

History

Before the Inca Empire added the territory in the Northwest in the 15th century, the population of what is now Argentina was made up of a number of thinly dispersed indigenous groups. Many of these had been conquered by the Mapuche who had spread into Central and Southern regions from present day Chile. The Incas control of a large region of Western South America lasted until their fall at the hands of the Spanish in the 16th century.

© Glaudia Califano, David Spinks 2021
G. Califano and D. Spinks, *Adopting Agile Across Borders*,
https://doi.org/10.1007/978-1-4842-6948-0_2

Chapter 2 | *Argentina*

Early Spanish explorations focused on the false premise that there were vast quantities of silver to be discovered – Spanish explorer Sebastian Cabot gave the river Rio de Plata (river of silver) its name, and part of the area was called *argentum*, Latin for silver. Once it was found there was little mineral wealth in the area, the port of Buenos Aires was considered little more than a backwater as the Spanish focused on the riches to be found in the gold and silver mines of present day Bolivia and Peru.

Buenos Aires turned out to be an ideal port for trade, but restrictions by the Spanish crown meant that most of this was in the form of smuggling. Either way, this contributed to the growth of the city. As silver mining declined in the 18th century, restrictions were relaxed and Buenos Aires was made capital of the new Viceroy of the Rio de la Plata in 1776. Attempted invasions by the British in 1806 and again in 1807 united the locals and contributed to growing confidence to become independent alongside a growing dissatisfaction with Spanish rule. A process began which was to lead to Argentina becoming the successor state to the Viceroyalty and formal independence was declared on 9 July 1816. Regional political differences meant that conflict and civil war followed for much of the 1800s.

During a period of relative peace and stability in the late 19th century, new laws enabled Argentina to open up to foreign investment. Cattle and cereals were exported, and the economy grew substantially. However, perhaps the bigger impact was on Argentinian culture and demographics, which were shaped by waves of immigration from Europe. This immigration was on such a scale that Argentina was second only to the United States in terms of the raw numbers of people coming into a country. Italians and Spanish led the way, with more people arriving from France, the United Kingdom, Germany, Poland, Ukraine, India, and others. Britain became Argentina's main trading partner up until World War II. There are even Welsh settlements named Y Wladfa[1] in the Chubut province that still exist, and a form of "Patagonian Welsh" as a language. Today, around 85% of the population of Buenos Aires is of European descent.

This age of prosperity in Argentina's history has been all too rare. The flood of immigrants that swelled the population of Buenos Aires, doubling its size to 1 million people, sparked a social crisis as it just could not cope with the numbers. After the military seized power in 1929, an obscure colonel named Juan Domingo Perón rose to power, who, together with his wife Eva (Evita) Duarte, influenced Argentine politics, arguably to this day. Both revered and despised, the Peróns social-welfare reforms have had a lasting effect on Argentinian spirits and economics.

---

[1] *History of the Welsh Colony in Patagonia.* Welsh-Argentine society. www.cymru-ariannin. com/en/hanesywladfa.php

Adopting Agile Across Borders

The 1970s and 1980s saw more violence, first the so-called "Dirty War" where the government – the result of another military coup – used brutal tactics to suppress the Montoneros – an extreme-left Perónist guerrilla group – whose own tactics consisted of bombings and kidnappings. Anyone thought to be associated with socialism or showing dissent were at risk of becoming victims of state terrorism. This was only ended when, after an ill-judged attempt to raise nationalist sentiment, the military-led government invaded the Islas Malvinas. The uncompromising British fought back, the Falklands War resulting in Argentine defeat and the military being forced to withdraw from power.

A history of conflict and uncertainty has meant the economy of Argentina has perpetually struggled. Since the 1980s, inflation has been difficult to control for successive governments. Private industry has been sold off and borrowing has soared. Periods of spiraling unemployment have been common. That is not to say that there have not been booms along with the busts. Following devaluation of the peso and the defaulting of AR$140billion of debt in 2002, a subsequent period of stability for the currency followed, making Argentina's exports suddenly cheap. Argentina enjoyed a booming economy during the mid-2000s, though the next economic crisis never seems to be far away. In 2018, inflation rose while the value of the peso plunged, sparking a new recession that was still ongoing when the coronavirus pandemic hit.[2]

Insights

We must acknowledge the scale of Argentina geographically (it is the eighth largest country in the world after all) with a diversity of people and cultures from the Gauchos, to the people of Tierra Del Fuego far to the South, and those of the northwest who have more in common with the indigenous people of Chile, Bolivia, and Paraguay than the so-called porteños people of Buenos Aires.

Given the dominance of Buenos Aires in commerce and international business, we were drawn to the Agile community in the country's capital.

By sheer coincidence, our time in the city coincided with the very first visit of all of the board members of the Agile Alliance who were flying in for a breakfast meetup with the local Agile community. We had been in Buenos Aires for just four days, but decided that this was enough time to consider ourselves as locals, so we joined the meetup. Figure 2-1 is a picture of the meetup attendees.

---

[2]Gillespie, P. (2020). *In Perennial Economic Crisis, Argentina Faces Worst Year Yet.* Bloomberg. www.bloomberg.com/news/articles/2020-06-23/in-perennial-economic-crisis-argentina-faces-its-worst-year-yet

Chapter 2 | Argentina

Figure 2-1. Desayunando con el Board del Agile Alliance Group meetup in Buenos Aires, Jan 2018. Glaudia is far left, David is slightly left of center at the back

When we first arrived, we felt a little bit like we were "crashing" the meetup. These concerns quickly evaporated due to the hospitality of both the Agile Alliance Board and the local Agile community. The porteños may just be the kindest and most hospitable people around. And as it turned out, crashing this meetup was the best thing we could ever have done as it kick-started our journey.

Perhaps it is the history of economic ups and downs that contributes to Argentina's passion for people. After all, economic security may come and go, but friends and family will always be there. Relationships are highly valued. People give each other kisses on the cheek regardless of gender or how well they know one-another. David was quite taken aback during our first meetings when he suddenly found himself exchanging cheek kisses with other men who were complete strangers! Not that they remained strangers for long – the warmth and hospitality shown to us by our hosts soon made us feel as if we were old friends.

If history is anything to go by, economic conditions in Argentina can change at any time. People in a good position one day may find their fortunes change quickly. Perhaps this is why there is such respect for others no matter their socioeconomic position. Anyone could find themselves anywhere on the rungs of the societal ladder in the blink of an eye.

**Adopting Agile Across Borders** 29

This could also be a factor in Argentine courage. Boom-bust cycles represent not just uncertainty, but opportunity as well. People display a curiosity, a willingness to experiment. Fortune may just favor the brave who foster the courage to innovate.

Argentina's software industry is much smaller when compared to those in other parts of the world such as India. However, it has seen significant growth since 2003, with increases ranging from 15 to 20% per year. Nearshoring is becoming more popular due to favorable time zone compatibility with the United States and Europe, the good quality produced, a high level of language skills of its IT professionals, the good level of education at local universities, and price competitiveness. This development of the software industry in turn sparked a keen interest in Agile ways of working in the country. It could be argued that Argentina is the breeding ground for Agile in South America.

The very first Latin-American conference on Agile development took place in Buenos Aires in 2008 with 900 people in attendance. Mary Poppendieck was the keynote speaker. Since then, Ágiles Latinoamérica[3] has been a recurring yearly event which has taken place across a host of different locations in South and Central America.

Despite the sheer geographical size of the continent, the Agile community in South America are very close to one another. The influence of Argentinian Agile practitioners could be seen in Uruguay, Chile, and all the way up to Colombia, where we would go on to meet teams who had been coached by people from Argentina.

Meeting facilitators are sure to be challenged in Argentina. Argentinian speech can be verbose, eloquent, rich, and passionate. The people have the courage to share their opinions. They are willing to experiment and take chances. This all requires a strong personality to keep minds focused and to respect timeboxes. When we asked people what teams in Argentina found most challenging, the word "focus" came up time and again. When digging deeper, we were told that the reason for this is that many people generate numerous ideas. A lack of communication was certainly not an issue; if anything, it appeared as if the opposite was true with many opinions and discussion points coming up that could result in a loss of focus.

---

[3]Ágiles Latinoamérica 2008 www.agiles.org/, http://agiles2008.agiles.org/en/

Chapter 2 | Argentina

> ■ **Takeaway** Use divergent and convergent thinking techniques. With creative teams that have no shortage of ideas, focus might be lost and it is unclear which ideas to pursue. We do not want to stifle this creativity, we do want to leverage it.
>
> Divergent and convergent techniques involve giving everyone space to capture and put forward ideas and then coming together to agree on the best ones. A simple example of this is to have individuals write on post-it notes and then stick them on a wall so that they are visible to the whole group (or replicating this in a virtual whiteboard tool). These can be grouped in an affinity map. By dot voting, you can quickly converge on which item to focus on first.
>
> Divergent and convergent methods also work really well when teams struggle to generate ideas, or with teams with dominant personalities and more passive ones.

A surprise to us, given the Argentine loquaciousness and people-orientation, were the reservations and feelings of discomfort expressed from team members in raising observations concerning their teammates. On further reflection, this does make sense; it is precisely because of the strong people-orientation innate in Argentinian culture that critiquing others, especially those that people are close to, would be uncomfortable to many. In this part of the world, people's social and professional lives are intertwined – people's work colleagues are also considered to be their friends. In an Agile environment where a drive for continuous improvement can sometimes be perceived as a personal critique of an individual's way of working, there can be a reluctance by people to be completely open, honest, and direct for fear of hurting the feelings of those that they care deeply about. This from a people that are usually passionate and outwardly display their emotions on most things.

While there are many strengths of Argentinian behavior that fit well with Agile values – focus on quality, satisfying the customer, willingness to experiment, courage, people-orientation, and teamwork – potentially resulting in highly performing teams, colleagues and partners from countries outside of South America are advised to invest some time in understanding the culture to avoid misunderstandings and strengthen the relationship.

> ■ **Takeaway** Build client-vendor relationships. When engaging with third parties, it is important to invest in building a relationship that goes beyond contracts and hand-offs. Include the delivery team in this – building a relationship between the team and client will pay off in the long run as everyone feels more invested in what the partnership is trying to achieve.

Adopting Agile Across Borders

Figure 2-2. People-orientation and relationship building is a big part of Argentinian culture (image courtesy of Tasia Graham)

The illustration of Figure 2-2 represents the people-orientation of the culture. For Argentinians, people come first, whether this is in the form of team members' well-being, or the customer's experience. These concerns are far ahead of considerations such as meeting a planned deadline. Use of raw metrics to win an argument will not win friends. Debates are won through charisma, emotional engagement, and building trust. In general, Argentines, with all of their sophisticated taste, care much more for human beings than for material things. We heard examples where software development organizations would not engage in a relationship with a client if their people felt uncomfortable working with them. Winning a contract and short-term profits are important, but good people are in demand, and keeping them engaged, motivated, and happy in their working environment is seen as a

Chapter 2 | Argentina

much more sustainable way of running a business in the long run. Losing people and having a high turnaround of staff adds risk to deliver for your clients and damages your reputation.

Good companies, aware of employment laws, invest in their people. They aim to keep people happy, motivated, and performant. In a country with such economical roller-coasters, waste cannot be afforded. At the same time, companies need to keep their talented people so investing in them makes sense as a strategy on multiple levels. We heard multiple times during our time in Argentina and beyond that finding good developers is hard, so building a work environment where people want to be, where they are given autonomy, mastery, and purpose, as discussed by Dan Pink,[4] is important for success.

10Pines is one company that is an exemplar of this. By sheer luck, when we sat down at the Meetup breakfast, we happened to sit next to Federico Zuppa, one of the partners at 10Pines. We got talking to Federico and later visited 10Pines. Here he talks about the Agile teams at the company.

Heart of Agile Teams at 10Pines[5]

Tom DeMarco coined the term "Jelled Teams" to define those teams that just feel good. Members are energized and motivated. They work hard and in a very disciplined way. They collaborate effectively, ending each day tired, but happy for what has been accomplished. Have you developed software in such teams? Is there anything more enjoyable?

What makes these teams great? What are their values? As leaders in our organization, what can we do to create them? I will describe our recipe using Alistair Cockburn's "Heart of Agile"[6] format. In this case, as I am focusing on the "collaborate" section of his model, I am calling it "The Heart of Agile Teams at 10Pines." I believe **great teams are made from its people, the heart, that work in a great environment, with a clear vision, self-organized, and effective communication.**

The heart, made together with these ingredients, looks like Figure 2-3.

---

[4]Pink, D (2011) *Drive*. Canongate Books Ltd; Main edition (13 Jan. 2011). ISBN-13: 978-1847677693

[5]Contribution based on the blogpost at https://blog.10pines.com/2019/05/14/heart-of-agile-teams-at-10pines/

[6]Cockburn, A. *Heart of Agile*. https://heartofagile.com/

Adopting Agile Across Borders

Figure 2-3. The Heart of Agile at 10Pines

People: At the heart, there's the people. There cannot be great teams without motivated and capable developers.

Great environment: These people need an innovative environment where they can thrive, feel safe, and be energized.

Vision: Teams focus on what needs to be accomplished. Having a shared vision enables our teams to be aligned and collaborate better.

Self-organization: Starting from this shared vision, we self-organize to devise a plan and we work together toward it. Empowerment is the best intrinsic motivator, for both the products we create and for ourselves.

Communication: Last but not least, we need to communicate efficiently. Our methodology maximizes the communication bandwidth, with open-space work areas, shortened feedback cycles, and the use of all available digital tools.

When I was thinking about our heart, I had an epiphany: I realized the people are the heart, and our values and practices are the same whether at team or company level. There is no friction between the company and the teams that self-organize to work on projects. They share the same values, do the same things, and organize in the same way.

Let's talk about each of these "ingredients" and what we do to enable and enforce each of them.

Chapter 2 | Argentina

People

Figure 2-4. People are at the heart of 10Pines

As illustrated in Figure 2-4, at the heart, there's the people. Teams are their people and the people are the company as well. It's not possible to develop software with unmotivated people that you can't rely on. Therefore, we put great effort into the hiring process. We don't search for experienced Java developers for an important project. This would be too ephemeral. We search for developers that are interested in developing their professional careers at 10Pines.

Based on these objectives, we have designed our hiring process. We want to see how candidates code, how they solve a problem, the process they use (e.g., Test Driven Development), the abstractions they choose, and the way they test their code. We don't pay attention to programming language details, but we are very thorough in discussing the way they design and test their code. Getting to know the human side of someone is both really important and really difficult in such a short period of time. We maximize the time between us and the candidate, carrying out a group interview with members of the team where everyone participates. It's important to get to know someone you'll be spending so many hours with!

After the candidate becomes a "pine," as we call ourselves, we need to set a path for growing. This is crucial for us. We want knowledge workers that care about self-fulfillment as well as 10Pines. We need competent software crafters that stay with us for a long time. Would it be possible to do this if there was no way to grow inside 10Pines? We have put great effort to create our career path, which we call the "pine's path," and that takes us from being "padawans" to "knights" and then "masters," after many years of programming practice. Our path has something peculiar compared to other companies I've been a part of in the past: because we are a self-managed company, our participation and responsibilities impact on our career paths.

Great Environment

Figure 2-5. A great environment at 10Pines

Figure 2-5 represents how I believe we work better when we feel good. And we feel good when there is a great environment. When we trust the company, we feel safe and we have the freedom to do our work the best way we can.

How can we have such an environment? What do we leaders need to do to accomplish this? When 10Pines was starting, we did a group activity that had the objective of answering the following question: What does your perfect job need to have? We arrived at the conclusion that we value the human aspect (the way we treat each other), empowerment (being able to participate), having interesting and challenging projects where we learn and grow professionally, getting paid accordingly and, last but not least, work comfortably.

These core values drive the way we work and our day-to-day decisions. We have a horizontal structure where we are empowered. We have open-book management, so everyone sees what 10Pines earns and spends on each project, including what each person gets. We do company standups weekly, and we use that space to give kudos. We choose the most interesting projects where we get paid fairly. And we take care of our comfort, having a great office with everything we need to feel well.

Each year, in our annual strategic planning retreat (which we term our "yearly strategic retirement"), we measure how we are doing for each attribute using the radar retrospective. A lot of honest and valuable discussions have arisen by doing this activity.

Vision

Figure 2-6. 10Pines vision

Empowered people, working in a great environment and having a shared vision as shown in Figure 2-6, is what gives rise to the collective intelligence. We all need to understand the objectives because this allows us to make better decisions.

For each new development project, we start with a phase that we call Product Discovery where all team members participate. We build a shared vision for the project, we get aligned and set up a basis of collaboration.

At 10Pines, we share a vision that all pines build and review each year in our yearly strategic retirement. We imagine the company's future and ourselves in it. We talk and dream.

Self-Organization

Figure 2-7. Self-organization at 10Pines

As represented by Figure 2-7, we all manage the company and therefore we all have lots of things to decide, organize, and work on. We self-organize to create teams for all new projects and we self-organize within the teams as well. The synergy reached by self-organized teams leads to better results and it makes us feel better. It intrinsically motivates and energizes us. It contributes to creating a great environment. This is what Mary Poppendieck tells us in "Empower the Team,"[7] Jim Highsmith in "Team versus Tasks,"[8] and Jurgen Appelo with the "Darkness Principle."[9]

The teams at 10Pines are very disciplined. They are rigorous in their technical practices because everyone enforces them. There is also strong leadership which is not from a given position, but from having knowledge and experience.

---

[7] Poppendieck, Mary & Tom. (2003). *Lean Software Development: An Agile Toolkit.* Addison-Wesley Professional. ISBN-13: 978-0321150783
[8] Highsmith, J. (2009). *Agile Project Management.* Addison-Wesley Professional. ISBN-10: 0321658396
[9] Appelo, J. (2011). *Management 3.0: Leading Agile Developers, Developing Agile Leaders.* Addison-Wesley Professional. ISBN-10: 0321712471

Communication

"Few of us are in the high tech business. Most of us are in the human communications business," said Tom DeMarco. I agree. The better teams communicate, the better they will work. Each team is different, so each team needs to have its own communication strategy that broadens their bandwidth and makes it as efficient as possible.

Figure 2-8 demonstrates how, at 10Pines, we start by creating a shared vision among everyone involved. We work closely with business members. We use an iterative and incremental process that shortens feedback cycles. We work in open spaces to improve osmotic[10] communication and we use all available tools (like Google Hangouts/Slack).

We understand the importance of communication and therefore we actively work to make it as effective as possible.

Figure 2-8. Communication at 10Pines

[10]Cockburn, A. (2004). *Crystal Clear: A Human-Powered Methodology for Small Teams.* Addison-Wesley Professional. ISBN-10: 0201699478

Conclusion

Great teams start with their people, those that are energized and empowered to give their best. There should be an environment that provides safety and encourages collaboration. It should also be an innovative place where people can grow professionally. Teams need to have a shared vision, to promote empathy and to activate collective intelligence. Members self-organize toward this vision. The synergy achieved because of the combination of multiple talents ensures the best results and motivates us intrinsically. Teams need a process that shortens feedback cycles and broadens the communication bandwidth.

10Pines is a great team, with its people, empowered and motivated at heart, a great environment that all of us co-create together, a shared vision and a strategy that maximizes communication.

—Federico Zuppa, Partner at 10Pines

■ **Takeaway**   Hire the right people from the start. Invest in getting your hiring process right. Involve the team. Bring agility into the hiring process itself (Agile HR). Align it with your company values (if you don't have clear company values, or they are no more than rhetorical, then work on these!). Company values can be used to discover who the right people are to join your team.

As Federico from 10Pines said, *"We don't search for experienced Java developers for an important project. This would be too ephemeral. We search for developers that are interested in developing their professional careers at 10Pines."*

If you have the right people in the right roles, agility – and more importantly your organization – is more likely to succeed.

The results of these kinds of work environments are happy people and teams that stay together for long periods, in many cases years rather than months. Unlike shorter lived teams, these teams have the chance to reach highly performing states. At 10Pines, for example, teams have reached such a high level of performance and self-management that a formal Scrum Master is not required for each team, let alone traditional managers. 10Pines has become known as "the company without managers."

■ **Takeaway**   Create an environment where people can grow. By this, we do not mean climbing a corporate ladder, but to grow valuable skills, knowledge, and experiences. To grow as a team member and to grow as a professional. In summary, to grow as a person. Extra responsibilities and promotion then become a side-effect of this approach, instead of basing such things on longevity.

Getting On and Around

Like other South American cultures, building relationships in Argentina paves the way for all else, whether it is winning a contract, penetrating a market, or the formation of a team. Establishing long-term connections is above any short-term goals, and the Argentine people's own personalities are fully on display as they do so.

In more than one of the companies that we visited, team morale was so important that teams would be involved in discussions with clients, and all parties would need to be happy with the relationship before the company would take the contract. Good developers are hard to find, so it is a commonly consciously strategic decision to get the thoughts and input of the teams and consider their welfare in key decisions.

This relationship-centricity applies at the enterprise level as well. Both clients and vendors seek to build long-term, mutually beneficial relationships based on trust.

Hiring and firing procedures more commonplace in other parts of the world are less accepted. Strong unions help to protect employees, while culturally, the natural tendency is to nurture.

Despite the outwardly cheerfulness of the Argentine people that we met, Buenos Aires reportedly has the highest ratio of psychologists per capita than anywhere else in the world. Perhaps this is not a coincidence given the country's history and the highly erratic changes in standards of living. However, as a foreigner, one should not dwell on the country's history of political and financial problems in conversation. Instead, appreciate and enjoy the courtesy of your hosts.

Agile Community Events and Meetups

- Ágiles Argentina: www.meetup.com/agiles-arg/
- Developers4Good: https://developersforgood.com/

CHAPTER

3

Chile

Chile is perhaps the country in South America that we visited that has most in common culturally with Europe. Compared to some other countries in South America the business setting in Chile is more formal. Punctuality is generally observed, while communication is more restrained and pragmatic.

Yet we found Chileans to be as people-oriented as the people that we met in Argentina, Colombia, or Uruguay. Focus is on the customer. Teams are like families. And business is built on earning trust and building relationships. This is a country that has much to contribute to the world, and we are not only talking about their exceptionally good wine.

History

Humans began to form settlements in some of the valleys and coastal areas of what is now Chile around 10,000 years ago. The Incas extended their empire into Northern Chile in the late 15th century to the early decades of the 16th century, but never exerted any control over the South due to the resistance of the Mapuche people of Central and South Chile. They were the only indigenous group to hold off the Inca.

The Mapuche's resistance to the Spanish conquistadors that began later in the 16th century led to the abolition of slavery by the Spanish crown who recognized that the policy was actually intensifying Mapuche resistance rather than intimidating them into submission. The Spanish efforts to colonize Mapuche territories continued all the way through to the 1880s without

© Glaudia Califano, David Spinks 2021
G. Califano and D. Spinks, *Adopting Agile Across Borders*,
https://doi.org/10.1007/978-1-4842-6948-0_3

Chapter 3 | Chile

success. The population of Chile today is largely of Spanish ancestry mixed with indigenous groups and the characteristics of pride, honor, and rebelliousness displayed by the Mapuche is rooted into Chilean cultural behaviors, as well as in those in other parts of South America. Centuries since the attempted invasion of the Inca, these characteristics are still very much in evidence.

A large part of Chile's economy is based on mining. Chile is the world's largest producer of copper, lithium, and iodine, and as of 2018, copper mining alone accounted for 30% of all exports (down from 60% in 1970).[1] The mines were controlled by the United States for much of the mid-20th century, but calls to "nationalize" them first came from reformist president Eduardo Frei, and this was later enacted under president Salvador Allende, leading to US hostility and sanctions. A period of economic instability followed. In 1973, the Supreme Court opposed Allende's government and, though against the constitution, supported a little known military general named Augusto Pinochet. Pinochet seized power following a military coup d'état.

Pinochet's era was marked by many human rights violations and Chile actively took part in Operation Condor, the US-backed campaign, to suppress the spread of communism in the countries of the Southern Cone of South America that also included Brazil, Argentina, Uruguay, and Bolivia. In parallel, Chile experienced what economists described as the "Miracle of Chile," where the economy was turned around by the implementation of free-trade agreements, the privatization of state-owned companies, and policies to control inflation. One view is that the free market conditions ultimately led to Pinochet's military junta being replaced with a free and democratic society, though others would argue a contrary view.

Today, Chile is one of, if not the most stable and prosperous country in the whole of South America. It leads the way in income per capita, it has the highest credit rating, and it has low levels of the perception of corruption. Since 2013, Chile has been considered by the World Bank as a "high-income economy." It was the first country in the continent to be a member of the OECD, a position it has held since 2010 (Colombian membership was agreed in May 2018 and finally became a member in April 2020). The economic policies in place since the 1980s under Pinochet have remained in force and have helped to fuel the country's steady economic growth.

Chile's unique triangle of trade with the United States, Europe, and Asia put them in a good place, and these relationships are something that they are determined to maintain. With the Pacific Ocean on one side and the Andes effectively cutting it off from the rest of the continent, Chile's geography has historically diminished its relationship with the other countries of South

---

[1] *This is Chile* www.thisischile.cl/economy/mining/?lang=en#:~:text=The%20country %20is%20the%20largest,more%20than%2060%25%20in%201970

America. Its chief trading partners in order include Japan, the United States, Britain, Brazil, South Korea, Germany, and Taiwan, its political stability helping its attraction as a trading partner with the rest of the world.

Britain had a major influence on the formation of the Chilean navy during the 19th century, a time that saw Chile at war with an alliance of Bolivia and Peru in the War of the Pacific. The French influenced Chilean architecture and the legal and education systems. Prussians trained and organized the army. German settlement had a long-lasting influence on the society, economy, and geography of Southern Chile.[2] Perhaps it is for these reasons that Chile feels more European-orientated than any other part of South America despite having had a lower level of migration from Europe than most of its neighbors. Between 1851 and 1924, Chile received just 0.5% of all of the European immigration to South America.

Situated on the Pacific rim of fire, Chile has been dogged by more than its fair share of natural disasters, primarily earthquakes and tsunamis. The 1960, 9.5 magnitude Valdivia earthquake is the most powerful earthquake ever recorded. An 8.8 magnitude earthquake hit off the coast of Chile in 2010, with over 500 people killed and US$30 billion worth of damage caused by the quake and resultant tsunamis. However, the Chilean people showed their spirit. Within a few months, ports, roads, and airports had been rebuilt and were back up and running largely due to how the citizens helped each other.

Later that same year, there was another show of national solidarity when a cave-in at the San José copper-gold mine trapped 33 miners 700 meters underground. The men were eventually rescued after 69 days. The incident united the nation and captured the attention of the media across the whole world. Widespread anti-government protests and riots across the country in 2019 and 2020 triggered the decision for a referendum to change the constitution. In a display of national unity, there was overwhelming agreement for a rewrite and the result included agreement that ordinary citizens would be included in drafting the new version which would then be voted on in a follow up referendum.[3]

Insights

Agile ways of working are on the rise in Chile, and more and more large global companies there are looking into adopting Agile. The Chilean Agile community "Chile Agil" exceeds 7400 members at the time of writing, with many

---

[2]Young, G. F. W. (1971). *Bernardo Philippi, Initiator of German Colonization in Chile*. The Hispanic American Historical Review, 51(3), 478-496. doi:10.2307/2512693

[3]Mishra, S. (2020). *Chile votes overwhelmingly to rewrite constitution from Pinochet dictatorship. Independent.* www.independent.co.uk/news/world/americas/chile-constitution-referendum-vote-polls-pinochet-plebiscite-b1334522.html#r3z-addoor

Chapter 3 | Chile

members actively attending local meetups, conferences, and events. And it is not just confined to the software development industry, Agile ways of working are being adopted by the Chilean government with the establishment of Chile's "Government Lab" in 2014.[4] The intention was to bring everyday people closer to the workings of government. A member of the government Lab sits down with advisors of the president to decide what the country's most urgent problem is and then they try to find a way to fix it. One such example was to deal with the national health insurance system, where one of the major problems was the time it took for people to get answers to basic queries which could take as long as a month. Based on user research and an incremental and iterative approach, a chat tool and online knowledge base were developed, aiming to allow branch officers to answer 85% of queries immediately, with more complicated ones answered within 24 hours. A key part to Chile's Government Lab was getting the buy-in at the highest possible level, including government ministers and heads of department.

The education system is highly regarded. There are 8 years of compulsory education followed by an optional four years of secondary or vocational education and additional higher education. Chilean universities are acclaimed throughout Latin America.[5]

Like in most South American countries, building relationships and loyalty is highly valued. An example of this comes from Continuum, a boutique software development agency that we visited in Santiago de Chile. They shared with us their approach to forming contracts with clients. For Continuum, it is important to build relationships with their clients based on trust. So instead of wordy and legally binding contracts, they prefer, especially with their smaller clients, to create what they call a working agreement. These focus primarily on working arrangements such as an expectation that the client will have someone act as Product Owner and that person is expected to be available to the Continuum team for an agreed amount of time. The working agreement sets out a clear objective to be achieved, with an expectation that solution details will emerge. Chilean reputation as fast payers helps to further establish trust. We will talk more about Continuum's approach to Agile contracts as well as some examples from other parts of the world later in the book.

The communication style is eloquent when it comes to both listening and speaking. Opinions may be concealed at first, but once friendship is established and trust has been built formalities fall away. In general people do speak up when it comes to business and politics. The last couple of generations have grown up without a dictatorship and so are far more questioning. There is not the same feeling of repression or fear of consequences that earlier generations

---

[4]Clement, M and Axelsen, A. (2019). *Agile working solves Chile's toughest challenges – fast. Apolitical.* https://apolitical.co/en/solution_article/agile-working-solves-chiles-toughest-challenges-fast

[5]*Chile Education. Britannica.* www.britannica.com/place/Chile/Education

had. Leaders consequently require a good balance of skills that include negotiation, facilitation, and displaying the right levels of authority to deal with people that have many different attitudes toward those in power.

Companies tend to be hierarchically structured with top-down control, especially in the larger organizations. This approach and mentality could prove to be a barrier to be overcome for widespread Agile adoption.

More work-oriented and with the harsh economic times within living memory, people are more mindful of building careers and having job security. We are often asked by people from many parts of the world questions like "How do I become a Scrum Master?" or "How do I become a developer?" While qualifications and certifications are important to demonstrate knowledge, it is very difficult to get into these careers without experience. While in Chile, we came across a story that demonstrates the perseverance, patience, and determination that is sometimes needed to get into these careers. The story, introduced by Andrés Peñailillo, Developer and Agile Consultant at Continuum, comes from Eugenio Lopez, who became a developer at Continuum. Eugenio tells a heart-warming story of his journey into starting a career in software development while demonstrating the continuous learning attitude that we would associate with the Agile mindset.

The Accountant That Automated Himself Out of a Job and Into Development

From the beginning, the way we approach candidate interviews in Continuum is with several members of the team in the room. This is because while working in the company the candidate may work with almost anyone in the company.

The procedure is simple, every hiring process is open to anyone in the organization and whoever wants to participate in the interview is encouraged to do it.

With several people, we can ensure that at least the new team member can match on a cultural level, we are sure this kind of match is much more important than technical skill, and that can be validated in another way.

This story begins with the process to hire a new developer for Continuum. Leo, the CTO, was in charge of this particular process. We were looking for someone with a profile with a strong JavaScript background.

We use GetOnBoard.com, a platform for managing every open position, and Leo asked for anyone who wants to participate in the next round of interviews for the people he selected from this platform. I (Andrés) reviewed the candidates myself and one in particular caught my attention. He was an accountant that in his free time started to learn about programming and all of

Chapter 3 | Chile

his technical exercises looked promising. My attention was captured by this profile because of my own history. I'm mostly self-taught, but my career path was always close to tech, so my curiosity was in the candidate's change of profession from accountant to developer. I joined the interview, alongside two other developers.

Here is the story in Eugenio's own words:

"I majored in Accounting in college and graduated with my Bachelor's in Accounting, immediately afterward I moved to Santiago and started working.

After some time I had worked on and left (both voluntarily and involuntarily) a couple of accounting jobs, and found myself as an internal auditor for a software development company, where my first assignment was to generate a weekly report that was a manual, slow, and very time-consuming task. It was an error prone process – an Excel spreadsheet had to be filled in, with all the data passed to a PowerPoint presentation, formatted and verified manually. Any new information meant everything had to be redone.

As a concurrent assignment, since I had told them that I was good at Excel, I had to find a way to automate the generation of this report.

I ended up making an "application" (actually a very big Visual Basic for Applications macro) with a database and an interface to manage the data. It automatically formatted and exported the data, solving both the Excel to PowerPoint problem and the need to manually verify that all data is correctly passed/formatted.

Unfortunately, after the report became easier to make, it was not possible to justify having both the senior auditor and me, a junior auditor, so I was laid off.

After a couple more accounting jobs, I got tired of accounting because I found the profession to be incredibly monotonous and I considered that whatever job I got in accounting would still be monotonous, even if I were promoted. I decided to take a break from accounting and work in general. However, after a significant time without a job, I ran out of my severance and I incurred a lot of credit card debt (pro-tip: don't incur a lot of credit card debt). I had to take on another accounting job.

That job lasted for four months, and I found myself without a job, in a lot of debt and with no clear way out of it. The only things I had were knowing that I really didn't want to do accounting anymore... which paradoxically was also the best way I could get out of debt... and the "goal" of not working in accounting by the time I was 30 (I was 28 at the time), even if it meant frying burgers at McDonald's.

I did remember that back when I was a kid I liked programming. I made a program that read user input from the DOS command line and responded to some basic things (like "What's your name?" then it'd reply "Hello <name>!"), and I managed to draw some lines on the screen using TurboPascal.

Adopting Agile Across Borders

My programming didn't progress much back then because there were no resources for me to keep learning and no one to help me learn either. While I still liked computers, and spent (too much) time using them, I was just a user, albeit a savvy one.

I decided to try to learn how to make web pages. A Google search told me I needed to start with HTML.

My attempt lasted 20 minutes.

To pay the bills I got another job as an accounting clerk. While procrastinating on the job, I saw that a friend that had started working as a photographer had made himself a website. Now, I'm no designer, but I considered that I could... improve upon it, so I started to work on creating a better version of his site from scratch, which required me to learn HTML, CSS, and eventually JavaScript.

I had made a decent amount of progress on the website, but my probationary period of my accounting job ended and I did not get my contract renewed (since I did almost none of the things I was supposed to do).

I realized that I had to do something or who knows how I'd end up. My parents, while supportive, weren't really happy that I had no job while in debt. At the same time, the family printing business was starting to wither because its work was drying up due to the transition to electronic documents.

I decided to start learning to program, almost 20 years after my initial foray into programming. I kept on working on the mock website I was making for my friend's business. The things I needed to do started to become more complex, I spent more time debugging, thinking how to do the stuff I wanted to do, researching and though frustrating at times, I really enjoyed the process, to which I initially dedicated about 6–7 hours a day.

The ideas I had for the project started to stray outside from what little I knew back then, which was HTML/CSS/JavaScript. Since I wanted to store stuff I needed to have a database, which meant I'd need a way to talk to the database, which Google said meant I'd need a "back end," where unlike my current learning path, there were many options to choose from with no real clear best choice.

After doing some research both on languages and the Chilean programming job market, I chose to learn Ruby on Rails. I stumbled upon Michael Hartl's excellent book Ruby on Rails Tutorial.[6] It took me about 11 days to finish following along with the exercises and trying hard, both to understand everything I was doing and finishing the extra exercises. Full of confidence after finishing the book, I set out to create a Rails project to integrate my work into... and found myself having to consult the book to remember exactly what I had to do even for basic stuff.

---

[6]Hartl, M (2012). *Ruby on Rails Tutorial: Learn Web Development with Rails* (Second Edition). Addison Wesley. ISBN-13 : 978-0321832054

Chapter 3 | Chile

Time went on, I struggled, I learned, I enjoyed the experience, and I managed to finish the website project to what I considered an acceptable feature set.

I tried to make a website for myself, as a resume. Now, I'm not a designer... and that was made more than clear in this case. After a month and a half, I dumped the whole project because everything I designed was awful. I did learn how to set up a website so it could be publicly accessible, so not all efforts were wasted.

I decided that, to get a better job, I needed to learn more. After visiting GetOnBoard.com and developer's websites like StackOverflow, I decided to learn a front end JavaScript framework. React was all the rage, so I hopped on the bandwagon. After an initial bit of trouble, I noticed that all the previous months of experience had been very productive for my learning, as I did not find React difficult at all.

As a practical application, I decided to create a project where I'd call the API of Chilecompra, the Chilean government's portal where they put contracts out to tender, and display the information, be able to filter it, receive notifications, etc., hoping that maybe it'd be useful for someone, that I'd be able to learn something useful out of the experience, and that maybe my parents would be able to get something useful out of it.

My mom got a minimum wage job at a competitor's printing business, my dad kept the family business alive taking whatever little work arrived, and I kept on learning, being a bit under pressure knowing that money was tight and that I was a burden to my parents, as they kept on paying the debt I'd taken some years before. I went from spending 6–7 hours a day programming to 8–10, and after finishing my "work" I'd spend a couple of hours reading or watching videos about programming or computer science.

When I finished the React project, I decided that I knew enough to be able to get a job. I went on GetOnBoard and applied for my first software development job at a company called Continuum. They invited me for an interview. I traveled to Santiago, a 12 hour trip, to attend the interview.

I made it to the office and was greeted, then led to the interview room. I was very surprised, and nervous, to find myself in front of four other people. Also, I was wearing a suit while all of my interviewers were wearing jeans and shirts, and one of them had a big not-acceptable-in-accounting beard. They were very nice though, and asked me about myself, about my programming experience, why I chose to change from accounting to programming, what problems I'd solved, or had difficulties with. Also, I told them that I automated myself out of a job and they laughed, then Leo, one of the interviewers felt bad for laughing about it. The interview lasted about an hour and a half, and afterward while on the bus home, I received a phone call from Leo, but the noise made it impossible to discern anything.

Adopting Agile Across Borders

Figure 3-1. Eugenio Lopez in the office of Continuum

When I got off the bus, I was called again by Leo, and he informed me that I was hired, asking me when I'd be able to join, considering I had to move from Valdivia to Santiago, and telling me stuff I should learn before day one.

I was elated."

—Eugenio Lopez, Full Stack Developer, Continuum

After meeting with Eugenio, we started to debate if this person can be moved to the hirable section of the process, personally, I was amused about his story about automating himself out of his own job, and I was really impressed with his understanding of JavaScript. But we in the team had concerns about if he would be able to work alongside other developers, mostly because his experience consisted mostly of working alone, also not having real work experience as a developer can come with a strong bias to working "by the book" and not adapting to the way of work of the real world. Another concern was that Eugenio was living in another city and if we hired him and he didn't adapt well, we would have made a person move for only a few months.

The positives outweighed the negatives. His willingness to learn and improve in his craft were obvious, he realized that his skills were more in line with a developer than with his profession as an accountant and this was a really bold and courageous move. We need more courageous people in the tech industry. Besides, he was still new to the programming world which was better for us, this way we are able to teach him at a time when he was still fresh. Sadly many developers work in a mediocre environment and it's harder to eliminate bad practices inherited from previous experiences.

Chapter 3 | Chile

Months later we found out that it was a good decision to hire Eugenio and now he's been working with us for the last two years; in this period, he has worked with several people of Continuum on multiple projects. Figure 3-1 shows a picture of Eugenio in the Continuum office.

—Andrés Peñailillo, Developer and Agile Consultant, Continuum

---

■ **Takeaway** The value of courage. Eugenio's story demonstrated courage in spades: Eugenio's courage to leave a career he was unhappy with and to persevere with a career change when there were no guarantees of success. Continuum demonstrated courage in seeing Eugenio's enthusiasm and passion for software development and took a chance in hiring someone inexperienced and without formal qualifications.

To enact change and achieve great things as individuals, teams' and organizations' courage and perseverance in the face of adversity are fundamental.

■ **Takeaway** Empower the team in choosing the people they work with. We have seen and heard many examples of how involving the people that new hires will be working with in the recruitment process leads to a better fit. After all, it is the people that they will work with on a day-to-day basis as peers that understand what is best for their team.

Getting On and Around

Putting effort into relationship building is important in order to build good collaboration, and can be harder earned in Chile than the other South American countries that appear in this book. People's true feelings may not be on full display, at least not until friendship and trust has been established. Trust and friendship are things that need to be worked on.

Building a relationship should be the primary concern if there are long-term goals to be achieved. Diplomacy should work both ways for the good of the relationship.

Admitting that there are challenges is not always an easy thing to do for people that have pride. Well run retrospectives are therefore important for Agile teams if they are going to get the best out of the event and improve. The following story comes from Renato Otaiza, Agile Coach at Scotiabank in Santiago, who talks about the importance of running retrospectives at every level of the organization.

Retrospectives at Every Level[7]

Giving ourselves the opportunity to stop doing whatever we are doing, breathe, make our ways of working visible for everyone, dedicate some time to talk, and ultimately elaborate on some improvement opportunities is something that used to be uncommon. And, more importantly, turning those opportunities into specific actions for becoming a better team, individual, department, or institution is far more uncommon to observe.

Retrospective is the word we use for describing the practice above. The concept was popularized by Norm Kerth back in 2001 in his book *Project Retrospectives: A Handbook for Team Reviews*, but it is in the 1990s that this practice started to be part of teams' behaviors[8]. Its purpose is actually specifically described by the 12th principle of the Agile Manifesto:

At regular intervals, the team reflects on how to become more effective, then tunes and adjusts its behavior accordingly.

I have been participating and facilitating lots of retrospectives during the last few years and I am proud to say that I haven't stopped since I started. Retrospectives have helped me and the people that I've been working with to become better people and to become better as teams. They have helped us to become more connected as a department and be a more conscious organization. There is no silver bullet here though; preparing a well thought through retro, developing deep and meaningful conversations, and following up properly with what's been discussed and agreed is the baseline for getting the right value from this practice.

A very useful thing I frequently use for getting people to connect, focus, and establish the feel of a retrospective environment is the retro's prime directive, proposed by Norm Kerth in his already cited book:

Regardless of what we discover, we understand and truly believe that everyone did the best job they could, given what they knew at the time, their skills and abilities, the resources available, and the situation at hand.[9]

Making this sentence visible and to openly talk about it is such a powerful way for getting everyone into a humble and transparent position. We can then be in a place to recognize what the main teachings about a given situation or period of time are. And, more importantly, we can recognize that we commit errors and we can learn from them. *After a battle, everyone is a general*, the Czech proverb says:[10] don't dismiss your past actions, decisions, and potential

---

[7]Contribution based on the blogpost at https://medium.com/@rotaiza/retrospectives-at-every-level-65f6369f3dd3
[8]*Heartbeat Retrospective*. www.agilealliance.org/glossary/heartbeatretro
[9]Kerth, N. L. (2001). Project Retrospectives. Dorset House. ISBN-13: 978-0932633446
[10]*po bitvě je každý generál.* WordSense. www.wordsense.eu/po_bitv%C4%9B_je_ka %C5%BEd%C3%BD_gener%C3%A1l/

mistakes, because although there is no way to change them now, there is a huge opportunity to learn from them. And don't judge what was done, because your actions and decisions were the best you could do at the time.

I've got used to retrospectives thanks to Scrum. Running team retrospectives every two weeks made me realize how powerful they can become if properly prepared, developed, and followed up. And I have also understood how powerful they can be for any individual, any kind of team and even any big group of people (i.e., organization departments, divisions, areas, units) as seen in Figure 3-2. When approaching a new person, team, or department seeking a new way of thinking and doing things, regardless what Agile framework or technique they implement for their daily work or at a strategic level, I always suggest running retros. And this is not only nice words, I've actually been doing it with teams, across multiple teams, across senior management – retrospectives at every level!

Figure 3-2. Holding a large retrospective with a large group of people from across the organization

Along with product teams having two-week Sprints that finish with a one- or two-hour retro event, imagine a whole ecosystem where there is cadence for running retros at multiple levels. A team of Scrum Masters and Agile Facilitators running retros every two months for getting more conscious about their impact on the environment they work in. A group of 40–50 people working on a strategic organizational challenge that stops every three months to learn about their actions and adjust their behavior accordingly. A C-level executive,

Adopting Agile Across Borders

seeking feedback from their reports, that gets a view about their leadership through retrospectives, promising actions back to the team based on what was encountered like the one shown in Figure 3-3. A whole department of around 150 people that organize their goals on a quarterly basis, who celebrate their achievements and learnings for the period through XXL retrospectives.

Figure 3-3. A C-level executive team retrospective

Having a retrospective culture then, is not only about Scrum Teams periodically running this event. Having a retrospective culture is about designing retros (choosing appropriate techniques for the relevant situation), properly developing its steps (set the stage, gather data, generate insights, decide what to do, and close the retrospective), and following up (defining relevant improvement actions and actually implementing them) at every level of the organization. Yes, at every level of the organization! Figure 3-4 shows a retrospective involving people in a huge department of the organization.

Chapter 3 | Chile

Figure 3-4. A group discussion in a retrospective of a huge department of the organization

I am currently preparing a retro for the Vice President and Directors of the Digital Banking Unit of a multinational bank. First thing to do, apart from reminding everyone of the retro's prime directive, is to follow up the team's actions from the last retro: launch a Community of Practice for sharing and aligning high-level strategies (i.e., digital products, digital technology, sales strategies), and have at least one team-building activity outside of the office. Then, we will spend some time generating deep and valuable understanding of current behavior, agree on actions to improve, and commit to implementing these actions. Retrospectives for every single team? Of course. Retrospectives at every single level? Of course too!

—Renato Otaiza, Agile Practitioner and Coach at Scotiabank

■ **Takeaway** Carry out retrospectives at all levels. In many organizations, retrospectives are carried out at the team level. But there are many impediments or potential improvements that are outside the team's sphere of control, but go nowhere because there is no forum for such impediments to be discussed. Retrospectives are all about continuous improvement, and for true business agility, the organization as a whole should seek to continuously improve. As described by Renato, holding retrospectives at every level is a great way to drive organizational continuous improvement and agility.

Agile Community Events and Meetups

- Chile Agil: `https://chileagil.cl/`, `www.meetup.com/chileagil/`
- Movimiento Ágil Chile: `www.meetup.com/MovimientoAgilChile/`
- Professional Scrum Chile: `www.meetup.com/ProfessionalScrum/`
- Agile Women: `www.meetup.com/AgileWomen/`
- Agile Open Camp: `www.meetup.com/Agile-Open-Camp/`

CHAPTER

4

Colombia

With a history of adversity, the Colombia of recent years is emerging with a sense of relief and optimism for the future. While Argentinians, Chileans, and Uruguayans have a strong European influence due to migration from across Europe, Colombia has been more closed. As a consequence, we found that Colombian people have a closer relationship to their traditions. Relentlessly friendly and helpful, it is perhaps no coincidence that we met with more Agile practitioners per unit of time in Colombia than in any other country.

History

Christopher Columbus saw the coastline of what is now Panama, Colombia, and Venezuela and gave the lands his own name, though he never actually set foot on Colombian soil himself.

Before Columbus's arrival, the land of present day Colombia acted as a corridor between the Caribbean Sea and the Pacific Ocean for a number of independently developing early civilizations. Some of these early inhabitants were highly skilled craftspeople when it came to the area's most valuable resources – gold and precious gems.

The Spanish conquistadors arrived in 1499 in search of gold and emeralds, and the area's abundance of both enticed them further inland. Colombia became part of the New Kingdom of Grenada which also covered present day Panama,

© Glaudia Califano, David Spinks 2021
G. Califano and D. Spinks, *Adopting Agile Across Borders*,
https://doi.org/10.1007/978-1-4842-6948-0_4

Chapter 4 | Colombia

Ecuador, and Venezuela. After several failed rebellions against Spanish rule, the Venezuelan general, Simón Bolívar led the fight against the Spanish, winning victory in 1819.

The territory became known as the Republic of Colombia, but controlling such a vast area was a task that the new regime was incapable of, and so the area was split into three new countries in 1830 (New Granada, Ecuador, and Venezuela). Shortly afterward, centralist and federalist political forces emerged, and there followed no less than eight civil wars in the second half of the 19th century. These in turn first created the United States of Colombia and then finally the Republic of Colombia. "The Thousand Days' War" helped to give an opportunity to the United States, who were looking to influence the region, including over the construction of a canal to link the Atlantic Ocean and the Pacific Ocean. The Americans supported a separatist movement in Panama that led to it becoming its own independent republic in 1903.

The 20th century saw continued conflict in Colombia. La Violencia, another destructive civil war, took place during the middle of the century. In an attempt to quash moves of liberal groups' independence, the leaders of the two main parties supported a brief military dictatorship before signing a pact to share power, essentially repressing political activity outside of their parties. This sowed the seeds for the formation of guerilla groups and then paramilitary groups by rich Colombians to protect their interests. Things were complicated further with the rapid rise of the drug cartels in the 1970s.

The early 21st century has seen Colombia turn a corner. A strong counter-terrorism and counter-insurgency campaign has led to peace agreements with the guerilla groups. Kidnappings and attacks have reduced drastically. Economic plans are attracting investors and the country has become accessible for business and tourism.

Insights

The education sector in Colombia has grown significantly in the last two decades. In 2015, education spending was increased significantly, part of a wider goal by President Juan Manuel Santos to make Colombia the most educated country in Latin America by 2025.[1] Not only is basic education free and compulsory between the ages of 5 and 15, but English is part of the state curriculum. Bilingualism is a criteria for accreditation of higher education programs.[2]

---

[1] *Strategic Framework* www.mineducacion.gov.co/1759/w3-article-356367.html
[2] Immerstein, S. (2015). *Education in Colombia.* World Education News and Reviews. https://wenr.wes.org/2015/12/education-in-colombia

Adopting Agile Across Borders

Modern and hip Medellin, where it always feels like springtime, has a distinctly different feel to eclectic, sophisticated Bogotá. Medellín is no stranger to reinvention. In less than three decades the city has gone from being described as "the most dangerous city on earth" to the "Silicon Valley of South America"[3] as symbolized in the illustration in Figure 4-1. In 2013 *The Wall Street Journal* and Citibank named Medellín the world's most innovative city in the world, ahead of cities like New York and Tel Aviv. It was therefore no surprise that we were invited to so many organizations that adopted Agile in Medellin that we ran out of time and were not able to honor all invitations. This is just one reason for us to go back sometime in the future!

Figure 4-1. Medellín, from "the most dangerous city on earth" to the "Silicon Valley of South America" (image courtesy of Tasia Graham)

---

[3]Kitt, J. (2018). *Medellín proves why it could be the "Silicon Valley of South America."* The Bogota Post. https://thebogotapost.com/medellin-proves-why-it-could-be-the-silicon-valley-of-south-america/32906/

Chapter 4 | Colombia

Formalities in the hierarchy of Colombian organizational structures are more akin to those seen in traditional American, British, or Japanese companies when compared to Colombia's neighbors to the south in Argentina or Uruguay. Business is conducted collaboratively. Yet, culturally, just like in Argentina, there is a reluctance to be direct to avoid hurting others. We met Dominic, an Agile Coach from Germany who had moved to Colombia, and he told us his story about implementing Agile at a company in a country where the culture was very different to his own.

Lean Change Management at a Hardware Retailer[4]

After several years experience in Europe in the software industry, first as a developer and then as a Scrum Master, in 2016 Dominic was offered a challenge by his father-in-law to come to Colombia and continue the family business. Plastinorte S.A.S. was not a software company though, instead it was a retail company selling hardware materials such as upholstery, flooring, and mattresses to name just a few. Even though the industry was quite different to the one of software that Dominic had known, he soon came to see the potential of Plastinorte and accepted the challenge together with his wife Catalina.

When Dominic first arrived at Plastinorte, he took the time to really understand the business, chatting to everyone no matter what their role was. He saw that his father-in-law had done an excellent job of building up the business, but he also saw that it would need to adapt to the new world of digital, and to a knowledge-based economy. Inspired by Jason Little and ideas from Lean Change Management[5] with the collaboration and the seeking of buy-in for change that the approach brings, Dominic, together with Catalina and the team at Plastinorte, evolved the business.

One of their foundations was to build upon open source software that Dominic encourages the wider community to get involved with, not for commercial gain, but to encourage feedback and to make the products even better. The result: Plastinorte has a system that lets them see reports and figures on everything, from accounting and inventory to payroll and much more. Catalina's father had a dream of being able to pick up his phone and quickly know what was happening in the business. Now the dream was real. The technology had taken them from a place where they did not know their own data, to one where it was available in real time and from anywhere.

---

[4]Contribution based on the blogpost at www.redtangerine.org/2018/05/02/plastinorte-lean-change-management-in-action/
[5]Lean Change Management https://leanchange.org/

In parallel to the technology, Dominic and Catalina are working to bring the people closer together for the good of the business. It is a big task as the company has about 70 employees and 13 branches. Despite the Lean Change Management approach he was taking, Dominic still faced cultural clashes at first. The Colombian staff were not used to his polite but direct German style. He told us about how when he was facilitating his first retrospective with the team, people were shocked by his manner, their emotions fully on display, which in turn was a surprise to Dominic. Realizing his mistake, and under the guidance of Catalina, he made adjustments to his approach. This included spending time building relationships with people and finding more constructive and less direct ways to critique, as well as being ready for people's real emotions to come out.

But Dominic does not want to be the boss, instead he wants to empower, including the store managers of the branches, encouraging them to own the direction but, and here is the key thing, to collaborate together for the wider good of the business and not just their own store, using the now visible data to support decision making. For example, where one store has a product that is selling well at a good price, another store manager who has unsold stock of the same item should now help with the supply of the item to the other store. Dominic told us that he believes "technology creates visibility," and this is just one example where it is making a difference to Plastinorte. Their journey continues, but as a result of the work over the last two years, Plastinorte is now the number one company of its kind in Colombia, way ahead of the competition.

Catalina's father had created the company with a desire to provide stability and security for the employees and their families. Dominic and Catalina want to continue the story. They want to continue giving people stability by growing and developing them, and making them adaptable in a world where permanent employment and a job for life is evermore uncertain. Dominic is not interested in qualifications, instead he looks for enthusiastic, adaptable people, keen to learn, and who would be a good fit with the rest of the team. He is proud of developing people and is happy if they leave the company to go on to do great things. Above all, he wants to grow the next generation of leaders.

Understanding that improvement never stops. Dominic spoke passionately about other ideas he had, discussing with us how the traditional Tayloristic hierarchical management structure is no longer fit for purpose. He offered us an alternative, drawing us a structure more like a multi-celled organism not too dissimilar to the ideas discussed in Holacracy[6] and by Niels Plaegling,[7] this

---

[6]Holacracy www.holacracy.org/
[7]Plaegling, N. (2014). *Organize for Complexity: How to Get Life Back Into Work to Build the High-Performance Organization.* BetaCodex Publishing. ISBN-13: 978-0991537600

Chapter 4 | Colombia

despite him not being aware of either of them. Dominic saw a future where the store managers could work as a kind of distributed Product Owner group, and drive the strategy of the business from the ground.

—David Spinks

■ **Takeaway**   Transparency is more than visibility. Transparency goes beyond having information available, to creating a shared understanding of everyone involved in, or receiving the value from our efforts. The transparency that Dominic created enabled better decision making, collaboration, and progress toward a shared goal. Without transparency, people cannot be properly empowered, and decisions and actions they take are likely to be flawed.

We also heard stories from the opposing perspective of a Colombian Scrum Master who had moved to Amsterdam, the Netherlands. His team and fellow Scrum Masters were puzzled as to why he was approaching subjects in such a careful, and in their eyes, convoluted way.

On the flipside, Colombians, though outwardly among the friendliest people in the world, have a defensiveness about them, borne in no small part out of the difficulties of the country's past.

In the Columbian culture, timekeeping is seen as more of a virtue than in some of the other countries in South America. They are good timekeepers when it comes to formal events. Like their neighbors though, strong facilitation is needed to keep conversations relevant and with suitable brevity; the Colombian communication style is among the most loquacious in the world.

Past conflicts have left remnants of secrecy and defensiveness that may be at odds with the Agile values, but qualities of pragmatism, compassion, and, most of all, respect make the Colombian professional landscape well suited to Agile methods as the stories from EPM, a giant energy and water services company, demonstrate. We will hear from Sebastián Pérez Jiménez, a Computer Specialist, and Liliana Zuluaga Hoyos, Agile Coach. But the first story comes from Claudia Liliana Toscano Vargas, Agile Coach.

Accelerating the Supply Chain of Goods and Services

The Cultural Transformation Unit within the management function of Human Resources asked me for help to apply some sort of collaborative work method in the supply chain of the Vice Presidency office. They looked to us because they were aware that we had four years of experience applying Agile frameworks such as Scrum, Scrum-ban, and the Kanban Method within Information

Adopting Agile Across Borders

Technology Management. They wanted to experiment with ways to guide the work of the teams involved in the supply chain process and to work more collaboratively in their recruitment processes.

I met with the entire team to understand what they needed, and we ended up defining an experiment.

The general objective of the experiment would be to have a first version of a collaborative work model based on Agile methodologies and guided conversations in the EPM supply chain process.

From the experiment, we would seek to verify the following hypotheses:

1. Increased collaboration and shared responsibility
2. Improved quality as perceived by the internal client
3. Reduced delivery times of contract completion

The steps to carry it out were as follows:

1. Diagnosis of the team and the process: Understand the hiring process, the way people interact, their understanding of what collaborative work means and their willingness to be part of the pilot.

2. Definition of strategy: Define the most appropriate frameworks and train people. In this case we had an "Agile Inception" session to introduce Scrum and how it works.

3. Execution of the experiment.

Throughout the execution I had two roles. First, I was to be the Scrum Master of the team, and second, to be the mentor of the people in the Cultural Transformation Unit so that they would be able to share the practices with the other teams in the unit.

In the Agile Inception, the team met face to face for the first time. It included all of the roles that participated in the hiring process: Negotiator, Glider (a role similar to a Project Manager), Lawyer, Auditor, and Requestor (the internal client). We built consensus in understanding the needs of the internal client, the initial scope of the documents that needed to be produced and procedures that were to be carried out during the experiment. Some of the output from the inception is shown in Figure 4-2.

Chapter 4 | Colombia

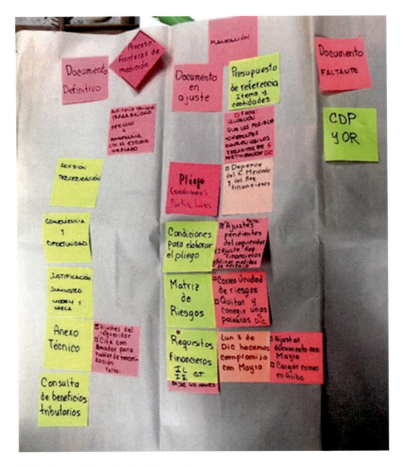

Figure 4-2. Output from the Agile Inception

In addition, we defined what collaborative work meant for us:

- We have confidence in each other's work
- We have valuable conversations
- We get to know our client
- We have respect for each other
- We verify instead of making assumptions
- We understand the context and why we are doing things

We agreed to do weekly Sprints since the deliverables could always be finished in less than five days. Mondays would be when we would hold the Sprint Review, Sprint Retrospective, and Sprint Planning events.

Adopting Agile Across Borders

In our first planning session, we defined our Story Map based on the known scope which is shown in Figure 4-3. Initially we defined the first three Sprints worth of work. During the following two iterations, we planned out the rest of the Story Map all the way to the stage of formalizing contracts. In total we predicted that there would be 12 Sprints.

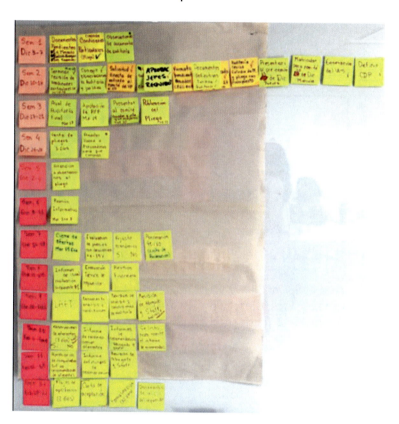

Figure 4-3. Story Map

In the retrospective of each Sprint we found opportunities to improve the process, and our behavior as a team quickly took us to greater productivity and effectiveness. From iteration 7, it was very difficult to find things to improve!

Figure 4-4 shows some of the improvements that were made.

Chapter 4 | Colombia

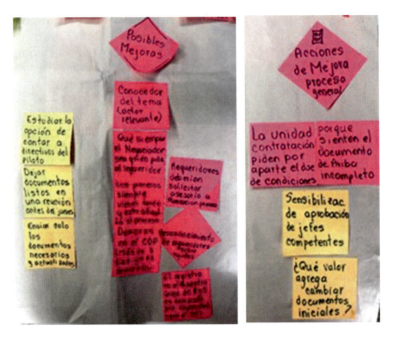

Figure 4-4. Process improvements

We decided that in Sprint 11 we were ready to validate the initial hypotheses of the experiment since there were only two final work items left to be delivered in Sprint 12 to finish successfully.

Although throughout the execution we saw continuous improvement, collaborative working, and a lot of commitment from the team, when we analyzed the results of the experiment, we were even more amazed. The three hypotheses were all validated!

Hypothesis 1 – Increased collaboration and shared responsibility

While this had already been evident during the experiment, we asked the team to describe, in their own words, how they believed they had collaborated and shared responsibility, and this was what they told us:

- We were able to understand the whole process and be clear about all of the steps and the different responsibilities.
- We had defined criteria to describe the whole process which facilitated common understanding and improved harmony.

Adopting Agile Across Borders

- We had timely feedback that contributed to the success of the deliverables.

- We understood the importance of all who participate in the hiring process.

- We avoid unnecessary rework and we made effective decisions as a team.

- We had valuable conversations and shared learning.

- We know each other as human beings. Knowing each other as people helped with collaboration as we better understood each other's thoughts and inclinations.

Hypothesis 2 – Improved quality as perceived by the internal client

This was what our internal client shared with us about the work carried out:

- Higher productivity was evident, possibly due to the fact that this system motivated the team to work only on achieving the desired results with high quality.

- All objectives were achieved while avoiding unnecessary rework… all processes should work like this!

- It was incredible to see responses quickly and timely where usually there would be a delay.

- We received support from all team members to help with our tasks.

- We did not feel like a client, but part of the same company.

Hypothesis 3 – Reduced delivery times of contract completion

Compared to historical performance, the supply chain Vice Presidency had defined set milestones to complete things by. When comparing our times in this experiment with the times that were expected by the historical processes, the difference can be seen in Table 4-1.

Chapter 4 | Colombia

Table 4-1. Comparison of times between Agile experiment and historical performance

Stage	Completion of previous analysis	Publication	Acceptance	Formalization	Start of contract
SLA Date	11/12/2018	18/01/2019	08/04/2019	14/05/2019	12/06/2019
Date Pilot	11/12/2018	20/12/2018	27/02/2019	08/03/2019	11/03/2019
Time Save		-28 days	-40 days	-67 days	-93 days

The improved timings were more than expected! The internal client simply could not believe it.

In addition to all of the above, the general objective of having a collaborative way of working based on Agile methodologies was achieved and there was something that could be replicated with other teams. The staff that I mentored in Scrum felt able to go on and support other teams.

In conclusion, the experiment was very successful. Scrum is already spoken very highly of in all of the places that it has been used. I have proposed further experiments with Scrum to refine its use and its further use in the Cultural Transformation Unit.

This experience has given me one of my greatest senses of satisfaction as an Agile Coach and specifically in the use of Scrum, since it was totally experimental for me and for the contracting area of EPM. I had no expectation that it could work for them. I felt fortunate to work with people of such high knowledge and experience in their roles. To this day, it is one of the Scrum Teams that I have most seen continuous improvement in, and who have achieved high levels of productivity in the entire company. I have come to realize that by creating a collaborative work environment, having the courage to sustain it, motivating people who have the right knowledge for a common purpose, and giving them guidance in Scrum, we can achieve amazing things.

—Claudia Liliana Toscano Vargas, Agile Coach at EPM

■ **Takeaway** Take a hypothesis-driven approach to change. Nobody can be certain that any change is going to work, all we can do is hypothesize, carry out the change and then look at the results. A good hypothesis should make it clear what will be measured to validate the experiment's success. For example, your hypothesis statement could be something like, "we believe by introducing pair programming, we will reduce the number of bugs in our software by 80% while continuing to deliver the same number of features." If the experiment proves that the change is not for the better, that should be celebrated as much as if the change did lead to improvement. There is as much value in learning what doesn't work, as to what does.

> ▦ **Takeaway** Create team alignment. Abstract values and talking about collaboration can mean different things to different people. As Claudia talked about in her story, she and the team defined what collaboration meant to them, for example. Various canvases such as the Team Canvas[8] can be used by teams to create a shared understanding and team culture so that all members know what is expected of them and what to expect from each other.

Geniio: Generating Integral and Timely Information

A process of transformation in an organization like EPM is a great challenge that goes beyond methodologies and technical processes (of software in our case). It extends to the purpose of the organization and its people.

An example of this process of change in the organization is the Geniio team who, with discipline and dedication, are today creating products of value, and are an example in the use of Agile practices.

The generation of electric power is a complex and extensive process. Groups of experts generate, store, process, and analyze large amounts of data to make decisions. In most cases this was carried out in diverse and basic solutions, often in Excel and PowerPoint. The result is a lot of waste, risk of error, and a reliance on people's knowledge, people who are working with scattered information. Making decisions in a timely manner and with the least possible uncertainty is vital for an organization such as EPM.

The Technology and Information Management group who, at the time were part of the wider plan to adopt Agile, were requested to provide a solution.

We began with an inception session where all of the key people that were identified to achieve the objective were invited. This included managers, software architects, and development analysts among others. The inception took three days and as a result we had determined the structure and identity of what was team Geniio, its purpose, an understanding of the general context of the problem, expected challenges and risks, and a high-level release plan for deliverables in chronological order.

The inception was challenging. The group was used to traditional projects. Achieving consensus on the purpose and priority of deliverables was difficult with such a large group, especially in a culture where the feeling is, "I need the

---

[8]Team Canvas http://theteamcanvas.com/

Chapter 4 | Colombia

whole system for it to work." We struggled to keep the conversation about value and purpose, and away from going into detailed discussions about very specific elements. Though this inception phase was difficult, it set the stage for the rest of the project.

The development team and Product Owner had very little experience of Scrum. It was necessary to spend the early days writing user stories and building trust that work could be done in increments without a complete architecture having been defined. Training that had been given previously had been given too long ago, ideally, it would have been delivered "just in time" and we would have had an Agile Coach giving training and advice.

Little by little the team began to get into a rhythm and establish discipline. The Geniio team showed great resilience in the first Sprints. While Sprint forecasts were not achieved, the team learned what their capacity was and the importance of making the whole team's work transparent. The team delivered early results in Excel that acted as a minimum viable product to get early feedback for the development team with a low amount of effort. Building in the agreed architecture would come later.

The Geniio team was supported in the roles of the Scrum framework by Agile Coaches as part of a mentoring scheme. During the first five Sprints, the mentor took charge, allowing others to observe and learn. Following this, they co-facilitated with others, for example, the Scrum events, or writing stories before taking more of an observation and advisory role, giving feedback and confidence to the team. Eventually the mentor would only be involved by invitation from the team.

The development of the Geniio team has been marked with a number of important milestones in the adoption of Agile practices, which act as inspiration for other teams at EPM that are starting their own journey. Among the many achievements, those that stand out are as follows:

1. Geniio has been active as a team for more than 60 Sprints. This has allowed them to continuously adapt their processes which is complemented by a long history of velocity and delivery metrics.

2. The team had made the concept of minimum viable product part of daily life and with it regular value-adding deliveries. This has helped the organization with a paradigm shift away from thinking such as "until I have everything, I cannot prove it or use it."

3. In all of its months of work, the Geniio team has undergone many changes to people and stakeholders due to changes on the part of contractors or organizational shifts. The team has assimilated these without compromising on the quality of the product or suffering considerable variations in its ability to deliver product increments.

Adopting Agile Across Borders

4. Geniio has positioned itself as an example as "the best way to solve problems." Because of this, there is a desire for other teams to achieve the same working dynamic.

5. Geniio has shown that it has brought down the previous organizational barriers and hierarchical separation. Geniio team members are like a family and it is difficult to differentiate where its people are in the organization, or if they are contractors. Everyone in the team contributes equally and shares the victories and opportunities for improvement.

The process of adopting Agile is challenging. Multiple dimensions need to be addressed, including the development and evolution of the team, and alignment with the organization as a whole. Patience and perseverance combined are needed to achieve success stories such as those of Geniio. In an environment such as ours which promotes development and self-exploration, learning is gained through experience complemented by training, and the motivation to follow the vision of the organization.

Our recommendations when adopting Agile is to allow everyone involved to have their say on the methods used. Following a single prescribed recipe will not work for everyone all of the time. Teams should be encouraged to mature their own processes with autonomy.

Finally, we recognize that all methodologies and frameworks are a means to an end, and not an end in themselves.

—Sebastián Pérez Jiménez, Computer Specialist, EPM

■ **Takeaway** Nail it before you scale it. No true Agile method provides a clear template to follow. Adopting Agile is a never-ending journey of discovery and experimentation to find what works within context. Start with a pilot team that still delivers value, but limits the risk. You can then build up experience with what works and what doesn't in your context over time. Changing whole departments or organizations in one big bang to work Agile rarely works out well.

■ **Takeaway** Learn through experience. While training is valuable, it is complementary to learning by doing. As we saw in Sebastián's story, the Geniio team's success came from learning through experience, by experimenting and trying out ideas for themselves. This takes time and so requires a culture of trust. There also needs to be an understanding that results do not come immediately following the completion of a training course. Practice over time supplemented by training is the way to long-term benefits.

Chapter 4 | Colombia

Scaling Agile at EPM

Fénix ATC is a system that supports office personnel attending to EPM's electrical power users. It was developed in Visual Basic 6.0 17 years ago, a language that is no longer supported by Microsoft. This represents a high risk of continuity for the business with fears that at any moment it could stop working, affecting the 151 offices across Antioquia that depend on it. This is why it became imperative to migrate the system to a more modern platform, where we could take advantage of modern technology as well as to have vendor support.

Although several alternatives were evaluated to carry out this migration, Microsoft Dynamics CRM was chosen due to the fact that EPM had already migrated water and gas services to the platform. This allowed reuse of some of the components already developed, as well as giving us a unified model of all of our products and services.

Fénix ATC is a huge system, and it integrates with more than 10 other systems. In a first planning exercise, it was estimated that the migration would take 22 months to be carried out, but this was based on five teams working in parallel with a total of 26 people. This estimate showed us the magnitude of the project, and why we needed a way of scaling our existing Agile process to enable parallel working and to manage dependencies.

At EPM, and specifically within Information Technology Management, we have been implementing an Agile adoption project since 2014, with a team of Agile Coaches supporting project and application support teams with Scrum and Kanban. We had never applied a scaling framework. When the project to migrate Fénix ATC arose, we in the Agile Coaching team were consulted on how to scale agility.

In our team of Agile Coaches, we had some knowledge in some of the scaling frameworks, specifically in LeSS and SAFe®, but we did not want to rule out others such as Nexus and Scrum of Scrums. In my role as an Agile Coach, I set myself the task of studying them all, in order to choose the framework that best suited the needs of the migration project. We had a single product with a single Product Owner, we wanted short feedback cycles for monitoring and adjusting the plan, and a strong communication mechanism between teams, due to the dependencies there would be between them.

We still took some elements from SAFe®, such as the Program Board that is shown in Figure 4-5, to help with the management of dependencies between teams. But overall, SAFe® was discarded, because we felt its strength is more in helping at the portfolio level, and its planning cycles were spread out too much.

Adopting Agile Across Borders | 73

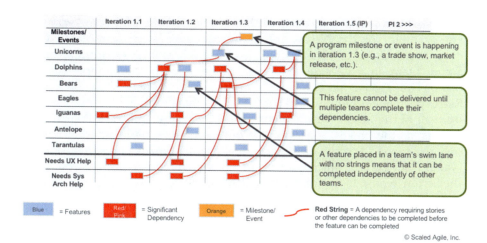

Figure 4-5. Program board[9]

We finally chose Nexus as the most suitable framework for us. Its additional roles and artifacts such as the Nexus Integration Team and the Nexus Sprint Backlog would help facilitate communication and dependency management. The Nexus framework is shown in Figure 4-6.

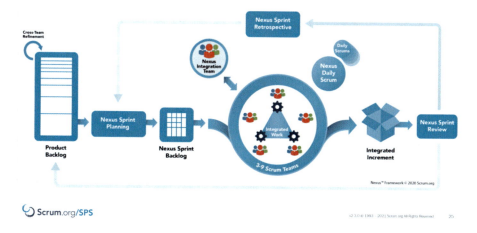

Figure 4-6. Nexus framework[10]

---

[9]Scaled Agile Framework® PI Planning www.scaledagileframework.com/pi-planning/
[10]The Nexus Guide www.scrum.org/resources/online-nexus-guide

Chapter 4 | Colombia

The Nexus events are versions of those in Scrum but with some variations. For example, for the Nexus Sprint Retrospective event, the Nexus Guide describes three parts. The first part is where representatives from across the Scrum Teams in the Nexus meet and identify issues affecting more than one team. The second part is where each team conducts their own Sprint Retrospective with input from part 1. In the third part, representatives again from all of the Scrum Teams meet again to visualize and track improvement actions for the Nexus as a whole. In our case, we experimented by applying only the second and the third part. Similarly, the Nexus Guide describes the Nexus Daily Scrum, which is a daily meeting with representatives from across the Scrum Teams. In our case, we wanted to try this new event, not on a daily basis, but twice a week. In both cases, the idea was to experiment and make changes where necessary that suited us as the project progressed.

We ran a "kick-off" day for the project. During the day we held a contest to determine the name of the project. From the different names proposed, by way of vote the project was to be called "Dynamo," due to its relationship with the generation of electric power, and our use of the Microsoft Dynamics CRM as the development platform. During the day we talked about the Nexus framework and our particular adaptations for the project. The days for the events and a Sprint duration of two calendar weeks were agreed upon. Then, the teams were formed and each of them chose their name and logo. They were named "Cosmos," "Orión," "Neutrón," "Voraz," and "Enchufados." After this session, the project began immediately.

The project has been running for a year, and to this day, we continue to use the Nexus framework without major modifications. Learning the Nexus framework has been easy, since it is based on Scrum. We have gone from teams of six to nine people, to five or more teams working simultaneously on the same project. Due to the larger scale that it has entailed, the facilitation of the Nexus has required greater preparation and organization in order for it to run smoothly.

The biggest challenge has been in managing the dependencies between the teams. It has required excellent coordination and a high level of commitment to ensure that teams do not block each other, and for teams to meet their forecasts for each Sprint. We have found that for Nexus to work well, the rigor in engineering practices is critical, as we must ensure a smooth integration of all of the team's work into the Increment to be delivered. Because there are several teams building on the same product, test automation, continuous integration, and continuous deployment are essential.

Perhaps the most novel part of the framework is the Nexus Integration Team and its events: the Nexus Daily Scrum and the Nexus Sprint Retrospective. Our Nexus Integration team is made up of the project leader, the Product Owner, the Scrum Master, and a member from each of the teams. Its function is to generate warnings of dependencies and problems between teams, help

Adopting Agile Across Borders

solve them, and remove impediments, always trying to ensure that there is a "Done" integrated Increment by the end of each Sprint. In addition, it must ensure the use of development standards, infrastructure, and architecture to ensure the construction of integrated quality Increments.

The teams adapted easily to working in the Nexus, due in large part to the fact that most of them already had experience working with Scrum. As an Agile Coach, I must say that these teams are made up of committed, open, and very creative people. The latter has been amply demonstrated not only in the product they are building but also in the way they carry out the Sprint Reviews. On many occasions the Sprint Reviews are based on specific themes. On one occasion, a story set in space was devised, in which the teams were protagonists in the story. On another occasion, during the football World Cup, user stories were presented on T-shirts that represented the different countries taking part in the competition. Picture from these are shown in Figures 4-7 and 4-8. This has brought dynamism and camaraderie, and has aroused the interest of all participants, especially the Product Owner and stakeholders. After each release, we usually prepare a celebration for all, in recognition of everyone's contribution to the excellent results that the teams have obtained so far.

Figure 4-7. "Space Story" Sprint Review

Figure 4-8. "Football World Cup" Sprint Review

Chapter 4 | Colombia

It is things like this that has kept the teams very motivated and happy, helping them to reach levels of high performance in their work as a team, both in terms of productivity and in building quality into the product. Team morale is monitored through surveys sent to the Scrum Teams, with results displayed in a radar, as shown in Figure 4-9. To measure the quality of the product, we have tools such as Sonar, which measures different quality indicators such as cyclomatic complexity, test coverage, and code duplication, among others.

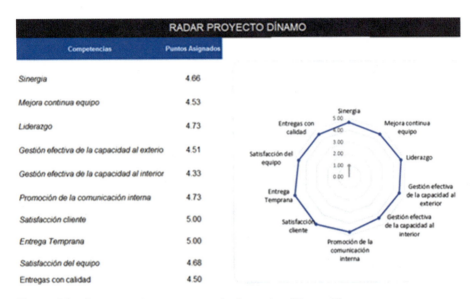

Figure 4-9. Continuous improvement radar for project "Dynamo"

The Nexus framework is helping to successfully execute the Fénix ATC migration project. We are fulfilling the expectations of our stakeholders, and also achieving our promise to the development teams of self-management, motivation, productivity, and happiness.

The success of frameworks such as Scrum and Nexus lies in the willingness and commitment of people to learn new ways of doing things, to experiment and to contribute, to achieve a shared vision, knowing that we are delivering a product of value to the business, and that we are contributing to make life easier for our users, and therefore, our energy customers.

—Liliana Zuluaga Hoyos, Agile Coach at EPM

> **Takeaway** Scaling depends on doing your research and good people. There are many scaling techniques out there, as well as Nexus, there is LeSS, SAFe®, Disciplined Agile, Scrum of Scrums, Scrum@Scale, etc. However, as Liliana shows in her story, success is still based on the commitment of the people involved, their willingness to explore, and their drive to continuously improve.

> **Takeaway** Take a systems thinking approach to change. We have seen companies that focus only on implementing a particular organizational restructure or adopting an Agile scaling framework that results in little improvement. In any such initiative, the likes of architecture, infrastructure, and development practices in a software development environment should be subject to just as much scrutiny for change. For example, redesigning architecture to enable teams to work as independently as possible from each other, or replacing tightly coupled legacy systems stacks with modern implementations that enables things like continuous integration, automation of testing, build and deploy, real-time monitoring, etc.

People tend to be passionate about what they do and act spontaneously over creating and following detailed plans. Most of all, people have a compassion for putting other people at the center of everything they do. Humor and storytelling is frequently used. While there is a strict adherence to written contracts, with nothing being sure until it is in writing, a concern for other people is the dominating influence on behavior. This was best summed up when we asked the Geniio team at EPM how they measured success. After a couple of seconds of thought, one of the team members answered us with, "we measure success by the size of the smile on our customer's faces."

Getting On and Around

While great talkers, many people in Colombia are also great listeners. A respect for allowing others to have their say through to completion should work both ways. Facilitators and decision makers should be well aware of the importance of allowing everyone to have their chance to talk and build consensus as a group ahead of just following the wishes of the most senior person.

Honor is important and there is a wish to avoid causing embarrassment to themselves or others. A strategy of building relationships and trust is important as people value long-term human relationships as the foundation of everything else. Critique with care, as we saw Dominic at Plastinorte find out the hard way in his story a little earlier.

Chapter 4 | Colombia

To foreigners, Colombia's history and politics may be fascinating, but keep in mind that many people have lived through the difficult times first hand. It is best advised to avoid starting conversations about politics and historical conflicts.

Agile Community Events and Meetups

- Agiles Colombia: `https://agilescolombia.org/`
- Scrum & Agil Colombia: `www.meetup.com/scrum-agil-colombia/`

CHAPTER

5

Uruguay

Uruguay, like its people, is a country that is calm and self-assured. The people are warm, sincere, open, and seemingly happy. It is one of South America's most progressive societies (Uruguay was the first country in the world to fully legalize cannabis in 2013). It ranks highly on global measures for personal rights, tolerance, and inclusion,[1] making it a perfect place for Agile to flourish.

Diminutive in size and sandwiched between the region's main powers, the question is how well Uruguay can punch above its weight.

History

The Charrúa, Chaná, and Arachán were small tribes of nomadic hunter-gatherers who were the inhabitants in the area of what is now Uruguay, as well as neighboring areas of present day Argentina and Brazil, before European colonization. It is estimated that the population of these tribes numbered no more than 20,000 people in total.

Colonization of this part of South America by Europeans occurred relatively late, partly due to the initially strong resistance shown by the indigenous peoples (who were later all but wiped out by European invaders), and partly due to apathy because of an absence of gold and silver in the area. The Portuguese and Spanish took an interest in the region in the late 17th and

---

[1]The Social Reference Imperative https://web.archive.org/web/20160305112007/http://www.socialprogressimperative.org/data/spi/countries/URY

© Glaudia Califano, David Spinks 2021
G. Califano and D. Spinks, *Adopting Agile Across Borders*,
https://doi.org/10.1007/978-1-4842-6948-0_5

Chapter 5 | Uruguay

18th centuries, the Portuguese establishing a base at Colonia del Sacramento and the Spanish founding Montevideo. The two powers struggled against one another for control of the area until Spain sided with France in the early 19th century, bringing them into the Napoleonic wars. Britain attempted several invasions of the River Plate area to gain control of Buenos Aires and Montevideo. Though the British had a presence in Montevideo for a few months in 1807, they were ultimately unsuccessful in occupying Uruguay. The struggles weakened the colonizing powers and sowed the seeds for independence movements to grow.

A concentrated campaign in 1825 against what was then Brazilian control led to a British mediated treaty that gave Uruguay its independence. The threat of further incursions from Brazil or Argentina subsided toward the end of the century, allowing Uruguay to emerge with a strong economy based on beef and wool – a legacy of the cattle that had been first introduced by the Spanish.

A period of relative stability and harmony was disrupted when, partly because of a drop in food prices in Europe and Asia after World War II, and partly due to a general worldwide decrease in demand for Uruguayan agricultural goods, the economy took a downturn. The subsequent drop in the standard of living led to civil unrest and the rise of an armed guerilla group named the Tupamaros who carried out robberies, kidnapping, assassinations, and made attempts to overthrow the government. Tensions escalated to the point where the government announced a state of emergency in 1968, introducing a number of repressive policies and the suspension of civil liberties in 1972. The following year, the military, on request of the then president Juan Maria Bordaberry closed down the congress and established a civilian-military regime. During this time, Uruguay participated in Operation Condor,[2] the US-backed campaign, to repress the political left by a number of right-wing dictatorships in South America. Democracy was not re-introduced in Uruguay until the mid-1980s following the rejection of the military's new constitution in a referendum.

Economic instability rose again at the turn of the millennium, when commodity prices dropped again and financial crises affected Argentina's, Brazil's, and Uruguay's other main export markets. Despite the severity of the financial situation, Uruguay fared much better than its neighbors, an indication of its stability and reputation to investors. In the global financial crisis of 2008, Uruguay was the only country in the whole of the Americas that did not fall into a recession going by the technical definition of two quarters of negative growth.

---

[2]Dinges, J. *Operation Condor*. Columbia University. www.latinamericanstudies.org/chile/operation-condor.htm

Power in Uruguay has historically been contested between the Blancos and Colorados parties (named after the respective white and red bands that their members wear). In recent years the first left leaning party, Frente Amplio (translated as "Broad Front") was elected in 2004, 2009, and 2014. They have introduced many cultural changes. The Frente Amplio government has overseen the legalization of marijuana, abortion, and same sex marriage. In 2005, they created the "Ministry of Social Development" to reduce the country's poverty rate.[3]

Uruguay is notable for the progress it has made in its development and use of renewable energy. It made the bold ambition to be carbon neutral by the year 2030. As of 2015, they were 95% there, an achievement made in less than ten years[4] by the development of hydroelectric dams, wind turbines, and solar panel parks. This has slashed Uruguay's cost of producing electricity and the country's carbon footprint.

Since its transition back to democracy, Uruguay has developed good relationships with the United States. Commercial trade has grown substantially between the two countries in recent years in particular, fueled by a bilateral investment treaty signed in 2004, and a Trade and Investment Framework Agreement in 2007.

This relationship between Uruguay and the United States was in evidence in the companies that we visited, nearshore software development companies providing services to US customers looking to lower costs while retaining quality and speed to market. The following story is told by Juan Rucks, Senior UX-UI designer at a company called UruIT based in Montevideo that we visited, and he tells the story about how at UruIT they build relations and trust with their overseas clients.

Building Trust, Learning, and Understanding: An Agile Approach to Project Discovery

Starting any new development project is a challenge. It's the kind of stuff that still keeps me up at night. There is that uneasiness in the air that is almost palpable: there's a lot of money on the line, anxiety is high, and trust still

---

[3]Meyer, P (2010). *Uruguay: Political and Economic Conditions and U.S. Relations.* https://fas.org/sgp/crs/row/R40909.pdf (page 2 *"...National Plan to Address the Social Emergency (PANES). PANES provided a monthly conditional cash transfer of approximately $75 to over 100,000 households in extreme poverty. In exchange, those receiving the benefits were required to participate in community work and ensure that their children attended school daily and had regular health checkups."*)

[4]Macdonald, F. (2015). *Uruguay Has Shifted to Getting 95% of Its Electricity From Renewables in Less Than 10 Years.* Science Alert. www.sciencealert.com/uruguay-has-shifted-to-getting-95-of-its-electricity-from-clean-energy-sources-in-less-than-10-years

Chapter 5 | Uruguay

needs to be won. Agile methodologies, User Centered Design, and Design Thinking are all things that sound great when you explain the theory, but for the person on the paying end who is unfamiliar or inexperienced in development of any kind, those first days or weeks can REALLY make you question your investment decision. It's not so hard to empathize with a client. As a client you want to see progress as soon as possible; you just shelled out thousands of dollars and in return the people you just hired are running "new-age" activities with post-it notes, asking to talk to users and telling you they are probably not going to do all the things you hired them to do in the time you hired them to do it. Wireframes, designs, prototypes, code, functionality, and releases are those tangible things that most clients in my experience consider "progress"; but Agile is not so good in providing "progress" in terms of delivering more features as it is in identifying value. Agile development if done right – in my opinion – is not faster than other methodologies but rather the opposite: it provides faster opportunities to learn and iterate on the thing you just built. You might actually spend more time ideating, testing, and measuring a particular piece of functionality than building it. If we compare development methodologies, I believe that in the same set amount of time using an Agile methodology, you will probably get less functionality done than in more traditional development, the difference being that the functionality that you do build will no doubt be more valuable and refined. This is an idea that is all well and good on paper, but telling the client that we will probably get less done than what they imagine is a really hard conversation at this stage of the project.

After many new projects, some more successful than others, I've come to the conclusion that the first few weeks of a project are about balance: interweaving things that the client wants to see with testing and research. Now all clients, all projects, and all teams are different, but I'll try to share our way of tackling these first few Sprints and why we do it in the way we do. It is in no way perfect; in fact, it is very much a work in progress which changes with every new project.

To understand why we do the things we do I figure it's important to first give you a little insight into our own particular context. We are a small development company based in Uruguay that works remotely principally for the US market. We tackle anything from small three-month startup projects all the way to partnership-like developments that span years. This means we meet all kinds of clients, from startups to well established companies, who have all types of previous experiences with development projects and who do business in all types of markets. However, although I can't say it is true in all cases, two particular patterns I've seen with our clients are that (1) they are looking for lower costs than what they can get back in the United States while still keeping quality and (2) they appreciate, or are interested in, an Agile methodology because they've been burned previously with the more traditional waterfall approach of developing.

Adopting Agile Across Borders 83

Lots of companies and people have different names for the initial project start phase, we in particular have started calling it the Project Discovery. It is very different from our actual development cycle and more often than not, we sell it as an entirely different project. The idea behind this is that we can't estimate what we don't understand. When a client comes to us asking for a price and time estimate, it's often – and particularly in bigger projects – that we back up and propose to do a Project Discovery instead.

This is in fact what gives us our first limitation: the Project Discovery cannot be a big investment for either the client or for us, both in terms of money and timewise. Coming from a non-Agile UX background on my first projects, it made perfect sense to me to analyze problems in detail: conduct user interviews and testing sessions, create personas, post surveys, do benchmarking, create user journeys, etc., and of course, create neat documents to gather all our findings before starting a project. If you take the time to do all these things – and we have! – you most likely are going to spend months in this endeavor. To top it off, the unfortunate truth is that most clients do not see the value in these things that we in the industry do. I've yet to see a client have a "eureka" moment based on user feedback that has drastically changed their way of thinking or their general approach to an idea; the truth is that the conclusions of good UX research rightfully get passed off as common sense in the final solution. So my advice here – and a general rule of thumb for everything in this initial stage – is to do only the essential. So how do we define what is essential? Basically by forcing our Projects Discoveries to happen within a week. An idea that we borrowed from the Design Sprint concept by Jake Knapp.[5] This not only keeps the cost of the discovery phase relatively low, but having a finite amount of time forces us to make conscious decisions on how to best spend that time.

Before I get into describing our Project Discovery, I must say that client involvement during the discovery week is an absolute requirement. Learning is mutual and intensive: the client has the business knowledge that we must absorb and we must teach the client how we work. This week offers some key insights into our daily work habits such as prioritizing, identifying value, building incrementally, and testing hypotheses. It is here the client begins to understand what to expect as far as working together if the project continues after the discovery phase. For these reasons we ask the client and the stakeholders involved to free up their schedule for this particular week. The reality, and one of the biggest setbacks we've had with the Design Sprint method mentioned before, is that it has been impossible to ask a client and the stakeholders to give us their undivided attention for an entire week. Additionally, if you've ever run any Design Thinking activities with someone

---

[5]Knapp, J. (2016). *Sprint*. Simon & Schuste. ISBN-13: 978-1501121746

Chapter 5 | Uruguay

from another business or background you'll agree with me that skepticism is a big obstacle to get over. Asking for an entire week is not only a huge investment of time and money, it begs the question of "is this the best use of my time?" right out of the gates; trust is a hard thing to win over, let alone win back. To this end, we defined that a single day of the discovery week can have no more than four hours of meetings or activities with the stakeholders; and we always divide those four hours into two or more intervals since it's hard to keep everyone involved and active for a longer period.

Despite our belief in collaboration and encouragement to run the discovery week in person, be it the client flies over to Uruguay or we send people over to them, this does not always happen. We are used to working remotely, but for many of these activities the distance issue can be quite a challenge. We've yet to find a way to get the same level of client involvement as we get in person. Nonetheless, it can be done, it is just a lot less effective and a lot more work. Another incredibly important and sometimes overlooked aspect of having this week in person is the empathic value of the meeting of the two sides. Development can seem pretty cold and distant through mail or even video conferencing; making a connection on a human level is the base of any good working relationship, it helps communication and motivation by creating a deeper involvement and understanding between everyone.

Which takes me to our team. Usually our Project Discoveries involve all of the team members that could eventually take on the project. This depends on the size of the project, but we are used to working in small autonomous teams from three to eight people made up of Product Owners, UX/UI roles, and full-stack developers. All the team is involved in most of the activities throughout the week to learn about the project firsthand, provide their perspective, and quite possibly to take turns facilitating the activities or meetings with the stakeholders. I believe having the whole team involved is key if you can spare it; everyone learning firsthand information and providing input from their different backgrounds is a real time saver in the end and keeps everyone aligned – plus it generates that all-so-important empathy and involvement I mentioned earlier.

As far as the discovery is concerned, to me it is like a conversion funnel: it starts off with the big picture, you prioritize something and add detail, then repeat until you have a small enough chunk of the most valuable part of the project with enough detail that you could create a prototype or wireframe with. A simple example could be an online travel agent, where as a group one could identify plane ticket sales as the most valuable thing to tackle first; then within the plane ticket sales, tackle round trip tickets and within that tackle frequent flyers. So you end up creating a pretty limited but fully working plane tickets purchasing platform or site only for frequent flyers and only for round trip tickets. This is important because not only does it become the backbone of the system, it is something much more graspable, estimable, and testable.

Adopting Agile Across Borders

What is imperative here is that everyone – client and team – is in agreement that this is the most important and valuable thing to tackle first. Prioritization in relation to value is an incredibly important lesson the client must learn about working in an Agile methodology so we try to introduce it to them as soon as possible. Our general goal in all development is to minimize what we build while maximizing the value it delivers; the idea behind this is that smaller and simpler things take less time to build, so if we identify and prioritize what is the minimum – and therefore fastest – thing we can build that provides the most value, we are making the best use of the project's budget and time.

The principal objectives of every discovery is to have a general understanding of the project and business, a prioritized backlog, an estimation of how long the project could take, and, above all, a general alignment between everyone of what is going to be built – if a discovery is done right, there are no surprises in the final deliverable. To this end, our first order of business after our initial talk with the client and getting a green light to begin a Project Discovery is to get together with the team internally and define the objectives of the discovery week. Our tool of choice here is Trello, where we create a column of objectives. Some are essential as I mentioned beforehand: "understand the business and its context," "align expectations," "define the project technology stack," "create a project roadmap," and "estimate size/cost," but, of course, depending on the size of the project, much more can be done in the week. Based on our initial talk with the client, we hopefully have at least a vague idea of the complexity and size of the project. It is with this intuition that we add new objectives to the week: "create a prototype," "identify aesthetics," "talk with users," "create a proof of concept," "conduct user testing" – anything we feel would add value to our final deliverable of the week to create a more valuable and solid project proposal. This is also where balance comes into play, we try to level out things the client might want to see with things that are more intangible or research based, and we may also end up challenging some of the client's original ideas and hypotheses on value.

Once we feel we have a good list of achievable objectives for the week, we begin planning the week and ideating the activities. We create columns for each day of the week and add activities to them. Using the aforementioned four-hour rule, we add those activities with the client and those without the client to the columns in an order that makes sense and that we consider achievable in an eight-hour day. We've taken activities to involve the client from several different sources: Jonathan Rasmusson's Inception Deck from the book *The Agile Samurai*,[6] the Design Sprint we mentioned earlier, some more traditional UX activities,[7] and some we actually borrowed and modified

---

[6]Rasmusson, J. (2010). *The Agile Samurai: How Agile Masters Deliver Great Software* (first edition). Pragmatic Programmers. ISBN-13: 978-1934356586
[7]*UX Design Methods & Deliverables* https://uxdesign.cc/ux-design-methods-deliverables-657f54ce3c7d

Chapter 5 | Uruguay

from other companies that have a similar "discovery" process. There are hundreds of different activities that have different goals, it's about experimenting and seeing which work best. The key concept in all of these activities is that both the team and the client are engaged and participating, if we start seeing that either side is waning, we either cut the activity short or propose a break. Some of our more tried and tested activities grouped by our more common objectives are as follows:

Understanding business context:

- "Where do you see the project in three months, one year, five years" activity taken from the Agile Samurai's Inception Deck. We ask the group to write their thoughts for each time period on post-it notes, post them on the wall, and then share.

- User journey mapping. Defining the start and endpoints of the customer journey as a group and then asking the client and stakeholders to fill in the middle with post-it notes.

- Stakeholder mapping. Identifying everyone involved and getting agreement on their level of involvement.

Align expectations:

- "What keeps us up at night?" from the Agile Samurai's Inception Deck. Write on post-it notes, share with the group and identify actions to counter them.

- Risk matrix. Write potential risks and worries on post-it notes and then identify their place as a group on a graph where "impact" and "probability" are the two axis. Those risks with high probability and high impact are discussed and we plan actions to counter or mitigate them.

- Google's HEART framework. You can read about the original activity[8] but we actually modified it to suit our needs. What we do is write objectives for the project on post-it notes and then later arrange them into the groups proposed by the framework. This, rather than forcing us to create goals for each category, helps us identify the overall category/theme of the project which we will later use to prioritize features.

---

[8]Rodden, K. (2015). *How to Choose the Right UX Metrics for Your Product.* Library.gv.com. https://library.gv.com/how-to-choose-the-right-ux-metrics-for-your-product-5f46359ab5be

Adopting Agile Across Borders

- IN/OUT from the Agile Samurai's Inception Deck. Here we discuss as a group what we will be doing, but more importantly, what we won't be doing.

Create a Project Roadmap:

- User stories. First identify the user archetypes and then as a group write on post-it notes things that these users will need to do in the form of user stories (e.g., As a frequent flyer I must be able to view my plane ticket purchases).

- Story mapping. Probably the most useful activity, but also the most difficult to explain and also the most time consuming. I won't try to explain it in detail, but you can find information online[9] or in Jeff Patton's book *User Story Mapping*.[10] We actually divide this activity into two parts, one for creating the story map of the flow we identified and a second part for prioritizing the cards into releases. This in fact becomes our initial backlog and also our source of information for wireframing and prototyping.

There are a number of other activities needed during discovery week, but the preceding are the main ones that require most collaboration. One final note is that we always finish off the week with a retrospective to collect insights on things we did right, things we can improve, and also to give thanks, but in a nutshell, this is how we run our discovery week. Once it is finished, we might add descriptions to the activity cards and time expectations for each. We then share the board with the client, present it to them and modify it based on their feedback so that everyone is aligned on what the proposal and objectives for the week are. Once validated, we schedule with everybody the meetings/activities for the first day.

I say only for the first day because in our experience, no discovery ever goes according to plan. The Trello board becomes a sort of living schedule. We are ready to change things up on a daily (or even activity by activity!) basis. As we start discovering the project and business, we soon find that we missed things, underestimated, overestimated, or just did not get the results we intended. This is why Trello is a good tool, since you can move, add or edit the cards as needed. We usually create a new column for those activities we did not get to since it is important to see them. Team and client decisions such as exceeding

---

[9]Bowes, J. (2017). *An introduction to user story mapping.* Manifesto. https://manifesto.co.uk/user-story-mapping/

[10]Patton, J. (2014). *User Story Mapping: Discover the Whole Story, Build the Right Product.* O'Reilly Media. ISBN-13: 978-1491904909

Chapter 5 | Uruguay

the time allotted, new activities, or new objectives all have an impact on what has been planned and it is important for everyone to understand and visualize that every decision has consequences. Nevertheless, it is imperative not to forget the essential goals. On bigger projects you can potentially take up the whole week just talking about the business or just understanding the project, it is key to just have a big picture understanding and quickly prioritize the most valuable user flows that need to happen within the system. This could be done in several ways, be it by general discussion or by using an activity like the aforementioned user stories activity followed by a prioritization of the stories. However, it is important to prioritize flows and not features, which is sometimes tricky when you talk in terms of user stories.

With any luck, by the end of the week we have all the information we need to create a document with all the work we did, its conclusions, a team proposal and time/cost estimations for the project. If the project is launched, we know exactly what we need to design, build, research, and/or test in its first Sprints. More importantly, the client gets a crash course of what working with us is like and a better understanding of the Agile methodology. There is a lot more trust and understanding by clients who we've run this type of discovery phase with. It makes easing into working with Sprints and increments of value a whole lot easier and smoother. That said, discovery is an ongoing process during the course of a project and having the experience of the activities makes doing them remotely later on much simpler. As I mentioned in the beginning, the initial discovery process itself is not perfect – there is no silver bullet when it comes to beginning a project – but hopefully it will give you some ideas into not only how to begin a project but also into how to establish a relationship with a client who is new to the Agile methodology.

—Juan Rucks, Senior UX-UI Designer at UruIT

■ **Takeaway** Get the whole team involved from the start. Involving the wider delivery team during discovery might seem like an inefficient use of people's time, but it pays off in the end. Everyone is more aware of the problem to be solved, instead of just being told what to build. We have seen and heard many examples where people are treated as order takers and the approach is to keep them focused on building stuff, only to find that features were delivered that went unused, or resulting products were different to customer and stakeholder expectations.

> **Takeaway** Find creative ways to engage with clients during discovery and keep this collaboration going throughout the engagement. Many clients find it hard to commit a lot of time and attention to their vendor partners. However, as UruIT shows, there are creative, flexible, and time-efficient ways to ensure the communication and feedback that is needed takes place.
>
> Examples include the following:
>
> - Keep meetings lean and worth doing
>
> - Agree regular meetings that are at the same time and place so a regular rhythm is established
>
> - Make it clear what the goals are for each meeting and what everyone should get out of it
>
> - A good facilitator can help the conversation flow and make the best use of time

Insights

The previous story, despite the humbleness of the teller, demonstrates a depth of understanding and commitment to Agile ways of working, perhaps more so in UruIT than with many of their US clients! We found the Uruguayan people to be warm, open, and sincere, traits shared by many of their fellow South Americans.

Perhaps despite its economic successes and stability, similarly to other South American cultures, friends and family are central to people's lives in Uruguay. Friendship and social interaction extends to the workplace. At UruIT, several people that we chatted with told us about how they felt like a family there. Their work colleagues were also their close friends away from work. The company operates a policy where people are free to work from home; however, the message that we got was that people wanted to come into the office (incidentally, an office that had been converted from a grand family home, giving it a very warm, friendly, and homely feel) to be with their teammates.

This interweaving of people's professional and social lives is well demonstrated by the following story, written by Gonzalo Barbitta, a Software Engineer at UruIT. Here he tells the story about an experiment run at the company where the team were empowered to control their own salaries.

Chapter 5 | Uruguay

Empowering Team Members to Control Their Own Compensation – What Happened When We Let a Team Evaluate Its Own Performance and Decide on Each Member's Pay[11]

We consider ourselves an Agile company, and therefore, every team inside UruIT is self-managed. This applies not only to development teams but also to HR, marketing, and finance. **Members of these teams take ownership of how their work is done** by planning and managing their day-to-day activities without any micromanagement from above. There's no boss sitting in an ivory tower, but instead, responsibility is distributed across all members of the team.

At UruIT, salaries are reviewed twice a year (in January and June) and, like most companies, raises are given based on performance. **But, if there are no "bosses" and everyone shares the responsibility for the teams' results, who should evaluate employees' work? Wouldn't it be better if your teammates were the ones who evaluated your work?**

The Context

Approximately a year and a half ago, our company decided to try and see whether empowering teams to self-manage their own salaries would be a good idea. Of course, this was not something that could be applied overnight. Instead, we had to start small, with maybe one or two teams who were willing to be the guinea pigs.

The experiment was very simple: **during each salary review, the team would have a certain amount of money to divide among its members.** This amount would be decided by management based on multiple factors, such as the period's revenue. How this distribution would take place was entirely up to the team; management would not weigh in in any way on their decision.

At that time, I belonged to a team of developers including Andrés Báez, Waldemar Lopez, and Gustavo Clemente. We had been working together for almost two years, but had known each other for much longer than that. It was safe to say that we really trusted each other and would be able to discuss without taboo such a sensitive topic as salaries. But most importantly, **we all agreed that our effort would be better evaluated by our peers, after all, it's they who see us work and progress on a daily basis.** So, with this in mind, we decided to go through with the trial of this experiment.

---

[11]Contribution based on the blogpost at https://uruit.com/blog/self-managed-teams-salary-transparency/

Transparency

The first thing we did was create transparency by **sharing our salaries with one another.** We strongly believed that in order to reach fair salaries, we needed to know this information.

As soon as we did this, we realized that one of us was earning less than the rest, mainly due to differences in our past experience and seniority by the time we all joined UruIT. But, even though our expertise at that moment may have been different, this person had shown great improvement, up to the point where there weren't any differences in our day-to-day activities.

We knew that if we were going to move forward with the experiment, **equality in salaries was essential as a starting base.** So, after the first review, most of the pay raise was used to bring our incomes closer together. The only reason why not all of it was given to one person, was the fact that at that time, one member of the team was in need of money because of a home emergency. Because of this, the income was finally split equally and given to the team members who either deserved it, or needed it the most.

Reward System

Now that we were in a more similar position when it came to salary, it was time to think about **how we would divide the raise during the next review.**

We knew that one of the variables we would consider was each person's effort throughout those months, so we needed to come up with a strategy to evaluate and keep track of such a subjective concern. After all, how does one measure other people's effort?

As we imagined, agreeing on a strategy turned out to be quite difficult. We met several times to discuss different ways in which we could approach this, but never managed to reach a consensus.

The first approach we thought about was to keep track of the number of points each person closed during a Sprint. However, we quickly dismissed this idea because we knew this was not a reliable measure of effort. If someone spends a big part of their Sprint helping a teammate, he'll be closing less points on his own. **Helping each other should be encouraged, not punished.**

For another option, we got in touch with a well-known Agile Coach from outside the company who also had a suggestion. At the end of every Sprint, each member would have 100 points to divide among his teammates. For instance, "Mel" would give "John" 60 points because of his effort and how effective his work was throughout the Sprint, and then 20 points to both "Jane" and "Richard." John, Jane, and Richard would then do the same.

Chapter 5 | Uruguay

We thought that this idea, even though it had its benefits, encouraged competition. Think about it: each member has only 100 (or X) points to assign. If you want to reward John, you need to punish someone else by reducing their points. We were afraid that in the long term, it might lead to undesired conflicts between us.

So, after a few more ideas, we came up with a solution that everyone could agree on: **a reward system**.

Basically, when someone contributed something valuable to the team, a point was awarded to that person. But how do we agree whether a contribution is valuable enough to deserve a point? Are all contributions worth one point? For instance, is spending an entire day helping a fellow dev in need worth the same as helping troubleshoot an issue which took five minutes?

Since this is too subjective, we agreed that no point would be questioned: if someone felt that a point was deserved for whatever reason, this was to be respected. Points were to be added individually and secretly.

In order to keep track of these points, we used a big letter box on our desk. Points eventually turned into post-its where someone would enter their name, its recipient and the reason for the reward. This would **help us know as a team what each member considers valuable**, so we could align on a direction.

Time for Review

Months went by, post-its were added into the box, and the time for review came. We had to decide how we were going to split the raise from the money that was given to us.

Theoretically, the number of post-its would be used to evaluate the contribution of each member throughout these months. However, we soon realized this system was not going to be a reliable measure of each team member's effort for different reasons.

For instance, two of our team members worked from home at least once a week. When this happened, the number of notes granted to them was much lower, mainly because it was hard for other members to see their effort throughout the day. The same applied to vacations – the person that was out of the office clearly did not receive any notes and was punished somewhat for their absence.

We knew we could not only rely on these numbers.

We reminded ourselves about each team member's salary, and after a brief discussion, it was clear that we were not going to reach a consensus on how to divide the income. So, to keep things as transparent as possible, each of us wrote down on a piece of paper how they thought the income should be split by allocating a percentage of the available raise among the four of us, which would then be averaged. The decision as to how this would be done was up to each team member and their reasoning would not be questioned.

Table 5-1 shows the actual result using fake names.

Table 5-1. Results of UruIT team's thoughts on how to split salary increase

	Mel	John	Jane	Richard
Mel	20	40	20	20
John	35	35	15	15
Jane	30	40	15	15
Richard	30	50	10	10
%	28.7	41.25	15	15

For instance, Mel decided that 20% of the raise should be for herself, 40% for John, and the remaining 40% would be split equally among Jane and Richard.

After revealing these numbers, we had a brief discussion about why each of us decided to split the income in that way. It was clear that each person's priority was to achieve equality in our salaries. Secondly, for those with a similar income, we took into account the number of notes from the experiment. So, **even though the system had its flaws, it still had an impact on our final decision.**

Some Thoughts

I was recently asked whether I think empowering teams to self-manage their own salaries works or not. To be honest, this is clearly not something that would suit every company. But when it comes to companies with self-managed teams with a high level of decision-making authority, **I do believe this can be a great fit that could benefit both employers and employees.**

For employers, salaries are no longer handled by them, which takes some weight off of their shoulders. Let's be honest, when that time of the year comes when performance is evaluated and raises are given, it's likely that some employees will be unhappy with the outcome. Either no raise will be given to them or not enough. Regardless, it's the company that has to deal with the consequences. From there on, employees may feel undervalued and their commitment to the company may be compromised. With this strategy, it's up to the team to decide.

If teams can decide about pretty much everything else, why couldn't they decide on each other's salaries as well?

Chapter 5 | Uruguay

For employees, it gives them the ability to decide on their own salaries. **Their raise is no longer determined by someone who may not be capable of evaluating their work.** This is even more noticeable in non-hierarchical companies such as ours.

At a team level, it also has a great impact. First, the notes **help everyone understand what other members consider valuable for the team.** For instance, in our case in which there was a high level of customer support, joining a teammate for a customer call was clearly something that was greatly valued.

Secondly, discussing such a sensitive topic as salary, definitely **helps bring the team together.** Deciding why someone deserves a raise more than others, it's something that cannot be taken lightly. You might be forced to leave personal interests aside, or put yourself out there by sharing private concerns.

It's been a year and a half since we started with this experiment and unfortunately, the team is no longer working together. Don't worry, this had nothing to do with the experiment, it's just how our industry works! But on the bright side, we are able to share our experience with new members and, hopefully, have other teams try it for themselves.

—Gonzalo Barbitta, Software Engineer, UrulT

Considering the preceding story, is it any surprise that a Latinobarómetro[12] poll in 2010 found that Uruguayans are the biggest believers and supporters of democracy in South America? What also stood out to us after meeting Gonzalo and the team was that their first thought was for each other; their first concern was to ensure equal pay. Further, as Ganzalo describes, they decided to award pay increases to the people that needed it most, as shown in the case when an increase was awarded to one of the team members that had experienced a home emergency.

■ **Takeaway**   Don't limit experiments to products or processes. We build minimum viable products to test ideas for products or features, and try improvements in how we do things. However, don't stop there. Designing safe-to-fail experiments that explore and push the boundaries within which teams self-manage, are empowered and are trusted, as we saw with Gonzalo's team, could lead to some groundbreaking advancements in motivation, creativity, and productivity. At the very least, they should result in some valuable learning.

---

[12]Latinobarómetro www.latinobarometro.org/lat.jsp

Other signs of the socially conscious and progressive nature of Uruguayan society include a wealth gap between rich and poor lower than any other Latin American country,[13] and a high literacy rate of nearly 99%.[14] In 2009, Uruguay was the first country to provide a personal computer to every primary school student as part of the One Laptop per Child program.[15] In an example of "take it to the team" on a national scale, the Uruguayan constitution allows citizens to change laws by popular consensus through national referendums. Examples of its use include votes that have stopped privatization of public utilities and protected pensioner incomes.

With a population of just 3.4 million people at the time of writing, half of which is concentrated in the capital, Montevideo, Uruguay is the smallest Spanish speaking country on the continent. Geographically speaking, it is the second smallest sovereign nation in South America after Suriname, and when taking account of French Guiana, it is the third smallest territory. This is "small" in South American terms; Uruguay is still about three times the size of Ireland and about 25% larger than England. However, it is nestled in-between Argentina and Brazil, two giants in geographical terms.

Relatively speaking then, the size of the Agile community is correspondingly small, limiting the range of opportunities to share ideas and experiences locally when compared to Argentina, Brazil, or Chile, let alone in comparison to the likes of the United States and the United Kingdom. However, AgileUY, the active local Agile meetup in Montevideo is growing, and as of 2019 it has a respectable 1400 members. As we have discussed, we discovered that the Agile community in South America is not restricted by borders; Agile practitioners often share experiences and knowledge across countries, making it a "small" continent after all.

Uruguay's small stature means it is less thought of; the likes of Buenos Aires, Santiago, and Medellin are more likely to jump to mind ahead of Montevideo as locations for clients looking for offshore partners, or for companies looking to grow their international operations on the continent. Uruguay does have a number of strengths as a nearshore/offshore location though.[16] Few other

---

[13]Tucker, D. (2014). *Uruguay Has Lowest Income Inequality in Latin America.* Nearshore Americas. www.nearshoreamericas.com/infographic-income-inequality-latin-america/

[14]Literacy rate in Uruguay www.statista.com/statistics/575271/literacy-rate-in-uruguay/

[15]Murph, D. (2009). *Uruguay becomes first nation to provide a laptop for every primary school student.* Engadget. www.engadget.com/2009/10/18/uruguay-becomes-first-nation-to-provide-a-laptop-for-every-prima/?guccounter=1&guce_referrer_us=aHR0cHM6Ly9lbi53aWtpcGVkaWEub3JnLw&guce_referrer_cs=cTyyjBy8VBviUHt21cFsrA

[16]Ammachchi, N. (2016). *Exclusive Report on Uruguay's Outsourcing Strengths.* nearshoreamericas.com https://nearshoreamericas.com/uruguay-outsourcing-strength-lpo-kpo-fao/

Chapter 5 | Uruguay

Latin America countries can rival Uruguay for their Internet infrastructure. While salaries are higher than in other parts of South America, the workforce is highly educated. English is taught from middle school through to university,[17] and many people speak Portuguese in addition, as well as the native Spanish. A number of free-trade zones have been set up with tax incentives and exemptions offered by the government to encourage the creation of shared-service centers in the country.

Getting On and Around

In our experience, the people that we met while in Uruguay were easy to get along with. Their hospitality and helpfulness are seemingly unbounded. When we visited UruIT, we were invited to make use of their office space when we were done interviewing people. In another example, at one of the homestays where we stayed, the owner went above and beyond the call of duty to ensure we had a comfortable and smooth stay, organizing taxis for us, and giving us detailed itineraries for where to go and what to see. When it became time to leave, we had purposely left a book behind for future for guests to enjoy. Shortly afterward, we received an email from the owner. She showed real concern about how and where she could return the book that she thought we had accidently left behind.

Coupled with its relative social and economic stability, and Uruguayans' easy-going nature, there seem to be few taboos to avoid in conversation. Perhaps the main guiding principle is to acknowledge Uruguay as the independent and distinct country that it is. Despite the temptation to group Uruguayans in with Argentinians culturally, to do so would not only be unfair, but would also be rather disrespectful.

Agile Community Events and Meetups

- AgileUY: www.meetup.com/AgileUY/

---

[17]*Language education policies in Uruguay.* Language Education Policy Studies. www.languageeducationpolicy.org/regionamericascaribbean/uruguay.html

PART III

Asia

With the world's largest continent by population, the size of Asia's workforce and the number of consumers cannot be ignored. Countries in Europe and North America surged ahead with development of their economies from the time of the Industrial Revolution, expanding and consolidating their power through empire building and colonization of other parts of the world. But as we move out of the industrial age it would seem that culturally, Asia is perfectly suited for the new age of knowledge work. Asian philosophies of paternalistic and supportive leadership, consensus building, people-orientation, teamwork, collectivism, and a balanced view between the short and long term are perfectly aligned with the Agile mindset.

That is not to say that there are no challenges to overcome for Agile adoption. Companies remain rigidly hierarchical. Attitudes remain repressive, with people wary of speaking out for fear of losing face – or worse. Authority figures are seen as the ones that are wise and are the source of all answers, a hangover of the teacher-child relationship while in education that carries over into the world of work.

At the same time, Asian companies have already infiltrated many of the markets of the world. Levels of English are on the rise and there is huge potential in such a large untapped consumer market and workforce.

Agile Community Events and Meetups

- Agile Asia: www.agileasiapacific.com/

CHAPTER

6

India

India has the world's second biggest population and the largest number of people living and working overseas. Its economy and technology sector has seen enormous growth in recent times, in no small part due to it being the go-to location for outsourcing services. Combined with a colonial past, the people have a certain level of cross-cultural integration, including with those whose culture is vastly different to their own.

In many aspects, agility would seem to fit well with the culture. The people are team-orientated, relationship-driven problem solvers. Yet, in other areas there are barriers to overcome. Either way, the importance of the country on the world stage and of its people all around the world cannot be ignored.

History

Homo sapiens had arrived in the Indian subcontinent by at the latest, 55,000 years ago. This length of time means that people in this part of the world are second only to those in Africa in genetic diversity.[1] Along with settlements in Ancient Egypt and Mesopotamia (an area in the Middle East roughly comprising modern-day Iraq, Kuwait, parts of Southeast Turkey and Eastern Syria),

---

[1]Dyson, T. (2018). *A Population History of India: From the First Modern People to the Present Day.* Oxford University Press, pp. 1. ISBN 978-0-19-882905-8

© Glaudia Califano, David Spinks 2021
G. Califano and D. Spinks, *Adopting Agile Across Borders,*
https://doi.org/10.1007/978-1-4842-6948-0_6

Chapter 6 | India

the Indus Valley region in the North of India and modern-day Pakistan was home to the first civilizations from around 3000 BCE. Records from Mesopotamia indicate that Kerala in the Southwest of India was a major trading center for spices between these early civilizations at this time.

As urbanization increased over several centuries, the traditions of "Śramaṇa" arose. Śramaṇa can be translated as "making an effort or exertion," or, "one who performs acts of mortification or austerity, an ascetic, monk, devotee, religious mendicant,"[2] and its traces are part of all major Indian religions and culture. Śramaṇa was to become central to the philosophies of Jainism and Buddhism, and of "Saṃsāra," the concept of all existence as perpetual cycles, of the sun rising and setting, of birth, death, and rebirth.

The Maurya Empire, the largest empire ever to have existed on the Indian subcontinent, was to dominate South Asia from the 4th to the 3rd centuries BCE. A number of kingdoms and other empires that ruled over the area were to follow, including the Gupta Empire. Historians refer to this time as the "Golden Age" when developments in areas such as administrative practices, science, mathematics, literature, architecture, and religion (Hinduism, Buddhism, and Jainism) spread across Asia. India's economy became the largest in the world, accounting for between one-quarter and one-third of the world's wealth over the first 100 years CE.[3]

Continued raids on Indian kingdoms in the North and West laid the foundation for The Delhi Sultanate. Based in Delhi, it ruled large parts of the Indian subcontinent between the 13th and 16th centuries, and created the conditions for a mix of ideas and philosophies between Indian and Islamic cultures. The Delhi Sultanate took India onto the international stage, accelerating the mix of people, trade, technology, and thought, and it was one of the few powers able to repel the Mongol Empire.

In the 15th century, Sikhism emerged. Some of the core beliefs of Sikhism includes a belief in equality for all of humankind, justice and prosperity for all, and engaging in "Seva" or "selfless service." Alongside this, prominent beliefs in Hinduism includes the concept of "Dharma" which includes behaviors, duties, rights, conduct, and virtue that makes an orderly universe possible, and "Karma," the theory of moral cause and effect. All of these beliefs are in evidence today, as shown in the following story from Kiran Divakaran, who writes about the Sri Sathya Sai Super Speciality Hospital in Bangalore.

---

[2] Sanskrit Dictionary. www.sanskritdictionary.com/?q=%C5%9Brama%E1%B9%87a%22&lang=sans&action=Search

[3] Maddison, A. (2013). *Word GDP, 20 countries and regional totals, 0-1998AD.* The World Economy. www.theworldeconomy.org/MaddisonTables/MaddisontableB-18.pdf

Adopting Agile Across Borders

The Sri Sathya Sai Super Speciality Hospital, Bangalore: A Harmonious Work Culture With a Clear Mission

A company without a clear mission and without a culture where people freely interact, mingle, and allow people's creative juices to flow freely cannot be in as good a position to create significant value compared to those that do. People should have freedom to express themselves without being threatened, judged, or ridiculed, and they should feel an innate sense of why their work is important.

I get to experience this firsthand as a volunteer, or "seva dal" as they are referred to, at the Sri Sathya Sai Super Speciality Hospital in Whitefield, Bangalore. I go there to do "seva" (service) whenever possible to do my bit for society. On each visit, volunteers are given a task on rotation. At times, it could be assisting the nursing staff, at others, it could be taking blood samples from one part of the hospital to another. It could be bookkeeping, or helping patients through different tests and taking test reports to other units for processing.

The hospital is unique, in that it provides free medical care. No billing counter can be found anywhere – quite strange for a hospital in a country where many commercial hospitals look at the patient as a device for making money. No charge does not mean low quality – the work done at the hospital is second to none. World-class care is carried out at the Sri Sathya Sai Hospital in the fields of neurology, cardiology, and ophthalmology.

I am used to going there amidst my work at IT companies in Bangalore. Working at the hospital is not in the least bit stressful. People work in shifts of reasonable hours. I see people who start work at 7.30 a.m. and finish by 3.30–4.00 p.m. although during peak times key personnel sometimes work beyond the call of duty when there are instances of an influx of patients. People give their soul for the betterment of their fellow man in an environment of trust. I have heard stories from doctors who told me that they were more efficient and performed at their best in this environment than in other purely commercial run hospitals where making money was the sole intent. The environment has brought out the best in people.

I have always wondered why companies big and small cannot have cultures such as the Sri Sathya Sai Hospital. My service at the hospital has left me thinking that this is how all work should be, instead of people being made to chase endless deadlines, having every last grain of effort squeezed out of them, and people left feeling discontented and empty.

Current Problems in Organizations

Many companies are dealing with unrealistic expectations from investors, and upper management that demand success too quickly. Workers that try to outsmart each other to win the biggest bonus. Wrong behaviors are rewarded and few companies measure true success holistically. Work environments are a far cry from being psychologically safe, and people have no sense of purpose beyond earning money. The Sri Sathya Sai Hospital is a real life example of an institution that has broken the pattern and acts as an example for all of us to embrace.

Agile Principles As a Basis

One of the principles of the Agile Manifesto states, "Build projects around motivated individuals. Give them the environment and support they need, and trust them to get the job done." Creating motivated individuals needs an environment of psychological safety and having the right vision and mission. According to Kahn,[4] "Psychological safety is being able to show and employ one's self without fear of negative consequences of self-image, status or career." Once you create the right environment with psychological safety, where everyone feels motivated to contribute their best to a clear mission, the results can be amazing.

A Clear Mission

At the entrance of the Sri Sathya Sai Hospital the following mission is enshrined: "Paropakartham idam shariram." In Sanskrit this means, "the body is for the service of others." High quality, cost-free medical care is provided to all people that come, regardless of caste, creed, religion, nationality, or financial status. Combining spiritual values and medicine, the hospital respects the patient as a human being. It views illness and diseases as a consequence of how people live in society and therefore, it is the duty of society to treat every person.[5]

When Isaac Tigrett, the founder of the Hard Rock Café, approached the World Health Organization (WHO) with the idea of a hospital that gave treatment for free, he was met with ridicule. Tigrett did not give up and was

---

[4]Kahn, W. A. (1990). *Psychological Conditions of Personal Engagement and Disengagement at Work*. Academy of Management Journal. 33 (4): 692–724. doi:10.2307/256287. ISSN 0001-4273. JSTOR 256287

[5](2005). *Interview with Dr. A. N. Safaya, Director of the Sri Sathya Sai Institute of Higher Medical Sciences*. Swiss Review for Medicine and Medical Technology 27 pp. 7–16. www.sathya-sai.ch/SWISS_MED_2-E.pdf

**Adopting Agile Across Borders** 103

to contribute enormously to the initial setup of the Sri Sathya Sai Hospital following the sale of the Hard Rock Café. The hospital is sustained by interest on its initial investments and the generous ongoing donations from society at large, not only in financial terms and equipment, but by the large number of volunteers, doctors, and medical staff who contribute their time at the hospital in response to an altruistic higher calling.

A lot of naysayers predicted the downfall of the hospital, but it has proven to be sustainable. It continues to serve and go from strength to strength. Rigid cost control, continuous innovation, and course corrections help to control the costs. Cured and recovered patients are asked to help in ways such as donating blood or returning to volunteer when possible, although this is not mandated. The hospital's mission ripples through to the patients, many of whom start to help to care for others, validating the model further.

A Harmonious Environment

Tigrett was introduced to Sir Keith Critchlow, Professor Emeritus of the Prince of Wales School of Architecture in London. Critchlow designed the Sri Sathya Sai Hospital in a way that makes it feel more like a piece of art than a hospital. Despite the ever increasing demand, the atmosphere is one of calm, assisting in the healing process of the patients. The staff are trusted and have the necessary tools to carry out their duties. The environment enables the people that work at the hospital to give their best. Whether patients, medical professionals, or volunteers, all feel cared for.

Agile Flywheel Effect

Fix the culture of your organization, and all else starts to fall into place. Figure 6-1 shows when the Agile principle, "Build projects around motivated individuals..." is applied, it creates a repeating cycle of psychological safety, reduced stress, better productivity, less attrition and people having a sense of ownership of their work, and greater customer satisfaction. All of this enables a harmonious work culture.

Chapter 6 | India

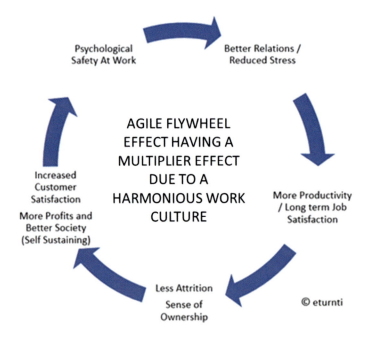

Figure 6-1. Agile flywheel effect

Environments where people are challenged without feeling threatened enable trust to be built and lead to organizations that can thrive.[6] These environments of psychological safety, where there is a harmonious culture, and where there is a clear mission is now increasingly a characteristic of successful digital companies.

—Kiran Divakaran, principal consultant at Eturnti Consulting Pvt Ltd

---

[6]Delizonna, L. (2017). *High-Performing Teams Need Psychological Safety. Here's How to Create It.* Harvard Business Review. https://hbr.org/2017/08/high-performing-teams-need-psychological-safety-heres-how-to-create-it

Adopting Agile Across Borders

▪ **Takeaway** Promote team psychological safety. Amy Edmondson, the Novartis Professor of Leadership and Management at the Harvard Business School,[7] talks[8] about three simple things that individuals can do to promote team psychological safety.

- Frame the work problem as a learning problem, not an execution problem.

- Acknowledge your own fallibility.

- Model curiosity and ask lots of questions.

Much of the approach and thinking that comes from the likes of Agile, Lean, Lean-UX, Lean Startup, and Design Thinking aligns perfectly well with the three elements that Edmondson describes. Work is seen as problems to solve. We accept "failures" (to learn fast). Proposed solutions are seen as assumptions to be tested. And the focus is on learning.

Continuing the history, at the end of the 15th century a Portuguese fleet discovered a route between Europe and India, paving the way for direct trade. The Portuguese set up a number of trading posts in coastal areas, and they were soon followed by the Dutch. War between the Dutch East India Company and the Indian kingdom of Travancore resulted in defeat on the Dutch side, and they never again posed a threat as colonizers. The French and the English also established their own trading posts, with the latter founding the East India Company (EIC) in 1600 to trade in the region.

The Mughal Empire conquered most of the Indian subcontinent in the 16th century and became the world's biggest economy, larger than that of the whole of Europe. The Mughals intensified agricultural production, moved the economy toward industrial manufacturing, and developed a unique style of architecture which included the design and construction of the Taj Mahal. The Mughal Empire broke up in the early 18th century, paving the way for the European traders to exert political influence over the split Indian kingdoms. The EIC gradually expanded its power and influence, annexing Indian states and agreeing treaties with others where local rulers deferred power to the EIC in return for a certain level of autonomy and protection. Following the abolition of slavery in the 19th century, millions of Indian people were transported under contract to various European colonies as a substitute for slave labor. Thus began the growth in the large number of overseas Indian people throughout the world.

---

[7]Edmundson, A. (1999). *Psychological Safety and Learning Behavior in Work Teams.* Administrative Science Quarterly, 44(2), pp. 350-383. www.jstor.org/stable/2666999?seq=1

[8]*Building a psychologically safe workplace.* TEDxHGSE www.youtube.com/watch?v=LhoLuui9gX8&feature=youtu.be

Chapter 6 | India

Grievances over land annexations, taxation, and cultural insensitivities saw growing unrest with the rule of the EIC during the 1800s. A large-scale rebellion by Indian soldiers employed by the EIC ran from 1857 to 1858 but was ultimately suppressed. As a consequence of the struggle, the British Crown took over all power from the EIC in what became known as the British Raj (Raj translates as "rule" in Sanskrit and Hindustani). Education was made a priority and would be based on the English language. Investment was made in infrastructure, including railways, canals, roads, ports, and telegraphy. However, India was made economically worse off overall because of the British. A series of diseases and famines killed tens of millions, but despite this, the population continued to grow.

To great outrage, Bengal was split into a Hindu Western half and a Muslim Eastern half in 1905. Though the British reunified Bengal in 1911, the action and the ongoing perception in clashes between Indian and British interests sowed the seeds for the independence movement. Under the leadership of Mahatma Gandhi, and inspired by the nationalistic leader Bal Gangadhar Tilak, who declared "Swaraj (self-rule) is my birthright, and I shall have it," the Indian National Congress (INC) emerged as the leading political party calling for independence. Their approach to use non-violent methods included non-cooperation and civil disobedience.

Around one million Indian troops served in World War I. Recognizing the part that Indian people played, the Government of India Act 1919 was created, in principle creating a system of dual-rule. A peaceful protest that resulted in the Jallianwala Bagh massacre, when troops were ordered to fire on protestors, led to Gandhi's non-cooperation movement. Meanwhile, Muslim communities were divided on calling for an independent and united India, or a completely independent new Muslim state as called for by the All-India Muslim League. Muslims had always been a minority and some were wary of the prospect of being governed by a Hindu state.

After World War II in which millions more Indian people served despite non-cooperation tactics of the INC, the new British Labour government declared it was to end British rule of India. In August 1947, the states of India and Pakistan were created. One of the effects was the large-scale migration of the Hindus, Sikhs, and Muslims moving between the two. In 1971, East Bengal, which had been part of Pakistan, became the independent state of Bangladesh following an independence war. The East Bengalis had support from India, and won their independence after growing international pressure on Pakistan.

India continues to have territorial disputes with Pakistan, most notably over the region of Kashmir, which resulted in three other wars between the countries before the end of the millennium. India has also had disputes with China, with the two going to war in 1962. After the United States and the United Kingdom refused to sell weapons to India, it turned to the Soviet Union with the two forming a strong economic and military relationship. India's support for decolonization in Africa and other parts of Asia has helped it to develop good relations in these areas, as well as with Latin America.[9] After the Cold War, India also developed relationships with the United States and the European Union.

Reforms and a liberalization of the economy that opened up foreign trade and investment in the 1990s has seen India become one of the world's fastest growing economies in the world. Hundreds of millions of people have been taken out of poverty as India's middle classes have grown. In addition, since independence, India has sustained the world's largest multi-party parliamentary democracy when measured by population.

Insights

In addition to its international presence, India has inherited many influences from the British. These include a democratically elected parliament, use of the English language in education, business, and administration, the love of tea, and a passion for the game of cricket. While Hindi is the most widely spoken language, India has no national language. Instead, Hindi and English are listed as "official languages" in the constitution.[10] In addition, the Indian caste system had many similarities with the British class system, and the British attempted to map Indian castes with British social classes. By introducing policies that gave preferential treatment to some castes over others and by using caste organization a central part of its administration, the British greatly influenced the system, resulting in lasting perceptions of superiority of one caste over another.

Since the 2010s, India has more people working overseas than any other country, with a diaspora population of around 17.5 million people recorded in 2019 according to the latest available data at the time of writing.[11] India itself has become an IT services and outsourcing hub. It is no coincidence that most of the people we have spoken to have at some stage worked with off-shore teams based in India, or worked directly with people from the country. A certain level of international and cross-cultural awareness has therefore been attained above that of other cultures, including that of their former rulers.

---

[9]Heine, J and Viswanathan, R. (2001). *The Other BRIC in LATIN AMERICA: India.* Americas Quarterly. https://web.archive.org/web/20170525115121/http://www.americasquarterly.org/india-latin-america

[10]*Languages of India.* New World Encyclopedia. www.newworldencyclopedia.org/entry/Languages_of_India#Hindi_and_English

[11]United Nations Department of Economic and Social Affairs, Population Division. *Twenty countries or areas of origin with the largest diaspora populations.* www.un.org/en/development/desa/population/migration/data/estimates2/estimatesgraphs.asp?3g3

Chapter 6 | India

The country has experienced rapid growth in its technology sector to begin to rival the United States and Europe. Bangalore is considered as a tech city and the "Silicon Valley" of India.[12] According to NASSCOM's report on the technology sector in India, the sector grew by 18 times in the first decade of the new millennium, with its Information Technology and Business Process Management industry worth US$191 billion and 4.4 million employees in 2020.[13]

A running theme in our conversations with people based in India or having been based there is the huge competition that there is between suppliers. This extends to individuals that feel they need to prove themselves to stand out from the crowd. Culturally, status is important, so the pursuit of certifications and qualifications to prove one's self is common. Organizations do what they can to be competitive, catering for overseas clients and partners who themselves are looking to outsource in order to reduce their own costs.

Closed questions such as "will you complete it this month?" or, "can you deliver it?" are commonly likely to be answered in the affirmative. This often results in misunderstandings and frustration in outsiders who feel that commitments have been broken or that interlocutors have been untruthful when it is perceived that promises have been broken. Losing any business is loathed, but this is only a small part of the picture. While we heard evidence that promises are made that cannot be delivered in order to beat the competition, this behavior is also part of a culture where pride, politeness, saving face, diplomacy, and harmony – especially when dealing with people perceived to be more senior – comes first. We were told that the customer is "seen as god" and "you do not say no to a god" so any request that comes from the customer is accepted, even if it is unrealistic. Besides which, what has happened and what will happen are things that are not considered to be simply black and white. Giving a binary answer ahead of time on what is possible is unnatural in a culture unconcerned with agendas, and instead views what will happen as something that will emerge in time.

Another common mismatch with other cultures is in the differing perception of time. While wanting to be accommodating to foreign partners, there are bound to be misunderstandings between a culture where the concept of saṃsāra is embedded, and others that believe that the future can be controlled. A belief that time is made up of perpetual repeating cycles that includes birth, death, and reincarnation is at odds with one that focuses on making detailed plans complete with milestones and deadlines, especially when such deadlines appear arbitrary.

---

[12]Saraogi, V. (2019). *How the tech city of Bangalore became the Silicon Valley of India.* Elite Business Magazine. http://elitebusinessmagazine.co.uk/global/item/how-the-tech-city-of-bangalore-became-the-silicon-valley-of-india

[13]Technology Sector in India 2020 – TECHADE – The New Decade Strategic Review. NASSCOM. https://nasscom.in/knowledge-center/publications/technology-sector-in-india-2020-techade-strategic-review

Despite the country's geographical size, people in the cities are used to crowded conditions and little privacy. Perhaps because of this, people are warm and sociable, and friends are made easily. The communication style is such that listening with great respect is appreciated while dialogue can be verbose with long monologues. Yet the content can often seem ambiguous and perplexing for those unfamiliar with the communication style. Emotions are usually out in the open. We heard stories where emotional attachments can cause problems in Agile teams; openness means that too much information may sometimes be shared. Critique in retrospectives for example can be taken personally and felt as hurtful. Therefore, criticism is rarely given for the sake of harmony. Instead the focus is on praise, respect, and making friends.

Though Indian culture has inherited a sense of a class system from the British, Indian teams have a strong sense of collectivism. People come to each other's aid when needed. We heard many stories of outside people working with Indian teams that were frustrated by the apparent silence of team members. People are used to command and control and defer to the leader. If someone is made a leader formally, they will act how they believe the leader should behave. Scrum Masters may act in a command and control way as it could be seen as a leadership position. If no leader is formally nominated, one will arise naturally from the collective group, and that person is expected to be the one to represent the team to outsiders.

Workplace trust is based on relationships ahead of tasks completed or achievements made, with nepotism a widespread factor. While great strides have been made, society remains patriarchal in varying degrees in different parts of the country. While India has seen spectacular economic growth in recent decades, poverty is also an ongoing and widespread issue.

Getting On and Around

Ziryan Salayi, an Agile Coach, Consultant and Facilitator from the Middle East but based in the Netherlands, shares some experience of bridging cultural differences with colleagues in India.

Understanding Culture Works Both Ways

As a consultant and an agilist, I have worked with people from all across the world. I have a Middle Eastern background, and my wife has a Vietnamese heritage. I also live in the Netherlands. So I have had many experiences understanding cultures from different perspectives. From all the stories I have to tell, I illustrate the power of cultural diversity with a description of my visit to Pune, India, with my previous colleague and manager.

Chapter 6 | India

This story highlights four essential topics some cultures might clash on with the culture of India:

- The power of hierarchical awareness
- Individual recognition vs. team recognition
- Work relationships before and after office hours
- Food as an elixir of trust

The Power of Hierarchical Awareness

My old manager is an example of an Agile leader. Her primary purpose is to make sure that people had all the expertise and freedom to deliver great products. She never used her hierarchical position in discussions and showed the courage to speak up to c-level management if decisions they had made would harm the team's ability to self-organize. To top it off, she did this with genuine passion, and from a deeply rooted belief that this is the way to "manage" within an organization.

One day, she and I discussed the next steps in our Agile transformation. We noticed that there were some issues between team members in India and team members in the Netherlands. Lack of trust was one of these issues. Although we had weekly video conferences to improve, we believed that addressing the issue of trust and collaborating to improve was more effective when we saw each other face to face. We therefore decided to schedule a week's trip to see our teams and team members in India and get to know them better. Management and team members in India were excited and happy to accommodate our stay. In preparation for our trip, the local managers in India planned a number of activities for our visit. My manager was surprised to see the first item on the itinerary was to "walk around the office and thank everyone."

Manager: Ziryan, they are not talking about me? Right?

Me: I am afraid they are talking about you.

Manager: But, I am not going to speak in front of them. What do I have to say which is of any relevance to them? I'd rather the time be spent giving the teams a podium to speak up instead of me talking in my business-suit.

As right as she was if this was the Netherlands, she was not aware of a difference in culture. A cultural collaboration starts with showing respect to the needs of both cultures. In India, a talk from someone in a position of authority is important to acknowledge the value of the team members' effort. Managers make the time to inspect the office and even take the time to thank everybody personally.

Adopting Agile Across Borders 111

After a discussion, we ended up with us both wearing our business-suits on the first day. But, instead of my manager, it was me giving a speech and thanking everybody in the office for hosting us. Although I wasn't a manager, they still treated me as higher up in the hierarchy. In order to respect the cultural expectations, the best alternative to my manager giving a speech was for me to give a talk. For the rest of the week, we could continue to work on gaining trust and have meaningful and open discussions despite the perception of a hierarchy.

Individual Recognition vs. Team Recognition

Being in an Agile organization, we value team effort and collaboration over individual targets and achievements. Yes, personal recognition is important, but team achievements are more important. We had this mindset, but we were in India where people have a different view.

On day three, we had a special event for the department. Everybody wore their best clothes and waited with full anticipation until it was 4.00 p.m. It was the annual event to look back at the results and communicate the plans for the rest of the year. Five minutes before the event, the manager in India approached us and told my manager that she had to make a special appearance. She had the honor of handing out the awards for individual achievements.

Manager: Ziryan, why are they asking me?

Me: Because you, as a manager from the Netherlands, are treated as a special guest.

Manager: But I don't know them that well and I have no idea what they have done.

Me: You will receive details, and the management here will say some nice words.

Manager: But we are working Agile now. No one individual can achieve things alone.

Me: You are right. What are you saying?

Manager: I think we should honor all of the team members.

Me: I think we should, but that would have less impact.

Again, my manager was absolutely right. An individual achievement award made sense back when we were handing out tasks and worked more individually. In this transformation, we were focusing more on team results. From the perspective of team efforts, an individual cannot have achieved the results alone. And yet, having personal achievements is essential to motivate

Chapter 6 | India

teams and team members in the Indian culture. Achievements like the employee of the month, best tester of the year, etc. are achievements one can take home so people's family can be proud. "Out of all the thousands of employees, my son or daughter has received this award"!

Given that in some cultures, recognizing individual achievements is a way of motivating people from childhood, we cannot neglect this and focus only on team achievements. Parents in the Middle East often want their children to have respected professions like doctors or lawyers when they grow up, so it is important for individual's efforts and progress to be rewarded. I remember how we had an annual "best student of the year" award in primary school in Iran and Iraq when I was younger. Before we came to the Netherlands, my brother and I were number one and number two in our class from the first grade to the third grade. Being awarded was a big achievement for me and acknowledgment of my effort, which made our parents proud.

Work Relationships Before and After Office Hours

My manager and another colleague arrived in Pune on a Saturday, and I arrived on a Monday. From day one, several colleagues from the Pune Office welcomed my manager and my colleague and gave them a city tour. They also took them to places to go shopping, go for food, etc. To my manager's surprise, throughout the week, the colleagues from the Pune office kept joining us, bringing us to restaurants and fun places in Pune. After three days, my manager started feeling uncomfortable and guilty at the same time.

Manager: Ziryan, what shall we have for dinner tonight?

Me: Our colleagues were talking about bringing us to a biryani place tonight.

Manager: Wow, are they joining us again? Don't they have a family to go to? I feel so guilty that they join us every day.

Me: It is their way to show their appreciation. They have arranged it with their families as well.

Often, in some cultures, working hours are for colleagues and outside office hours are for family. Occasionally you take people out for dinner or to a company event. However, usually, these are planned in advance. In Middle Eastern and Asian cultures, you see a different pattern. If you have visitors, you make sure they feel at ease and don't get bored during their stay. When the colleagues from India visited us in the Netherlands, I had to explain to them that there would be evenings that they were on their own. Not because our colleagues didn't value them, but because of the work culture in the Netherlands.

Adopting Agile Across Borders

Food As an Elixir of Trust

Office hours in India start around 9.00 a.m. and end around 6.00 p.m. During these working hours, there are two very important moments – lunch and mid-afternoon chai. When we were working from a distance, colleagues in the Netherlands were agitated by colleagues' work-ethics in India. Colleagues in India were often not available after the Daily Scrum. Also, they would not be available for 45 minutes just after our lunchtime. This behavior was high on my manager's agenda to discuss with the managers in India. In preparation for our stay, my manager and I had a little discussion.

Manager: Ziryan, I hear many complaints about the work-ethics and availability of our colleagues in India. This is a high priority to discuss.

Me: OK, that is not good. What ethics are we discussing?

Manager: Team members are gone for hours, and I don't think they are working the 8 hours they claim to do per day.

Me: Hmm… that sounds disturbing. What times are they absent?

Manager: Often after the Daily Scrum in the morning and after lunchtime.

Me: Ah, I see. I think they have very good reasons for this. They need this time!

Manager: What do you mean?

Me: Wait and see when we are there.

On the first day, we were invited to lunch with the local management team. They had taken 1.5 hours for this lunch. My manager was surprised. What are we going to eat that takes longer than the regular 45–60 minutes? However, she understood that it would maybe take more time because we were having lunch with the management team. On the second day, we had a 1.5-hour lunch and a long break in the afternoon for chai – this time with only two managers and some team members. The third day it was the same.

Manager: Ziryan, I still do not see why we have to have these long lunches and breaks in the afternoon.

Me: Why not?

Manager: It is affecting our effectiveness and productivity.

Me: OK, how much have you heard about our colleagues during these lunches?

Manager: I have heard a lot about their passion, their family, and their background.

Me: Would you have heard this if we did not have lunch?

Manager: I guess not.

Chapter 6 | India

Me: Exactly.

Although it sounds very unproductive, these moments are there to create a bond between team members. Team members share food and share moments. In Eastern cultures, food is the elixir of trust. When you have nothing in common, the love for food brings people together. If you investigate the time people are spending on breaks, lunch, and chai, it is probably less than people in the Netherlands office spend on chit-chat, coffee breaks (every hour), smoke breaks, lunches, and more coffee breaks in between meetings. The only difference is that in India, formal breaks take longer and contribute to the team building relationships and trust with each other.

Takeaways About the Difference in Cultures

Our issues between teams in the Netherlands and teams in India are not unique. For us to work together effectively, we need to change our perspective about the way we perceive different cultures. I often encounter that we want to get to know the other culture to find ways to get things done in the way we are used to in our own culture.

The trip in this story, among others, raised awareness for us to approach cultural diversity differently than we were used to. Understanding how another culture works is not sufficient to collaborate on an equal level. It takes openness and respect. For me, effectively collaborating in different cultures means I have to respect and be open to others' habits and comply as much as possible with the other culture. Only then can I be seen as an equal and gain trust.

—Ziryan Salayi, Agile Coach, Consultant,
and Facilitator at Scrum Facilitators

Several factors including past colonial rule and an embedded class system has instilled hierarchical systems and perhaps a cautiousness in the psyche. Hierarchical systems are common in organizations, and this helps to provide a sense of structure. In our discussions with practitioners, there was evidence that leaders who are open, eloquent, humble, provide safety, and take a carrot before the stick approach are loved. This style of leadership is likely to build trust and loyalty.

Establishing a trusting and psychologically safe environment where people are empowered may take time for those unused to such environments. Pranshu Mahajan, a Scrum Master with many years of experience working in various capacities in India, shares his story on the importance of learning to navigate Indian company hierarchies and building trust in Agile teams.

Trust: The Basic Building Block of Agile Teams

Scene 1

A group of young developers are sitting in a training room in Bangalore. They are eagerly awaiting the Agile Coach from another office of the company who is coming to help them start their team's Agile transformation.

The team's Scrum Master (who is new to the role and still learning how to be awesome) is sitting with them, finally able to see the process that she believed in and pushed for getting started. A point to note here: The team's managers were not a part of these workshops.

The Agile Coach arrives and introduces the Agile Manifesto and what Scrum is, and then goes on to talk about how the team currently functions to explore ways to improve together.

The participants are a little shy when it comes to talking about their current problems. The Scrum Master keeps that concern on-hold considering this is their first session.

It is a 2-day training. On the second day, they continue from where they had left off. They speak at length about how they as a team can drive changes and make things better.

They discuss initiatives they could try and changes they could make starting tomorrow, etc.

The session ends on a high, and from the Scrum Master's perspective, the training was great. Nobody raises anything major when feedback is asked for at the end of the sessions. It feels like people are happy with it.

So the day after, the Scrum Master decides to ask the team again what they thought of the training. He did this by organizing a variation of Rocket Retrospective to keep things quick, time-boxed, and get some feedback. Put simply, each member of the team writes anonymously on a post-it note their thoughts and all notes are placed face down on a table. The notes are then shuffled and revealed.

The responses:

> *"It was great in theory but the Agile Coach doesn't understand our problems."*

> *"How can someone from outside tell us how to fix stuff?"*

> *"Until he works with us and sees our reality, he will propose a theoretical solution not applicable to us."*

Chapter 6 | India

"Let's see what our site lead has to say about these changes that are being proposed from outside."

"How can we agree on something when our manager is not here?"

Two things happened here:

- Someone the team doesn't trust came in and told them how to improve.
- Indian companies are used to hierarchies. With management missing, telling the team to drive improvement on their own did not sit well with them.

It seems like the transformation stopped before it began. A rocky start.

This is a real story without making reference to anyone involved. I was part of this team of developers back then and went through my first "Agile Transformation" experience. I would like to point out that after this, it took a considerably long time for this team to get started with an Agile adoption again.

Scene 2

The same company, another department, another team. This team has heard a lot of things about how some of the other teams in the company have been transformed. And they are looking to start their own journey.

The new Scrum Master for the team discusses how they can kick things off. They talk about how they can learn this "Agile mindset" and about the potential improvements that they could make, etc.

Even though the Scrum Master is new to the team and the company, she has already accomplished her first step in a short period of time: to build trust with the team by showing that she is part of the team and will be going on the journey with them.

The next few weeks sees her organizing workshops to educate the team about Agile methodologies, the Agile mindset itself, ways of working such as Kanban, Scrum, etc. She and the team have intense discussions about how they can improve the current ways of working. And how to take the first step.

These workshops are messy and what comes out is not the answer to the team's problems. But the first step toward a goal they envision together.

Next up, the Scrum Master takes these outcomes and gets the managers on board. She gets the managers excited about the things they agreed with the team. This excitement trickles down to the team (which is always a good thing).

Adopting Agile Across Borders

The team commits and starts working toward their goals. There are a lot of arguments, some restructuring of the team, some people moved to other teams, and others joined this team. But they manage to pull through and achieve a lot of the things they highlighted in the Agile workshops.

One day, the Scrum Master decides to talk to the people about how they think this transformation journey is going. She decides to facilitate a retrospective focusing on how the team feels about how things are going.

The responses:

"I did not know it was going to be so hard. But since we could focus on the problems we wanted to solve, it became worthwhile."

"This only happened because we did it together. We all work together and it's easier to communicate."

"I was telling our management to stop sending consultants from outside. We know the situation better than they could. See, this worked out beautifully."

"It's great that we have someone who knew our situation before they decided to start solving problems for us."

Two things happened here as well:

- The team discussed and figured out the next steps together. There was no one from outside of the team telling them what to do. The Scrum Master was already part of the team.

- The management being on board and supporting the team meant everyone was all in and committed. We do not skip hierarchies in India.

This team had a great start to living the Scrum values. I was part of this team. I was transitioning from being a development team member to a Scrum Master and this was a great learning experience. Later when I started supporting a different team as a Scrum Master, I relied on this experience a lot and it helped me grow into the role.

This team hasn't stopped improving to this day. The last time I spoke to them, they were trying to make things better for themselves every week and trying to make things easier for the people who use their products. And they were living the values of commitment, courage, focus, openness, and respect.

Chapter 6 | India

The Lessons

The first, and most important step that you need to understand while trying to drive changes in India is building trust.

I cannot emphasize this step enough. For as long as I have worked in India (almost a decade) in a variety of roles, ranging from software development and support, to leading people, to functioning as a Scrum Master, this one factor has stood out to me the most.

Trust alone transcends the role that you have in a company. Be it a Scrum Master/Agile Coach, People Manager, Director, etc. Unless you have your team's trust, things will not go smoothly.

This becomes especially true if you want to drive a transformation.

The second thing is to learn how to work within hierarchies.

This might sound a little weird considering the Agile methodologies talk about self-organizing and self-managing teams. In Scrum, for example, the emphasis is on three roles, each with their own accountabilities.

Again, start by building trust with managers. Keep them in the loop and make them understand the what and why of the Agile approach before you start with the team.

You might at this point say – moving away from command and control hierarchies is exactly what we are trying to achieve.

To which I say – yes, I agree. Also, a Scrum Master/Coach has to be tactful. Understanding the art of the possible is a skill Scrum Masters need to learn.

My third tip is to give feedback one-to-one in person.

Indian people generally don't do well in giving or receiving feedback in an open setting. This is something to watch out for. For feedback of an individual (not team-related), make a note, have a one-to-one with them, and talk.

Then help the team and the individuals grow. Help them create an environment where exchanging feedback is appreciated and safe. It's not easy, but the journey is a great one to take because what you get in the end is a psychologically safe, self-managing team who can be constantly improving to deliver great quality products to customers.

The final piece of the puzzle – build relationships outside of work.

We Indians value our relationships a lot. Be it personal or professional. Unless we get along on a personal level, we will not really get along professionally. We believe the people we trust would do no harm to us. One example in a professional context where trust would be broken is yelling at an individual in-front of the rest of the team. We need to build trust, and see others

Adopting Agile Across Borders 119

wherever they are in the hierarchy as a friend (and it is not super hard to make friends here). Once you penetrate the circle of trust, it is effortless to discuss, implement, and drive improvements.

—Pranshu Mahajan, Scrum Master (Helping teams in their journey from being good to great)

■ **Takeaway** Hierarchical structures do not automatically prohibit agility. Though we have spoken about hierarchy in organizations as a barrier to adoption in a number of instances in this book, how they work in practice can take many forms. As we saw in many South American companies, the structure may appear hierarchical on paper, though the organizational culture allows things such as horizontal communication, and peers resolving issues rather than escalating to a manager. In Japan, we saw hierarchical structures, yet the focus is on consensus building, getting people involved, and managers as servant-leaders. Building trust and respect, as we saw in Pranshu's example, helps everyone to get into the desired mindset for servant-leadership and self-organization to succeed.

Many may feel uncomfortable transitioning to a self-organizing state, and will search for a leader for guidance. As mentioned earlier, in the absence of a formal leader in a group, one will naturally emerge. There may be a temptation to push against this for an Agile team, to insist on equality, but it could be argued that this is an acceptable form of self-organization. The team itself has agreed that this is the way they want to operate. As an outsider, it is advised to first build a relationship with the individual that emerges as leader – everyone else will follow.

Historically in hierarchical organizations, team members are used to, and feel the need to be given, explicit instructions to carry out. However, as in every culture and organization, when an environment of trust and safety has been established, people can prove themselves to be accomplished and skillful problem solvers.

A desire to deliver a good service, combined with business partners eager to progress, as well as the communication style, means there can be a tendency for overcommitting. Planning will be more successful when using open questions such as "How long do you think we will need?" This gives team members more room to express reality than questions that corner them into having to give a yes or no answer, such as "Will it be ready by X date?"

People are warm, respectful, communicative, and quick to share what they have equitably. It is relatively easy to build good relationships. Life is centered around family, so enquiring about people's family and showing respect for

Chapter 6 | India

their achievements will win hearts. It is unlikely to take very long before enquiries are made about your own marital status, children, etc. Marriage is so central to life that it is a point of fascination in many conversations.

Making friends and building relationships for the long term are more important than any short-term deal. Oral agreements are just as valid, if not more so, than written documents. People are used to uncertainty and ambiguity being part of life; the future is seen as uncontrollable, and truth does not have a binary answer. Facts and appearances have many moving parts and are open to interpretation and negotiation, so some decisions should not be made quickly. Acceptance of these factors has led to a flexibility in dealing with and managing uncertainty that perhaps other cultures could do well to learn from.

Agile Community Events and Meetups

- AgilityToday: http://agilitytoday.com/
- Agile Software Community of India: https://agileindia.org/
- Agile Network India: https://agilenetworkindia.com/
- Discuss Agile Network Bangalore: www.meetup.com/discuss-agile-network-bangalore/
- Agile Transformation Minds (ATM) – India: www.meetup.com/atminds/
- Scrum Bangalore: www.meetup.com/ScrumBangalore/

CHAPTER 7

Indonesia

Deserving of attention, not least for its population of over 270 million people, the Agile movement is in its infancy in Indonesia. Like the Philippines, after centuries of colonization, Indonesia is a cultural hybrid. There are literally thousands of subcultures spread across its estimated 17,500 islands[1] that cover an area stretching 5,000km east to west and 2,000km north to south. Its multitude of values and behaviors adds even more complexity in efforts of cross-cultural understanding.

People are embracing Agile with a mixture of excitement and apprehension. Growing in experience, pockets of Agile communities are forming and Indonesian teams are revealing themselves to be highly collaborative, innovative, creative, adaptive, resourceful, and courageous with a great sense of fun. This is coupled with a thirst for practical examples and a desire for answers for their immediate needs. Given a level of empowerment and an environment of safety, we believe teams in Indonesia have great potential to be great agilists.

History

Humans arrived by sea from mainland Asia to the islands of what is now Indonesia some 45,000 years ago. Indian culture was to come to dominate here and much of Southeast Asia from the 2nd century onward. Indonesia's

---

[1]Bland, B. (2017). *Indonesia starts count to solve the riddle of the islands.* Financial Times. www.ft.com/content/3acc43f0-45f5-11e7-8519-9f94ee97d996

© Glaudia Califano, David Spinks 2021
G. Califano and D. Spinks, *Adopting Agile Across Borders*,
https://doi.org/10.1007/978-1-4842-6948-0_7

Chapter 7 | Indonesia

name actually comes from the Greek for the Indos (Indian) nesos (islands). A number of Hindu and Buddhist states came and went across the archipelago in the centuries that followed. The spice trade brought Muslim traders through Southeast Asia, and Islam began to spread among the Indonesian island's inhabitants from the 13th century.

It was Portuguese traders who were the first Europeans on the scene in 1512. The French and British were also to have a presence, but over the next few decades, it was the Dutch that became the dominant power through the formation of the Dutch East Indies Company. This lasted until the company's financial collapse in 1800, and the Netherlands went on to establish the Dutch East Indies as a colony.

The idea of Indonesia as an independent nation state began to emerge in the early 1900s. The Dutch introduced policies to improve education and welfare, aimed at preparing the islands for self-government, albeit under Dutch control. This sparked movements for complete independence, only for the country to fall under the occupation of Japan during World War II. Just two days after the surrender of Japan, nationalistic figures such as Kusno "Sukarno" Sosrodihardjo and Mohammad Hatta declared Indonesian independence from the Netherlands. In 1945 Sukarno and Hatta were appointed as the first President and Vice-President of Indonesia, respectively. There followed a period of armed and diplomatic struggle, but in the face of growing international pressure, the Dutch eventually declared recognition of Indonesian independence a few years later.

The late 1950s saw the country move from a democratic regime to one of authoritarianism, the military stamping out the Communist Party of Indonesia following an attempted coup in a period of violence that left at least 500,000 dead, with some estimates as high as 3 million.[2] The head of the military, General Suharto, formally became president in 1968 and established what was informally termed the "New Order" administration. Indonesia experienced a sustained period of considerable economic growth,[3] thanks largely to the New Order administration opening up the country to foreign investment as well as it benefiting from two oil booms during the 1970s.[4] This enabled a process of industrialization and urbanization. During the 1980s, lower oil prices led to a government focus on diversification of the economy with a greater emphasis on manufacturing.

---

[2]Henschke, R. (2017). *Indonesia massacres: Declassified US files shed new light.* BBC News. www.bbc.co.uk/news/world-asia-41651047

[3]Elias, S. and Noone, C. of the Reserve Bank of Australia. (2011). *The Growth and Development of the Indonesian Economy.* www.rba.gov.au/publications/bulletin/2011/dec/pdf/bu-1211-4.pdf

[4]*New Order Miracle of Suharto's Indonesia.* Indonesia-Investments. www.indonesia-investments.com/culture/economy/new-order-miracle/item247?

Adopting Agile Across Borders 123

Years of accusations of corruption, human rights violations, and suppression of political opposition accumulated. Things came to a head in the late 1990s, with the additional impact of the 1997 Asian financial crisis which hit Indonesia hard. Sharp price increases led to rioting in the streets. President Suharto was forced to step down and the country returned to a genuine democracy for the first time since the election of Sukarno.

Issues such as corruption, terrorism, and social and political instability has slowed progress, but the economy has performed strongly in recent years. Annual growth has been between 4% and 6% since 2007. In 2018, Indonesia was ranked as the 16th largest economy by nominal GDP. Progress was halted by the impact of the coronavirus pandemic in 2020 which pushed the country into recession for the first time in 22 years.[5] While investment into science and technology remains low, there is a software development industry emerging. Further still, there are definite Agile communities that are appearing. Organized meetups and conferences for Agile practitioners to share their experiences and ideas are already regularly taking place.

Insights

Despite its Dutch colonial past, Indonesia's geographical location and the country's main religions – Islam was first introduced to the area by passing traders long before the arrival of Europeans – have been important factors in the shaping of Indonesian culture.

Status is not achieved through competition. Conformity and obedience are seen as greater virtues. Authority is instead usually transferred smoothly through a process more akin to inheritance. Promotion is awarded from above from those in positions of authority and the award is usually based on age, experience, and seniority. There are clear chains of command in Indonesian organizations. However, Indonesian people are consensus-driven decision makers.

Punctuality is not something that is high on people's agenda. Time is seen as a limitless commodity. A well-known phrase is "jam karet" which literally translates as "rubber time," meaning that time is regarded as something that can be flexible. People may arrive an hour late to a meeting and such tardiness is routinely accepted. In Jakarta, a ready – and perhaps overused – excuse is the traffic, which is always bad no matter the time of day. Yet, Jakartans are unbelievably patient in traffic.[6] Indonesians in general are a tolerant people

---

[5](2020). _Indonesia in recession for first time in 22 years._ BBC. www.bbc.co.uk/news/business-54819898

[6]Dunning, B. (2020). _10 things I wish I'd known about Jakarta (before moving here)._ The Jakarta Post. www.thejakartapost.com/life/2020/01/13/10-things-i-wish-id-known-about-jakarta-before-moving-here.html

Chapter 7 | Indonesia

that may not seem to have a sense of urgency. On the other hand, professionals who are used to working with foreigners such as Japanese people or Westerners are putting more value on punctuality.

People are less concerned with the pursuit of material things, profit, and professional success than they are with maintaining their various circles of relationships. There is as much value – perhaps more – placed on deepening interactions with colleagues or clients through playing sports such as football or badminton, or by dining together, than there is for working.

A large Chinese presence has formed in Indonesian industries. Along with large amounts of investments, a large number of Chinese companies and people have come into Indonesia. The Chinese are strongly involved in the business management, ownership, and shareholding of Indonesian companies. Consequently, there is a high number of Chinese people in professional class jobs living within the country. This has given Indonesia international connections and presence that it may not have otherwise had. This has not really impacted the workplace, where the workforce was already diverse.

People are comfortable mixing in groups, and experience being in crowded conditions means people have become accustomed to having little personal space. This familiarity with each other and sense of the group above the individual help make for great team players. The country possesses a relatively young population and we saw an eagerness in the younger generations to embrace Agile ideas from those that we spoke to, as well as judging by the attendances at the meetups and conferences that we attended. We attended the very first DevOps Days in Jakarta and were amazed by the enthusiasm of the people and the local talent. The same could be said when we were invited to speak at the Scrum Day Bandung 2018 conference. It was refreshing to see how many development team members were attending and participating in these events, and not just managers and consultants. The following story from Danny Wuysang, an Agile Coach, is an example of the growing enthusiasm for agility and continuous learning.

The Impact of Book Reports: A Story on Continuous Learning

I went to the same college as a bunch of my high-school friends. One day during my freshman year, which is not so long ago, we had an assignment to make a book report. I had gone to high school in Indonesia where we were rarely tasked to make book reports, let alone write one in English. So it was a daunting task for most of us. We had another friend who is also an Indonesian but he had gone through high school in the United States. He was not the smartest in the gang, but to our amazement, he breezed through the report. It was well written: good flow, minimal grammatical errors, and well structured. Of course, he got a good grade, while most of us struggled. When we asked him, he explained that he had been doing book reports throughout his schooling.

Mrs. Jean P. Powell, in her article "Why Book Reports?"[7] wrote: "For the serious student who will continue to learn, literature opens countless doors." Teachers expect that by writing book reports, students will read the book. Or at least some portions of it. And in the process, "expose them to literature, a storehouse of knowledge." For me, reading books and writing reports is one of the most important lessons toward self-learning. We are challenged to understand literature, offered information and ideas, then we need to communicate and express what we think about it. I am amazed by teachers' resources like "How to Make a Book Report, Grades 1-3."[8] For me, it is a wonder to read that first year elementary school students are expected to write a book report, however simple the report may be. This kind of education system surely challenges people's minds from such an early age. From my experience, the Indonesian education system did not really challenge us in that way.

Jumping forward, I am now an Agile Coach for a financial service institute in Indonesia. Yes, even without writing a book report in school, you can be an Agile Coach... One of the issues I face, and have heard my fellow Agile Coaches face, is people's eagerness to continuously learn, furthermore to self-learn. Most of us are used to being fed information by someone else. We wait to be ordered to do something. Seldom do we find ourselves exploring new stuff on our own that would improve how we are doing things in our job. The Manifesto for Agile Software Development starts with "We are uncovering better ways of developing software by doing it and helping others do it." For me, "uncovering better ways" means continuous learning, which is one of the most important Agile values that I practice and teach. To support this value, a mentality of self-learning is crucial. People in the organization should be encouraged to self-learn and be empowered to experiment. I believe this is a worthy challenge that all us Agile Coaches around the world should accept.

---

[7]Powell, J. P. (1969). *Why Book Reports?* Peabody Journal of Education, 47(3), 164–167. www.jstor.org/stable/1491920

[8]Prior, J. O. (1999). *How to Make a Book Report, Grades 1-3*. Teacher Created Resources. www.teachercreated.com/products/how-to-make-a-book-report-grades-1-3-2503

Chapter 7 | Indonesia

Some Ideas to Spark Self-Learning

- A community of practice is a great way to spark learning and sharing. It could be one that is internal within an organization, gathering those in the wider community who are interested to know more about Agile. Or it could be an inter-organization community.

- In the community, plan for a series of learning steps. A good series to follow is the Scrum.org Scrum Master Learning Path[9] if you use Scrum. Let these serve as an inspiration, and you can discuss in your community what you really need to learn.

- Take turns facilitating the sessions on different topics. At least every session, one person will learn something new by facilitating a session on something new.

- One important lesson I learned is to practice what we learn. After each topic, discuss with community members how each person will immediately put into practice what they have just learned. Next session, discuss how it went.

Personal Retrospective

When I started the journey with my current organization (or others before), I had a plan in mind. But as I gained more information, as I received feedback, I very often replan what I have to do next. I have to process this information and feedback, study more to gain ideas and insights, and go back with a hypothesis for the next experiments. This is my personal retrospective. A tool for my self-learning, my continuous learning.

Change the Environment

I grew up in an environment that did not really support continuous learning. An education system that did not really support self-learning. I am used to people teaching me stuff, rather than explore and find things out for myself. I have worked in similar environments. Now, I am trying to change this environment with the hope to evoke people's curiosity on a better way of working. A journey where we advance through continuously learning. A path of continuous learning. You are most welcome to join.

—Danny F. Wuysang, Agile Coach, BFI Finance Indonesia

---

[9]Scrum Master Learning Path. Scrum.org. www.scrum.org/pathway/scrum-master

> ■ **Takeaway** Treat continuous learning as part of everyone's job. Agility is about continuous learning, so it should be encouraged and made a natural part of how the organization works. In some companies, where learning has not been part of the organizational mindset, be aware that it takes time and conditioning for learning to become part of the cultural fabric. People cannot be forced into it, and everyone learns in their own way and at their own pace.

We saw signs of an emerging tech startup scene, new companies with innovative ideas that meet real people's needs. These startups are starting to make waves, and can be seen as a threat to, for example, the traditional big banks of the country. This in turn is spurring those same banks to adopt a more Agile approach. There are already Indonesian unicorns, privately owned startup companies that have grown to a valuation of over US$1 billion. Tokopedia and Bukalapak are two examples of these organizations that specialize in ecommerce. Traveloka is another that started out as an airline and hotel-booking platform, now expanding into other areas such as car rental and tourist attraction tickets. It is also now growing beyond Indonesia to other parts of Southeast Asia and into Australia.

Perhaps the most well-known Indonesian unicorn is Gojek. Founded in 2010 as a call center to connect people to courier delivery and ride hailing services, Gojek's apps have transformed life for many, offering more than 20 services across Indonesia, Vietnam, Thailand, Singapore, and the Philippines. Apps include "Go-Pay," an e-wallet service - crucial in a country where many people do not have a traditional bank account - "Go-Food" is a food delivery service, and then there is Gojek's "Go-Ride" service, an online moped taxi service. The Gojek green jacketed moped riders are ubiquitous in Jakarta, Bandung, and many other cities across Southeast Asia.

A growing software industry and a strong team ethic gives Indonesia many opportunities to develop their IT industry and Agile adoption. However, along with the potential, they face unique challenges. Indonesia is a very poor country when viewed on a per capita basis, and its wealth is unevenly distributed, geographically and socially. Several areas in the islands of Sumatra, Kalimantan, and Bali are economic centers in their own right, but it is on Java where many of the main cities are located. Jakarta feels like a city that would not be out of place in the West – there clearly is wealth there. Bandung, Yogyakarta, and Surabaya are also very significant. Java draws people to its dense population centers from the rest of the country, while areas such as Papua are disadvantaged and sparsely populated. Figure 7-1 illustrates a typical scene of Indonesian suburban life.

Chapter 7 | Indonesia

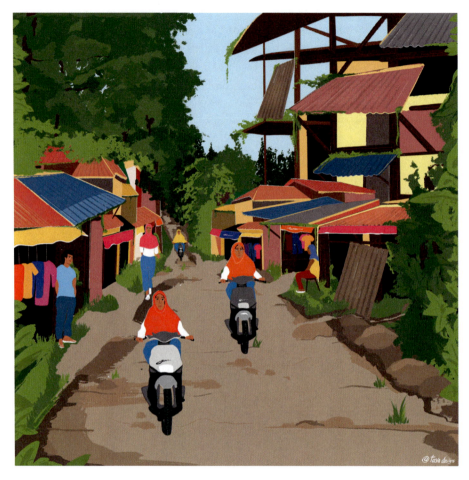

Figure 7-1. A suburban scene of a city in Indonesia (image courtesy of Tasia Graham)

Wherever they are, for most Indonesians, life is a struggle when it comes to financial security. As we will discuss later, talk of Agile, motivation, empowerment, self-organization, and the like must be a frightening prospect for people whose lives and those of their family depend on their job security. There is little state aid to fall back on. And this in a country on the Pacific Ring of Fire and close to the equator: earthquakes and tropical cyclones are a fact of life. Indonesia was the country that was worst hit by the 2004 Boxing Day Indian Ocean earthquake and tsunami for example.

Indonesian organizations are typically structured to be controlled from the top down in a command and control manner. Many leaders require a radical shift in thinking and mindset to truly embrace Agile. Hierarchically structured companies are common worldwide, but the expectation of authority and status through inheritance that is embedded into Indonesian culture is likely to make this mindset even harder to break.

Teams may struggle when given autonomy. Rather than a sense of freedom and motivation, people may well instead have a feeling of fear of the consequences of greater responsibility if things go wrong. In the Agile community we often talk about teams needing psychological safety, and in a culture where mistakes can ruin your reputation, establishing a culture where failure means learning will certainly be challenging. There is a valid question of whether Indonesian organizations are culturally ready and able to accept and embrace the Agile mindset.

■ **Takeaway** Learn fast. To build resilience in our teams and organizations, Agile encourages the concept of "fail fast". Maintaining a status-quo is not a sustainable long-term business strategy, so companies need to constantly innovate and reinvent themselves. This involves trying things that might not work. By accepting that failures happen, but designing experiments so that these failures happen sooner rather than later, learning is faster and long-term risk is reduced. The word "fail" may have negative associations in some cultures, so perhaps a better way of thinking about it is "learn fast"!

Despite these questions, the cultural challenges, and the infancy of the Agile movement in the country, there is evidence in the growing communities that we saw that the Agile movement is taking root. There are two clear communities centered in Jakarta and Bandung that are emerging and helping to drive Agile adoption. We met with Hugo Messer, Agile Entrepreneur and originally from the Netherlands, and he shares his experience with building an Agile company in Indonesia.

Experiences of a Dutch Guy Building an Agile Company in Indonesia

In 2016, my wife and I (plus three kids) decided to move to Bali. Our main objective was to change our environment and embark on an adventure. I had no clear-cut idea what to do in Bali business-wise. The year before, I had experimented with talks at Agile conferences and running some Scrum training. When I arrived in Indonesia, I figured out Agile was still new. People asked me to help them in their Agile journey. So I started Ekipa.co. Today, we have a team of 15 coaches helping larger Indonesian enterprises with Agile Innovation.

While reading the Indonesian part of this book, I realized that in the Western world, we like to look at a culture and state how things work. We create stereotypes and recognizable behaviors. Western thinking is rational, explicit. Most cultural models are also developed in the West. One thing I've learned

Chapter 7 | Indonesia

while living in Asia is that things don't always need to be explicit. Things "are" and don't necessarily need to have a name or label. There may be many layers of truth underneath someone's appearance or statement. This creates discomfort in people with a Western, explicit paradigm. I've made many mistakes because I couldn't read between the lines. Over time, we learn how to move along with this. Call it cultural agility.

When I started working in Jakarta, I ran Scrum training, mainly for technical people. One of the things I encountered was followership. A teacher in Indonesia is always right. From a young age, we're taught not to question the teacher. The same applies to other people with authority (a father, a boss). Technical people are often thinking black-white. The world of a programmer consists of 0 and 1. These two behaviors pose an interesting challenge to the central theme of agility: self-organization. At the same time, Indonesia is built on teamwork, on community. If there is no obvious leader in a group, things work out. Over time, I've learned that teaching people Scrum black and white as the Scrum Guide describes it, leads to friction. Teaching people how to change their behavior, how to speak up, how to lead their own team without a "boss" works. People need to learn the bigger picture of agility for "it" to work.

Another stereotype is the reliance on authority, hierarchy, and command and control. Teaching people how to self-organize brings us a step in the right direction. But leaders need to change as well. Which is why Agile is about transformation, not (only) about one aspect like a specific practice. It's a collective change of mindset, structure, and practices (in that order). Strong Agile leaders understand this. They drive change because they see a better future. A future in which they make themselves redundant and become true leaders. While the stereotype is easy to recognize in many leaders and organizations, things can change. If the leader at the top has a strong drive toward agility, "followership" works in their favor. Adding the right mix of education and support for the wider group of leaders can bring about the desired change.

Time and planning is different in Indonesia if compared to some Western countries. Relationships and enjoying life take precedence. Even in office life, a healthy balance between "fun" and "work" is normal. At the same time, the energy of the Indonesian economy, the spirit of people to create a better future is everywhere. While it may appear as if people prefer to sit still, have fun and not work, as a group, we get things done. Value is created, problems are solved, startups scale. And yes, traffic jams sometimes cause delays. But I've experienced a surprising timeliness when meeting people. And if we're late, it's okay, no judgments. Meetings can move and change, which works both ways. Overall, I have experienced this makes life more pleasant and less stressful.

Adopting Agile Across Borders | 131

Lastly, fear of failure. I hear people talk about this everywhere. And I never understood it. The antidote seems straightforward: create an environment of trust and empowerment. And above all: remove the thought "us vs. them." As long as we have "us" (e.g., the team) and "them" (e.g., the leaders), tension will remain. If we instead think about "us," we'd see a group of people trying to align and collaborate toward a common goal. While in an environment with a lot of authority and power-distance this seems challenging, the sense of community helps. Communities exist everywhere: mosques, Balinese temples, Agile communities. I believe it's a leader's role to recognize this. The leader needs to stimulate openness, empower people to try new things, and fail and accept failure as a means to learn. The leader needs to see this as a communal effort and drive this mindset in any interaction.

I'm currently leading a transformation in a large state-owned telco. As can be expected, there are many forces working against agility: bureaucracy, leadership changes (even on the board level, decided by the Ministry), strong hierarchical positions and roles. To make the transformation work, we've provided help at different levels: leadership, middle management, and team level. For the leadership level, we've set up a center of excellence. The people in that team come from different departments. They're all supporting different aspects of the transformation (talent management, partnership, Agile scaling, product portfolio, architecture). With the CoE, we are able to orchestrate everything; since we're cross-functional, we can address different challenges one by one. At the middle management level, we have an executive Agile Coach doing one-on-one coaching. This helps leaders see what changes they need to make in their leadership. At the team level, our Agile Coaches help different teams adopt Agile practices and change their way of thinking.

This particular case is interesting because a state-owned enterprise isn't the easiest "target." But many factors help drive the change: the ministry "rejuvenates" ministers as well as directors in state-owned enterprises. Recently, a successful (young) entrepreneur joined the company's board to drive the digital transformation. The leaders in the digital division have all been "exposed" to Agile and innovation for years. As the company is on a quest to become the "engine" for the digital ecosystem, everyone keeps pushing forward. Agile is connected to the broader theme of digital and innovation. This leads everyone in the company to change, because it's not an "IT game."

Becoming Agile is challenging and takes time. It also needs leaders to stick around and see it through. I haven't led transformations outside Indonesia, Singapore, and Malaysia. But I'd think in any country, changing a large group of people takes persistence. Some things help and some things don't. What I strongly believe is that the culture of a company can overcome any "national behaviors."

Chapter 7 | Indonesia

As a final point, here are some short perspectives from Rez Hardityia, one of my colleagues in Ekipa:

> "As someone who recently returned to Indonesia, I do see some cultural challenges. But culture-specific challenges happen in every country, not just Indonesia. It's a matter of understanding the culture and knowing how to move forward.
>
> I get asked a lot about challenges in implementing Agile in Indonesia compared to Australia. Here's how I normally respond.
>
> - From what I've experienced, the main cultural challenge of Agile implementation in Indonesia is in the feedback and communication. This can be broadly generalized into two causes:
> - Hierarchy: Many Indonesian companies have a strong hierarchy culture with top-down control – where ideas and action need to come from the top. This comes from the values where elders are always to be respected.
>
> Communication: Indonesian way of communication is often indirect and they don't always say what they mean. This is deep-rooted in Indonesian culture and it comes from the value for being polite to everyone.
>
> Although those values mean well, they can hold teams back from reaching bigger goals. Agile is based on strong collaboration and open feedback from people regardless of their hierarchy or departmental position. In practicing Agile, open and honest feedback is key.
>
> But two things I also know about Indonesians; they're very resilient and have a huge appetite to learn and grow. We just need to support them in doing it."

—Hugo Messer, Agile Entrepreneur

Antony Marsh, Agile and Lean Coach from Australia, is another one of the people helping with the adoption of Agile in Indonesia, and he shares his view of Agile communities and coaching in Indonesia.

Agile Communities and Coaching in Indonesia

First, the community side of things. There is a very strong meetup and conference culture in Jakarta, with Agile, DevOps, and technical meetups every week. Coming from Australia I'm used to meetups of around 10–20 people – in Indonesia you can expect anything from 50 to 300 attendees.

Adopting Agile Across Borders

Because of traffic, meetups tend to start late and finish very late – this shows true commitment from the attendees who often have a commute home of 1–2 hours after events like this.

Given the growing interest in technology generally, there is strong interest from many companies in Agile and Lean. This either comes from people who have worked overseas in Agile contexts or those who are aware of technology and management trends and want to implement these ideas in their tech development processes. So often the push into Agile and Agile transformations is top-down in Indonesia.

In Hofstede's model of national cultures, Indonesia is a high power distance culture, meaning that people perceive and act on roles, hierarchy, and seniority in a stronger way than most Western cultures. This means that the manager or leader is in a position of power and it is hard for Indonesians to challenge or disagree with their opinions. This can impact on values and principles required by Agile in terms of openness, honesty, transparency, and so on. Indonesian managers also have a tendency to impose control, so this is an important factor when trying to influence change.

Some aspects of traditional Indonesian culture are more in sync with Agile however, as my colleague Karim Jonosisworo points out:

- *Musyawarah*: Discussion that involves all stakeholders to achieve a decision, normally to solve certain issues

- *Gotong Royong*: Literally meaning communal work, where people collaborate on achieving a certain goal

Musyawarah and *gotong royong* are often combined to solve problems in communities and work together regardless of race, religion, or tribe, for the mutual benefit of all. In a culturally diverse nation like Indonesia, there is certainly a strong approach to inclusion and consensus-building.

—Antony Marsh, Agile and Lean Coach

Agile Coaches that we met during our time in Indonesia revealed a pattern of organizations engaging them, looking for concrete examples and clear instructions on how to implement Agile practices. The common story seemed to be a missing focus on embracing the Agile mindset, to study the principles and understand the "why" behind the various practices. There is perhaps a lack of confidence for people to experiment, to find out what does or does not work in their context.

Chapter 7 | Indonesia

■ **Takeaway**   Have patience and perseverance. An Agile journey is exactly that: a journey. And there is no right end destination.

Putting some standard practices in place to get started while people grow their understanding of the Agile mindset is a perfectly good place to start. Over time, allow people the space to explore and discover what Agile means. For example, encourage continuous improvement. Allow growing autonomy by having a shared vision and a bounded environment within which people can self-organize.

It is common for people to be risk-averse because of a high level of fear of failure and the possible consequences for their reputation and their position. This leads to people taking less risks and the reluctance to try out new practices. At the same time though, due to constraints on being able to get things done, such as rules, regulations, and bureaucracy that slow things down, people can be creative problem solvers.

We found that, like in many organizations in other parts of the world that are new to Agile, people were looking and hoping for a "silver-bullet" for their problems. While there was certainly a willingness and excitement for Agile in the people that we were meeting, our experience suggests that the Scrum value of courage can be a challenge. Courage to really enact change, likely missing due to not wanting to fail or to lose face. Uniformity, calmness, and to "blend in" are often deemed much more appropriate behaviors in most situations than to challenge or speak out.

A discussion on the effect of diversity in teams will come later. Suffice it to say for now, diverse teams that are coached well, that have built an empathy and understanding for each other can outperform homogeneous teams. However, diverse teams that have not got good cross-cultural awareness generally perform worse. In Indonesia, because of the difficulty in finding qualified people, we spoke to many companies who are widening their search across the country and beyond for people to join their organizations. In so doing, they face a challenge in building teams of people that will complement one another; Indonesia itself is a vast country made up of thousands of islands with a broad array of subcultures.

However, those teams that can overcome their differences can reap the rewards of their diversity with a wider range of backgrounds giving a wider set of points of view which can ultimately lead to greater innovation. We will discuss this further later, but for now we share the story of PT Bank Central Asia Tbk, a huge organization that would seem to have the right culture in place for Agile to thrive, despite its scale. The story is told following our meeting with Ferdinan Wirawan, now VP of Information Technology Group, who shared the story of Agile adoption at the bank from his own perspective.

Bank Central Asia, Jakarta – A Journey to Agility[10]

Among the skyscrapers in Central Jakarta, one tower stands out from its neighbors. The modern Menara BCA building rises proud and tall, its exterior of innumerable glass windows reflecting the sunlight, making the streets of Jakarta seemingly brighter.

BCA (Bank Central Asia) is an Indonesian private bank founded in the 1950s and is the largest private lender in the country. Its size now means that its movements can have an impact on the whole of the Indonesian economy. With such responsibility, you would think that change would be carefully considered, detailed plans need to be made, experimentation unheard of, and Agile practices feared.

We met with Ferdinan, one of BCA's Scrum trainers in the Menara building, in an office room so underused that the PC equipment hadn't even been set up. "This is supposed to be my boss's office," Ferdinan said, explaining that managers spent very little time in their own offices. Instead, they spend their time in the open spaces with the teams. The use of the word "boss" was a bit of a misnomer; "the higher up you go," Ferdinan told us later, "the more you serve."

Ferdinan himself joined BCA in February 2010, having started his career as a video game tester and IT professional in Canada. He felt a culture shock upon his return to Jakarta a year prior, finding himself adrift, unsure how to best pursue a new career in a city of 10 million people. The shining light that he and many people saw was that at BCA, its reputation as an employer meaning that there are thousands of applicants eager to join at any given time. Ferdinan was not a software developer, he was not highly technical, he was not a manager, yet those at BCA who he met with saw something in him, that he could add value, and most importantly fit in with the company culture.

Company culture is key at BCA. They have had values of customer focus, integrity, teamwork, and a continuous pursuit of excellence in what they do and more for a number of years, long before they started to adopt formal Agile practices. Early on, Ferdinan found himself playing a role in IT project management, which involved gathering data for reporting and creating Gantt charts for estimating project completion dates.

At the time, BCA processes were very document-heavy. There was a feeling that the way they were working was mechanical and not being embraced. One of the development teams had heard about Scrum and had been experimenting with it – after all, they were in a place where experimentation was encouraged. They reported some successes. Inspired by what he was reading, Ferdinan set his mind to leading an Agile transformation.

---

[10]Contribution based on the blogpost at www.redtangerine.org/2018/11/20/bank-central-asia/

Chapter 7 | Indonesia

Things did not go to plan, however. They sent several key leaders on Scrum training in December 2014. Those that attended were inspired; however, many didn't know what to do practically to get started. They made kanban boards and used sticky notes but Scrum values were not really embraced and things were not changing. There were multiple projects on the go that they were struggling with and people were still getting burnt out. More training was arranged specifically for Product Owners and development team members, but again, they lacked the concrete direction that they desired – wanting concrete examples and certainty is a cultural characteristic of people in Indonesia. Despite the false start, the understanding of the need for change was still there, as was the space and trust to keep trying.

Ferdinan took it upon himself. In June 2015, based on his meticulous reading of the Scrum Guide and experience in practicing LEGO® Serious Play®[11] facilitation, Ferdinan ran his own Scrum workshop. The result: disaster. Following the workshop, he reflected on what went wrong, kneeling in piles of disordered Lego in a huge ballroom that had been full of people, where nobody could hear themselves and the message of delivering value was lost in the debris of Lego bricks, Ferdinan was determined not to give up. He realized his mistakes, gathered up the Lego, and went back to the drawing board.

As 2016 rolled around, Ferdinan was putting more work into the design of his workshop, with clearer objectives and a plan to run them with smaller groups of people. He ran a number of sessions. Groups were kept to a maximum of 20. By the end of the year, over 300 people had been through the training. And they were beginning to get it. Ferdinan got his Scrum.org PSM I (Professional Scrum Master I) certification that same year and set in motion a program where, in turn, each newly certified member of his team would become trainers for others in upcoming workshops. At the time of writing, there are now 17 PSM I certified people (one trainer even obtained a complete set: PSM I + PSPO I + PSD I). Scrum Teams were springing up. They were gaining momentum.

One of the issues they needed to address was the question of how to scale. They didn't believe that SAFe®, Nexus, or any of the other scaling frameworks were right for them, so they experimented to work out what would work for their context. Out of the experiments came what they term "mini-companies." A mini-company can be made up of multiple Scrum Teams. In each mini-company, there is one Chief Product Owner overseeing one central backlog which is split into team-specific backlogs. These are managed independently by Product Owners that work at the team level. Mini-company backlogs are fed from other backlogs from all around the company, with requirements flowing into the mini-company backlogs by collaboration between the Product Owners and all relevant stakeholders. All backlogs are visible to everyone.

---

[11]LEGO® Serious Play® www.lego.com/en-us/seriousplay

Adopting Agile Across Borders

Teams are not in silos away from the business though. Everyone involved in an initiative, including business people, is seated with the team while it is being worked on.

Mini-companies are (usually) completely independent from each other. Sprints are two weeks long and produce potentially releasable product increments. As alluded to earlier though, they need real care on what is released. BCA's reputation and the wider economy is on the line. Work of compliance, review, and approval procedures does not need dedicated Sprints though; they are embedded as part of each team's Definition of Done. Not bad for such a large and complex organization.

In the four years since the start of their Scrum adoption, people are more engaged. They have a process that is working better for them and which they embrace. They feel safe. Teams are trusted and empowered, each is free to experiment and decide on its own engineering practices, with communities of practice set up to share learning across teams. Scrum has even spread to the central HR department. IT and HR work closely together and look carefully at how candidates will fit into the team, as they did with Ferdinan, with tools such as the four colors personality test[12] used to build teams with a variety of characteristics. The list of applicants to BCA grows, and part of the attraction is the use of Scrum, but most of all, they have a foundation of attractive company values and culture. "Most companies want to do an Agile transformation to change their company culture," Ferdinan told us, "but we already had it. Scrum blends into the culture that we already have."

We were feeling very inspired as we left, back out into the heat of the day with the sunlight continuing to reflect off of the Menara BCA building and across Jakarta.

—David Spinks

Getting On and Around

The Indonesian national motto is "Unity in Diversity," an acknowledgement of the range of ethnicities in the country. Managers and facilitators would do well to recognize the need to build strategies for dealing with a range of diversity in their teams and organizations. Creating a culture of understanding, empathy, and integration would help to avoid misunderstandings, resulting in getting the best out of people.

---

[12]*Which Color Personality Are You: Red, Blue, Green or Yellow?* https://knoji.com/article/which-color-personality-are-you-red-blue-green-or-yellow/

Chapter 7 | Indonesia

Bluntness and directness can cause discomfort and embarrassment. Instead of confrontation, problems should be referred to in an indirect manner. The workplace values harmony, understanding, and mutual respect, and recognition of achievements will usually be well responded to. People need to feel safe, encouraged, and given direction to grow their confidence. For all teams in the world, clarity of direction is essential, however, perhaps few more so than teams that live in a culture unforgiving of mistakes.

On a personal level, people are extremely friendly and this should be responded to in kind, though it is considered to be bad manners to ask personal questions. There can be some fascination with foreigners who are visiting places off of the usual tourist maps. We were stopped more in Bandung than in any other part of the world that we have been by passers-by wanting to have selfies taken with us. David, standing at just over six feet, appeared to be of particular fascination, with many people wanting their photo taken with him in particular. We soon learned to allow extra time for our journeys to take account of this!

A note of caution: the head is regarded as a sacred part of the body that should not be touched by others. This extends to children, so ruffling a child's hair as a form of affectionate greeting should be avoided. Seniority is respected by holding your head lower than those in positions of greater authority, so bowing is common. Shaking hands is usually an acceptable way to greet others. In Jakarta, women often do so, though they will more often greet with a bow and with their hands folded. The right hand should always be used for interactions, whether when shaking hands or when passing or receiving objects. This is because the left hand is assumed to be reserved for "bathroom duties" and so its use in relation to interacting with other people is considered to be impolite.

The communication style is loquacious with emotions on display. Discussions are respectful; they are not aggressive, and people listen without interruption to the point where long monologues are tolerated even when they are not being completely understood. Checking for understanding is therefore important. Indonesian teams are comfortable with, and even embrace, ambiguity and loose ends. At the same time, people do not want to lose face or cause disappointment by admitting that they do not have answers. Therefore, when working with teams, try to ask questions in a more open way, instead of in a form where they can answer with a yes or a no.

People like to work in groups and make decisions in numbers. Conformity and alignment on decisions is important. More senior and older people are expected to do most of the talking and drive the direction of meetings, so creative facilitation is advised to enable everyone to express their thoughts, while also maintaining harmony.

Agile Community Events and Meetups

- Scrum Day Bandung: `www.scrumdaybandung.com/foundation`
- DevOps Days Jakarta: `www.devopsdaysjkt.org/`
- Agile Circles Indonesia: `www.meetup.com/AgileCircles Indonesia/`
- Agile Circles Bandung: `www.meetup.com/AgileCircles Bandung/`
- Komunitas Scrum di Indonesia: `www.eventbrite.com/o/ komunitas-scrum-di-indonesia-15945747321`
- Agile BSD: `www.meetup.com/Agile-BSD/`

CHAPTER

8

Japan

Japan can legitimately lay claim to being the source of thinking that most influenced the creation of the Scrum framework, the most popular manifestation of Agile in the world. It is also the birthplace of the Toyota Production System whose methods are the principal source for Lean.

Yet Japan's economy, booming from the 1950s to the 1990s has now been stagnant for decades. The adoption of Agile is nowhere near the level of the United States or Europe, while innovation in the country is seemingly at a standstill. At the same time, Japanese people's nature of respect, courtesy, collaboration, and sheer hard work seem to be a perfect fit for Agile ways of working. The paradoxes are many in this unique and fascinating country.

History

Japan remained relatively isolated during its early periods and the feudal era – a time when the warrior class, the samurai, emerged to become dominant. It wasn't until the 19th century when the "Black Ships" – the name given to the US Navy vessels – arrived, forcing Japan to open up. Through a period of treaties with Western countries and civil war, Japan actively became westernized, adopting political, economic, judicial, and cultural influences from the West on its way to industrialization.

Japan became a world power, seeking to expand its interests and influence through expansionism and military force. This included conflicts with the Russian Empire for control over areas that included Korea and Taiwan in the

© Glaudia Califano, David Spinks 2021
G. Califano and D. Spinks, *Adopting Agile Across Borders*,
https://doi.org/10.1007/978-1-4842-6948-0_8

Chapter 8 | Japan

Russo-Japanese War from 1904 to 1905, and in World War I when they sided with the Allies. Their defeat in World War II left the country devastated, and in 1947, they adopted a new constitution that focused on liberalism and democracy.

The Japanese economic miracle that took place after World War II took a country that was on its knees to one that had the second biggest economy in the world. It was partly sustained by US assistance to counter Soviet expansion, and partly by the characteristics of the Japanese people themselves. Manufacturers, suppliers, financiers, and distributors formed groups called keiretsu,[1] essentially groups of informally interlocked businesses with lasting relationships with each other and a focus on long-term sustainability rather than short-term profits. Unions had good relationships with government, who in turn stimulated growth through regulations and protectionism. Companies offered lifetime employment and support in exchange for loyalty and dedication.

With so much money in the economy, an asset price bubble formed in the 1980s, during which assets and real-estate were deemed to be greatly overvalued. Lending and subsidizing to failing banks and businesses created "zombie" organizations. Loans went unpaid and the banks delayed decisions to collect on collateral. Funds for economic growth dried up.

It was in 1986 that two professors, Hirotaka Takuchi and Ikujiro Nonaka had an article published in the Harvard Business Review titled The New New Product Development Game.[2] Takuchi and Nonaka looked at a number of practices of successful manufacturing companies, such as Honda, 3M, Hewlett-Packard, Fuji-Xerox, and Toyota, drawing attention to the use of overlapping processes instead of sequential ones. They stressed the importance of speed, flexibility, and teams of autonomous people for successful product development, likening the approaches they were seeing to a game of rugby, where a team "tries to go the distance as a unit, passing the ball back and forth." Several years later, Jeff Sutherland and his team at Easel Corporation began practicing techniques inspired by the article to develop software.[3] Sutherland went on to refine the approach with Ken Schwaber and together they developed the Scrum framework.

---

[1]Twomey, B. (updated 2018). *Understanding Japanese Keiretsu*. Investopedia. www.investopedia.com/articles/economics/09/japanese-keiretsu.asp

[2]Takuchi, H. and Nonaka, I. (1986) *The new new product development game*. https://hbr.org/1986/01/the-new-new-product-development-game

[3]Sutherland, J. (2014). *Scrum: The Art of Doing Twice the Work in Half the Time*. Random House Business Books. pp. 32–33. ISBN-13: 978-0385346450

Meanwhile, the 1990s for Japan became known as the "Lost Decade," though many would regard the stagnation continued to 2010 and beyond. The 1997 Asian financial crisis and the general global slowdown of growth in the early 2000s hindered Japan's recovery. Though the country returned to growth after 2005, the effects of the Lost Decade continue to be felt today.

On April 30, 2019, Emperor Akhito abdicated the throne. Akhito's son, Naruhito, became the new Emperor of Japan and this marked the passing of the Heisei imperial era to the new Reiwa era. The Prime Minister, Shinzō Abe said that the Reiwa era represents "a culture being born and nurtured by people coming together beautifully."[4]

We could not visit Japan without visiting Toyota and seeing the famous Toyota Production System[5] for ourselves. Based on the philosophies of Toyota's founder Sakichi Toyoda, it has evolved over decades from the approaches developed by Sakichi Toyoda's son, Kiichiro Toyoda and the engineer Taiichi Ohno.

The Toyota Takaoka Plant Tour[6]

From a high steel walkway, we looked down on the long production line, starting at the point where the first fittings are made to the shell of the car. We saw the use of kanban cards, sheets of paper several times bigger than a standard sized post-it note, with all kinds of instructions laid out in a standardized format on the card. Several kanban cards were attached to the shell of the body of the car, one for each assembly station, and we were told they convey information that included the model (the production line will have different models and specifications coming through, depending on orders to be fulfilled) and the intended market of the car so that the workers know to apply any context-specific configurations needed.

I liked that the cards were information radiators and not merely instructions, trusting assembly workers' knowledge and expertise. As the work is done, the kanban cards are taken off the car and put to one side. They are then collected regularly and taken away to trigger the restocking of parts – the ordering done 'just in time' to eliminate the waste of over-stocking.

---

[4]*Bidding goodbye to Heisei; saying hello to Reiwa.* Japan Times. www.japantimes.co.jp/opinion/2019/04/01/editorials/bidding-goodbye-heisei-saying-hello-reiwa/#.XOmJTrzYrnE

[5]Toyota Production System https://global.toyota/en/company/vision-and-philosophy/production-system/

[6]Contribution based on the blogpost at www.redtangerine.org/2018/08/07/toyota-plant-tour/

Chapter 8 | Japan

At each assembly station was the "Call Switch" which workers could use to signal a problem. We saw the "Andon Board," each station represented by a row with a color giving the status on the electronic board. Everything was green. Should a Call Switch be triggered, the corresponding row representing the workstation on the Andon Board would turn amber, notifying everyone that there was an issue. The station's team leader would discuss the concern with the team member and try and resolve it immediately. If they can resolve the issue then the line continues without a stoppage.

Our tour guide pointed out the yellow marks on the conveyor belt. Should the Call Switch have been pulled and the issue unresolved by the time the yellow mark reaches another mark at the side of the belt – which indicates the start of the next assembly station – the row representing the station on the Andon Board turns red and the whole production line is stopped and remains so until the issue is resolved. This is part of the principle of "Poka-yoke", a Japanese term for any mechanism that helps someone avoid (yokeru) mistakes (poka), to eliminate product defects by drawing attention to errors as they occur.

Assembly teams are five to seven people, plus a team leader and a group leader (group leaders have more authority than team leaders). Teams are rotated around workstations several times per day to spread knowledge and so workers do not lose concentration doing the same thing all day. Two shifts run for nine hours with a 45-minute lunch break and a 10-minute break every hour. If someone is losing concentration or needs a rest break, they can pull the Call Switch and the team leader can step in. A nice touch was that people could wear whatever they wanted, as long as they didn't have accessories such as belts that could get caught up in any of the machinery. This was refreshing after being in Tokyo where, almost without exception, we were surrounded by the white shirts and black or navy-blue trousers or skirts of the city's office workers.

Decades after the TPS was first thought up, continuous improvement is still at the heart of what Toyota do, and everyone is encouraged to share ideas of how to eliminate waste or work more efficiently. Improvement opportunities seem limitless with every detail, no matter how small, open for analysis and improvement. We could see at each station, trays containing parts laid out in well-thought-through configurations.

We were shown one idea that was adopted where a worker needed to pick up five bolts for a task, but raised an issue that when he reached into the tray of bolts he would not always grab the five bolts required, slowing him down on completing his task. To demonstrate the problem, a tray of bolts was provided for us to try. On my first effort, I retrieved three bolts. On my second attempt, I got the five. On my third, I had picked up four. An obvious solution would have been to supply the bolts in trays of 5, but this would have caused waste elsewhere – someone else would have to set the tray up, not to mention the waste in transiting the trays of bolts back and forth to the workstation. The

Adopting Agile Across Borders | 145

solution was a contraption, a mechanical arm consisting of five "fingers" with small magnets on each end. Work the lever and the fingers would dip into the tray of bolts and snap back, dropping excess bolts back into the tray leaving five bolts for the worker to pick off the magnets, every single time.

I was struck by how relatively quiet the plant was. In my younger days, I worked in factories to pay my way through my student years. While there was the expected whirr of machinery, what was missing compared to my experience was the sound of human voices, usually loud and barking orders. We saw robots, small cars like something from Star Wars, dragging huge pallets of parts around the factory floor. We saw robot arms spinning and moving, beavering away packing boxes. They almost had their own personalities. Mechanical rigs did the heavy lifting. It turns out that 90% of the production line is automated. This includes much of the continual inspection, which were other variants of the Call Switch and Andon Board that we had seen but automated. For example, at the engine assembly area there were traffic light displays showing the status of the emerging engine after the latest checks at each point of the production line. The automated quality checks together with all workers taking collective responsibility for quality, never knowingly allowing defects to be passed onto the next process has meant that Toyota produces an end product that has a defect rate of close to 0% on final inspection.

Some of the other impressive stats were: a cycle time of one day – the time it takes to build a car, from stamping the body shell to completion, a throughput of 1200 vehicles per day, or put another way, one car delivered nearly every minute. And these rates have flexibility too. The production rate is based on one month of real orders, plus a projection for the following two months of orders – capacity is balanced with demand. Flexibility is built into this plan if these projections are inaccurate.

The Toyota Takaoka plant tour showed us so many ideas and practices that demonstrated Lean principles, principles that can be applied to the work of software development teams and beyond. Toyota certainly live by their company motto which translates to "Good thinking, good products."

—David Spinks

Takeaway Build quality in from the start. When done right, Agile is about ensuring quality throughout your process. At Toyota, the line is stopped when major issues are found. In software development we have practices such as Test Driven Development, Continuous Integration, and test automation. Quality is an ongoing concern for everybody and not something that is left toward the end of our processes, no known faults or bugs are allowed to go downstream.

Chapter 8 | Japan

Insights

Japan is considered unique, both by the people themselves and by outsiders looking in. Culturally, while there are some similarities in behavior with other Asian cultures, Japanese people are quite unlike all others. The country is an isolated island. The language can be vague and ambiguous. Communication with Japanese people can be perplexing to foreigners, for example their use of impersonal verbs make it unclear who or what is being referred to, so communication is highly contextual.

The people have learned to live together in crowded conditions – only about a quarter of the land is habitable due to the mountainous terrain – leading to the need for conformity and harmonious living. The constant threat of earthquakes adds to their collaborative nature. The ability of the Japanese people to bounce back and rebuild roads, buildings and homes after natural disasters is well known, not just in terms of the speed in which they can do so but also often rebuilding with better quality than what was there before. This is in no small part due to the camaraderie and the determination of the Japanese people who are perhaps the greatest and most well-intentioned team players in the world. The behavior of Japanese at the 2018 FIFA World Cup[7] impressed the world when fans and the team themselves cleaned up after themselves, leaving spotlessly clean stadiums and dressing rooms in their wake.

We saw evidence of this collaboration spilling over into the software development realm. Pair Programming is a common technique in building software across the world, but during our time in Japan, and in more than one company, we saw Mob Programming[8] in action.

Mob Programming in Japan

Following our hosts on a tour of the office on many of our company visits in Japan, one of our immediate observations was how some of the work areas had been arranged. In one office's large open-plan space shared by several teams were not just the usual rows of individual workstations and mobile whiteboards, but separate areas set up with a number of comfy looking seats arranged informally facing a large screen. As we walked through, we saw what appeared to be one small Scrum Team standing around a mobile whiteboard to the side of one such area. At another, the team appeared to be seated, but

---

[7]Illmer, A. (2018). *Japan fans impress by cleaning up stadium*. BBC News. www.bbc.co.uk/news/world-asia-44492611

[8]Mob-programming www.agilealliance.org/glossary/mob-programming/

Adopting Agile Across Borders

fully engaged in discussions. Our host confirmed that the first group were in their Daily Scrum, but that the other team were "mobbing." He pointed out the Product Owner, standing by the screen upon which the display was being switched back and forth between what appeared to be an IDE, and a running version of the web application that the team were working on. A couple of the team were seated to one side, seemingly in deep discussion on a particular detail of what was being built, while the rest of the team's attention was on what was happening on the screen. One or two of them – "Navigators" – made suggestions to the sole person that had a keyboard in front of them – the "Driver."

We had coached and encouraged Pair Programming with teams that we had worked with, but this was the first time we had seen the development practice expanded to include multiple people. Here, and in other companies that we visited, Mob Programming stations had been specially created for the whole Scrum Team, including the Product Owner, to work together. These mob stations enabled everyone to gather together in a shared space around one large screen, but were set up with just a single development machine so that the entire Scrum Team could continuously collaborate to get one feature at a time to "Done" – fast. Semi-circular seating aided whole team communication and allowed the team to rotate the driver role.

Mob Programming enhances many of the core Agile principles: face-to-face communication (business people, customers, or customer representatives can be part of the mob), collaboration, self-organizing and cross-functional teams, regular reflection, building quality in, and doing only the minimum necessary to name a few. It reduces communication problems and delays, enables quick decision making, builds in a code review process at the point where it is most efficient to do so (i.e., as the code is being written), helps to keep technical debt down and helps to share knowledge.

The practice of Mob Programming has gone on to spread rapidly throughout Japan since Woody Zuill's keynote talk "Mob Programming and the power of flow" at Agile Japan 2018.[9] There can be few better examples of collaboration in action than Mob Programming, and given their cultural context, it would appear that the Japanese – when given the right environment – are the masters at it.

—Glaudia Califano

---

[9] (2018). *Mob programming and the power of flow agilejapan 2018 Mob-programming.* Slideshare.www.slideshare.net/hiranabe/mob-programming-and-the-power-of-flow-agilejapan2018keynote

Chapter 8 | Japan

Transparency, one of the three pillars of empirical process control theory that Scrum is founded upon, risks disrupting the harmony that is so sought after by Japanese people in their lives. To them, harmony takes precedence over clarity, even affecting the Japanese language which, as noted previously, can be vague and ambiguous. Transparency, and even truth, are secondary concerns to harmony. Saving face for one's self and for others comes before all else. An example of this is that many Japanese people will rarely say "no" directly for fear of causing upset. Instead, they will answer with silence, or they will give indirect messages and a range of subtle expressions to convey a message of "no" such as "I agree... 30%." Or they will promise to give an answer at the next meeting, only for you to find they are never available when trying to schedule something.

The characteristic of conformity and harmony in Japanese psyche means that decision making is done by consensus. There is even a term for it – Nemawashi. Nemawashi is literally translated as "going around the roots" and refers to a Japanese gardening technique where the tree is prepared to survive transplanting in a new location at a later time.

In organizations in Japan, the term Nemawashi is used to describe an informal process of laying the groundwork and building consensus before making formal decisions. Support for a particular point of view is built subtly through informal meetings or corridor conversations, for example. And although this process can take time, it is thought to reduce the risk of resistance. In the end, successful application of Nemawashi allows changes to be carried out with consent of all relevant parties and everyone aligned on the direction.

Adopting Agile Across Borders

Figure 8-1. Formal meetings to build harmony and relationships (image courtesy of Tasia Graham)

Formal meetings on the other hand, as illustrated in Figure 8-1, are to unveil decisions, not to debate them. These meetings allow for ceremony and relationship building, and an invitee will bring whole entourages with them made up of people of different specialisms or perspectives to show solidarity and harmony. Stating one's own position and the exchange of platitudes may need to be repeated a number of times at a succession of meetings as the entourage expands. Meetings may also contain periods of constructive silences to allow reflection on the content.

Nemawashi can mean that things take time, but in the end, a solid consensus has been reached with everybody aligned on the direction. The agreement that has been built is combined with a pragmatism and flexibility. A signed contract is seen only as a starting point and can be rewritten in time.

Chapter 8 | Japan

Long-term goals and relationship building are much more important than contract negotiation or following a plan.

Japanese people, like many South Americans and other nationalities, will continue to regard time in ways that will conflict with other cultures, especially those in the West. Japanese people hate to be rushed into a decision. For them, the solidarity and consensus derived through the process of Nemawashi is worth the time it takes. This can however be considered as counterintuitive to the very essence of Agile thinking.

The Scrum role of Product Owner, properly enacted, and with full empowerment to make decisions could be the antidote to the agonizingly slow process of Nemawashi, but this would require a huge cultural shift. Another remedy to this could be to have very clear long-term goals, or a vision that everyone agrees with from the outset. Once this is in place, it should be relatively easier to build consensus on decisions, as they should be aligned to the clearly stated goals.

Nemawashi exists despite companies in Japan being generally hierarchically structured. People influence their peers and direct managers in the hierarchy. Ideas and suggestions flow up the chain for ratification, with acceptance and policies flowing back down for action. Contact is never made beyond the immediate rungs above or below a person's place in the hierarchy.

Much is built around the hierarchical nature of company structures and the two-way loyalty between people and the company that they work for. We heard stories about how graduates would join companies that would not just provide them with a job and a career, but also support them in their wider lives. This could include helping them in finding a home and organizing social activities. We even heard of an example where the company assisted employees in finding their life partners.

The loyalty between employee and employer goes well beyond that of those in other parts of the world. Traditionally in Japan, companies have provided stability, support, and certainty to their workers and dependents. In return for this, they get loyalty and complete allegiance from employees. It is rare for people to move from one organization to another. Someone with roles at more than two or three companies on their CV would be looked at suspiciously. It has been a long-established norm for people to have dedicated themselves to one company, with seniority determined by age and longevity. It is not uncommon for mediocre people to climb the ranks due to their patience rather than through any merit.

This loyalty to the company and the previously discussed group mentality are factors that contribute to the infamous Japanese culture of long working hours. It is such a part of Japanese culture that many companies expect it as a matter of course. We heard stories of employment contracts being written with clauses included that explicitly stated the number of extra hours

Adopting Agile Across Borders

expected to be worked per week. It is not as simple as blaming corporate pressure though. In a culture where honor and saving face is so important, pressure from peers plays a major part. People feel compelled to stay in the office just because their colleagues are, regardless of what the actual work demands are. We even heard stories where husbands would loiter in the city after leaving the office, spending time in bars so as to not appear at home too early and bring disgrace to the family by giving the impression that they are not working hard.

These attitudes are changing though. Old attitudes are sometimes referred to as "Shōwa," in reference to the Shōwa era that preceded the Heisei era, and corresponding to the period between 1926 to 1989 when emperor Hirohito reigned. The younger generation want more freedom, leisure time, and life experiences. They do not want the lifestyles of their elders. Employers are recognizing the problems – not least because of the country's high suicide rate. There is even a term, karoshi, that describes people working themselves to death. We heard about a company that had created a drone to fly around the office, playing loud music to encourage people to leave on time[10] – at the risk of increasing stress levels even more.

Perhaps another contribution to the long working hours culture – and the stress – is the expectation of perfection. There is little room for safety to experiment. For example, we heard about a Scrum Team that abandoned a Sprint because of a reported bug in their web application in production. Fixing this bug was seen to be so important that the current Sprint Goal became obsolete. The problem only affected the application on an early version of Internet Explorer and a small number of users, but the company risked bad reviews, upset customers, damage to their reputation, and loss of face. The likes of Facebook and Twitter are powerful tools in Japan, with a company's reputation very much dependent on word of mouth on social media and other communication channels. In other countries, organizations may have just asked users experiencing the issue to upgrade their browser version, or to try an alternative browser, but in this case, fixing the bug was seen as of greater value than continuing to work toward the current Sprint Goal.

As a result of Japanese people's need for perfection, it could be argued that innovation is actually repressed. Failure and losing face are too much of a risk to experiment. It is still common for many traditional Japanese companies to treat QA as something to be done toward the end of the development cycle,

---

[10](2019). *Japan turns to tech to cut long working hours.* BBC News. www.bbc.co.uk/news/av/business-47209793/japan-turns-to-tech-to-cut-long-working-hours

Chapter 8 | Japan

with the existence of an independent QA department that does not understand Agile, and who proudly retain ultimate authority on whether to release. Alternatively, QA is often outsourced to a specialist company.

Realizing that they needed to adapt to stay competitive in a fast changing industry, KDDI, one very large company that we visited, was well into their Agile journey. They were adopting and scaling the Scrum framework, with help from well-renowned Agile Coaches from the United States and Japan.

KDDI: Designing the Future Using Scrum[11]

There is a place in Tokyo that is full of energy and activity, with many people moving around with purpose, some in groups, some on their own. Early morning appears to be one of the busiest times as people walk hurriedly with their coffee to get to work. Despite the activity, the scene is organized, the movement of people is smooth as everyone passes one-another with a practiced, calm, agility. I could be talking about the Shibuya Crossing, said to be the busiest road intersection in the world, with up to 1000 people crossing in all directions at peak times and a stone's throw from Shibuya station, one of, if not, the busiest station on the planet. However, I am in fact describing one of the offices of KDDI, one of Asia's largest telecommunications providers a few kilometers away from Shibuya.

We had been invited to the KDDI office for a tour that had been organized for the visit of Avi Schneier, Principal Consultant, Agile Transformation, and JJ Sutherland, CEO, of Scrum, Inc. who KDDI had partnered with for their Scrum adoption with local support from ESM, Inc.

KDDI had seen that the innovators – from and inspired by Silicon Valley – were coming. There had been very little investment in R&D and innovation in Japan in recent decades, and KDDI saw that they had to change. KDDI began their Agile journey in 2013, part of a strategy to change the reliance on 3rd party vendors and move development in-house, starting small with one pilot team and building up from there. They recognized that they needed to create empowered, autonomous teams with management's role as facilitators and enablers, inverting the traditional hierarchical pyramid. The collaboration with Scrum Inc. began at the start of 2017. A year and a half later, the partnership is strong, with Scrum Inc. paying regular visits to the KDDI Tokyo offices to see how things are going and to continue supporting them, the visit from Avi and JJ was just the latest example of this. With an employee base of over 35,000 people, KDDI have since become one of the main examples in Japan of rolling out and scaling Scrum in a large company.

---

[11]Contribution based on the blogpost at www.redtangerine.org/2018/09/24/kddi/

Adopting Agile Across Borders

We didn't know where to begin with our questions as we chatted with Yoshinobu, KDDI development manager, while regularly stepping out of the way of people passing by. We didn't really need to worry about asking questions though, we were getting a good idea of what was happening just by being there. We were shown a number of different offices, and throughout them all we could barely see any wall space that was not used for the display of Scrum boards, story maps, burndown charts, or other information. Rolling whiteboards and electronic screens were dotted around. The whole place was one giant information radiator, with everything displayed with the meticulous tidiness so typical of Japan, swim lanes drawn perfectly level, and post-it notes stuck up in neat rows, for example.

It wasn't just the high level of transparency that impressed us, but also what we saw people doing. One team were Mob Programming in a specially designed area with sofas and a big prominent screen, a technique heavily used at KDDI. A few meters away, another team were similarly gathered in their Sprint Planning event. Around the other side of more rolling white boards, another team were gathered around another screen, the technology utilized to dial in remote team members for the team's Daily Scrum. KDDI has 26 teams in all, just three of which have offshore team members, a mark of how far they have come to create in-house capability.

Avi told us about some of the other changes that had occurred over the last year and a half. He pointed out one board that had three columns with headings "To Do", "Doing" and "Done", saying that when he first arrived the board had 14 columns on it, a hint perhaps of the waterfall process that KDDI were trying to get away from. Avi told us about another breakthrough, product managers that had moved from their previous offices to sit in the same room as the development teams, the greater face-to-face communication between business people and developers real progress for a company the size of KDDI that had traditional company structures historically. This product management group sits together with the Chief Product Owner, a gigantic user story roadmap on the wall by their desks. They were working with three Scrum Teams on a single product using practices from Scrum, Inc's Scrum@Scale framework.[12] For example, Scrum of Scrums and MetaScrums (where a group of Product Owners align the teams' priorities) help to coordinate, communicate, and bubble up impediments to the Executive Action Team, a group with the empowerment to remove impediments that cannot be removed by the Scrum of Scrums group. There was no need for inspirational posters on the walls for these teams; there is little that can be more motivating than seeing how your product is performing. Electronic screens in the office were giving feedback on the state of their applications in production in real-time.

---

[12]Scrum@Scale Guide www.scrumatscale.com/scrum-at-scale-guide/

Chapter 8 | Japan

As well as their work supporting a range of services for network, mobile and cloud for their corporate customers, KDDI support ICT solutions and have been contributing to the establishment of an Internet of Things environment. They are also interested in partnering with, and co-creating new businesses to provide services and solutions in the digital space. The KDDI Digital Gate is a major part of this strategy and we heard more about this later in the day. In partnership with JBPress, KDDI had organized a conference titled "Digital Innovation Leadership" and we had been invited to attend after the office tour and lunch. JJ Sutherland gave a talk, introducing Scrum and its benefits for innovation, and there were other speakers, thought leaders in digital innovation in Japan. Among them, we heard from Akihito Fujii, General Manager of the KDDI Solutions Business Planning Division, and Takayuki Yamane who spoke about the KDDI Digital Gate.

The KDDI Digital Gate is designed to be a space for innovation, where people can come together to create new products and services in a concept not too dissimilar to the Nordstrom Innovation Lab.[13] The mission is not technology led, instead the starting question is always, "How can we create value?" Design Thinking is encouraged to develop ideas that can be quickly turned into prototypes which are quickly turned into products with direct feedback from customers evolving the product as it is being built. KDDI wants to make the Digital Gate truly open, inviting partnerships and collaboration from anyone with a hope of spawning new startup businesses.

In a few short years, KDDI have become one of the leaders in digital innovation and Agile in Japan. What we really liked was their openness and willingness to share. They are passionate about spreading the use of Agile outside of KDDI and supporting the new wave of innovation emerging in Japan.

—David Spinks

■ **Takeaway**   Use information radiators. The transparency that comes from having key information available at a glance – such as current work in progress, health of applications, and how products are currently performing and being used in real time – increases shared accountability, motivation, and quality to name just a few benefits.

---

[13]Nordstrom Innovation Lab www.youtube.com/watch?v=2NFH3VC6LNs

Adopting Agile Across Borders

One of the biggest challenges facing Japan is its aging and declining population. The birthrate in Japan has been below sustainable levels since the mid 1970s, resulting in a population that has been in decline since 2011. The number of Japanese people aged 65 years or older has nearly quadrupled over the last 40 years and accounts for more than a quarter of the total population.[14] Japan is the most rapidly aging country in the world. Concerns are growing about the change in demographics and the increasing stress on the economy and social services.

The government has responded to these concerns with policies designed to encourage fertility, including laws to limit working hours. These policies include those to encourage women into motherhood and the workplace, but they have struggled to overcome traditional behaviors and entrenched stereotypes. Traditionally, women become housewives, and those that do work are in low-paid, part-time jobs worked in around their children's or husband's needs. While men are expected to start a career at a well-established corporate company, there are no such expectations for women. In general, anyone aiming at becoming an entrepreneur is looked at with suspicion.[15] But a woman starting her own company is looked at as taking up a hobby rather than developing a real business or career, though women embarking on forming startups is growing.[16] In either case, entrepreneurship comes with high risk costs of social failure, which can have serious social implications in a culture that sees "failure" as deeply negative.

In reality, the country faces a difficult choice between accepting the decline in population and subsequent effect on economic growth, or open the country to migration – a historically unpopular move in such a relatively closed society. The thought of immigration brings with it concerns about rising crime, the loss of cultural traditions, and the effect it may have on the ethnicity of the country.

The discipline and conformity of hierarchical Japanese society, together with Lean manufacturing principles worked brilliantly during the Japanese economic miracle. However, it has left the country, and many others like it, ill-prepared and ill-structured for the new world of complex knowledge work.[17] Of as much concern is the effect of complacency from the culmination of the previous successes.

---

[14]*Total population of Japan from 2000 to 2025, by age group.* Statista. www.statista.com/statistics/612575/japan-population-age-group/

[15](2014). *Japan's Startup Scene.* Emperics Asia. www.asianentrepreneur.org/japan/

[16]Birmingham, L. (2016). *Japanese women crowd into startup lists.* Nikkei Asian Review. https://asia.nikkei.com/Business/Japanese-women-crowd-into-startup-lists

[17]Snowdon, D. and Boone, M. E. (2007). *A Leader's Framework for Decision Making.* Harvard Business Review. https://hbr.org/2007/11/a-leaders-framework-for-decision-making

Chapter 8 | Japan

Following decades of stubborn stagflation, the country's demographics and complacency combined with one of the highest rates of public debt to GDP in the world,[18] Japan has many challenges ahead. The widespread adoption of Agile could be just the stimulus needed to put Japan back at the forefront of innovation and productivity.

Getting On and Around

The sound of many people slurping bowls of soup or noodles may border on being repulsive to some, but in Japan it is a sign of appreciation and enjoyment of the food. Be aware that this behavior is perfectly normal when dining in a restaurant in Japan. The food in Japan, whether at a restaurant or even from a supermarket, is so good that showing such appreciation is warranted.

Japanese people may sometimes appear to be aloof and may not initiate conversation. Language may be ambiguous and reserved. In fact, people are, in general, extremely shy. Perfectionism makes people reluctant to speak in languages other than their own in case they disgrace themselves by speaking imperfectly. Japanese people are taught to be polite and that it is disrespectful to stare so they purposely avoid eye-contact. Visitors are advised to reciprocate to avoid making their guests uncomfortable. Show respect by trying to understand the rituals of communication and relationship building. For example, be humble, don't interrupt, listen intently, and learn to be comfortable with silences. At the same time, people are forgiving of any faux pas.

The meaning behind words and phrases do not always translate well between English and Japanese, and vice-versa. In the Agile community we use phrases such as "fail fast," where failure is seen as an opportunity to learn and improve. Translating "failure" into Japanese results in a term that is regarded as deeply negative.

■ **Takeaway** Watch out for hidden meanings in language. Sometimes literal translations between languages can result in very different perceptions of meaning including many words and phrases commonly used in the Agile community. "Failure" is a deeply negative word when literally translated into Japanese. To "experiment" is natural to talk about alongside inspection and adaptation, but is often seen as not being in control and an act of incompetence by the Dutch. Items on the "backlog" could be construed as being on the back burner and will never be done in Germany as well as in the Netherlands. Product Backlog grooming is a common term the world over, but was replaced by Product Backlog refinement in the 2017 version of the Scrum Guide due to the connection of the term "grooming" with child sex offences in the United Kingdom.

---

[18]IMF government gross debt across the world www.imf.org/external/datamapper/ GGXWDG_NGDP@WEO/OEMDC/ADVEC/WEOWORLD

Adopting Agile Across Borders 157

A reluctance to be open, and the difference between internal feelings and what is displayed in public is described by the two words, Honne ("the true sound") and Tatemae ("the façade"). Honne Tatemae describes how Japanese people reserve the sharing of their emotions and feelings with close friends and family only. Asking Japanese people about how they are feeling in a workplace setting makes them deeply uncomfortable as the following story from Donna Marie Lee shows. Donna is an Agile Coach working in Japan, but she is originally from the Philippines.

Glad, Mad, Sad in Japan

Japanese people are well mannered to a fault. Usually calm and polite in every situation (except when a production error occurs, as with everybody else). After being here for four years, I have witnessed an interesting facet of the Japanese culture, like their constant need of perfection, the omotenashi* culture, and the myriad of ways of saying "No" without saying "No." I have never seen a Japanese person blow their top in public or at work, and they are quite cautious of saying what they truly feel. This is quite a significant revelation for me when I started working as a Scrum Master in Japan when the majority of the team is Japanese.

Just to give a brief background, I have been working as a Scrum Master in the Philippines before moving to Japan to join a large ecommerce company back in 2015. The organization had quite an international setting. However, the first team I worked with were mostly Japanese and a few foreigners who have lived in Japan for a while and have grown accustomed to the culture. I was to replace their former Scrum Master who was moving to a different department and they were mildly interested in what I can do for them.

After observing their Sprints, I asked them if they were willing to try a new format of retrospective. They agreed to the idea, so I prepared the same format (based on Esther Derby's five stages of retrospective) that was popular back home with the same activities:

> 0. Goal of the retrospective
>
> 1. Set the stage (check-in question)
>
> 2. Gather data (Glad Mad Sad)
>
> 3. Analyze data (5 whys)
>
> 4. Decide what to do (SMART goals)
>
> 5. Close the retrospective (+/Δ)

After review, I gave them an introduction on what it means to have a great retrospective, the new format, and we proceeded without issues until we got to step 2.

Chapter 8 | Japan

I drew three columns with a happy face, a sad face and an angry face. I told them to write on the post-its provided what made them glad, sad, and mad during the Sprint.

Their faces changed from neutral to perplexed to downright uncomfortable.

"Mad..?"

"Really? We need to say what we are mad about?"

"How to do this…"

"Oh, I don't know…"

My supposedly effective retrospective format immediately backfired. You idiot! I thought to myself. You forgot one vital point: work and emotions do not mix with these people. They were fiddling with the markers, having a difficult time trying to express something that is obviously so unnatural for them that I wanted to sink into a hole and stay there from such a careless mistake.

During the closing of the retrospective, I asked them what they would like to change in the retrospective format, even though I already knew the answer. They told me this way of gathering data was not a good fit for them. I apologized to the team, telling them that I will think of a better format that suits their style for the next Sprint.

In a work setting, Japanese people were more inclined to state facts and leave their emotions at home. So instead of such a "controversial" way of gathering data, I decided to use Keep, Drop, Add, and Improve for their next retrospective.

And indeed it was successful. They had absolutely no problems giving input in this manner. They were much more comfortable in sharing their insights which resulted in good, lengthy discussions. They told me that they want to keep this style, and of course, I happily obliged.

This experience affirms that it is vital to understand the culture and the behavior of people to decide activities that would be most effective for them. What may be successful for one team and one country might not be true for another. There is a phrase in Japanese that aptly points this out called "kuuki wo yomu" that literally translates to "read the air," meaning to understand the situation around you and act accordingly. This unique Japanese societal behavior complements an indispensable quality that any Agile Coach or Scrum Master should hone, which is the powers of observation.

* Omotenashi translates as "hospitality" in Japanese.

—Donna Marie Lee, Agile Coach

Jean-Baptiste Vasseur, originally from France but now living and working in Japan, shares another retrospective technique for getting people to open up, share ideas, and come out with concrete actions for improvement.

Fun/Done/Learn: An Alternative for Sprint Retrospective Events[19]

In October 2018, I participated in a Scrum Alliance retreat in Okinawa. The retreat was a good opportunity for Agile Coaches to gather, share experiences, provide or be provided with some help, and, of course, to have some fun together.

During the three days, we split into teams of six members to address an initially agreed set of topics. My team came up with some interesting discussions around teams who tend to resist the adoption of Scrum. While we were exploring the reasons to explain why such teams resist, we ended up defining a framework that teams could use to self-assess their Scrum maturity based on three criteria:

- How much the team is able to deliver ("Deliver" was revised later to "Done")

- How much the team is learning and improving ("Learn")

- How much the team is enjoying their work and workplace ("Fun")

We realized later that this aligns well with Daniel Pink's ideas on autonomy, mastery, and purpose as motivators, but also that this self-assessment could be used during a Sprint Retrospective (or at a project, or phase level). And, this is how we gave birth to the Fun/Done/Learn retrospective (FDL).

How to proceed:

1. Use a large white board, or put together some large paper sheets to make the frame.

---

[19]Contribution based on the blogpost at https://medium.com/@jb.vasseur/fun-done-learn-an-alternative-for-scrum-retrospective-events-b3c175d2f20c

Chapter 8 | Japan

2. Draw three circles, crossing each other so that the overlapping areas are large enough to place some sticky notes inside later. Label the circles as "Done," "Learn," and "Fun."

3. Gather your team around a table, each participant having a pen and some sticky notes (you can limit the number of sticky notes per person if necessary).

4. Each participant will write down on the sticky notes all activities and Product Backlog items that they have been working on, or anything that happened during the Sprint (no more than three to five minutes should be needed).

5. Participants will then take any sticky note that they did not write, and place it on the frame, where they consider it belongs. Continue this until all sticky notes have been placed on the frame. For example:

   - A sticky note that refers to a feature implemented with a new technology that was successfully delivered would make sense to be placed where the circle Learn and Done overlap each other.

   - Some other activity may have been fun, and helped the team to learn a lot, but did not result in a significant output. In this case, it could be placed across the Fun and Learn overlap.

6. Participants take some time to review, share, and discuss by the frame. We observed that this was a good exercise to help the team discuss the topic of definition of "Done," but also definition of "Fun." ;)

7. Participants then each indicate (by placing a dot with a pen) which category they think the Sprint as a whole belongs. They then discuss where they want the next Sprint to go, and how they can achieve this.

Adopting Agile Across Borders

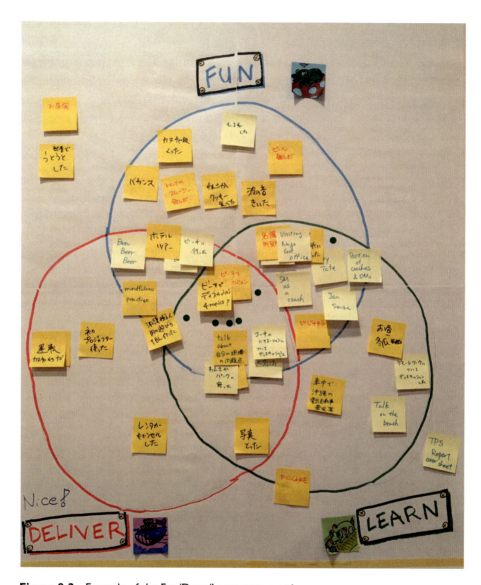

Figure 8-2. Example of the Fun/Done/Learn retrospective

Figure 8-2 shows an example of the results generated from a Fun/Done/Learn retrospective.

—Jean-Baptiste Vasseur, CEO/Agile Coach at Yamaneco

Chapter 8 | Japan

> ■ **Takeaway** Use a variety of retrospective formats. Retrospectives can become repetitive with little value derived from them if the same format is being used time after time. There are many great resources out there to give you fresh ideas such as those that can be found at funretrospectives. com, tastycupcakes.org, or in books like *Agile Retrospectives: Making Good Teams Great* by Esther Derby and Diana Larsen[20] or *Getting Value out of Agile Retrospectives – A Toolbox of Retrospective Exercises* by Luis Gonçalves and Ben Linders.[21]

Politeness and humbleness are core to interactions with Japanese people. They are likely to apologize for rudeness that they haven't committed, minor transgressions, your sports team being beaten, or anything else they can think of. Reciprocating with similar self-deprecation will endear you to them.

Following ceremonial protocol is important. A simple example is the ritual of exchanging business cards on first meeting, where the card is presented with both hands and with a bow. The recipient takes it with two hands and is expected to take some time to study it. This is a good example of how Japanese people are more concerned with symbolism than substance in their meetings. Harmony, courtesy, and following established rituals allow them to understand where they are in the sequence of the different phases of an event. Establishing a repeatable ritual for the Scrum events, for example, may make the Japanese more comfortable. Too much experimentation with different retrospective formats could throw them. Expect the major decisions to be taken outside of formal meetings as we discussed with the concept of Nemawashi.

Direct criticism, or the forcing of opinions would be considered impolite. For Japanese people it is appropriate to nod and smile, and avoid conflict at all costs. Creativity is needed to get people to open up and relax. In retrospectives, use of games and gathering data anonymously may help. It is important to be conscious of language used and to avoid emotional language as Donna's story demonstrated.

Great sensitivity is paid to the hierarchy with high levels of respect shown to those in higher status positions. Subordinates defer to those above them, often waiting to be invited to share an opinion or to elaborate. It could be easy to miss important insights, simply because people have not been given permission to speak by those perceived to be more senior.

---

[20]Derby, E. and Larsen, D. (2006). *Agile Retrospectives: Making Good Teams Great. Pragmatic Bookshelf.* ISBN-13 : 978-0977616640

[21]Gonçalves, L and Linders, B. (2014). *Getting Value out of Agile Retrospectives – A Toolbox of Retrospective Exercises.* lulu.com. ISBN-13 : 978-1304789624

Whatever the level of cross-cultural awareness, those from outside of Japan are never likely to master the Japanese art of "reading the air," the subtle body language, phrases and idioms that only other Japanese people are likely to pick up on. The risk of being labelled as Kuuki Yomenai[22] ("cannot read the air") is almost inevitable.

It is however entirely possible for relationships between Japanese and outsiders to form, as the following story about how a Japanese company grew a community around its product demonstrates.

How Building a Strong Product Community Put Astah on the Map[23]

"So where are you planning to go next?" asked the hotel receptionist in Tokyo, expecting us to list some of the usual tourist places.

"Fukui!" both David and I responded, full of enthusiasm.

The receptionist looked confused. "Why? What is in Fukui?" he asked.

We could of course have mentioned the famous Tojinbo cliffs, Fukui castle or the prominent dinosaur museum. Those are exciting attractions, they were just not the reason that we were going to take the Shinkansen (bullet train) from Tokyo to Fukui. We were more interested in meeting with trend-setters than dinosaurs – we had a meeting with Kenji Hiranabe, CEO of ESM, Inc. and CTO of Change Vision, Inc.

Change Vision, Inc was founded by Kenji Hiranabe in 2006 to develop and market Astah. As an engineer, Kenji worked with many software tools that were mechanically right but not user-friendly. He dreamed of something more intuitive, something that would align with developers' logical thought processes and their imagination, something that would allow them to share these thoughts with others. He decided to create Astah, an editor for creating UML diagrams, mind maps, flow diagrams, use cases, and much more. Models and diagrams can be shared among teams, integrating with several tools such as Confluence. Astah Professional is built in close collaboration with users, it consistently scores highly in user reviews and it is regarded as a high-quality and user-friendly tool. Simplicity, quality, and community were, and still are, the top priorities of Change Vision and Astah.

---

[22]Spacey, J. (2009, updated 2015). *Why You Need to Read the Air in Japan.* Japan Talk. www. japan-talk.com/jt/new/kuuki-yomenai

[23]Contribution based on the blogpost at www.redtangerine.org/2018/09/11/change-vision/

Chapter 8 | Japan

Satomi Joba, Head of Communications, gave us a tour around the office and explained a bit more about Change Vision, Inc. and how a smart strategy of building a strong community around the product helps them to succeed. She told us that one of the Change Vision team's strengths is the ability to build and maintain strong relationships with their users. Over the years they have built up an Astah community, one that everyone involved with the product is a member of: end users, programmers, marketing, communications, and resellers. The close collaboration between community members contributes to Astah's continuous success. An example of this collaboration is the "Friends of Astah"[24] initiative, launched in 2011 to thank and strengthen the Astah community further. As a friend of Astah, members are encouraged to spread the word about the product, for example, in blogs, at conferences and meetups, etc. As a reward, the member receives benefits such as a free Astah Professional license. The Friends of Astah initiative helps Change Vision, Inc. kill many birds with one stone. Satomi Joba's passion for the product and infectious personality made me want to become a friend of Astah even though my profession is not the main target audience. I was happy to settle with becoming a personal friend of Satomi and Kenji.

This word of mouth approach is a relatively inexpensive way for Change Vision, Inc to reach their worldwide target audience and potential prospects. And the friends of Astah truly believe in the product, all are users and are highly knowledgeable about the product. Who else would be better to promote Astah? As the number of license holders increases, the number of users that actively participate in the community increases, giving more visibility on how users from various industries and countries use the product, and what their needs are. This enables the Change Vision, Inc. team to continuously adapt and improve their products. Existing Astah users are kept engaged and happy, and Friends of Astah can also give the Change Vision, Inc. team visibility of the latest trends in their industries.

Satomi told us that the Friends of Astah initiative has been phenomenal. The initiative has been rewarding in ways that they could never have imagined. One friend of Astah in Brazil, Carlos, told Satomi and the team how he used Astah to create a "flood-alerting" system[25] as an open source project. It made everyone at Change Vision Inc. very proud to be part of a project that is actually helping people's lives on the other side of the world.

Satomi also recalled another milestone. A few years ago Change Vision, Inc. had its ten-year anniversary, and they wanted to mark the occasion with an anniversary party. To the surprise of Kenji and all of the team, Satomi asked

---

[24]*Friends of Astah* https://astah.net/about/friends-astah/
[25]*Case Study: Weather Warning Project (Brazil)* https://astah.net/astah-users/individuals/case-study/

Adopting Agile Across Borders

the Astah friends to create a short video message. She did not have to wait too long for a response, the next day the numerous video messages started to pour in from all over the world. Satomi called upon her media editing skills and the result was a heart-warming video compilation that was watched by Kenji and all of the team members at the party. Everyone was touched by the enormous love and support from the Astah friends. Special moments like this gave Kenji, Satomi, and all the team the courage and desire to go on for another ten years at least. It was truly powerful and not something anybody at Change Vision, Inc. imagined would ever happen when launching the Friends of Astah program. Figure 8-3 shows one of the messages that was sent by some of the friends of Astah.

Figure 8-3. Celebration of the tenth birthday of Change Vision, Inc

Satomi showed us the Friends of Astah world map, displayed in the middle of the office so everyone could see it as shown in Figure 8-4. The map is continuously updated and shows all of the friends of Astah, a license holder indicated with a small sticky dot and grouped by country (as a Dutch citizen I was very pleased to see our little country doing well on the Astah map). Different color dots showed us the new license holders by year.

Chapter 8 | Japan

Figure 8-4. Friends of Astah world map

The map indicated that the userbase in Germany had been growing significantly. Satomi explained that the main factor of this growth was due to HIS GmbH, a company based in Hannover that provides a Campus Management System for higher education institutions across the country. HIS GmbH has used Astah to develop a web-based system for the administration of the student life-cycle, from enrolment to graduation. As their standards have spread, more universities have adopted Astah to refine their own systems. A few years ago, Kenji and Satomi flew all the way from Japan to Germany to pay HIS GmbH a visit[26] and learn more about the work they do. Additionally, they also wanted to express their appreciation to the people at HIS GmbH for being such a long-term loyal user of the product. This is part of Kenji's philosophy of fully embracing the principle of face-to-face communication which helps to build trust and relationships with users. Since the visit, Satomi told us that more communications between Change Vision, Inc and HIS GmbH emerged, and sales in German academic institutions keep on increasing.

---

[26]Joba, S. (2013). *Making business process transparent with users – Interview with HIS, GmbH in Germany.* Astah Blog. https://astahblog.com/2013/07/16/interview_with_his_first/

With a great product, a strong community, and smart initiatives, Change Vision, Inc. have put themselves prominently on the world map.

—Glaudia Califano

Agile Community Event and Meetup

- Tokyo Agile Community: www.meetup.com/Tokyo-Agile-Community-TACO/

CHAPTER

9

The Philippines

Colorful jeepneys, vehicles left behind by the United States after World War II, are a popular form of public transport all around Manila and the rest of the Philippines. The illustration in Figure 9-1 depicts a colorful vibrant scene that can be seen in many places. The decision to phase the jeepneys out[1] could be seen as a metaphor for the country moving on from its colonial past.

The US occupation of the Philippines has had a lasting effect. In general, there is a good proficiency with the English language, and American influence can be seen in aspects of the Filipino culture. The Philippines is a democracy and freedom of speech is written into the constitution. American style coffee shops, diners, and fast food restaurants are not hard to find in Manila.

Centuries of Spanish colonization has also influenced the culture, such as in the way people communicate and interact with each other. A mañana tendency has also been inherited from the Spanish. Yet, the Philippines is growing economically and becoming a player on the world stage. A combination of cultural influences, combined with a concerted adoption of Agile could be a winning combination to help get them there.

---

[1]Mercurio, R. (2020). Traditional jeepney phaseout to proceed. *The Philippine Star.* www.philstar.com/headlines/2020/06/03/2018383/traditional-jeepney-phaseout-proceed

© Glaudia Califano, David Spinks 2021
G. Califano and D. Spinks, *Adopting Agile Across Borders*,
https://doi.org/10.1007/978-1-4842-6948-0_9

Chapter 9 | The Philippines

Figure 9-1. A scene including colorful jeepneys in one of the cities of the Philippines (image courtesy of Tasia Graham)

History

Modern humans are believed to have inhabited the islands of the Philippines for tens of thousands of years. Arrivals from Taiwan advanced rapidly southward from around 2200 BC, diversifying the population. Indian traits spread across the Philippines during the 10th century, and by the 14th century Islam was also expanding in the region. Around this time, coastal areas of the islands were becoming trading centers with societal structures, communities, alliances, and conflicts developing from there.

The period of history following European arrival to the islands was full of conflict between the Spanish colonists and the indigenous population. The first explorers, claiming the islands for Spain, arrived in 1521. One of the colonizers, Ruy López de Villalobos, named the Islands after King Philip II during an expedition in 1542. It wasn't until 1565 when the first Hispanic settlements were formed. The conquistadors invaded Muslim occupied Manila, establishing it as the capital of the Spanish East Indies in 1571.

The Spanish brought unity to the Philippines which had previously been a collection of fragmented states. It can be argued that it was the Spanish occupation from the mid-1500s to the 19th century that molded the archipelago into a nation, with the establishment of international trade and immigration, especially between Manila and the Mexican city of Acapulco. The 19th century saw an explosion in population as Philippine trade opened up across the world, and the Spanish introduced hospitals, free education, and a number of other policies aimed at social welfare.

Throughout their rule, the Spanish fought off military challenges from the Dutch and the British (who briefly succeeded in occupying Manila between 1762 and 1764), as well as from Chinese and Japanese pirates, all the while continuing to contain Muslim uprisings. However, during the 19th century, feelings of resentment grew against the Spanish from those native to the Philippines, including those of Latino origin, as their rulers were seen as exploitative who gave preferential treatment to people from Spain itself.

While independence movements and wars spread across South America, tensions in the Philippines grew as propaganda for Filipino self-governance spread. The Spanish reacted with brutality, including the carrying out of executions of leading revolutionaries. This actually made matters worse; the repressive actions turned more of the people against the Spanish. A militant secret society called the Katipunan was formed in the 1890s and they started the Philippine revolution. The Spanish-American War started in Cuba and spread to the Philippines. After the defeat of the Spanish, it seemed as if the independence of the Philippines was inevitable.

The revolutionary leaders declared Philippine independence in 1898 and the First Philippine Republic was formed the next year. The new nation's status was short-lived, however; the United States had paid Spain the sum of US$20 million in compensation for the possession of the islands (along with Puerto Rico and Guam thrown in for good measure) in the aftermath of their conflict. The United States did not recognize Philippine independence claims, resulting in the Philippine-American War that ran between 1899 and 1902, and the defeat of the First Philippine Republic.

The 20th century saw the US rule influence Philippine culture and psychology. The Americans introduced democratic elections, capitalism, and the English language – which became widespread. There was a resurgence of the Philippine culture in literature and cinema to counter the effect. In 1935, the United States declared the Commonwealth of the Philippines, giving it the status in preparation for full independence. These plans were interrupted by World War II and the invasion by the Japanese. Throughout the occupation, many

Chapter 9 | The Philippines

Filipinos remained loyal to the United States, believing that liberation from Japan would at long last bring them independence. The Philippines suffered many atrocities at the hands of Japan, and Manila itself was badly decimated by both American bombs and the fleeing Japanese during the liberation of Manila.

The Philippines was officially recognized as an independent nation in 1946. For a time, things looked promising, and the economy did well in the years after the war. Ferdinand Marcos won the 1965 presidential election and initiated a number of major infrastructure projects. However, his presidency turned into a dictatorship. He was accused of corruption and mismanagement of the economy which was to have a lasting impact on the country. Marcos was eventually ousted following an uprising after the assassination of his main political opponent and what was regarded to be a fraudulent election victory in 1986. It was only in the 1990s that the country began to recover when the government relaxed regulations and restrictions, while encouraging private investment and entrepreneurship.

The Philippines' colonial past, firstly from more than 300 years of Spanish rule and then that of the United States from 1898 after the Spanish-American War, has had a lasting impact. Fidel Ramos, the president in the 1990s, went as far saying that the country could not be governed in the same authoritarian way as other Asian countries such as Japan, China, and Korea in acknowledgment of the influence of the United States on the Filipino mindset.[2]

Rodrigo Duterte won the 2016 presidential election. One of his initiatives was to launch what was called the "Build! Build! Build!" program, a policy aimed at reducing poverty, increasing jobs, economic growth, and reducing congestion to usher in a "golden age of infrastructure" in the Philippines. He launched a crackdown on criminality and also brought in the Universal Access to Quality Tertiary Education Act, providing free education for Filipinos in the country's public universities and colleges, and grants to students in private higher education institutions. The growing quality and innovation in Philippine education is exemplified by Asia Pacific College which we visited during our time in Manila.

---

[2]Lewis, R.D. (2006) *When Cultures Collide: Leading Across Cultures, page 475 (Third Edition)*. First published in hardback by Nicholas Brealey Publishing in 1996. ISBN-13: 978-1-904838-02-9

Asia Pacific College: Bridging the Gap Between Academia and Industry Through Information Technology[3]

After checking into our hostel in Manila we went to find our next temporary virtual office, a.k.a. coffee shop. Here we met with a fellow "virtual office colleague" from Manila to talk about our research. While enjoying our coffee we also came to know more about his life, work, and how he earned his BS in Computer Science and Information Technology with Specialization in Systems Software Engineering eleven years previously from Asia Pacific College (APC) in Manila. After he gave us a brief and very enthusiastic explanation of APC, we realized that this college is something unique. Seeing that we were intrigued, he offered to message his contacts at APC to see if they were open for a visit. And that's how two days later we arrived at the APC premises and sat down with Executive Director Rhea-Luz R. Valbuena, and Director for MIT/MIS/MSCS Graduate School and BS Computer Science Ernesto "Boogie" C. Boydon to talk about APC.

We learned that APC was established in 1991 as a non-profit venture between IBM Philippines and the SM Foundation, which is an organization that is committed to supporting and empowering their host communities through education, healthcare, shelter, disaster response, farmers' training, environmental programs, and care for persons with special needs in the Philippines. Their vision: "A Philippines where everyone has the opportunity for self-improvement and the environment is sustained for future generations." One means to work toward their vision is to provide college and technical-vocational scholarship grants as well as access to primary education.

Nowadays APC is recognized as a Center of Excellence in IT Education. It has grown from a mere "IT training center" for corporate employees, to one of the premier colleges in the Philippines, offering Bachelor's degrees, Master's degrees, and Senior High School courses.

APC bridges the gap between academic learning and Information Technology industry by:

- Industry guided curricula
- Faculty that consist of professionals and industry practitioners
- Project-based learning
- Six-month, full-time internships

---

[3]Contribution based on the blogpost at www.redtangerine.org/2018/06/11/asia-pacific-college/

Chapter 9 | The Philippines

APC has an industry-guided curriculum, and through continuous feedback loops, APC ensures its curriculum and learning materials are up to date with IT industry requirements. APC is envisioned as a learning institution that brings graduates to the job market who fulfill the information technology skills that industry needs. APC works together with 220 industry partners using continuous feedback loops to adapt and improve the curricula to the latest industry technologies, methodologies, tools, and requirements. The APC advisory board meets regularly to discuss the feedback. They update the curriculum and learning materials to keep up to date with the latest IT industry trends. As a result, new specializations have been added to the curriculum over the years. One example is the addition of the Cyber Security and Forensics specialization that was created as an elective but has now evolved into its own specialization.

Faculty consist of professionals and industry practitioners that are able to impart real world experiences into relevant and effective education. When we were introduced to Ernesto he handed over three business cards to us. One for his work at APC, one for the company of which he is CEO, and one for the Philippine Computer Society where he is a member of the Board of Trustees (we felt quite inadequate presenting only one business card).

The college believes that professional competence is best fostered by coupling teaching with hands-on training. The curriculum is taught using project-based learning. Project-based learning is education that goes beyond the academic realm, classroom, and theory. It is practical learning. One project-based learning project we discussed with Rhea and Ernesto, was developing a product using Scrum. As part of the Bachelor's degree, students are introduced to Scrum, a Scrum Team is formed, and a product is built using iterative development. The Scrum Team consists of computer science or information technology students who work together for one semester. There are times that these computer science/information technology teams include members from different programs (e.g., business, animation, etc.) in the case that the project requires specific skills. A semester is ten weeks and is divided into five Sprints. During those Sprints, the Scrum team works closely with Masters in Information Technology (MIT) students who act as Product Owner/project stakeholders. Both undergraduate and MIT students are introduced to the values, principles, and practices of Scrum. They also write user stories, refine a Product Backlog, and use Agile engineering practices. Ernesto told us that the students are fully committed to what they are doing and enjoy working together in this way.

Another aspect of hands-on training is the 6-month, full-time internships program. Senior students (those in their final year) are assigned to work full time in industry for a period of six consecutive months where they are completely immersed in a real working environment experiencing hands-on

Adopting Agile Across Borders

training, helping with actual projects and dealing with clients. APC has more than 200 internship industry partners offering senior students an opportunity to work with them.

The industry-led curriculum, training by industry professionals, project-based learning, and internships all result in companies being able to recruit graduates from APC that meet their needs. It gives students an opportunity to get a degree, be prepared for working life, and make themselves highly employable. It looks like this is a win-win situation for all.

Students are granted scholarships, helping young people reach their full potential. APC graduates are high in demand, being known for their passion, adaptability, and mindset. The SM Foundation believes that when one family member graduates from college, the graduate can help another sibling to go to school and serve as a key to lift their family out of poverty. A belief that is affirmed by over two decades of scholarship programs.

I could go on to write many pages about APC, but instead I will bullet point a few of its initiatives and achievements:

- The opening of its own consulting department

- Tech talks from industry professionals are held regularly at APC for students

- The career placement office that APC runs that actively helps students find employment

- Collaboration programs with a number of non-government and government agencies, other schools, colleges, and universities such as those with the School of Engineering for the Internet of Things and the School of Multimedia Arts for Animation and Creative Arts

- In 2017 APC received autonomous status from the Commission of Higher Education (CHED), the highest recognition that the CHED can grant any private higher education institution in recognition of APC's accomplishments, quality, public responsibility, and commitment as a higher-education provider

Many months after our visit, and just as we were completing the manuscript of this book, the world was hit by the coronavirus pandemic. Rhea got back in touch with us to tell us about the latest initiatives at APC and how they were making adjustments due to the pandemic.

"Due to the pandemic situation, APC became more Agile than ever.

Chapter 9 | The Philippines

Prior to the region's Enhanced Community Quarantine (ECQ), APC has introduced our next-level Project Based Learning - we call it PBL2. Just like the original PBL, the students work on real projects set by our industry partners but this time, the projects are much bigger in scope and the composition of the teams of students is a mix from various programs. Students come from Computer Science, IT, Business, Engineering, Psychology and Multimedia Arts, and each has a role to play in the project. The Computer Science and IT students took on the roles of developers, Business students prepared marketing research or business plans (based on what may be required in the project), and Multimedia Arts students are in-charge of the creatives side. Psychology students perform some research in the projects. During the quarantine where face-to-face contact is not allowed, the students have continued to be able to work on their projects together with the clients by using collaboration tools effectively, and still taking an Agile approach.

With the quarantine in effect, APC transitioned to a Home Study Flexible Learning approach where agile teaching has been very effective in our programming classes. Regular coordination between students and the faculty is made, with consultation and review of progress. Students with the highest grades in the class are identified and become mentors, enabling peer learning which has become an effective approach for learning for both mentors and mentees, not to mention how this helps the faculty have a systematic way to oversee the class.

Education tools were maximized in the classes, taking into serious consideration the limitations that students have with resources and Internet access. For students who were not able to access coursepacks or modules online, APC provided printed copies of the materials to these students, sending this to their homes via courier. We also prepared softcopies on flash drives for the students that may prefer this option as downloading at home could be an issue due to limited bandwidth. Since not all students have laptops, we made it possible for most modules to be accessible via a smartphone, so materials were carefully chosen that produce the least amount of data as much as possible.

Operationally, there were a lot of process adjustments as well. We were not strict with submission dates although we encourage the students to submit coursework by certain target dates. But because of resource issues, we allow submission to be made within a year, in which case, students will receive an "In-Process" grade. We deemed it necessary to not give any "Repeat" or Failing grade this semester due to the adjustments and challenges.

With our Home Study Approach, we have been invited by the Philippine Commission on Higher Education to demonstrate our Home Study Program Model for Information Technology Education to 300 faculty members from different Higher Education Institutions in Metro Manila (National Capital Region).

There is still a lot to do to polish the procedures and to provide better assistance to students. I have witnessed APC's innovation and constant reinvention of education in response to changing times. We never stop trying.

APC's first class of students graduated right in the middle of the Asian financial crisis of 1997. APC trained more than 500 Y2K COBOL programmers to help the world overcome the Year 2000 bug. APC easily survived the 2008 Philippine financial crisis. APC quickly recovered from the devastation of Typhoon Ondoy and other catastrophic floods.

APC survived all these and continues to thrive – because we are Rams, Agile and resilient in times of adversity."

—Rhea-Luz R. Valbuena,
Executive Director at Asia Pacific College

Hearing more from Rhea about how APC is adapting so quickly to the pandemic goes to show their ability to respond to change. Even without this, they are showing how they continue to innovate and evolve their learning programs, encouraging collaboration between students studying in different disciplines on cross-functional teams with PBL2.

—Glaudia Califano

■ **Takeaway**   Build bridges across education and industry. The gap between academic theory and real world industrial experience can be a big one, and a common problem that we have seen the world over. Initiatives such as those at APC that mix education and work experience are emerging in different parts of the world.

APC's project-based learning approach teaches not just technical skills but also gives their students crucial experience in the so-called soft skills, such as collaboration, communication, negotiation, and facilitation. In the future workplace when more and more tasks will be automated, these are essential human skills that no machine is ever likely to be as good at as a well-rounded human.

Filipinos represent one of the most scattered populations in the world. It could be said that the Philippines' main asset is people.[4] At the time of writing, the last official figures for Filipinos overseas was released in 2013

---

[4]Asis, M. (2006). *The Philippines' Culture of Migration. Migration Policy Institute.* www.migrationpolicy.org/article/philippines-culture-migration/

Chapter 9 | The Philippines

with the number put at 10.2 million people[5] (with the population of the Philippines at just under 99 million at the time). Approximately four million citizens of the United States have Philippine ancestry. At the same time, the number of Americans living in the Philippines numbers around 350,000.[6]

The Philippine overseas population continues to grow, a big part of this is due to continued government policies and campaigns to promote working abroad. People living and working overseas are highly regarded by their nation, doing good by sending money home and acquiring new skills that they can then bring back to the country on their return.

Insights

US policy during the years of its colonization means that English is one of the official national languages of the Philippines. This has helped the Philippines to be, by population, the second largest English-speaking nation in the world. This language proficiency also means that companies from English speaking countries outsource to the Philippines in areas such as call centers and IT.

A typical communication style in the Philippines is heavily influenced by the Spanish, with verbose dialogue, though it tends to be less animated and excitable. Speeches can be lengthy, but verbal communication is highly valued. Overall, people come across as polite and attentive listeners, rarely interrupting each other, yet they do have some courage to provide respectful feedback. Open criticism of others is avoided though. Instead, disapproval is indicated indirectly, through what is not said, or accompanied with compliments in other areas. One team we visited in the Philippines told us all about working with colleagues located in Australia. The difference in time zone between the two was not the biggest issue. What was a problem was the direct style of feedback given by the Australian team, which was quite a shock to the team in the Philippines.

During our visit we discovered that the Philippines has a fairly new, but thriving Agile community. The Scrum movement began to get real traction from around 2012. Nowadays there is a great deal of interest, and its popularity is on the rise, especially in the younger generation. Evidence of this is the Agile Philippines Meetup in Manila that we joined, where more than 110 people attended. This meetup is very active, with events organized around different subjects each and every month. This includes running the meetups virtually since the onset of the coronavirus pandemic.

---

[5](2020). *Stock estimate of overseas Filipinos.* https://cfo.gov.ph/yearly-stock-estimation-of-overseas-filipinos/

[6](2020). *US relations with the Philippines. US department of state.* www.state.gov/u-s-relations-with-the-philippines/

**Adopting Agile Across Borders** 179

There are various reasons why companies in the Philippines decide to transform to Agile. Management at some companies realize that to compete they need to change the way they work. Others are following the trend. Now, more people are understanding the benefits of Agile ways of working and are eager to move to it. Collaboration between development teams and client customers is greater. Lessons of discipline in ensuring quality of product have been learned. And we also saw signs that companies in the Philippines are evolving engineering practices, adopting ideas such as Continuous Integration, Continuous Delivery, and Acceptance Test Driven Development.

In the Philippines, where traditionally company structures are hierarchical, it is essential that top management is fully behind an Agile transformation. Employees are very much open and adaptable to change; however, in general they will in the first instance seek for active buy-in from their management. This alignment and encouragement from top management where it happens, has enabled those that have gone on the journey to have a much smoother ride. On top of that, as an outsourcing hub, many clients of Philippines companies have started their own Agile transformation journey at the same time, strengthening the collaboration between the client and their partners in the Philippines with Agile ways of working even further. They are in it together.

▇ **Takeaway**   Get started with practical experience. We are often contacted by people that are new to Agile who want to get their first role in an Agile team, very often as a Scrum Master or a Product Owner. Even when having completed a training course and earned a certification, it is very tough – though not impossible – to get a role on an Agile team without relevant experience.

We suggest going to meetups and building your network. Volunteer to help at these meetups and at conferences. Look for opportunities to shadow and observe. Or start experimenting with Agile practices in your current work together with others that you work with. Very often, we see that people first work as team members in an Agile team before taking on the Scrum Master or Product Owner.

The concept of family is very important in the Philippines. In order to support their families financially, monetary rewards and career progression are seen as important. But it is not only blood relatives that are regarded as family. As we also experienced across South America, work and social lives are intertwined in the Philippines. Work colleagues, especially team mates, can be regarded as "family" resulting in teams that are strong in collaboration and knowledge sharing, with a lot of respect and empathy for one another. This, in combination with the innate politeness of Philippine culture, means that true openness can sometimes be compromised, making retrospectives a bit tricky for example. Nobody wants to be seen to be openly criticizing or risk hurting their "family" or friends.

Chapter 9 | The Philippines

■ **Takeaway** Use retrospective formats that enable deep analysis. The retrospective is all about making improvements, it is certainly not a place to apportion blame. There are many different retrospective formats, many of which can be used for the team to analyze deeply what has happened so that everyone can focus on improvements without passing judgment, while avoiding emotional conflict. Examples include the "5 whys" or the "strengths-based retrospective." Bringing in and analyzing metrics with tools such as burndown charts and cumulative flow diagrams can also be used to focus minds on logical discussions.

Agile teams that stay together for long periods of time, have the chance to learn the best ways of working together. However, sometimes an Agile team needs to be broken up and new teams are formed. As often team members in the Agile team in the Philippines are so close, they can feel as if they are being ripped away from their "work family," which can be hard for some people. It takes time for new team connections to be made, but over time, not only can strong new teams be formed, but strong inter-team relations and communications, as people stay connected with their former teammates.

Leadership and status is generally won through age, connections, and the reputation of the family name. Older and more senior people are expected to be people with wisdom which they pass down to younger and more junior people. In return, they expect their status to be respected. Paternal leadership styles are common, in that leaders have the employee's best interests at heart in return for their loyalty, respect, and deference.

Managers provide clear instructions in order for progress to be made. Teams have no problems when carrying out instructions, and in many organizations people are used to managers giving explicit orders. Some employees may feel lost without such clear direction. This also means that there is quite a mindshift required to get people to think creatively for themselves in terms of what needs to be done to achieve outcomes, instead of focusing on the completion of tasks.

One of the big cultural barriers to Agile adoption in the Philippines is managers' tendency to adopt traditional command and control leadership styles, with managers that desire holding onto power. Efficiency is affected by having to consult with the appropriate person with the right level of authority to get things done. At the same time, the Philippines' history has fed people's desire for democracy, freedom of speech, and other traits that clash with their managers' autocratic styles. In this respect, Agile practices of empowering the team, self-organization, and more can be a natural fit with the array of cultural aspects in the Philippines when given the chance.

**Adopting Agile Across Borders**

There is cause for optimism in that many cultural behaviors we see in the Philippines seem to be naturally aligned with Agile ways of working. It may take a cultural shift to enable people to feel empowered and take more ownership of decisions for example, for Agile to truly flourish. Key to Agile adoption in the Philippines is for companies to create "safe" environments to give people the courage to challenge, think for themselves, and to say "no" openly.

The Philippines is overall a developing country, and its people are concerned with the basics of life. Concern for job security and providing for family is the primary motivation, and a fear for one's position is an impediment to the courage and openness needed in Agile. However, underneath the surface there are people ready, willing, and able to embrace the Agile mindset.

Getting On and Around

Politeness and showing respect is central to Filipino life, especially more so toward elders and to people that are more senior.

Heated discussions, open disharmony and strong opinions can make people uncomfortable. Instead, the skill of reading the subtle, hidden signals, by what is not being said, and reading between the lines is key. Praise for educational achievements, qualifications, and English ability are celebrated. Showing concern and interest in people's well-being and families is appreciated. When discussing timings, try to make expectations explicit as lateness is commonly accepted as normal.

Agile Community Events and Meetups

- Agile Philippines: www.meetup.com/AgilePhilippines/, https://agilephilippines.org/

- Agile Leaders PH: Chapter: www.meetup.com/Agile-Leaders-PH-Chapter/

CHAPTER

10

Singapore

Singapore, its people instilled with Confucian values of respect, duty, moderation, and a strong work ethic, is one of the so-called Four Asian Tigers. In return for a booming economy, good education, security, and affluence, the people of Singapore are attuned to a disciplined and work-oriented existence. Laws are strict, perhaps most infamously is the outlawing of chewing gum. Climbing into positions of power is the ambition of many, not just to keep up with the high cost of living, but also for being seen to have a position of high status. However, in the rush for roles that are seen as important, well respected, and highly paid, respect has been lost for the roles that do. Building things, software included, has not been regarded as a desirable long-term career path.

With a scarcity of good software developers, the question is whether Singapore can wake up in time to embrace knowledge work for what it is and Agile thinking before it gets left behind.

History

Singapore derives its name from the Malay name for the country, Singapura, which in turn comes from the Sanskrit, Simapura. Sima meaning "lion," and pura meaning "town" or "city."

This small island (actually one main island with dozens of smaller ones dotted around it), just off of the southern coast of the Malay Peninsula was an insignificant trading port, left abandoned after Portuguese forces raided it and

© Glaudia Califano, David Spinks 2021
G. Califano and D. Spinks, *Adopting Agile Across Borders*,
https://doi.org/10.1007/978-1-4842-6948-0_10

Chapter 10 | Singapore

destroyed the settlement that was there in the early 17th century. It was the arrival of a British statesman and representative of the British East India Company named Thomas Raffles in 1819 that set the island on a path to be the country that it is today. Raffles saw the potential of the geography; he understood that it was a perfect place for a new port and colony. Timed with a growing industry of sorting and exportation of Malaysian produced rubber, Singapore quickly developed, growing in size to a population of 80,000 people by 1860 from the mere 1,000 inhabitants that were in the area at the point that Raffles had first arrived.

The British East India Company collapsed in 1858, and control of Singapore was transferred to the British Raj. World War I had very little impact in the area since the conflict did not spread to Southeast Asia. However, Singapore was captured by Japan during World War II. The failure to defend the country damaged Britain's credibility in the eyes of many Singaporeans, and thus began a movement for independence. Singapore left the British Empire in 1963, in a short-lived merger with Malaysia that lasted just two years before disagreements over a number of policies, including restrictions of trade from Singapore to the rest of Malaysia, led to clashes and riots. The Malaysian parliament, without Singaporean representation, voted to remove Singapore from its federation and, in what is arguably the only occurrence, Singapore became an independent country against its own will.[1]

Under the leadership of its first Prime Minister Lee Kuan Yew, Singapore, in the span of a single generation, effectively moved to a status of a developed country when measured by ways of the advancement of its economy, gross domestic product, and its technological infrastructure. Between 1965 and 1995, the growth rate averaged around 6% per year.

Lee served as Prime Minister for a total of 31 years, from 1959 until he stepped down in 1990. His policies focused on economic growth, support for entrepreneurship, discipline, and an intolerance for civil disobedience of any kind. This set the backdrop for the country's staggering economic success. Many wrote off Lee's vision, after all, Singapore had few natural resources. But with steadfast determination, he saw that the people of Singapore were his greatest asset and he inspired the populace to fulfill the ambitions that he had for the country. By several measures, Lee Kuan Yew could be regarded as one of history's greatest leaders.

---

[1]Soniak, M. (2013). *Was Singapore's Independence an Accident?* Mental Floss. https://www.mentalfloss.com/article/52146/was-singapore%E2%80%99s-independence-accident

> ■ **Takeaway** An empirical leadership approach can lead to dramatic success. Traditional management relies on the wisdom of the leader who gives orders based on belief in theories and processes. An empirical leader on the other hand sets a vision and the boundaries, accepts that the future is unknowable, solves problems and makes decisions based on evidence, just as Lee did when leading Singapore.

Lee's "stop at two" policy in the 1960s and 1970s, designed to slow and reverse the population boom that had been building since World War II, was arguably too successful. The birth rate declined rapidly, falling to the lowest in the world. For the last few decades, the Singapore government has been encouraging immigration of foreign workers to stabilize the population. As a result, present day Singapore is made up of people with an extremely diverse range of origins and cultures, including many people of Chinese, Malay, Indian, European, and Eurasian origins.

Insights

Lee Kuan Yew had a clear vision for what he wanted for Singapore.[2] He was known for being disinterested in theories, and instead talked about solving problems – he thought of himself, and was widely regarded, as an empiricist.[3] He understood that diversity could be harnessed and become one of Singapore's strengths as well as keeping the population stable and from aging too dramatically in a country with such a low birth rate.

It could be argued that much of Singapore's success is due to its diversity. For example, it could be said that Singapore has had an advantage with the historical commercial experience from the West, in combination with the diligence and discipline of the East. This, along with the Singaporean model of a strong authoritarian government providing stability and a harmonious society has helped its growth.

The Singaporean meritocratic approach is evident in the society as a whole. Like most of Asia, the people of Singapore are comfortable in hierarchical structures in their government, organizations, and in wider society. The ambitious Singaporeans accept that a high work ethic is required to progress. The people of Singapore not only place a great deal of value on wealth, but also on "linear time," a trait very much inherited from the West and one that

---

[2]Sigdyal, A. (2008). *A transformational leader: Lee Kuan Yew.* ResearchGate. www.researchgate.net/publication/327790824_A_transformational_Leader_ Lee_Kuan_Yew

[3](2013). *What's the big idea?* The Economist. www.economist.com/banyan/2013/09/17/ whats-the-big-idea

Chapter 10 | Singapore

is uncommon in many other parts of Asia. They are in general, extremely punctual. They are mindful of sticking to schedules, timeboxes, and deadlines.

Overall, Singaporeans typically have good manners when it comes to being careful and courteous listeners. A Sprint Planning event that we observed while in Singapore was one of the most orderly Scrum events that we have ever seen. The team listened, did not interrupt one another, but still gave honest and polite feedback to each other. It was the epitome of respect. The language used was unambiguous yet humble with language used such as "my modest opinion on this is...."

The strict laws of the country are about instilling discipline and order. There is little to suggest that the laws have acted to repress people. Corporate culture would seemingly be more of an influence on how open people are.

Lee Kuan Yew once stated, "The greatest satisfaction in life comes from achievement. To achieve is to be happy... Achievement generates inner or spiritual strength, a strength which grows out of an inner discipline."[4]

Lee certainly inspired the people of Singapore. Ambition is seared into the national consciousness. Manufacturing work, such as software development, has traditionally been seen as a phase in one's career to be endured on the way to something more important such as analyst, marketeer, or manager. Many drive toward leadership positions, not necessarily because they actually want to do the job, but for the status that being a manager brings, and the higher salaries that come with such positions. The illustration of Figure 10-1 serves as a metaphor of Singaporean people's desire to climb to higher positions.

---

[4]*Prime Minister's New Year Message, 1973.* National Archives of Singapore. www.nas.gov.sg/archivesonline/data/pdfdoc/lky19730101.pdf

Adopting Agile Across Borders

Figure 10-1. Impression of the Gardens by the Bay area and workers of Singapore (image courtesy of Tasia Graham)

Consequently, many are in roles that suit their ambitions but not necessarily their passion or their competency. This is commonly reflected in software development not being regarded with the professionalism it deserves.[5]

The policies of the ruling People's Action Party (PAP) can certainly be credited for much of Singapore's spectacular economic growth and success. Policies have included a social engineering system that steers the population to study and train in particular industries. In the past there have been pushes toward manufacturing, design, and biomedical science as well as IT. However, the

---

[5]Vodde, B. (2012). *Singaporeans, wake up! Why software is eating your island.* www.odd-e.com/material/2012/eat_singapore.pdf

Chapter 10 | Singapore

Singaporean meritocratic approach has resulted in people of lower privilege and lower skill being left behind. Singapore has one of the biggest gaps between the rich and the poor of any of the developed nations.[6]

Sydney Brenner, the Nobel Prize–winning biologist, when he met Dr. Goh Keng Swee, then Deputy Prime Minister of Singapore, alluded to Singapore's success not being sustainable in the future. To paraphrase Brenner, he said that it would be important to transition from a nation of technicians to a knowledge-based economy.[7] This was back in 1985.

Three and a half decades on, and Singapore's IT industry, like many others around the world, has yet to make the shift in thinking as described by Brenner. Knowledge work is still managed in the same way as manufacturing work. Engineering practices that are being taught in universities lag behind what is going on and needed in industry. The Agile mindset, principles, and practices are not on university courses at all. At the same time, most companies continue to operate with top down hierarchical structures. The idea of creating environments of empowered, autonomous teams with managers as servant leaders is rare, though we did find some examples to the contrary while in Singapore.

Yves Lin, Strategic Consultant at Titansoft Pte Ltd, an information technology and services company based in Singapore, shared with us the following lessons and the effort involved in the Agile transformation at Titansoft.

Eight DON'Ts in Agile Transformation[8]

I was holding the role of General Manager in Titansoft when I first encountered Agile in 2014 – and I felt as though Agile (Agile development, Agile management) depicted an ideal world. Just take as an example, in the most popular Agile methodology, Scrum, there is no Team Leader and projects are completed through the division of labor within the Scrum Team. Members have the option to choose the task they work on rather than having a supervisor assigning work. Team members are motivated and strive to perform, with results shared by the entire team.

In other words, it is similar to the presentation of an ideal society in communism which reads

---

[6]Einhorn, B. (2009) *Countries with the Biggest Gaps Between Rich and Poor.* https://web.archive.org/web/20111008055647/http://finance.yahoo.com/banking-budgeting/article/107980/countries-with-the-biggest-gaps-between-rich-and-poor

[7]Khew, C. (2015). *Mentor to a nation's science ambitions.* The Straits Times. www.straitstimes.com/singapore/mentor-to-a-nations-science-ambitions

[8]Contribution based on the blogpost at https://blog.titansoft.com.sg/2018/12/27/more-waterfall-8-donts-in-agile-transformation/

> *From each according to his ability, to each according to his needs.*
>
> —Socialist slogan of Étienne Cabet, Louis Blanc, and Karl Marx[9]

However, it was only after we took the first step when I realized that reality can be very different from initial expectations!

The team gets caught in a decision-making dilemma; without a Team Leader, a discussion about a small decision can drag on for three or four days. Without a supervisory role to communicate information, the team's direction is not aligned to the department and company's direction. Daily stand up meetings are just for the sake of putting on a show as team members work separately. Senior members feel that it is a waste of time to coach the juniors, whereas junior members feel that the seniors are just doing what they like instead of attending to their duties. All this, let alone the departure of Titaners who are not accustomed to the new way of working during this phase of transformation, created a period of turmoil in the company.

It was only after a year or two into our Agile transformation that the chaotic situation gradually resolved as we internalized the spirit of Agile. Nevertheless, it took an unimaginable amount of our time, attention, and effort.

Reflecting on our past five years of experience with Agile, if it were possible for us to start all over again, there are some practices we might have changed to simplify the process, such as follows.

1. DON'T eliminate supervisors; DO let supervisors do the right things

When Agile transformation was first introduced to Titansoft, we eliminated the management position in teams – the Team Leader. The smooth transition was thanks to the understanding and support of Titaners who held those positions. In spite of that, this was a dangerous move as it would likely have incurred great resistance and led to serious consequences in most organizations.

If we could start all over again, we may not have eliminated all the Team Leader positions. Instead, we would have provided all members the opportunity to take turns being the Team Leader and perform supervisory duties. Equipped with leadership experience, members would have a better understanding of the company's operational situation and perspective. At the same time, it serves as a succession planning opportunity for senior leadership roles.

What are the responsibilities of a supervisor?

---

[9]Bovens, L. and Lutz, A. (2019). *"From Each according to Ability; To Each according to Needs" Origin, Meaning, and Development of Socialist Slogans.* History of Political Economy. https://philarchive.org/archive/BOVFEA

Chapter 10 | Singapore

Aligning company goals and values, sourcing for talent, securing resources, helping internal and cross-team communication, supporting the growth of team members, and making high-quality decisions about organizational system issues.

2. DON'T be an all-rounder; DO be willing to do anything when the team needs it

At the beginning of our Agile adoption, we hoped that members of the team can be full-stack developers, meaning that everyone can perform front-end, back-end and testing. Therefore, we eliminated the job titles of Front-end Developer, Back-end Developer, Testing Engineer, etc. and renamed all software development–related job titles simply to Product Developer.

The advantage is without a doubt, the removal of the job function barrier. Yet, it created a misconception that everyone has to know everything, and everything has to be perfect.

If we could start all over again, we would still eliminate those titles but focus on contributing our own expertise, learning others' expertise, and helping out when necessary, rather than having everyone learn all skills.

What we require is for teams to possess an end-to-end skill set as a whole, instead of requiring everyone to be an end-to-end expert.

3. DON'T put the customer first; DO fully grasp dynamic market changes

Agile places great emphasis on collaboration with customers. As a B2B company, we are often at the whims of customers. As a result, we have forgotten that customer collaboration is merely one of the many possible methods to search for a good product-market fit which in turn ensures that our products are profitable.

If we could start all over again, we would pay more attention to the value generated after the delivery to customers' requirements, review the effectiveness of each requirement with the customer, and even consider meeting with the actual end users in the market instead of just receiving second-hand feedback from customers.

The customer is not the priority, generating profits for survival is.

4. DON'T make everything transparent; DO enable easy access to information required for work

In an attempt to implement organizational transparency, we made salaries transparent by publishing the salaries of 80% of our developers. In practice, there are many more details to be considered such as the publishing of only entry and middle level employees, adjustments for the same job grade to receive the same salary, and the withholding of publication of individual bonuses.

In my opinion, the overall impact of salary transparency is neither good nor bad. It did not bring about many benefits and likewise, did not cause any negative reactions. Nevertheless, it ensures that supervisors do not have to worry about gossip surrounding salary. Besides this, we have numerous other attempts at information transparency.

If we could start all over again, we would pay more attention to information integration rather than focusing solely on information publishing. Too much information coupled with a limited time results in information overload and key information being obscured. In my view, one of the supervisor's essential responsibilities is to assist the team with filtering, organizing, and translating of information.

Transparency is a means to improve effectiveness in order to achieve the organizational goal, transparency in itself is not the goal.

5. DON'T seek consensus; DO collect different opinions before making decisions

Zappos[10] and Morning Star[11] are notable for being highly Agile and liberal companies. Yet, they both retained the operational decision-making role in their teams and departments. Agile organizational structures such as Holacracy[12] and Sociocracy[13] also have a specific role for operational decision making. In Holacracy, it is known as Lead Link, whereas in Sociocracy, it is known as Operational Lead.

Upon elimination of the Team Leader position after introducing Agile, teams were given free rein to self-organize and make their own decisions. Inevitably, the results were atrocious. Teams either took a long time to discuss without reaching a consensus, otherwise nobody took the lead in making a decision. Or decisions resulted in blame with claims of "it was the team's decision" when problems emerged.

If we could start all over again, we would first introduce the concept of Consent Decision Making[14] to our teams and separate the decision-making system into governance and operational. Consent is applied in governance (such as developing game play rules) whereas the supervisor (or Team Leader, Lead Link, Operational Lead) would make the final decision after considering everyone's opinions in the operational context (following the game's rules).

---

[10]Ward, C. (2017). *The Zappos story: Is holacracy a proven structure for improving customer experience?* mycustomer.com www.mycustomer.com/service/management/the-zappos-story-is-holacracy-a-proven-structure-for-improving-customer

[11](2016). *Morning Star's Success Story: No Bosses, No Titles, No Structural Hierarchy.* https://corporate-rebels.com/morning-star/

[12]Holacracy www.holacracy.org/

[13]*What Is Sociocracy and Why Does Democracy Need it?* sociocracy.info www.sociocracy.info/what-is-sociocracy/

[14]Consent Decision Making https://thedecider.app/consent-decision-making/

Chapter 10 | Singapore

Never ever use consensus as not everyone has the same level of investment and risk tolerance toward the job. People with more impact on the company's future should have a greater decision-making power.

If it is not possible to apply consent decision making, choose autocracy over consensus.

6. DON'T be anti-bureaucratic; DO let the people doing the work design processes to solve problems

After exposure to Agile concepts, I envisioned an ultra-flat, non-hierarchical world.

However, after reality starts to sink in and once the organization starts expanding, some form of hierarchy is required for resource integration and scheduling to ensure the effectiveness of the overall organization. Hierarchy closer to the customer would handle more concrete affairs, while hierarchy further away from the customer would handle more abstract affairs.

If we could start all over again, our focus would not be on eliminating the bureaucratic system but on finding ways for more effective operation of the bureaucratic system, more effective integration of resources, smoother flow of information, and greater authority for front line staff to service customers.

The problem lies not with a bureaucratic system; rather, it is a bureaucratic mindset that is the problem.

7. DON'T spend on providing lots of training; DO reflect and grow from daily work

In my opinion, the purpose of an Agile transformation is to become a learning organization. In order to achieve that, Titansoft spent a lot of resources and time for Titaners to attend classes and enroll in training courses. This eventually led to the condition of "over learning" – being overwhelmed with new knowledge due to attending too many classes, reading too many books, and listening to too many shared ideas without sufficient time to digest, absorb, and apply insights gained to work.

If we could start all over again, we would place much more emphasis on solving problems at work, focusing on learning and growth through daily work instead of concentrating on providing opportunities for education and training.

Real learning would bring about organizational changes, otherwise, it is just an illusion of learning.

8. DON'T build spiritual camps; DO learn to face the cruelties of reality

During our Agile transformation, I realized that being Agile requires effective communication. Thus, I participated in an array of communication courses, including Focused Conversation method ORID,[15] DISC personality profile,[16] coaching, facilitation, Satir Model,[17] and so on. Among these, the DISC and ORID courses have been introduced to Titansoft as part of the internal foundation training courses conducted annually.

Without a doubt, these courses have been of great help to my personal growth. However, in terms of Return on Investment (ROI) from a business perspective, I feel that besides the basic communication courses, other classes do not bring about any significant financial outcome.

To make matters worse, these courses end up creating an expectation of "you need to care about my feelings" in participants, although they were initially meant to help set self-expectations rather than to make demands of others.

If we could start all over again, we would focus more on ways to resolve conflict, create healthy conflict, and cultivate a culture of dealing with matters as they are and discussing them on their own merits. This is not to say that we should not care about others' feelings. We should instead discuss work-related matters backed up with data. Opinions can be expressed with a softer edge, but the reality is what it is and will not change with feelings of happiness or upset.

Surviving is the top priority, only when we survive can we have opportunities to seek spiritual growth.

Eight DON'Ts in Agile Transformation

Those are the Eight DON'Ts of Agile gained from my personal experience. I hope this will be a helpful reference for people who wish to adopt Agile into their organizations.

DON'T eliminate supervisors; DO let supervisors do the right things

DON'T be an all-rounder; DO be willing to do anything when the team needs it

DON'T put the customer first; DO fully grasp dynamic market changes

---

[15]Grayson, R. (2010). *ORID – strategic questioning that gets you to a decision*. Pacific Edge. https://pacific-edge.info/2010/08/orid/

[16]*DISC Personality Test* 123test.com. www.123test.com/disc-personality-test/

[17]Smith, S. The Satir Change Model. https://stevenmsmith.com/ar-satir-change-model/

DON'T make everything transparent; DO enable easy access to information required for work

DON'T seek consensus; DO collect different opinions before making decisions

DON'T be anti-bureaucratic; DO let the people doing the work design processes to solve problems

DON'T spend on providing lots of training; DO reflect and grow from daily work

DON'T build spiritual camps; DO learn to face the cruelties of reality.

—Yves Lin, Strategic Consultant, Titansoft Pte Ltd

Another example of an Agile thinking organization in Singapore is PALO IT. We were particularly interested in, and impressed with, the approach that they used in keeping teams together and stable so that they could reach the highest possible level of performance. This is despite PALO IT serving the needs of several clients.

PALO IT – Valuing Creativity, Positivism, Team Spirit, and the Capacity to Deliver[18]

In downtown Singapore, both parallel to the Boat Quay and within walking distance of the Clarke Quay parts of Singapore River lies Circular Road. In the last few years especially, it has become one of the hippest places in the city, with quaint ramen bars, unpretentious burger joints, chic Italians serving pasta and pizza, Thai restaurants, and quirky Irish pubs among other places to hang out. As such, Circular Road has become the go-to spot for many people in the area for a lunchtime meeting.

It was here that I was treated to French crêpes by Sylvain, Agile Enterprise Coach at PALO IT, whose office sits in among the buzz of Circular Road. Sylvain had invited me to lunch and a tour of the PALO IT Singapore office. We had first met at Scrum Day Bandung 2018.

The international flavor of the dining options on Circular Road reflects that of PALO IT itself. With a leadership team from France founding the company in 2009, PALO IT now has 25 nationalities represented among its almost 500 employees (as of June 2020). Thirty percent of the company's activity takes place in Singapore and Hong Kong, with further operations in Australia, Mexico, Thailand, Colombia, and, of course, their home country of France.

---

[18]First appeared as a blogpost at www.redtangerine.org/2018/07/18/palo-it/

Adopting Agile Across Borders

A Friday lunchtime is probably not the best time to get a feel for the activity taking place in any office. When Sylvain, originally from France himself, toured me around, there were a few empty desks, though the buzz of an energetic work space was still palpable from those that were in. It is a beautiful office, cozy furniture, exposed brick walls and large wooden desks, seemingly more used for hot-desking than as fixed workstations made it feel every bit as nice a place to be as the bars and restaurants downstairs. I loved the decor of the place. Displayed prominently on one wall was the office kudo tree in full "bloom," as can be seen in Figure 10-2.

Figure 10-2. Palo IT office with Kudo Tree

The majority of PALO IT staff were not at the crêperie, however, nor were they at any of the other places on Circular Road for lunch. It all became clear once Sylvain explained how many of the teams at PALO IT operate. It is a model that I have not encountered anywhere else, but one that I myself have been pondering on as an effective way to work. They are not a software house, building solutions internally with a Product Owner proxy-like interface with the client. They do not send developers or consultants to clients to work on site. No, what they do is send fully formed Agile teams to the client.

The benefits are clear. These teams have worked together for a long time and reached a high level of maturity. They know how each other work. They know what they as a team are capable of. There is no period of team formation, as described by the Tuckman model,[19] at the client's expense.

---

[19] *Tuckman's stages of group development.* Wikipedia. https://en.wikipedia.org/wiki/Tuckman%27s_stages_of_group_development

Chapter 10 | Singapore

Teams work in close collaboration with the client at their premises. This is the embodiment of *customer collaboration over contract negotiation* from the Agile Manifesto for Software Development. Of course, this model brings with it many other benefits that we would expect from teams embracing Agility: highly motivated and high performing teams, greater predictability of deliverables, and transparency between the developers and the customer teams to name a few.

It is not just about producing lines of code though. PALO IT puts emphasis on "the emergence of disruptive ideas," and they encourage the mentality from the Lean Startup movement.[20] A range of innovation practices such as Innovation Games, Business Model Canvas and Design Thinking and more are used. A digital innovation lab was created to work with clients on prototyping and analysis of ROI.

With the success and continued growth of PALO IT, Circular Road is not just the go-to place for bars and restaurants, but for business and IT solutions as well.

—David Spinks

■ **Takeaway** Agility is a continual journey, not a destination. These journeys involve ups and downs, successes and failures, and every such journey is unique. It is the journey itself that will shape the Agile mindset of those involved.

There is much that can be learnt from studying other's journeys, but to quote Michael Bassey Johnson, Nigerian playwright, "When you are gunning to be like other people, you are foolishly repeating their mistakes, and the worst of it all is that you can't even correct yours." The value with any Agile initiative is in the learning in your own context through trial and error.

Copying and pasting of someone else's model not only means you have not gone through the learning that they did, but in all likelihood, those that you are copying from have already moved on!

Sylvain Mahe, Agile Coach and Conscious Leadership Coach at PALO IT from the previous story, originally from France but now working in Singapore, shares his personal Agile journey, and how tapping into the "consciousness in organizations" has allowed him to develop further as a coach to help those that he works with.

---

[20]The Lean Startup http://theleanstartup.com/

Adopting Agile Across Borders 197

Agile and Consciousness in Organizations
Midlife Crisis

Where I question my impact and deeper purpose.

I had been helping organizations adopt Agile for about ten years when I started questioning the impact I was making and more generally the success of Agile adoption initiatives.

Don't get me wrong, I'm not saying I was having no impact. I certainly saw positive change. Better collaboration and more transparency, leading to better and faster decisions. Less waste in the system and less work in progress, leading to shorter lead times. More feedback loops leading to less rework and increased satisfaction of stakeholders.

I guess many would have been quite happy with such results. And indeed my clients were quite happy. But for some reason, I felt that I was falling short of delivering the promise of Agile.

To me, Agile had always been much more than a way to deliver products and services more effectively and efficiently. Agile is about bringing pride and meaning to our work. It's about giving power back to the people who do the work to make decisions instead of others telling them what to do. It's about truly reconnecting with the people we serve: users, customers, whatever you call them. It's about joy, humanity, and respect. If you focus on those things then high performance – better time to market, customer delight, or increased employee engagement – will happen, almost as a side effect.

It's within that frame that I felt that I was failing, that we were failing as a community. Call it a midlife crisis.

At one point I thought it was just me, that I was too much of a dreamer or idealistic. But after so many years in the industry and a countless numbers of meetups, conferences, and working with other Agile practitioners, I knew that for many of them as well Agile was much more[21] than a set of practices.[22] It was literally a way of living and a way to make the world a better place, one stand up at a time.

So here I am, ten years in the job and wondering what I could do to be a more effective coach. Looking for solutions and asking myself if I should just lower my expectations. Or maybe find another job.

---

[21]Sheridan, R. (2015). _Joy, Inc.: How We Built a Workplace People Love._ Penguin Publishing Group. ISBN-13: 978-1591847120

[22]Hseih, T. (2010). _Delivering Happiness: A Path to Profits, Passion and Purpose._ Business Plus. ISBN-13: 978-1455508907

Chapter 10 | Singapore

The Consciousness Lens

Where I finally find the key that will bring me to the next level.

And then came the book *Reinventing Organizations*[23] by Frederic Laloux. In this book the author explains that organizations – like individuals – evolve following levels of consciousness from where they derive their identity: organizational models, processes, culture...

Levels of consciousness are stages of development based on evolving world views (beliefs, values). Each level focuses on specific needs and defines how much complexity an organization can handle – lower levels tend to be more reductionist, whereas higher levels are more systemic.

Frederic Laloux describes five levels that I have summarized in Table 10-1.

Table 10-1. Frederic Laloux's five levels of organizations

Color	Metaphor	Attributes	Breakthroughs	Examples	% Organizations
Red	Wolf Pack	Constant exercise of power by the chief to keep foot soldiers in line. Highly reactive. Short-term focus. Thrives in chaotic environments.	Division of labor Command authority	Organized Crime Street gangs Tribal militias	<1%
Amber	Army	Highly formal roles within a hierarchical pyramid. Top-down command and control. Future is a repetition of the past.	Formal roles, stable and scalable hierarchies Stable and replicable processes	Church Military Government organizations	20%
Orange	Machine	Goal is to beat the competition, achieve profit and growth. Management by objectives.	Innovation Accountability Meritocracy	Multinational companies Investment banks Charter schools	60%

(continued)

---

[23]Laloux, F. (2014). *Reinventing Organizations*. Nelson Parker. ISBN-13: 978-2960133509

Adopting Agile Across Borders

Table 10-1. *(continued)*

Color	Metaphor	Attributes	Breakthroughs	Examples	% Organizations
Green	Family	Focus on culture and empowerment to boost employee motivation. Stakeholders replace shareholders as primary purpose.	Empowerment Egalitarian management Stakeholder model	Businesses known for idealistic practices (Ben and Jerry's...)	10%
Teal	Living organism	Self-management replaces hierarchical pyramid. Organizations are seen as living entities, oriented toward realizing their potential.	Self-management Wholeness Evolutionary purpose	A few pioneers (Buurtzorg, Patagonia...)	<1%

The levels are like Russian dolls. It means that if you operate at a certain level, you are also able to operate at lower levels. The opposite is not true. Also, operating at a certain level means that you benefit from all the breakthroughs unlocked at lower levels.

Using this lens it becomes clear that not all consciousness levels are "Agile-friendly." I'll consider Red organizations as out of scope in the context of Agile adoption. By far most of the organizations we work with are Amber or Orange whereas the Agile territory is Green and Teal.[24] We could even say that in many ways Agile was a reaction to those types of organizations that tend to value the right hand side of the Manifesto.

As a result, if you try to grow Agile in such organizations – and I did try many times – you'll face many challenges. The pattern I see the most frequently is that Agile is primarily (or uniquely) seen as a way to deliver more efficiently and "installed" as a new process with new roles and procedures. They approach an Agile adoption as they approach any change initiative: by following a recipe.

In my experience, the recipe never fails: it tastes bad 100% of the time.

---

[24]*Lean and Agile Adoption with the Laloux Culture Model (copyright Agile for all).* www.youtube.com/watch?v=g0Jc5aAJu9g

Chapter 10 | Singapore

Agile: The Magic Recipe

1. Define new roles and responsibilities.

    1.1. Map current and new roles (e.g., Business Analysts become Product Owners, Project Managers become Scrum Masters...).

    1.2. If possible, encourage double-hatting (one person – multiples roles).

2. Document Agile as a new process (similar to Standard Operating Procedures): planning, reviews...

    2.1 Precisely define who should participate in meetings, when they take place, their duration, as well as their input and output. Provide templates for everything. Force the teams to use them.

3. Hire a team of Agile coaches with the mandate to push and make change happen.

4. Don't communicate the new way of working to the other parts of the organizations or partners (vendors) – that will slow you down.

5. Define KPIs focusing on output (number of Agile teams, number of people trained, number or story points completed) so that you'll quickly show progress.

6. Roll out.

    6.1 Tell people what to do. Do not co-create.

    6.2 Expect teams to learn the new way of working on top of their normal work. Don't accept any dip on productivity.

    6.3 Challenge teams to be Agile in a fixed-scope, fixed-schedule, and fixed-budget context.

7. Accept concepts to be corrupted for the sake of "being flexible and Agile" (e.g., MVP is just a new name for release, Product Backlog for specifications documents and coaches are asked to normalize story points across teams).

8. Blame Agile and abandon it when things don't work.

The emergent nature of Agile is ignored and teams have very little space to experiment, learn, and find their way. Very often Agile is "installed" in a big bang manner and the one size fits all approach creates a lot of friction across the organization. The focus on doing (new practices) instead of being (the mindset) leads to a misunderstanding of the intent behind the practices. Agile often becomes an excuse to squeeze more out of people. Thanks to motivated individuals and an army of Agile coaches, things change locally for a short time; however, slowly but surely the system returns to its previous state.

This approach is doomed to fail for many reasons. I'll just highlight the main ones:

- Ignorance of the J-Curve[25] of change ("Slowing down to speed up" is not an option)

- Misunderstanding of what Agile is

- Non-Agile way of adopting Agile

- Lack of clarity on the Why[26]

- KPIs not aligned (focus on output vs. outcome) with new ways of working

I found this frame provided an elegant explanation to the most common challenges faced in Agile transformations that had been highlighted for years in studies such as the Business Agility Report[27] or the State of Agile Report:[28]

- "Leadership style" (Business Agility Report 2020)

- "Agile Mindset" (Business Agility Report 2020)

- "General organization resistance to change" (14th State of Agile Report)

- "Not enough leadership participants" (14th State of Agile Report)

- "Organization culture at odds with agile values" (14th State of Agile Report)

Frederic Laloux's model gave me a new lens to understand corporate culture and I became more empathetic of how each organization approaches change depending on their level of consciousness.

The Role of Leaders

Where I connect the dots.

---

[25]*The Change Curve.* Mindtools.com. www.mindtools.com/pages/article/newPPM_96.htm
[26]Sinek, S. (2011). *Start with Why: How Great Leaders Inspire Everyone to Take Action.* Portfolio. ISBN-13: 978-1591846444
[27]Business Agility Report https://businessagility.institute/
[28]State of Agile Report. VersionOne. www.stateofagile.com

Chapter 10 | Singapore

I had been reading Michael K Sahota's blog for a few years when I decided to fly to Melbourne to take his Certified Agile Leadership Course. Saying that it was a great decision is an understatement.

What makes this course unique to me is that it stitches together many disparate pieces – some I knew and some new ones – in a coherent whole. The kind of feeling you have when you complete a jigsaw puzzle and finally see the big picture.

Let me highlight a couple of key light bulb moments and insights I got from the course (I highly recommend the Certified Agile Leadership Course from Michael K Sahota to any agilist who wants to reflect on her approach and reinvent it. There is much more than what is highlighted in this contribution).

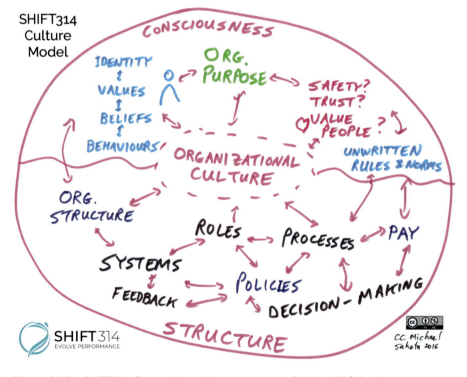

Figure 10-3. SHIFT314 Culture Model (image courtesy of Michael K Sahota)

Adopting Agile Across Borders | 203

The first one is a model[29] to understand culture. As shown in Figure 10-3, Michael presents corporate culture as being the combination of Consciousness (values, beliefs, psychological safety... – what is invisible) and Structure (processes, roles... – what is visible). The model helped me understand that while one goes with the other, if we focus too much on the Structure, for instance by bringing new practices that don't match the underlying level of Consciousness, then eventually the system will go back to its natural state by dropping – or corrupting – the new practices. It's like trying to run an app without the supporting operating system.

Fractality and the Role of Leaders

The work of Frederic Laloux had already equipped me with a good lens to understand culture and why I was struggling to make amber and orange organizations adopt Agile (and if you are not convinced yet, Michael K Sahota's detailed analysis[30] of the Agile values and principles with regards to Laloux's model should make it crystal clear).

The second aha moment was about the fractal nature of organizations. What Michael K Sahota articulates very well is that because organizations are fractals – as collections of individuals – their level of consciousness is the expression of the level of consciousness of its parts – the people. This is illustrated in Figure 10-4.

At this point it became clear to me that in order to make a bigger impact on organizations I had to focus more on the individuals.

But which ones? Is the level of consciousness of an organization simply the average of that of its people? Well, not really. It turns out that the leaders have much more weight and influence. They are the ones who primarily shape the culture. What Michael K Sahota summarizes by saying that "Organizational Behavior Follows Leadership Behavior"[31] and, as a result, "Leaders Go First"![32]

---

[29]*Culture is the Core of Your Organization – V2.* SHIFT314. https://shift314.com/culture-centre-organization/
[30]*Agile Culture -> Self-Managing People.* SHIFT314. https://shift314.com/agile-culture-self-managing-people/
[31]*Organizational Behaviour Follows Leadership Behaviour.* SHIFT314. http://agilitrix.com/2016/08/organization-follows-leadership/
[32]*Transformation? Leaders Go First!* SHIFT314. https://shift314.com/transformation-leaders-go-first/

Chapter 10 | Singapore

Figure 10-4. Organizations are fractals (image by Sylvain Mahe based on the concept by Michael K Sahota)

Our behaviors are a reflection of our internal beliefs and world views (for more on levels of consciousness and adult development, I recommend the work of Robert Kegan and Lisa Lahey[33]). To change the outside, we need to work on the inside first. It means that the leaders need to work on their Consciousness.

Everywhere I looked I read the same message: we need more Conscious Leaders if we want organizations to evolve. I knew I was on to something. And I was not going to be disappointed.

Beyond Agile: The Dawn of Conscious Leaders

Where I find my tribe.

I believe the need for Conscious Leaders goes way beyond Agile. I feel that in order to tackle the greatest challenges of our time, we need a radical shift in our level of consciousness. What do I mean by "the greatest challenges of our time"? The United Nations' "Global Goals For Sustainable Development" (SDGs) are a good place to start, as shown in Figure 10-5.

---

[33] Kegan, R and Lahey, L.L. (2009). *Immunity to Change: How to Overcome It and Unlock the Potential in Yourself and Your Organization (Leadership for the Common Good).* Harvard Business Review Press. ISBN-13: 978-1422117361

Goals for Sustainable Development

Figure 10-5. The United Nations' Global Goals for Sustainable Development (Source: www.un.org/sustainabledevelopment/ The content of this publication has not been approved by the United Nations and does not reflect the views of the United Nations or its officials or Member States)

To succeed, we need to grow Conscious Organizations, organizations that care about employees, customers, partners, communities, and the planet. Organizations that go beyond the quest for infinite growth in a finite world – a quest that is doomed to fail. Conscious Leaders are the leaders who will spearhead this movement and create organizations that commit to focus on social and environmental concerns as much as they do on profits: the triple bottom line, as shown in Figure 10-6.

The Triple Bottom Line

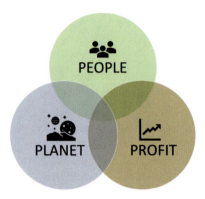

Figure 10-6. The triple bottom line for sustainable management

It's at this point in my journey that my employer decided to become a B Corporation[34] (a movement of organizations using business as a force for good). The stars were aligning.

So what are the attributes of Conscious Leaders I've been talking about? I won't go into the details in this contribution, but you'll find in the following the key aspects of Conscious Leadership as I see it.

Conscious Leadership
Self

- Emotional and body awareness
- Knows their purpose and values, and uses them as a compass when making decisions
- Awareness of their triggers and how to shift from reaction to response (self-regulation)
- Practices centering/grounding/intention setting to get clear head space and tap into intuition
- Doesn't identify with thoughts/inner critic/stories
- Practices self-care

---

[34] Certified B Corporation https://bcorporation.net/

Adopting Agile Across Borders

Relationships

- Knows how to give and receive feedback
- Empathy through presence, intuition, and deep listening
- Courage: (to be authentic, to be vulnerable, to explore their (leadership) edges)
- Unconditional responsibility
- Clear boundaries

World View

- Abundance[35] (vs. scarcity) mindset[36]
- Sees below the surface and beyond the obvious
- Cultivates kindness, gratitude, and compassion
- Wants well for others (positive impact): awareness of the impact of their actions on others and the environment
- Knows that output is not outcome, intention is not impact

For those who want to learn more on this topic, I highly recommend the work of the Conscious Leadership Group[37] and Eric Kaufmann.[38]

Conscious Businesses are organisations with Conscious Cultures catalyzed by Conscious Leaders.

—Jeff Klein

Where to Start? How Embodied Practices Helped Me Become More Conscious

The new set of skills Conscious Leaders are invited to develop may seem overwhelming at first and many readers may be wondering where to start. I have good news for you! It's not that difficult and you already have everything you need. Because all you need is your body.

---

[35]Stinson, N. (2017). *10 Steps to Develop an Abundance Mindset*. The Chopra Center. https://chopra.com/articles/10-steps-to-develop-an-abundance-mindset
[36]Castrillon, C. (2018). *How to shift from a scarcity to an abundance mindset*. Thriveglobal. com. https://thriveglobal.com/stories/how-to-shift-from-a-scarcity-to-an-abundance-mindset-3/
[37]Conscious Leadership Group https://conscious.is/
[38]Erik Kauffmann www.erickaufmann.com

Chapter 10 | Singapore

What do I mean by that?

What I mean is that most of those skills can be developed through simple practices involving the body. To be honest I even believe it's a compulsory stop if you want to become a more conscious leader!

The body is a powerful way to become more aware of yourself, others, your hardwired reactions to events, and, more generally, your way of being. And this is where the magic happens. As my teacher Mark Walsh[39] explains, this increased awareness will in turn allow you to develop a broader – more skillful – range of responses and eventually give you more choices – more options – in your life. This is immensely powerful. This is shown in Figure 10-7.

Figure 10-7. Awareness allows a wider range of responses and more choice

Let me illustrate with an example.

I worked with a leader that was triggered when he received what he considered as negative feedback. Even if he intellectually knew feedback is important and actively promoted it with his teams, inevitably he reacted with sarcasm or an attack when someone suggested he could have done something better. The work we did together allowed him to notice what was going on in him, verbalize it, and connect it with past experiences. This new awareness gave him the strength to have a conversation with his team, and he became more attuned to himself so that he could recognize the early signs of being triggered. Now he's able to slow down and create a space for a new response, one that is more skillful and more aligned with the leader he wants to be. When I talked to the teams he works with, many people told me they see and feel the difference, they know he's not faking it and that he's been growing a new way of being. That's the magic of embodiment.

So, more concretely, which practices are we talking about?

There are plenty of practices out there that can help you achieve shifts in awareness: meditation, yoga, dance… However, there is one called centering that I've found is the most easily accessible for beginners and with the greatest "return on investment." Centering is a regulation technique that will help you restore emotional balance, shift to a more resourceful and creative state, and overall develop a more intimate relationship with your body.

---

[39]Embodied Facilitator https://embodiedfacilitator.com/

Adopting Agile Across Borders

I know it may seem too easy or even a bit silly. Maybe you don't have a strong connection to your body, emotions, and sensations and think it will never work for you. All I can say is that when it comes to living a disembodied life, I've come a long way. For the longest time I was mostly unaware of my emotional states (beyond basic emotions like sad, angry, or happy), with a very limited vocabulary about my sensations and almost no access to my intuition (you know, the gut feeling). And one practice at a time, it improved. Now I'm a much more balanced person, I show up differently and I have access to resources that were not available to me before.

Three courses have been instrumental in my journey (in chronological order):

- Vipassana silent retreat
- Wendy Palmer's Leadership Embodiment
- Mark Walsh's Embodied Facilitation Course

The practices I've learnt there are true superpowers and they are easily accessible as long as you commit to doing the work.

So I just invite you to give it a try. Do it, practice, and see what unfolds for you. Then if you want to explore more, I strongly recommend you study the field of embodiment.

A New Conversation

Where I learn how to show my clients that what they want may not be what they need.

All those insights radically changed the way I approach change in organizations. The focus is not Agile anymore – or any desired state with a strong cultural component (Digital, DevOps, Customer-centric…) – the focus becomes the awareness of the leaders about themselves and the level of consciousness of their organization.

For a very long time, when I trained and coached leaders to be "more Agile," I was using concepts such as leadership vs. management, servant leadership or Goleman's leadership styles,[40] I educated them on the concepts of self-organizing teams and nitty gritty details like story points or cost of delay. Now I invite them to work on themselves and as a result on their organization's culture.

So how do we shift the conversation, as indicated in Figure 10-8? This is my approach today.

---

[40]Goleman, D. (2000). *Leadership That Gets Results*. Harvard Business Review. https://hbr.org/2000/03/leadership-that-gets-results

Chapter 10 | Singapore

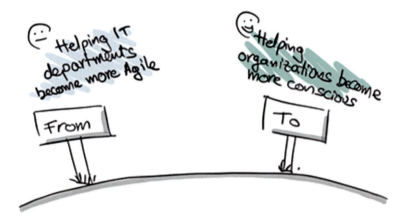

Figure 10-8. Shifting the conversation

Ten Tips to Shift the Conversation

1. Start from a clean, centered, and neutral state. A strong centering practice (like the one presented earlier) is very helpful here.

    This will allow you to better listen, create psychological safety and engage from a place of service (instead of following your agenda).

2. Bring the leadership team into a room to discover what they are trying to achieve. Get clarity on the Why.

    Once the leaders know what the North Star is, help them reframe the conversation: it's not about their want (be it Agile, Digital, DevOps..), it's about their need.

3. Make leaders aware of their current corporate culture and level of consciousness.

    I find that The Leadership Circle[41] assessment is a wonderful tool to achieve this.

    Ask them if their goal is compatible. Help them see the gap.

4. Explain their role as a guiding coalition.[42]

---

[41] Leadership Circle https://leadershipcircle.com/
[42] *The 8-Step Process for Leading Change.* Kotterinc.com. www.kotterinc.com/8-steps-process-for-leading-change/

Adopting Agile Across Borders

They shape the culture and therefore will have to embody the new ways of working. The key question here is: which behaviors are they willing to change?

5. Explain that first they need to create a movement[43] that will help the organization be ready for deeper change. Rolling out a recipe will not work.

   This movement should focus on identifying, educating, and connecting the pioneers who will become internal change agents.

6. Define a measure of success.

   Help them identify a good set of leading indicators measuring output and lagging indicators measuring outcomes.

   (Leading indicators measure what we do in order to achieve a certain goal. They are predictive by nature. Example: handwashing rate. Lagging indicators measure how we performed. They are indicators of past performance. Example: infections.)

7. Create the Transformation Backlog.

   I like to use Impact Mapping[44] for this and I invite them to create their personal transformation backlog as well.

8. Create a roadmap (three to six months is more than enough. Remember, we're Agile) and agree on a cadence to steer the initiative:

   - Planning: Discuss and agree on next actions

   - Review: Showcase the results accomplished

   - Retrospective: Inspect and adapt the way the guiding coalition works

9. Get them to commit (I usually facilitate a ritual where they write down their commitment on an index card and then we peg all the cards on a string).

   Leaders will be leading the change and literally need to embody it. Human beings are great "BS detectors." If

---

[43]Walker, B. and Soule, S.A. (2017). *Changing Company Culture Requires a Movement, Not a Mandate.* Harvard Business Review. https://hbr.org/2017/06/changing-company-culture-requires-a-movement-not-a-mandate
[44]Impact Mapping www.impactmapping.org

they see that the leaders are not walking the talk, they know it's not real. Change fatigue in organizations makes the problem even more acute.

10. Iterate over the transformation backlog to implement the change.

The least I can say is that my impact – and sense of fulfillment – has drastically improved since I applied this approach. My clients achieve greater outcomes and I feel much more aligned with what I think Agile truly is. More on this later.

The business that leaders are in today, is the business of transforming awareness...There is a deep longing for more meaning, for connections.

—Otto Scharmer, Author of *TheoryU*

Looks like I've finally got over my midlife crisis.

And Does It Work in Singapore? My Experience As a French Agile Coach in Asia

After eight years working as an Agile coach in Singapore (and a few countries in Asia) I've stopped counting how many times I was asked this question (or its variation "Does it work in Asia?").

The short answer is: from my experience so far, I believe the challenges to Agile transformations are quite universal.

The main reason I see is that the dominant model of organizations is similar to the one we know in the West: hierarchy-based, focused on maximizing resource utilization, expecting compliance, and with little room for autonomy and creativity. I know I'm simplifying, but you get the idea.

Of course, some say that "Asian cultures" – whatever this generalization means – with their emphasis on respecting the boss and elders, favoring group harmony, or avoiding saying no makes Agile adoption efforts even harder. I tend to disagree with this view as I also see positive factors.

- Most Agile transformations here have started around 2010–2015, at least ten years after the first ones in Western countries. Even today, most organizations are still running their first transformation or about to start the second wave. I see it as a blessing as I believe organizations here benefit from what we've learned a lot as a community in the past 20 years.

Adopting Agile Across Borders

- As I often explain in my training courses, Agile is firmly rooted in Lean, and Lean was developed in Japan. This fact is often an eye-opener for my clients.

- Most organizations I've worked with are more and more multicultural these days, making the lines blur between East and West.

- Last but not least, many of the practices that are key in Conscious Leadership are strongly influenced by Eastern practices like meditation, yoga, or martial arts and land very nicely here. I've found leaders to be particularly receptive to embodied practices and many of my peers who work in the West tell me it's more difficult for them.

If the challenges are universal, the solutions are not and a mistake would be to copy and paste what has worked in other parts of the world. My experience and that of other Agile practitioners in Asia is that we tend to invest significantly more on aspects like building trust, psychological safety, and one-to-one conversations.

Each country, organization, or team is unique and it's a key part of the job of being an Agile coach to sense the environment and respond in unique ways. In that context, I haven't found my work to be more challenging here than in Europe or Africa.

The Most Important Work of My Life

Where I know what I'm meant to do.

To conclude, I'd like to quote Gandhi. *"Be the change you wish to see in the world."* We are all leaders and if we can't change others, we can change ourselves – and by doing so we inspire others. So if we want to shape corporate cultures where Agile will thrive, I invite all readers to embark on this journey of exploration and develop their awareness and consciousness. It's a very rewarding journey and the benefits abound: a greater sense of purpose, joyful workplaces, a sense of fulfillment by doing meaningful and impactful work… and helping create a better world.

I think no work is more important than this.

More and more people are already on this journey, but organizations are lagging behind. Together, we can change this.

Chapter 10 | Singapore

Show Me the Results! What I've Seen So Far in the Organizations I Work With

Since I've implemented this approach, I've been delighted by the results.

I've seen "tough managers" become compassionate coaches, sales targets fade into the background in favor of more holistic positive impact dashboards connected to the Sustainable Development Goals and innovative ideas flourish.

How so? To me the answer is quite simple. As the leaders, teams, and the organization at large develop a higher level of consciousness, then collaboration naturally improves, political games tend to dissolve, silos break down and more meaningful conversations happen all over. Ultimately, the organization becomes ripe to question its purpose and impact.

It becomes obvious to many that the traditional KPIs don't measure the right things – that we should focus more on outcomes and impact rather than output – that vendors should be truly treated as partners, and that we can achieve much more if we allow everyone to bring their whole self to work.

But be warned though, the adoption may seem slower at first and without strong support it may feel very uncomfortable. But it eventually picks up, and ends up being much stickier and sustainable. Another great aspect is that because the people – including the leaders – become the agents of change, you don't need an army of Agile coaches anymore. You're not applying brute force anymore. Instead it feels like playing chess in the organization, something I enjoy a lot. Moving one piece at a time and seeing how the game reconfigures.

The "Transformation Backlog" I put in place at the beginning of any engagement and that we use as our compass to steer the transformation has drastically changed. You will still find the typical training and coaching activities to help teams apply Agile practices or awareness sessions on the Agile mindset, but they are augmented with activities focusing on helping the organization and its people reflect on their sense of identity and ways of being. Now the transformation backlog contains items such as:

- Emotional Intelligence
- Personality types (using the Enneagram,[45] the 4 Elements Model[46])
- Vulnerability

---

[45]*The Nine Enneagram Type Descriptions*. The Enneagram Institute. www.enneagraminstitute.com/type-descriptions

[46]*The 4 Elements*. Embodied Facilitator. https://embodiedfacilitator.com/the-4-elements-mark-walsh/

Adopting Agile Across Borders

- Team toxins[47]
- Nature immersions
- Mindfulness practices

And where is Agile in all of that? Well, as I mentioned in the first section, its benefits come as a side effect. Engagement improves, increased collaboration reduces waste, lead time shrinks, products or services improve as feedback loops are naturally put in place, and it gets much easier to attract and retain talented people.

It's a different game. One that I find very fulfilling.

—Sylvain Mahe,
Agile Coach and Conscious Leadership Coach, PALO IT

■ **Takeaway**   Change is not something that should be forced. It is human nature for us to react with our "fight or flight" mechanism when confronted with change that is outside of our control and may be perceived as a threat to our security or status. Any change that is imposed is therefore likely to be resisted. We cannot change others, we can only change ourselves, and by doing so we may inspire others to take our lead. The most successful change initiatives are done by including those involved in change decisions and by leading by example.

Whether or not these examples are the exception to the rule, or if these are a sign of change in how software development and knowledge work is done in Singapore remains to be seen.

Getting On and Around

Singapore has one of the best education systems in the world.[48] As part of a continent where culturally, courtesy and status is important to people, Singaporeans will appreciate the showing of respect for their academic and professional achievement. At the same time, recognition is given to those that show great teamwork, a trend especially true with the younger generations. The value for showing respect to elders is very much part of Singaporean culture, despite Singapore's meritocratic nature.

---

[47]Calabrese, J. *Team Toxins and Team Conflict*. jakecalabrese.com. https://jakecalabrese. com/team-toxins/
[48]Graham, L. (2015) *Singapore tops OECD's global school ranking*. www.cnbc.com/2015/05/13/ singapore-tops-oecds-global-school-ranking-us-placed-28th.html

Chapter 10 | Singapore

In business and in people's professional lives, there is an expectation for conformity; enigmatic behavior or eccentric appearance will lose trust. People are expected to be clean and well-dressed in the workplace. This is despite the country lying just one degree off of the equator and the year round heat that comes with it.

The rich diversity of cultures from all around the world puts managers, leaders, and facilitators with cross-cultural awareness at an advantage. Those that can build empathy and understanding within these culture-rich teams and organizations can take advantage of a broader spectrum of backgrounds, world views, and experiences, resulting in greater input of ideas and innovation – a huge component for knowledge work. And yet, there is a lack of evidence of many having developed these skills, not just in Singapore but throughout the world.

Agile Community Events and Meetups

- Agile Singapore: www.meetup.com/Agile-Singapore/, http://agilesingapore.org/

- Startup Agile Group – Singapore: www.meetup.com/Startup-Agile-Group-Singapore/

- Agile Circles Singapore: www.agilecircles.sg/

- Singapore Lean Startup Circle: www.meetup.com/Singapore-Lean-Startup-Circle/

CHAPTER
11

United Arab Emirates (Dubai)

The population of the United Arab Emirates is overwhelmingly made up of immigrants. Workers come from countries such as Pakistan, India, the Philippines, Korea, Europe, and the United States for jobs in oil, construction, or knowledge work. Managing cross-cultural differences then, would appear to be one of the main challenges for organizations based in the country.

Our own visit was limited to Dubai, but our time there and the conversations that we had with the people in the local Agile community offered a fascinating insight into this part of the world.

History

The area of land that makes up the United Arab Emirates today has had human occupation for thousands of years. Groups of nomadic tribes survived through agriculture and the raising of animals for their milk, eggs, meat, and other products.

As European colonists expanded their reach, the likes of the British, Dutch, and Portuguese began arriving in the Persian Gulf leading to conflicts between the European powers and the local Emirati traders. The Portuguese conquered

© Glaudia Califano, David Spinks 2021
G. Califano and D. Spinks, *Adopting Agile Across Borders*,
https://doi.org/10.1007/978-1-4842-6948-0_11

Chapter 11 | United Arab Emirates (Dubai)

coastal communities in the 16th century, while British interest was in protecting the Indian trade routes which included military operations along other parts of the coast. It was in 1820 when the British signed a maritime truce with local rulers that led to the term "Trucial States" which came to be used to define the coastal area. Further agreements were made during the 1800s which effectively established an arrangement whereby the British provided protection of the Trucial coast in return for the Trucial sheikhs agreeing not to enter into relationships with any other foreign government without British consent.

Dubai itself is believed to have been established as a fishing village in the early 18th century with a population of 700–800 people. In 1901, Dubai was established as a free port with no taxation on imports or exports. It became particularly well-known for pearling and the export of pearls in the 1930s.

During the early 1900s, the British became aware of the potential for oil in the region. The Anglo-Persian Oil Company (APOC), which was later to become British Petroleum (BP), had a large share in the Iraq Petroleum Company (IPC), and they led the IPC operations to drill for oil. Eventually oil was discovered off of Dubai's waters in 1966, accelerating the plans of Sheikh Rashid bin Saeed Al Maktoum, the ruler of Dubai, to carry out massive infrastructure and construction projects. This boom led to a great influx of immigrant workers. Between 1968 and 1975, the city grew by more than three times.

By 1966, it was becoming clear that the British could no longer afford to protect the Trucial States. In 1968, then British Prime Minister Harold Wilson announced the government's decision, reaffirmed in 1971 by his successor, Edward Heath, to end the protection treaty that it had with the seven Trucial Sheikhdoms, Bahrain, and Qatar. The ruler of Abu Dhabi, at the time, Sheikh Zayed bin Sultan Al Nahyan, tried in vain to persuade the British to keep the protection treaties in place by offering to pay the costs of keeping the British Forces in place, but the offer was rejected. The relationship with the British ended on December 2, 1971, and the United Arab Emirates became an independent nation, made up of the six emirates of Abu Dhabi, Dubai, Sharjah, Ajman, Fujairah, and Umm-al-Qaiwain, with Abu Dhabi chosen as the capital. Ras al Khaimah became the seventh emirate in 1972.

Revenues from oil were poured into healthcare, education, and infrastructure. Dubai became an international hub. Economic growth in the United Arab Emirates has been impressive and steady over the last 50 years, with only a few blips along the way, such as during the global financial crisis in 2008-2009. Average GDP growth between 2000 and 2018 was around 4%.[1] In parallel, the

---

[1] Dobrovolskij, T. (2009). *United Arab Emirates – Economic, Social, and Institutional Analysis.* Empyrean Advisors. www.empyrean-advisors.com/united-arab-emirates-country-analysis/

population of the UAE increased from 550,000 in 1975 to around 10 million, mainly due to immigration, with expatriates making up around around 88% of the population.[2]

Insights

With a backdrop of tribalism and the country having been made up of seven distinct emirates, the United Arab Emirates has a very traditional and conservative society. Leadership is authoritarian. However, in 2016, the country appointed a Minister of Happiness,[3] responsible for boosting the joy and mood of the country's citizens. There is also a Ministry of Tolerance[4] and 2019 was designated the "Year of Tolerance."

There are attempts to diversify the economy away from the dominance of oil, with the country able to entice business with its political stability, forward thinking government, favorable economic conditions, improving regulatory environment, and generally good infrastructure, including that of Information and Communications technology. Dubai itself has become a hub for service industries and knowledge work, including finance and IT. Dubai Internet City[5] along with Dubai Media City were set up as free economic zones. Rules here give companies a number of taxation and customs related benefits which are guaranteed in law for at least 50 years. IT companies with a presence in Dubai Media City include Google, Microsoft, Oracle, IBM, Dell, and Hewlett Packard. The UAE government also set up the world's first Ministry of Artificial Intelligence.[6] Dubai is at the forefront of the county's efforts of technological advancement and has been in and around the top five fastest growing cities in the world in the last few years.[7]

The UAE has one of the world's highest net migration rates, with the highest numbers of people coming from India, Bangladesh, and Pakistan. Immigrants from Europe, Australia, North and Latin America make up about 500,000

---

[2](2020). *UAE Population and Demographics.* Dubai Online. www.dubai-online.com/essential/uae-population-and-demographics/

[3]Chew, J. (2016). *This Country Just Appointed a Minister Of Happiness.* Fortune. https://fortune.com/2016/02/10/uae-minister-happiness/

[4]Muhammad, A. (2019). *UAE's tolerance model has "potential to become a global movement for good."* Emirates News Agency. http://wam.ae/en/details/1395302752575

[5]Dubai Internet City https://dic.ae/

[6]Galeon, D. (2017). *An Inside Look at the First Nation With a State Minister for Artificial Intelligence.* Futurism. https://futurism.com/uae-minister-artificial-intelligence

[7]Everington, J. (2015). *Dubai enters top five ranked fastest growing economies.* The National. www.thenational.ae/business/dubai-enters-top-five-ranked-fastest-growing-economies-1.116265

Chapter 11 | United Arab Emirates (Dubai)

people of the population. More than 100,000 British people live in the country[8] and English is widely taught in schools as a second language. The United Arab Emirates also has close strategic ties with the United States.

Dubai is one of the most popular tourist destinations in the world, with people visiting it for its aquaparks, indoor ski slope, the world's tallest building, desert tours, and of course the opulent shopping malls. The approach of attracting high spending tourists has evolved the Dubai culture to one of extravagance and luxury.

Private sector employers tend to be more inclined to hire overseas workers because of cost, but also because of employee rights. For example, foreign workers can be made redundant more easily. UAE locals tend to go into government or public jobs. However, there is a perception that pay is based on people's nationality[9] instead of competence, with some evidence emerging to back this up.[10] Those from India, Sri Lanka, Nepal, China, and Africa would be paid at a much lower rate in comparison to someone from the United Kingdom to do the same job for example.

Getting On and Around

Where organizations in the United Arab Emirates already have a challenge of building effective teams from a pool of such diversity, the inequality in pay that we were told is common knowledge, must be a significant barrier to building team cohesion. Among the other anecdotes that we were told were stories where tensions were often caused by cultural clashes. Assertiveness and truth in some was incompatible with expectations of compliance and diplomacy in others for example. We heard stories where siloed groups had formed with a real reluctance to share knowledge – an obvious impediment to creating an Agile environment.

■ **Takeaway** Coach teams to empathize with each other. As we will discuss in part 6, diverse teams that are coached well, that learn to articulate their differences that have the biggest impact, who truly empathize with each other, and who leverage their diversity can reach higher levels of innovation and performance.

---

[8]Sambidge, S. (2009). *UAE population hits 6m, Emiratis make up 16.5%.* Arabian Business. www.arabianbusiness.com/uae-population-hits-6m-emiratis-make-up-16-5--12137.html

[9]Janardhan, M. (2004). *UAE: Forget the Experience. It's Your Passport That Matters!* IPS News www.ipsnews.net/2004/10/uae-forget-the-experience-its-your-passport-that-matters/

[10](2017). *Revealed: Average Western expatriate salaries in the Gulf.* Gulf Business. https://gulfbusiness.com/revealed-average-western-expatriate-salaries-in-the-gulf-2017/

Adopting Agile Across Borders

Another hurdle that we were told about, perhaps because of the autocratic nature of the culture, was that overseas companies operating in Dubai feel outside pressure to act in a command and control way. A fear of failure appears to be common within company cultures where there is a low tolerance for things going wrong. And with few employment rights as foreigners, the threat of losing a job carries with it losing the right to stay in the country. This is an unfortunate mix that means that values such as courage, transparency, and experimentation that are commonly advocated with Agile methods are repressed.

In one example, we heard about a software engineer, an expatriate who was part of a team that were being pushed to deliver more and more features on top of a product already saddled with technical debt. In what is a rare case, they stood up to the Product Owner and company managers, insisting on an agreement where 50% of development capacity be reserved to manage and tackle the technical debt problem over time. We can only imagine the courage that this took; however, people standing up for what they believe in like this rather than playing it safe is the exception rather than the rule.

When it was talked about, as acknowledged by those telling many of the stories that we encountered, Agile was referred to as being in name only, with waterfall processes in place but repackaged as Agile. Some teams in organizations may be "doing standups," but it didn't take long for us to hear anti-patterns emerge such as the segregation of the "development Sprint" and the "test Sprint." Some of the blame is pointed toward a lack of maturity in the knowledge of Agile in the region, with a reliance and expectation on many of the people coming in. These people are judged on their Agile certifications and attracted by the money on offer, but in many cases have little or no actual practical experience, let alone a true understanding of agility. It is a common problem worldwide, but more acute here, whereby there is a shortage of experienced practitioners that understand agility, compounded by organizations, especially larger ones, not understanding what they are recruiting for and what to look for.

Dubai is an international hub with massive multinational companies operating in the city. Any large-scale organization that has established corporate cultures and embedded ways of working formed over decades is going to have struggles adopting Agile, especially when there is a shortage of practitioners. There are startups in Dubai, and they are proving to be successful by adopting an Agile approach,[11] and we believe this will gain attention and help build momentum.

---

[11](2020). *UAE start-up Fruitful Day triples business by remaining agile.* Arabian Business. www.arabianbusiness.com/startup/446586-uae-start-up-fruitful-day-triples-business-by-remaining-agile

Chapter 11 | United Arab Emirates (Dubai)

The main need here is for education, gaining agreement for real change and for sharing experiences. For Scrum Masters or Agile Coaches going into any of the major companies, what is needed is a lot of patience and understanding what is possible.

■ **Takeaway** Seek organizational agility. We see many "Agile teams" that are formed in environments where the rest of the organization lacks agility. The team soon finds itself hindered from becoming truly Agile by organizational policies such as how people are recruited, performance reviews, progress reports, how contracts are agreed, how individuals are rewarded, etc. How these policies are chosen to evolve or not alongside Agile adoption in the teams are important aspects that can determine the success or downfall of adopting Agile in an organization.

Agile Community Events and Meetups

- Agile ME Dubai Chapter: www.meetup.com/AgileME-Dubai/

- Agile ME Abu Dhabi Chapter: www.meetup.com/AgileME-AbuDhabi/

- Dubai Future Startups: www.meetup.com/Dubai-Future-Startups/

- Abu Dhabi Agile Scrum Exchange: www.meetup.com/Abu-Dhabi-Agile-Scrum-Exchange-ADASE/

PART
IV

Europe

Culturally rich, with a multitude of countries in a relatively small geographical area when compared to other continents, agility is well established in many of the Northern and Central countries of Europe.

Many of the countries of the continent are in the fortunate position of having strong economies and high standards of living. Incomes and wealth are generally high compared to most other parts of the world. European brands are known the world over. Decades-old, even centuries-old, organizations have an accumulation of wealth and success.

The main barrier to Agile adoption in many cases could therefore be complacency. True Agile companies can be found in small start-ups, but these are easily swallowed up or swatted aside. Many Agile adoptions in the big organizations are localized in a few pockets in IT departments, or are in name only. Nevertheless, Agile is not niche; conversations, conferences, and meetups span far and wide, and the momentum of the Agile movement has it on the precipice of becoming the default way of operating.

Europe has had a long and lively history, culminating in a relative period of calm and cooperation in recent decades. The expansion of the European Union (that was until the decision of the United Kingdom to leave) acts as a symbol of international and cross-cultural collaboration. European diversity and the continued development in the abilities to communicate, collaborate, negotiate, and work together could well prove to be their greatest strength in the future world of work.

Part IV | Europe

Agile Community Events and Meetups

- Agile Lean Europe: https://agilelean.eu/
- Europe Women in Agile: https://womeninagile.eu/
- Agile Testing Days: https://agiletestingdays.com/
- Agile Leadership Europe: www.agile-leadership-europe.com/

CHAPTER
12

Germany

Germany is one of the biggest economies of the world, built through the establishment of efficient processes that ensure quality. There is a belief in a world of order, symmetry, rules, and procedures. There is even a German expression for it – "Ordnung muss sein" which translates to, "there must be order." The saying is so embedded in the culture that it has become a cliché for Germans all over the world.

German brands are players on the world stage. It is difficult to argue with methods that have led to such success, methods that are now ingrained. Yet attempts at adopting Agile are seemingly as ubiquitous as other countries where Agile has taken off.

Perhaps more so than any other country on our radar, certain cultural traits that we discovered in Germany are a great fit with Agile adoption, while at the same time others would seem to be a barrier.

History

The German Confederation, a collection of sovereign states, was founded in 1815 by the Congress of Vienna after the demise of Napoleon's First French Empire and the end of the Holy Roman Empire. In 1871, most of the Germanic states unified into a nation referred to as the "German Empire" or "Imperial State of Germany." Its power grew based on the growth of its industry, contributions in scientific advancements, rail network, and the strength of its army.

© Glaudia Califano, David Spinks 2021
G. Califano and D. Spinks, *Adopting Agile Across Borders*,
https://doi.org/10.1007/978-1-4842-6948-0_12

Chapter 12 | Germany

What became known as "The German Revolution" began toward the end of World War I, resulting in the end of the German monarchy, and the declaration of Germany as a republic with a democratically elected parliament. The new leadership signed the Treaty of Versailles and accepted defeat by the allies – an act seen as humiliating in the eyes of most Germans.

Severe inflation led to radical economic reforms and the introduction of a new currency in 1924. The 1920s became known as the Golden Twenties, and the country went through a period of growth, innovation, artistry, and expansion of liberal values until the Great Depression in 1929. After the governing coalition collapsed, leading to a fragmented parliament, the Nazi Party became the largest party in the parliament in a specially called election, and its leader, Adolf Hitler, became the Chancellor of Germany.

The regime became a totalitarian state, and began a program of economic renewal. It withdrew from the Treaty of Versailles. The invasion of Poland in 1939 sparked World War II. After their victory, the Allies split Germany's territory into four zones, the West occupied by France, the United Kingdom, and the United States, while the East was under the control of the USSR. The Berlin Wall became a symbol of the split between East and West.

The Marshall Plan was an American initiative designed to aid the economic recovery in Western Europe. It encouraged a reduction of cross-border barriers, deregulation, increasing productivity, and the adoption of modern high-efficiency American business procedures and processes. The Americans recognized that the reconstruction of Europe depended on a strong German industrial base.

A long period of economic growth for West Germany followed. GDP grew at a rate of 9–10% a year. Unions did not oppose policies such as postponement of wage increases and minimized strikes in support of seeing technological advancement and worker participation. This included workers having the right to vote for representatives on boards of directors and workplace rights. West Germany joined NATO in 1955 and was a founding member of the European Economic Community.

In 1989, Hungary opened up its border with Austria, enabling thousands of East Germans to immigrate to West Germany via Hungary and Austria. Under growing pressure, the "Two Plus Four Agreement" was negotiated where the four occupying powers renounced their rights and allowed for the reuniting of East and West Germany, with the fall of the Berlin Wall a symbol of the reunification and the end of the Soviet Union.

Germany has since become the economic powerhouse of Europe. At the time of writing, as well as having the largest economy in Europe, Germany has the fourth largest economy in the world by GDP. The standard of living is high, there is a universal healthcare system and tuition-free university

Adopting Agile Across Borders

education. It is a leader in advancing European integration, transitioning to sustainable energy, smart technologies, the Internet of Things, and the automation of manufacturing and industrial processes. Berlin has become a hub for startup companies.

Levels of immigration have consistently been among the highest in the world, a policy used to offset a long-standing low birth rate.[1] This has resulted in Germany having a highly diverse population with around a quarter of the population immigrants or of migrant decent.[2]

Insights

Berlin transcends international borders. The city has rapidly become a diverse melting pot and one of Europe's main technology hubs, attracting people from all around the world, with substantial investment and a vibrant startup scene.[3] Munich too is an important technology center with hundreds of startups of its own.[4] Figure 12-1 represents Berlin and Munich's café culture, where startups may be being run from a coffee shop. While these two cities have their fair share of established companies too, other parts of the country rely more on long-standing organizations and industry, such as Wolfsburg that is the headquarters of Volkswagen, and Stuttgart, home to Daimler and Porsche.

---

[1]*Germany Population.* World Population Review. https://worldpopulationreview.com/countries/germany-population

[2](2020). *German population of migrant background rises to 21 million.* dw.com. www.dw.com/en/german-population-of-migrant-background-rises-to-21-million/a-54356773

[3]Staff, M. (2020). *Berlin breaks the national mould to become a global hub.* Computer Weekly. www.computerweekly.com/news/252484438/Berlin-breaks-the-national-mould-to-become-a-global-hub

[4]Renoldi, M. (2020). *Is Munich Europe's #4 tech hub after London, Paris and Berlin?* Dealroom.co. https://blog.dealroom.co/munich-is-europes-4th-tech-hub-after-london-paris-and-berlin/

Chapter 12 | Germany

Figure 12-1. Berlin and Munich are examples of cities with many startup companies, some of which may be being run from a coffee shop (image courtesy of Tasia Graham)

German organizations and culture are built on structure and established processes that to them have been proven to work – for German leaders and employees, there is no substitute for experience. That is not to say that formal qualifications are not seen as important, but status is earned through achievement, length of experience, and how well established processes are applied and monitored. As such, historically, people stay at the same company for long periods of time and are reluctant to give up positions that they have achieved, though this is rapidly changing. Companies are commonly structured in a vertical hierarchy, where people feel comfortable knowing where they stand and what they are expected to do through clear instructions. We heard stories where Sprint Reviews were treated more as demonstrations of work completed instead of the two-way conversation and feedback cycle intended

Adopting Agile Across Borders

by Scrum. On many occasions, improvement actions are seen as something for managers to take care of, so the Agile ideal of teams owning improvement is hard to adopt.

Knowledge and information is shared on a need to know basis. Controlling the messaging is a normal way of behaving, both in business and in private. Few German companies share information for consumption for the wider public and their own employees. Many people and companies are unfamiliar with having full transparency, with real fears of how information could be misused. Information considered relevant to be shared is passed down through the hierarchy, with communication lines following reporting lines. It is atypical for communication channels to be with equals horizontally across departments.

Despite these hierarchical structures, building consensus for decisions in organizations or teams is paramount. Debate could be seen as involving communication that is blunt and direct to those unfamiliar with the German communication style. However, this is an example of where truth comes before diplomacy. Consensus building can be achieved through giving detailed clarification and justification based on facts and logic. Agreement is not made through negotiation and persuasion. Decision making in general involves extensive research, analysis, and "sign-off" from superiors. The aim remains to create alignment, solidarity, and comfort with the chosen direction while, at the same time, being fair to everyone involved.

Ordnung is achieved through looking at details closely and ensuring that there are sufficient plans and procedures in place. People will commonly pour over any artifacts or documentation produced, looking at it in detail no matter how long or boring it is. Oversimplification can lose trust. The way German sentences are structured obliges listeners to pay full attention in order to get full meaning. This helps to make German speakers good listeners and partially explains a distrust of the use of simple sentences. Advertisements in Germany are quite different to those found in the United States and the United Kingdom, where simple, catchy slogans are swapped for ads that are more formal, informative, and focus more on product features.

The Scrum value of focus would seem to be tailor-made for the German psyche, yet even here it is common to find teams working on many things at once. Completing planned steps one at a time and finishing projects according to schedule is a typical approach. When it comes to complex knowledge work however, what will actually happen in the future is unknowable and therefore uncontrollable through an up-front plan. When trade-offs are required, delays are more acceptable than compromising on technical excellence – German brands are known for their high quality. Part of this is fear and loss of face for producing inferior results, but it is also about playing the long game, with concern more for the plans that reach far into the future rather than immediate results and deadlines. We heard stories about how releasing products in an iterative and incremental way was met with suspicion at best, as a concern would be to be seen releasing an "incomplete" product.

Chapter 12 | Germany

The following story is about Filestage, a company based in Stuttgart that we visited, whose Agile approach to product development is based on feedback through user research and building good relationships with their customers.

Filestage: Streamlining the Creative Workflow, Based on Customer Feedback[5]

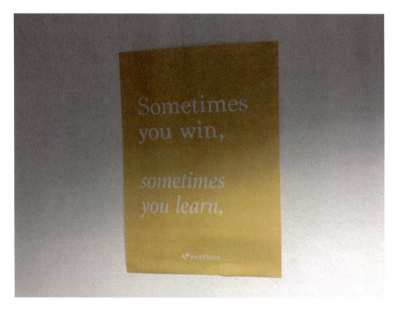

Figure 12-2. "Sometimes you win, sometimes you learn" poster at the office of Filestage

"Sometimes you win, sometimes you learn," reads one of the posters on the office wall.

The poster in question can be seen in Figure 12-2. Glaudia and I were located in a quiet street just outside of the center of Stuttgart, Germany, in an office that could have been mistaken for being someone's home if not for the number of desks, office chairs, and PCs in most of the rooms. Numerous potted plants received plenty of light through the ground level windows. In the entrance hallway, a monitor was showing KPI measures toward the current company goals. A cork board had pinned to it photos of the 16 employees and other associates, a clipping of a magazine article on the company, a picture of Niklas, the CEO, speaking at an event, and a blue Santa Claus hat, despite it being the middle of August.

---

[5]Contribution based on the blogpost at www.redtangerine.org/2018/11/06/filestage/

Adopting Agile Across Borders 231

Filestage is the name of the company that created this homely office space, the cork board, and a product of the same name. Filestage the product is a tool for people to review and give feedback on e-media such as videos, audio, design documents, PDFs, and more. After we tried it out to see if it would be useful for a retrospective exercise with a distributed team, the team at Filestage reached out to us for feedback. Not in the usual cold way using a standard feedback form, but contacting us personally to ask us how and why we were using it, and how they might make it better for us. Excited by a company taking such care over customer feedback, we made contact with Niklas and arranged a visit.

Niklas started by giving us some of the company history. Niklas, together with his university friend Maël (who unfortunately was not available during our visit), wanted to create something of their own rather than work for a corporate company. They experienced for themselves that "sometimes you win, sometimes you learn." Niklas and Maël started out by building an app for a retailer. The idea was for an app that helped people to find misplaced phones or tablets. The app worked well, but it was simply not popular. Niklas and Maël quickly realized that they had developed what their retail partner thought their customers wanted, not what their customers actually wanted.

With this lesson learned, Filestage was conceived by Niklas and Maël going out and talking to real people that had real problems to solve. Given their backgrounds in marketing and media, respectively, Niklas and Maël interviewed more than 40 people working in these industries. They identified problem areas of inefficiency in feedback cycles, for example, lots of emails being sent back-and-forth between people as a marketing campaign develops. They saw an opportunity for technology to streamline this process. This customer-led approach to product development is quite radical in Germany, where the norm would be to perfect a product before taking it to the market and hoping it is successful.

During the visit, we were joined by Anne, the Customer Success Manager, a role that includes helping Filestage to understand their customers better. Anne and Niklas recognized the importance of building relationships and not just making sales. "We are in a service industry, we need to build relationships and trust," Niklas said.

The product is evolved based on the feedback of the many. They want to stick with a standard product avoiding what many companies do in diverging their code base and ending up with customized products for each customer and the exponential maintenance costs that brings. Developers use tools such as use cases so that they have a good understanding of who is using the tool and why. The developers are empowered to challenge the requirements, and they have a healthy drive to create solutions that give the most value with the least possible amount of complexity in the product. Niklas told us that he has "many healthy debates" with the CTO on getting this balance right, to the overall good of the product and the company.

Chapter 12 | Germany

Niklas and Maël had no background knowledge of Agile and Scrum. They only became aware of it and how it complemented their own approach when they started building the development team. Experienced and knowledgeable developers shared their Scrum practices, and this fed into how the company is now run. As well as daily meetings in each team, retrospectives are done across disciplines so that people of different competencies understand what they need from each other. At Filestage, the retrospective is always started by talking about the positive things that are happening before looking at what could be improved. The impression is of a company with clear goals and where communication is efficient.

Filestage has practiced working and collaborating remotely since 2015. Niklas has three recommendations for creating a successful remote working culture. Firstly, sharing a clear vision that explains the why, with supporting KPIs that are accessible to everybody. This gives people ownership and results in people doing the best work they can towards the shared goal. Secondly, company culture should be worked on by leadership, with colleagues encouraged to socialize and get to know each other. Thirdly, great tools are needed that make information visible, accessible, and transparent, so there is an understanding of why decisions were made. Companies should have nothing to hide, according to Niklas. Shortly after our visit in the autumn of 2018, Filestage switched to working fully remotely.

With such focus on providing a product based on customer feedback, continuous improvement, and delivering valuable features with the least amount of complexity, it looks like Filestage are on to a winner. The company continues to grow, and when we caught up with Niklas toward the end of 2020, he told us that Filestage had grown to 24 people.

After our chat with Niklas and Anne, we stepped out of the meeting room, back into the hallway and over the text on the floor that reads "This is a bullshit free zone" as shown in Figure 12-3. Filestage is our kind of place.

Adopting Agile Across Borders

Figure 12-3. Stepping out of one of the offices at Filestage

—David Spinks

Work is a serious business. The universal use of the formal "Sie" (you) in business reinforces this and the hierarchical form of communication. Use of small talk, humor, sarcasm, and wit at work may be seen as unprofessional. The stereotype of German people not having a sense of humor is a myth that is rightfully slowly dying out, it is just that there is a time and place for it. Indirect communication, such as use of coded speech and relying on reading the air can be construed as dishonesty and can result in a loss of trust, so directness is welcomed overall. People are open to having mistakes pointed out, believing that criticism is constructive and that this helps drive improvement in a team or organization.

To make change, arguments often need to be backed up with facts. Such arguments need to be strong and well thought out; tried and tested procedures are in place from the long experience of Germany's established companies. These same companies may seem rigid and full of inertia to people pushing for agility. The perceived inefficiencies of practices such as Pair Programming or Mob Programming, for example, could meet strong resistance from traditional management that views programmers as only adding value when they are writing code.

> **■ Takeaway**   Manage the work, not the people. Value delivered and success is determined by getting things done. When the focus is on keeping people busy, the tendency is for more work to be started and not finished as it waits in queues for other busy people to pick up. Thus, it can take longer and longer for actual value to be delivered.
>
> When the focus is on managing the work, and when the people doing the work are empowered to self-organize to achieve collective goals, quality and time to completion improves because the system is set up to focus on the delivery of value.

We spoke with Daniel Hauck, at the time CTO of a startup in Germany, though he has had a range of titles and roles throughout his career, most of them working with Agile teams. Daniel has worked with a number of different nationalities, different team sizes, and in different industries, so is well experienced in understanding how to lead Agile teams. Here, he shares some of his tips for Agile managers.

Tips for Agile Managers

When I built my first teams, I made them co-located and I paid a lot of attention to bringing together similar people that might even share the same interests so they could relate to each other. Up to a certain point this is possible.

Later, due to the market situation and availability of developers in our area, it was not possible to have a team sitting in the same office (this was all before the coronavirus pandemic). There basically was only one option: build a distributed team with members overseas. The first half-Indian, half-German team in my organization was born.

Since the team members hadn't met each other face-to-face before and probably would not in the near future, they had to find their own way of working together remotely. I didn't force the team to work in a certain way or to have certain rituals.

The team had their daily meeting and besides that, some of them used Slack or Zoom calls during the rest of the day. They got along well with each other.

It took me a while to figure out what was happening. The team was multicultural, multi-language, multi-location, multi-skilled, multi-everything. More diversity would not be possible.

And the team made great use of it. People took up informal roles. The most "social" guy who was from Brazil was getting all of the necessary information from other teams and also acted as the informal leader. The conscientious

Adopting Agile Across Borders 235

Indian guy took care of the annoying little front-end bugs in the morning. The Turkish "mother" of the team kicked asses and held everybody in the team to account.

Another thing that the team did, and it was very important for them, was creating their own identity. Officially, the teams were named after their primary stakeholder. But of course that's not cool. The team came up with their own name, their own logo, and also invested their personal money for ordering stickers and cups.

The team together was more than the sum of its members and it also outperformed other teams in a number of ways: faster cycle times, higher activity recorded in a number of tools, noticeably more communicative and helpful, and they were much more sociable with other teams as well.

Everybody in the team felt responsible. They shared success, but also failed together and learned from it.

This is not only a great example of how a remote team can be built, but also generally how a very diverse team can build one team identity and one team consciousness.

Give Context, Not Just Skills

The first time I worked with people from different countries it wasn't a big deal. I took some time to show them our system and explained to them what the business' goals were.

After that was done we talked through the setup – the tech stack, environments, build steps, and so on. Soon the team started working on their own tasks and we advanced quickly.

Even through gaining that experience, next time I made a mistake. I had a large growing team abroad in India, and I thought I would just do things the same way as I did in the past, and send a developer from the team in Germany to onboard the teams there.

After some time I was wondering why the team wasn't performing too well. I talked to some engineers in the team and they told me that they had a hard time understanding our code and an even harder time figuring out what we mean with certain terms.

The key thing that I missed here was setting the context of the whole business. In the past I showed the teams our entire platform. But this time I had just sent engineers to explain the tech stack.

Chapter 12 | Germany

I assumed that the team members would somehow magically understand a platform built in Germany with German variable and database field names. But to build great products, it is necessary for those that are building the product to understand what the goals are, and how the customer will use the product.

It's also way more satisfying for people to know what they are working on and why, than for them to have to make assumptions about how the product they are working on will be used.

Instead of getting developers to explain to new team members what the business wants, we now let the Product Owners explain what the business wants. The Product Owners of our company have put a lot of time and effort into showing the engineers how certain features work and why they work that way. A lot of things here in Germany also have to follow certain rules or laws, which can also be unrelatable for people in other parts of the world.

If you want to take the test yourself, go to `www.nettolohn.de/` and figure out how to use the salary calculator and what are the rules behind it. Unless you are from Germany or have studied German taxation system you won't have any idea what the heck is going on there.

You hired your team for software development skills, so don't try to teach them technical skills. Try to teach them the context of your business and why it works that way.

Figure Out What People Want or Need

Starting with a new team is always hard. Either you are the new one or maybe the entire team has only come together recently.

You don't know the people, the people don't know you. There is something missing: relationships with each other.

For me this was the case when I took over a team in India. Previously, I had met the team as a tech lead, telling them how to do proper code reviews and how I would like the software architecture to be. Now I was standing in front of them as their manager. It was a sure thing that they had no idea what would come next.

Before it was "only tech" that I talked about with them, and I didn't need to build relationships. Now I was responsible for the team as a people manager.

On one hand, I had to catch up quickly with the needs of the people in the team, on the other, I had to set out what I expected from the team.

What should I do?

**Adopting Agile Across Borders** | 237 |

I called the whole team into a meeting room. As the great storyteller I am, I told them something like the following:

"I am really thankful to have been given the opportunity to lead this great department. For me this is a chance. But this should not only be a chance for me, but also a chance for you."

Now a dramatic pause, in this moment I pulled a bunch of index cards out of my pocket and handed one of them to each team member.

"I want to get to know each of you better and I want to know who you want to be in the next two to five years. It doesn't need to be a job title or any designation, just write down what you really want to do. Be it a software engineer, be it a designer or something entirely different.

"There is only one rule. You cannot write down that you still want to work for me in five years. That I will consider as a lie.

"Please take some time and think about where you want to be in the next few years and write that down. I will have a talk with each of you and we will discuss what you have written here."

In the evening I arranged a dinner with the whole team where I received the first feedback of the activity. It was positive. In most organizations or countries it is not common to ask what people really want. You have a job to do and you are paid for doing that job.

In the next few days I planned meetings with every team member and everybody brought their index card back to me. (I still have them in my drawer, by the way). Nobody had written that they wanted to work for me in the future. Check.

Some wanted to grow in their current career, some sought a promotion, some wanted to switch career paths, from tech to people management, like I had. And some wanted to get into a role where I already had a position open – even better.

We created roadmaps together and talked through possibilities. With some people, I had very honest talks and both of us knew that we wouldn't have a future together. Well, that's also an outcome. Instead of someone just quitting the job and me not understanding why, we could honestly look into each other's eyes and talk about it. For both sides, that's worth a lot. I could plan the replacement early and the team member could also plan accordingly.

The outcome of the story was a stronger bond with everybody on the team. When you ask people what they really want and don't plan to abuse this information, both sides win and it will lead to a fruitful relationship.

—Daniel Hauck, Agile Enthusiast

Chapter 12 | Germany

■ **Takeaway**   Allow teams to build their own identity. As we saw in Daniel's story, giving the team space to discover each other's strengths, to be able to relate to one another, to understand how to leverage their differences builds stronger teams. Simple activities like the team giving themselves a name and designing a logo, creating skills matrices together, and discussing their relative strengths with each other, or team activities such as going to lunch or work drinks are investments that can pay back with higher levels of team performance.

In general, people's personal lives and work lives are kept separate. We spoke to many people working in Germany that gave examples of how they knew very little about their colleagues personal lives. Leisure time is valued and, like work, compartmentalized.

In the realm of software development, specialist roles that were common are giving way to full stack developers who get involved in owning deployment and operations. Agile thinking and ways of working is more popular with software engineers, however, in many quarters, Agile has a bad name. It is seen as an excuse for ill-discipline, allowing people to do whatever they want and "inspect and adapt" used as an excuse for interference at any point in the process – a myth that needs to be busted.

In the following story, Resmi Murali shares her experience arriving at a company in Germany where Scrum was in name only, the patience she needed as an Agile Coach to build momentum for change, and the importance of management support.

Building Momentum for Change As an Indian Scrum Master in a German Company

Before I start, a little bit about my background. I was born and brought up in India. I moved to Germany ten years ago. You may be wondering why this is important. Well, Indians and Germans live in two different worlds when it comes to the culture. Indians are vivacious, speak loudly to make their point clear, use gestures when excited, and are very much into the topic being discussed. Germans are just the opposite, so it took me some time to adjust to being a Scrum Master in Germany.

I started at a company where there were three development teams, with a separate QA team and an Operations Team, all with their own Team Leads. "Product Owners" sat in a separate team and acted more like traditional managers. Zombie Scrum/Scrum Fall was being practiced and, you got it right, the teams were not cross-functional, not self-organizing, and not collaborative. For example, the QA team wanted to introduce an additional column to the

Adopting Agile Across Borders   239

Jira workflow. Without consulting the other teams or the Team Leads, they set about implementing this change. I came to know about it too late, two hours before the next Sprint Planning.

I tried to make the QA Team understand how important it is to have everyone's participation in such decisions. But because the Team Leads accepted the change without question, that was the end of the matter. I became a bit too loud in vouching for collaborative decision making. In Germany, if you are loud, you might be thought of as arrogant and ill-mannered. So sadly, I also lost the trust of this particular team and it took me ages to regain it.

I found out that the teams never had any Scrum training and they didn't have Scrum Masters. So Team Leads and Product Owners were sort of playing the part of Scrum Master, but so woefully that the teams had no idea why in the first place they were having Scrum Events, and how they should be run. For them, the Scrum Events were just more meetings among the thousands of others they seemed to be having.

As a duty-bound Scrum Master, I pointed out to the management the flaws of the Scrum implementation. The message I got was to not change anything, just to make myself somehow useful for the teams. In my pursuit of making myself useful, I thought of making the Sprint Retrospectives better.

All three teams were using a common retrospective format. A team member would prepare a confluence page to capture outputs, and the team would take an hour at the end of the Sprint to come together and talk. They started with a check-in on how they felt the Sprint went, scoring it on a scale of 1–10. Then they would move on to the format of "Start Doing," "Stop Doing," and "Keep Doing." The last part would be to create action items.

I got in touch with each one of the teams (let's call them A, B, and C) and asked them if I can take over facilitating their retrospectives. Team B agreed to give it a try. Teams A and C actually shared the same Team Lead, and he took a poll asking for the team's opinion. The poll had interesting options like "I know how retrospectives work" and it turned out that my help was not wanted. Since I got zero support from the management, I thought of waiting for the right time with teams A and C, and focused my effort in supporting team B. Over almost three months, I introduced new retrospective formats and helped the team to explore Scrum and their working processes. The feedback I got was very positive. Based on the recommendations of the team B members, I gained acceptance from teams A and C to start working with them.

In many of the discussions we had during this time period, I always felt that being a Scrum Master with a foreign background made discussions a bit more tense than if the teams had a German Scrum Master. Me being loud and open,

Chapter 12 | Germany

using gestures when communicating, and talking most of the time, led to comments like, "calm down," "don't be nervous," etc. I learned to adjust how I communicated, and I think that this helped me gain acceptance.

All these were my initial difficulties. A happy ending now! Toward the middle of the year in 2020, things took a 360 degree turn. There is a new CTO who lives and breathes Agile. In our first conversation, he made it clear that he would give me full support and authority for the Scrum process. Now we are in the middle of a true Agile transformation. Our plans for proper cross-functional teams are being put in place, and from February 2021 there will be five cross-functional Scrum Teams.

What I have learnt: change takes time, the importance of understanding the team's culture, especially as a Scrum Master with a foreign background, and the importance of having management support.

Scrum On!!

—Resmi Murali, Agile Coach

■ **Takeaway** Remember the principle of "the art of the possible." In his book **Agile Project Management with Scrum**,[6] Ken Schwaber, the co-creator of Scrum, often uses this phrase, and it is one that has helped us both over our careers.

Sometimes people or organizations are just not ready to change, whether we are talking about expectations on how much a team can realistically achieve in a Sprint, changing the organizational structure to create cross-functional teams, or empowering Product Owners. So learn to pick your battles and find the little wins that *are* possible while challenging the status-quo in a constructive way without losing trust or putting your own position at too much risk. To quote from Ken's book again, "a dead sheepdog is a useless sheepdog."

Change takes time, patience, and perseverance. Understanding the art of the possible given current circumstances at a point in time, as we saw in Resmi's story, is an invaluable skill for any Agile practitioner.

Getting On and Around

Time keeping and punctuality is valued. People do not like to be kept waiting for any length of time in case it affects their schedule, so sticking to timeboxes is important. However, in some organizations punctuality is actually a problem because people are having to multi-task, resulting in increased chances of

---

[6]Schwaber, K. (2004). *Agile Project Management with Scrum*. Microsoft Press. ISBN-13: 978-0735619937

people missing deadlines or being late to a meeting. Since work time and personal time is segregated, any work time that cuts into personal time will not be appreciated. Any change to schedules can be seen as a disruption. This could be one reason why, in general, change is felt to be uncomfortable.

People and organizations like to feel prepared, and though direct open communication is valued, showing vulnerability or admitting at not being "adequately" prepared can be hard in a business environment. For example, in many cases there can be a reluctance to ask for more time to complete a project. Creating a safe environment where people learn to be comfortable with "just in time" planning, understand that the future is unknowable in complex knowledge work, and taking an empirical approach are areas that Agile Coaches may want to focus their efforts on.

People in German organizations are driven by facts, logic, and are data-orientated, though we did come across examples where decisions were not data-driven. To enact change or influence any kind of decision, arguments need to be backed up with sound logic and ideally, good data to stand a good chance of acceptance. Emotional or speculative arguments do not have the same impact. Be direct and constructive with critique; subtlety may result in feedback not registering at all.

The focus brought by Agile methods such as limiting work in progress is sure to hit a chord with teams that like to work on tasks through to completion, though they may desire more detailed information at the start to guide them. We encountered many teams in German organizations that are most comfortable working on one thing at a time and unhappy having to context switch, leave things unfinished, or multi-task. Whatever is promised must be delivered.

The majority of people in Germany are multilingual and English is widely spoken. When applying for a role in a German organization, it is advisable to demonstrate adequate formal qualifications and experience. Sloppiness in appearance, timeliness, behavior, or effort is likely to have a detrimental impression. If you can penetrate the divide between work and personal life, German friendships can be deep and rewarding.

Boris Steiner, Agile Coach and Professional Scrum Trainer, shares a story of an activity that he used to integrate and build cross-cultural integration between his team with members based in Germany and Portugal, which resulted in team members developing their relationships with each other.

A Recipe for Cross-Cultural Integration

When it comes to distributed teams, some things are more complicated then if you just have everyone at the same place. Although I really appreciate the freedom of working from wherever I want, I believe that sometimes nothing

Chapter 12 | Germany

beats face-to-face communication. Whenever you work together with people that are not physically in the same room and from the same culture, you will have to face something that is called virtual distance. There are a number of different aspects to virtual distance, which are

- Operational distance: Having difficulties due to technical hurdles or communication problems

- Physical distance: Being apart from other people which might lead to time zone problems, for example

- Affinity distance: Finding it hard to connect to other people, for example, due to cultural differences

Challenges

I want to give you one particular exercise I did with a team facing these problems. We found it helpful to reduce affinity distance. I was working as a Scrum Master within a product development effort for a customer in Germany. We used Scrum as a framework to organize ourselves. The Product Owner role was fulfilled by someone from the customer's side. Historically, the development team consisted of developers from our company only. Over time, we grew from a small team to a bigger one (co-located), and later on, developers of our customer joined the team. Since they were located at a branch in Portugal, we had to come up with a lot of solutions for problems that previously did not exist to keep communication between everybody running smoothly. To give you an impression of what we had to deal with:

- Different time zones (if only of one hour) left us with limited spots to have interactions with everybody

- Written and spoken communication in a non-native language and all of the possible misunderstandings that can come with it

- Information radiators that needed to be virtual or physically duplicated in both locations

- Communication channels that needed to be easy to use and a low barrier to adoption so that people on the team wouldn't hesitate to use them

- Cultural differences between Germany and Portugal

Given all those circumstances and the pitfalls that come with them, imagine yourself being in the role of Scrum Master and helping a bunch of individuals to grow into a team. Together with a Portuguese colleague, I evolved a plan to strengthen team cohesiveness, awareness of cultural and communicational differences, and last but not least – to have a lot of fun!

The Idea

Figure 12-4. The plan for the cross-cultural cooking workshop

It all started with one thing on our mind, something that was very important to the both of us and something that we were sure was also important to our team: food! Why not have a joint cooking session with all of the people at one of the times when we are all co-located? So far, so standard. However, where would the fun be, if we didn't make it a little bit of a challenge? We scratched our heads, scribbled away on a whiteboard as shown in Figure 12-4, and came up with the following session.

Our vision was to map and apply Scrum to the process of producing a meal for the whole team and bring in some of the problems that we are usually faced with. We did not stick perfectly to what we came up with originally and did some inspection and adaptation of our own as facilitators. You'll find some more detail on this later on.

The Cooking

We used the next opportunity when the whole team was co-located in Germany to announce a "surprise timebox" well before lunchtime. As this was approaching, we found ourselves looking into some curious and hungry eyes. Finally it was revealed that this session was about cooking a joint lunch

Chapter 12 | Germany

for the whole group that consisted of a Portuguese and a German main dish as well as a dessert. To add a little bit of spice, the Portuguese colleagues were handed the German recipe and vice versa. Each group was therefore faced with making sense of a recipe in a foreign language, to buy all of the ingredients and to finally cook. We built three teams:

- All Portuguese with one German to help in translations and shopping (German dish)

- All German with one Portuguese to help in translations and shopping (Portuguese dish)

- Mixed team of Portuguese and German (dessert)

From there we let things go with the flow. As facilitators, the main thing we had to handle was trying to integrate the quiet team members. Besides that, the teams pretty much self-organized perfectly well. Of course, all the typical behaviors, ups and downs, patterns and anti-patterns that occur in a team when creating a done increment of software were also visible in creating an edible increment of food. Nevertheless, all three teams succeeded with their tasks at hand and our culinary review was enjoyed by everyone! We followed it up with a small retrospective of the exercise with the whole team.

Prerequisites for Your Own Session

So if you want to use the very same exercise within your team, what will you need?

- A time and place, where the whole team can spend some time co-located. You might think of only sending some representatives from one location to the other. However, I advise on bringing the whole team together as this is all about bonding, having fun together, and creating stories that the whole team will talk about when being distant from each other again.

- Two – not too complicated yet not too easy – recipes that are typical for your teams' nationalities.

- A more or less fully equipped kitchen. Make sure it can host enough people to actually interact and work together. If one of your recipes requires special equipment, be sure to provide it!

- A place to shop nearby. Going for the shopping spree, maybe not finding all ingredients, not being sure what the best ingredients to use are, needing to improvise – this is all part of the fun!

- A big table to have a feast with your team.

Adopting Agile Across Borders

So are there any hidden pitfalls and things that might go wrong? Of course. Tons of them. And for some of us, preparing a meal is nearly as complex as writing software. So be prepared to improvise. Let me share what we experienced in facilitating and how we adapted our initial plan.

Pitfalls

Originally we planned to keep people with different first languages apart from each other most of the time, only providing some "Joker-Cards" (imagine them as calling a friend when participating in "who wants to be a millionaire") to get some native speakers help for the recipe or cooking. That plan went in the bin quite fast since we thought translating the recipe from another language would have been too difficult, disrupt our timebox and result in a not-so-pleasant meal. Therefore we decided to include at least one native speaker of the recipe language in each team. But if you really want to challenge your team, give it a shot!

We also skipped the formal part of "review." Originally we had in mind to do some kind of evaluation of the various meals afterward. Something in the fashion of rating it with points. That idea just did not feel quite right the closer we came to the end of the session and it started feeling wrong when the whole team was sitting there, eating their meal and having a great time. What we wouldn't do again looking back, is when we tried to facilitate a discussion after the meal on how to apply the learnings from cooking to daily practice. So basically asking questions like: "OK, that thing about good communication about when the noodles will be done, what do we take out of that for our daily work?" Our facilitation skills failed pretty miserably with all those filled stomachs of the team. So food coma sure had its part to play in the failure, but transferring lessons from cooking to a work context might only ever work to a certain extent. I'd rather recommend to just run a feedback wall alongside cooking, or do a very quick flashlight (everyone just giving a quick impression of the exercise in one sentence) at the end, ideally combined with some kind of physical activity (like taking a short walk). As always, your context may vary. Feel free to experiment on your own and tweak what we did!

Quotes from a Portuguese Colleague

- *"Many of us Portuguese, were expecting that our German colleagues would be very cold and strict people (again a stereotype of North European people). It couldn't be farthest from the truth. All preconceptions have fallen away once we met and got to know each other better. In fact, I have found many of the German colleagues to be some of the kindest and cool people I have met in the last 4 years."*

Chapter 12 | Germany

- I was really surprised to learn that our Portuguese colleagues considered themselves as being pessimistic people. A thing that I thought would rather be a prejudice about us Germans. Although sometimes confronted with this trait that I kept being warned about, I found that it was not too bad at all. It was more of an ironic way of seeing things, with an acknowledgement of Murphy's Law that I learned to appreciate and get used to really fast!

- *"Time keeping and popularity: Here I think our cultures are very different. While in Portugal we have a more loose concept of time, where being late by a few minutes (let's say 5) is not a big deal and in some social situations it's even considered polite - in Germany on the other hand, if I'm not mistaken, being on time or ahead of time is paramount. I think we definitely improved together."*

Over the time we worked together, I would say that while we (Germans) got a little bit more relaxed with timing, our Portuguese colleagues got a little more disciplined and we met halfway. Nevertheless, this was something that needed some getting used to from both sides. While they had to learn that we consider punctuality quite important we needed to learn that them being late sometimes was by no means meant to be rude or offensive.

- *"Daily routine: Here I think we are also somehow different. From what I observed, we Portuguese wake up a bit later, lunch later and end the working day later. I'm always surprised how soon some of you start to think about going out to lunch. :) This together with the 1 hour difference we have, did not make things easy to schedule some meetings."*

I remember those shocked faces of the Portuguese when one of our team here in Germany said: "Hey I'm gonna be leaving soon after lunch today." Their faces were turning almost pale when they learned that he had already been at his desk since 6.00 a.m. and therefore his workday would be over at 2.00 p.m. This, combined with the fact that in our part of Germany - and in our team in particular - lunch was due as early as 11.30 a.m., led to some really funny conversations.

I hope some of you find this exercise worth giving a try! Another distributed team I was in touch with (consisting of people from Germany and Spain) already gave it a second test run and also had great fun! Whatever you end up doing, have fun on the way!

—Boris Steiner, Agile Coach and Professional Scrum Trainer

Negotiate German hierarchies with care. Communication across departmental boundaries is rare, and while departmental rivalries are common in a lot of countries, it can especially be so in German companies. There are clear reporting and communication lines vertically along chains of command. It is not unusual for Scrum Master and Product Owner roles to be regarded as "more senior," and this is before we consider "Agile Coach." We heard one story of a company where the senior managers, without any ill-intent, took the Product Owners to dinner, leaving the team behind.

At the very least, for agility to succeed, those in senior leadership positions need to embrace the mindset. In other cases, we spoke to Agile Coaches that talked about the need to split out entirely new companies in order for new ways of working to be used.

■ **Takeaway**   Create new structures when it is impossible to change existing ones. A pattern that we have seen being adopted more and more when organizations have become very large with traditional hierarchical structures that are hard to break is for the organization to start new companies within the company. The aim should be to create a new company that is as independent and self-sufficient as possible. This technique creates an unimpeded opportunity to structure the company in a new way, with new rules, values, and with people that have a mindset that is aligned.

That is not to say that the cultural leadership style is command and control. Fairness and seeking consensus with all people concerned is valued. Managers provide clear tasks, help, and advice to those that report to them, but in general once a task is fully explained, people like to be left alone to get on with it.

Agilists arguing against comprehensive documentation are advised to pick battles wisely. It is desired for things to be written down and documentation will be read. It is seen that written content that gives detail and clarity helps to avoid misunderstandings. Showing a lack of detail or simplification can be seen as being naïve. The change of mindset is to teach people to become comfortable for documentation to emerge instead of creating it all upfront.

Agile Community Events and Meetups

- Agile Learning Lab Berlin: www.meetup.com/Agile-Learning-Lab-Berlin/

- Agile Munich: www.meetup.com/AgileMunich/

- Agile Augsburg: www.meetup.com/de-DE/Agile-Community-Augsburg/

Chapter 12 | Germany

- Agile by Nature: https://agile-by-nature.de/

- Agiler Stammtisch Düsseldorf: www.meetup.com/de-DE/
  Agiler-Stammtisch-Duesseldorf/?_locale=de-DE

- ScrumTisch Stuttgart: www.xing.com/communities/
  groups/scrumtisch-stuttgart-ab4d-1008108/
  about

CHAPTER

13

The Netherlands

The iconography of the Netherlands hints at a country whose people are highly practical. Ubiquitous canals throughout the nation enable travel, irrigation, and the removal of water in a country where a significant percentage of the land is below sea level. Polders, artificially created areas of land reclaimed from bodies of water enclosed by dykes has created more space for development and agriculture.

The flatness of the land itself could be a metaphor for how the Dutch like to arrange themselves in society. Aside from the very biggest conglomerates (and the Netherlands has produced more than its fair share of those, including the world's first), Dutch companies are flat in structure, with people known to be tolerant and open. It is little wonder that in many ways the Netherlands is one of the world's Agile hotspots.

History

The words "Neder," "Nieder," and "Nedre" were used throughout Europe in place names to describe areas of low-lying land. It was in the middle of the 17th century that the Netherlands actually became an independent country.

A sparse population of Frisians, Low Saxons, and the Franks existed in the area following the end of the Roman Empire with feudal systems emerging over the next few centuries, and areas of land presided over by various lords. As trade increased, cities such as Bruges, Antwerp, and Amsterdam grew, with Amsterdam becoming the most important trading hub in Europe by the 15th century. Through a series of conquests and inheritance, the Burgundian

© Glaudia Califano, David Spinks 2021
G. Califano and D. Spinks, *Adopting Agile Across Borders*,
https://doi.org/10.1007/978-1-4842-6948-0_13

Chapter 13 | The Netherlands

Netherlands emerged, a union of territories that covered present day Belgium, Luxembourg, and parts of Northern France as well as the Netherlands. Control passed from the House of Burgundy to the Austrian House of Habsburg and Charles V, ruler of the Holy Roman Empire and King of Spain, in an era known as the Seventeen Provinces.

The merchant traders of the North embraced Protestantism, polarizing them from the Catholic people of the South and their rulers. The Northern provinces united in the Union of Utrecht against the Spanish backed Union of Arras in a war between 1568 and 1648. The war has been called The Dutch War for Independence, the Dutch Revolt, and the 80 Years War. The Spanish forces took most of the South (what is approximately now Belgium and Luxembourg) and the war became about the Dutch-speaking North securing their declaration of independence as the Dutch Republic in what was called the Act of Abjuration in 1581.[1]

Protestant Queen Elizabeth I of England supported the Dutch and the war continued until Spanish King Philip IV finally recognized the independence of the Dutch Republic, which later became known as the Netherlands. The new country entered what became known as the Dutch Golden Age, when the Dutch Empire became one of the major seafaring and economic powers. In areas such as art, science, medicine, architecture, education, and military, the Dutch were rivals for any in the world. The Dutch East India Company that had been created in 1602, and the Dutch West India Company were formed to establish colonies and trading areas throughout the world. Dutch settlements included those in North America, with the founding of New Amsterdam on what is now the southern tip of Manhattan. In Asia, they established the Dutch East Indies which was later to become Indonesia.

England was a major rival for world trade and the Anglo-Dutch Wars were fought, mainly at sea, in a series spanning the mid-17th century toward the late 18th century. 1672 became known as the Disaster Year when the Third Anglo-Dutch War coincided with a simultaneous war with the French. Continued competition with the English cemented a general Dutch decline in the 18th century.

French revolutionaries overthrew the Dutch and created the Batavian Republic, annexing the Netherlands into the French empire in the early 1800s. After Napoleon's defeat, the congress of Vienna created the Kingdom of the Netherlands, adding the Southern Netherlands to the north. The French-speaking, catholic South were very different culturally and rebelled, fighting an independence war and breaking away from the Dutch to form the nation of Belgium in 1830.

---

[1] Motley, J. L. (2008). *The Rise of the Dutch Republic (reproduction).* Bibliolife. ISBN-13: 978-0554314273

The Netherlands remained neutral during World War I, and it declared neutrality again at the start of World War II; however, it was invaded by Nazi Germany in 1940. Exiled in London, the Dutch government declared war on Japan who went on to occupy the Dutch East Indies. Following liberation by the allies, the Netherlands soon went on to fight independence movements in Indonesia, and under growing international pressure, recognized Indonesian independence in 1949. Decolonization continued as Suriname, and the Colony of Curaçao and Dependencies (which became known as the Netherlands Antilles) also became countries with more autonomy within the Dutch Kingdom.

A shortage of housing and goods, combined with a high population density, led to mass emigration, with Canada, Australia, and New Zealand as popular destinations. Despite this, a period of booming birth rates and economic growth followed, together with a period of great cultural change. Young people and students pushed for changes in areas such as equal rights, LGBT rights, disarmament and environmental policies. Dutch liberalism is perhaps most internationally symbolized in De Wallen, Amsterdam's red-light district, where consensual prostitution between adults is legal and there is a policy of tolerance toward soft drugs.[2]

Historically, the Netherlands has been a cultural melting pot. In the 19th century, significant numbers of people from China came to the country. In the 1950s, people moved from Indonesia. A shortage of workers in the Netherlands in the 1960s meant people were recruited from Morocco and Turkey as well as Italy and Spain as "gastarbeiders" (guest workers). The 1970s saw immigration from Suriname. With the expansion of the EU, an increased number of migrant workers arrived from Central and Eastern Europe. Significant numbers of people with heritage from outside of Europe make up the population in the likes of Amsterdam, Rotterdam, and The Hague.[3, 4] All of this has contributed to the Netherlands being a highly multicultural society.

Politically, the Netherlands is characterized as achieving broad consensus in its multi-party parliament and wider society. No single party has held a majority since the 19th century, and so governments have been formed of coalitions. The Netherlands became one of the founding members of the Benelux Union with Belgium and Luxembourg, NATO, the ECC, and the European Union.

---

[2]*Toleration policy regarding soft drugs and coffee shops.* Government of the Netherlands. www.government.nl/topics/drugs/toleration-policy-regarding-soft-drugs-and-coffee-shops

[3](2006). *Half of young big-city dwellers have non-western background.* CBS. www.cbs.nl/en-gb/news/2006/31/half-of-young-big-city-dwellers-have-non-western-background

[4]*Multicultureel Nederland.* UCL. www.ucl.ac.uk/dutchstudies/an/SP_LINKS_UCL_POPUP/SPs_english/multicultureel_gev_ENG/pages/allochtonen.html#:~:text=The%20Netherlands%2C%20the%20most%20densely,is%20of%20non%2DWestern%20origin

Chapter 13 | The Netherlands

Today, the Netherlands ranks highly for GDP, competitiveness,[5] and happiness indices.[6] The Netherlands came fifth in the 2020 Global Innovation Index.[7] Despite the relatively small size of the country, many Dutch brands such as Philips, Shell, ING, Unilever, Aegon, and Heineken are recognized the world over.

Insights

Ajax, the Dutch association football club, and the Netherlands national team made "Total Football" famous in the 1970s. The tactic involved any outfield player being able to take the position of any other player in the team in what is an analogy of the compatibility of Dutch culture with Agile thinking. People in the Netherlands are generally team-orientated and will take action rather than procrastinate. They are practical, persistent, have a low tolerance for waste, and strive for quality.

Management structures are largely flat, with leaders chosen based on merit, education, and the demonstration of competence.

Elroy Jumpertz, a professional software engineer shares the following story with his own experiences of how some of the organizations he has worked in has enabled those with leadership qualities to emerge.

Agile Organizations Set the Stage for Emergent Leaders

In my career as a software engineer I've been lucky enough to have had my first two jobs at relatively flat organizations, which at least partially embraced the Agile principles on the teams level. As a junior I started at Philips Lighting. What was remarkable about the team I was part of is that it consisted of junior developers only (at that time) and the team lead, who had a lot of experience managing software teams. In hindsight, I would say he was a Product Owner and Scrum Master combined. The team lead also strongly influenced how we thought about software development in a team. I don't

---

[5]Schwab, K. (2019). *The Global Competitiveness Report 2019*. World Economic Forum. ISBN-13: 978-2-940631-02-5

[6]Helliwell, J. F., Layard R., Sachs, J., and De Neve, J. (2020). *World Happiness Report*. New York: Sustainable Development Solutions Network. ISBN-13 978-1-7348080-0-1

[7](2020). *The Global Innovation Index 2020: Who Will Finance Innovation* (13th edition). Cornell University, INSEAD, and WIPO. ISBN- 978-2-38192-000-9

think we ever called ourselves a Scrum Team (even though we pretty much were), but as junior developers we were intuitively aware that there were some very specific things in our everyday behavior that gave us the label "Agile." For example, we worked on the highest-risk items first and made frequent deliveries to the master branch, such that if we would have to shift priorities, we would have maximized the business value up until that point. We focused on test automation, build pipelines, took the Sprint Goals seriously, and were very conscious about avoiding introducing technical debt as much as possible.

Our team lead took a very hands-off approach when it came to engineering work itself, while being very specific about the rules for team events such as the Daily Scrum, the Sprint Retrospective, and so on. Nobody on the team had ever heard of the Scrum Guide, and some of us were only vaguely aware of the Agile Manifesto, but even without that formal basis we all knew we operated with an Agile mindset.

Even though there was a large difference in experience between the team lead and us developers, he never treated us as people who were only given information on a "need-to-know-basis." We were encouraged to understand the business value of the functionality we were going to implement, the reasoning behind prioritization decisions, which stakeholder held which position, the financial situation of the team, and so on. In turn, responding to that trust, it felt only natural for us to be completely transparent and honest in what we shared with each other, the team lead, and the rest of the organization.

What I realized only much later is that the team lead, by taking this leadership stance, not only ensured that the right product was built, but he also shaped every single team member into well-rounded engineers who could potentially go on to take a leadership role in an Agile environment themselves. This is what I would call a Senior Engineer – someone who masters their craft (e.g., software development), but also understands the larger context in which engineering takes place, understands the Agile values, and is able to make meaningful contributions toward team performance in terms of self-organization.

Which aspects of that particular team made it such a breeding ground for emergent leaders?

- We were free to make our own choices with respect to the way we built the product. Our team lead, having about 20 more years of experience in software engineering than us, obviously provided some guidance from time to time, but otherwise gave us freedom.

- We felt a strong sense of ownership and responsibility. This really was our product.

Chapter 13 | The Netherlands

- The team lead knew that the occasional failure is unavoidable. Failures were managed in two ways: (1) making sure that a failure would not cause too much damage and (2) giving us an opportunity to learn from failures without personal repercussions.

- Since we were provided with a safe environment for the occasional failure, we developed a culture that embraced creativity and allowed us to act with courage.

- By allowing us the opportunity to reflect on failures (as well as on successes), the team lead invested in natural personal growth of every team member, as well as in ever-increasing maturity of the team as a whole.

After having spent four years in that team, it was time to move on. I became a software engineer at Thermo Fisher Scientific, in many aspects a similar organization as Philips Lighting. At Thermo Fisher I joined a new development team that was tasked with creating software for a new flagship product. The team consisted of three developers (including myself) at the time. The startup phase was chaotic and there was no clear leader, and only a little sense of direction. So intuitively I stepped up.

One of my first observations was: "I can't believe that our "backlog" consists of post-its on that one developer's screen." Enter a centralized backlog in the form of an Excel sheet and the polite request for every developer to add all their ideas and to-dos there, to be used when planning the next Sprint.

"We should at least have some daily check-in during which we plan the day." Enter the Daily Scrum.

"Periodically we should demonstrate what we're doing, at least to some people outside the team." Enter the (rudimentary) Sprint Review. And so on.

So what happened? Based on my experiences at Philips, and the fact that both Philips and Thermo Fisher encouraged emergent leadership, I had taken the lead in organizing our work without even thinking about it.

Only after a few months, when the engineering community was getting more serious about applying Scrum in all teams, did I enroll for a Scrum Master training. Needless to say, the Scrum mindset was a natural fit with my personal style, and the training served not to change my way of thinking, but to strengthen it. After completing the training I asked for the "official" role of Scrum Master for the team, and I got it.

Thermo Fisher shared some of the same values as Philips, such as:

- Management gave individuals lots of freedom to explore their interests.

- It was OK when somebody would step up and request a certain role. Proactiveness was encouraged.

Adopting Agile Across Borders

- Not all role changes were treated as promotions, with all their formalities. Having the role of Scrum Master meant nothing in terms of position in the company hierarchy, job title, or pay grade. It was just a "hat" someone would wear, simply because everybody agreed on it.

Additionally, my peers were immediately OK with me taking that role, because I had already demonstrated my abilities and they saw value in it. Management understood that they would be taking a manageable risk by making me Scrum Master. Teams didn't operate in silos, and there were enough eyes on any single team's output, as well as on individuals' well-being, to be able to detect well ahead of time if things would derail.

In conclusion, I think the following organizational traits support individual development and emergent leadership:

- Give individuals lots of freedom to make everyday decisions. Set boundaries within which they are free to tackle problems as they see fit.

- Have a role model who embodies the Agile mindset from whom the team can learn. Scrum training is a nice way to strengthen a team, but falls flat without role models. (Or, if I were to phrase it like the Agile Manifesto: *"everyday exposure to the Agile mindset over a theoretical basis – while there is value in the item on the right, we value the item on the left more"*).

- Create a team or company culture based on openness, honesty, and person-to-person communication.

- Embrace failure as an inevitable part of any complex product development, but ensure that the impact of failures are limited, and that teams and individuals are given an opportunity to learn from them.

- And finally, when someone requests a certain role or responsibility, keep an open mind. They might not have been your preferred candidate for the job, but if those directly affected by the role change are supportive, and as long as performance can be monitored honestly and openly, there is probably not much risk going forward.

—Elroy Jumpertz, Software Engineer

Chapter 13 | The Netherlands

Figure 13-1. Impression of making decisions through consultation and consensus building in Dutch culture (image courtesy of Tasia Graham)

Decisions are made through consultation and consensus building. People are open to, willing, and often expect to give their opinions. This idea of bringing people together for consensus building is illustrated in Figure 13-1. Everyone is regarded as equals, which may go some way to explain a rebellious streak toward hierarchy and status.

■ **Takeaway** Encourage engagement through self-organization within clearly defined boundaries. Creating environments where self-organization can thrive can be a challenge in certain cultures, not least for people in a leadership role. However, it is something that is relatively natural in the Dutch culture.

Adopting Agile Across Borders

It is no surprise that Management 3.0 has its roots in the Netherlands. Many management and leadership strategies are strong on theory, but lack a lot of practical guidance. Management 3.0 is not a framework or management method, more a mindset involving an evolving set of tools and practices to help manage within an organization. To quote from the Management 3.0 website,[8] "management is not only the manager's responsibility, but everyone's job!" Our favorite tool from Management 3.0 is Delegation Poker.[9] Delegation Poker is a great way to enable self-organization and get employees engaged.

People's rights and their role are respected. There is professional training required and an expectation of quality regardless of the job. There is an ideal of equality, and the underlying Dutch morality to ensure everyone's basic needs are met is demonstrated in a welfare state that is one of Europe's most comprehensive and expensive.

Dutch education is geared toward the needs and the development of the student, with pupils enrolled on programs and more specialist subjects based on their ability as they progress through the secondary education system. The system produces high quality engineers and technical people. Teaching foreign languages is embedded into the education system with English widely spoken. Reforms in the education system in the 1990s placed more of an emphasis on teaching management skills and increasing student's autonomy and responsibility for their own learning.[10] In general, people growing up in the Netherlands show a thirst for knowledge and new ideas. Adaptations of Scrum in the eduScrum[11] and ScrumatSchool[12] Initiatives demonstrate how the Dutch are applying Scrum in education and that they are ahead of most in applying Scrum methods outside of IT.

Directness and use of short sentences in the communication styles in the Netherlands is well known and takes some getting used to for those from more diplomatic cultures. Unfiltered critique, bluntness, and conversations on subjects that others may feel as embarrassing is as natural to the Dutch as discussing the weather. In many ways, this means that transparency is absolute; any critique is aimed at the idea or subject in question and are never intended as personal attacks (if opinions are of a personal nature, you are likely to know about it!). Such openness allows healthy conflict and debate with anyone

---

[8]*What Management 3.0 is About.* https://management30.com/learn/
[9]*Delegation Poker & Delegation Board* https://management30.com/practice/delegation-poker/
[10]*History of Education in the Netherlands.* K12 Academics. www.k12academics.com/Education%20Worldwide/Education%20in%20the%20Netherlands/history-education
[11]eduScrum. www.eduscrum.nl/
[12]ScrumatSchool. https://scrumatschool.nl/

Chapter 13 | The Netherlands

able to offer their opinion, and given the chance, most Dutch will offer theirs. Well-reasoned arguments backed with convincing evidence is the advised tactic in debates, which can turn quite lengthy, as consensus is built while all need to have their say. Some people will stick to their opinions despite pressure tactics, lengthening the process. Facilitators may need to resort to tactics to democratically gain the consent of the majority to keep things moving. Dutch pragmatism allows an opportunity to make up time, however. Discussing non-essential items, such as things that have already been agreed, processes that are known to be running smoothly or talking about "what is going well" is seen as a wasteful.

Amsterdam was once the center of trade for Europe and beyond, and home to the world's first true stock exchange.[13] A sense of internationalism has never left the Dutch – they are among the keenest and most adventurous of travelers. They are also a big immigration destination and large parts of the society of the Netherlands are not of Dutch descent, making teams and organizations highly diverse relative to those in other countries.

There also remains a financial and business savviness about the Dutch. They have a desire to make a profit or get a good deal, though never at the cost of compromising quality, reliability, or having a good relationship. They have a reputation for, and are mocked by their neighbors, for being frugal, somewhat of a paradox given the generosity of the state and the related high taxes that this brings.

Getting On and Around

Scrum Masters and Agile Coaches will generally need to be strong facilitators to allow fair Dutch debate while keeping to timeboxes. Techniques such as fist of five or roman voting can be useful to allow everyone a fair and democratic way to come to decisions without burning up too much time in building consensus.

Consensus building is important. Teams generally struggle with authority and command and control hierarchical styles of management. That is not to say that teams are not structured and organized; they are indeed detailed in how they carry out their work, but wish to do so without unnecessary micro-management or managerial overhead. It is surely no coincidence that the Netherlands has more than its fair share of companies practicing Holacracy[14] (Bol.com being one of the most well-known examples), a disciplined method where management is decentralized and teams operate with full autonomy.

---

[13]Petram, L. (2014). *The World's First Stock Exchange* (Illustrated edition). Columbia University Press. ISBN-13 : 978-0231163781

[14]*Holacracy Success Stories.* Holacracy.org. www.holacracy.org/whos-practicing-holacracy

Adopting Agile Across Borders

In the following story, Sander Hoogendoorn shares his own journey of going beyond following the mechanics of a particular Agile framework and allowing teams to discover the best ways of working for themselves.

Different People and Fewer Rules

Exactly two years ago at the time of writing this, I was in a small car with a local driver making our way across the impressive Indonesian island of Sumatra. My driver barely spoke any English, a fact that he compensated for by continuously smiling.

By the end of the afternoon, after an extremely bumpy five hours drive through back roads and gravel paths, we reached Medan, a big three-million people, dusty, and chaotic anthill of a city with barely any traffic signs or road marks to guide us. Using their horns as sonar, thousands of friendly smiling traffic participants stream through this city every day. Being used to mostly well-ordered European traffic, Medan became an experience I cherish to this day.

You probably wonder why I bring up Medan traffic in a post about Agile and culture. Am I going to talk about the difference between Indonesia, or Asia in general, and the Netherlands, or Europe in general? Yes and no. Bear with me.

Developer Productivity

In late 2016, I started an assignment as the Chief Technology Officer for a software product company that was a leader in their market in the Netherlands. Having been active for over forty years, the company's products ranged in technology stack from COBOL but compiled to Java every night, to low-code solutions, to PHP and JavaScript on the other end of the spectrum.

One of the challenges the management put on my plate was developer productivity. According to the company's CEO, productivity could and really should be much higher. The CEO was truly disappointed about the slow time-to-market of the new features the teams were building into their products. Especially since he, by decree, had ordered his management team to implement Scrum. "Surely that should have boosted productivity," he said to me.

Much to his surprise, productivity hadn't increased. At all.

"We Should Have Been There Already"

To get acquainted with the organization and its people, I started my new role with a series of interviews with semi-randomly chosen employees. People from the management, but also sales, product management, architects, and developers and testers from the various teams.

Chapter 13 | The Netherlands

Even though a number of these interviews surprised me quite a bit, I think it was the interview with the software development manager that stood out. A friendly gentleman in his mid-fifties, grey hair, glasses, suit, tie. "We have successfully implemented Scrum," the manager emphasized to me. "We hired a specialized Agile agency that trained us. They for instance taught us how to write user stories, how to estimate in story points, how to set up Jira, and how to do Sprint Planning and Sprint Retrospectives. Then we started to use Scrum in the teams. The consultants stayed on for another six months and coached us on the implementation. We even certified our Team Leads as Scrum Masters, and we certified our Product Owners too."

"So, how are you doing now?" I asked him, with the CEO's remarks in the back of my mind. The manager took off his glasses and wiped them with the flipside of his necktie. He sighed.

"Well," he said, "we did everything right. The consultants even told us so. All the teams work in Sprints, hold Sprint Planning meetings, have stand-ups. We have backlogs, do retrospectives. But still, after eighteen months, we don't see a rise in productivity." The manager stared at me with a worried look on his face.

"We should have been there already, shouldn't we?"

At Different Speeds

You might ask yourself why this company's story is remarkable enough to share. So many companies are implementing textbook Scrum. Some succeed, and Scrum helps them achieve whatever goals they have. Some of them fail. For different reasons. Sometimes because Scrum doesn't fit them. Sometimes because Scrum is not the right means to their ends. And sometimes even because they "implemented Scrum wrongly."

The next step in my onboarding was to get acquainted with the teams delivering the company's products. The teams, titled product lines, were organized by the product they were building. Maybe even more relevant is that these products, despite all dealing with the same business domain of insurance, were built on various technology stacks. The oldest product was, and still is, built with COBOL. Their CRM system was constructed in PHP. One product was based on a business rule engine and a low-code tool. And the most recent one was set-up in Java, while we started building the new microservices-based platform in TypeScript on node.js.

This is where you might ask if the technology stack is relevant to the way of working on the product lines. Scrum fits everybody. Right? To be honest, the stacks are not always relevant, but in this particular situation, they mattered.

Adopting Agile Across Borders 261

As I was soon to find out, these different teams, the product lines, producing different generations of products on different stacks, were populated by different kinds of people. And these different kinds of people felt at ease with different ways of working and at different speeds of delivery.

Too Slow and Too Fast

In order to decrease the company's time-to-market, which appeared to be the main challenge for this company, the CEO reasoned that team productivity needed much improvement. Hence, my first assumptions were that all product lines should move toward Continuous Delivery, thus releasing more often, leveraging automated tests, automated pipelines, and infrastructure as code. This is typically the world I live in. I am used to teams releasing to production with every single code check-in. In this world of Continuous Deployment, the typical Scrum process quickly becomes redundant, with its many events that are usually highly ceremonial. Teams whose process constrains them to, for instance, bi-weekly deliveries of "shippable product increments" are sluggish compared to teams who are able to deliver many times per day.

But the product lines at this company, as in many, many other organizations, were completely different teams delivering at different speeds.

Some of the product lines really entrenched my views on Continuous Delivery and they soon let go of the mandatory Scrum ceremonies and indeed moved toward delivering new versions of services multiple times per day. Those were the teams building the new platform.

However, the CRM and business rule teams did not feel at ease with this increased delivery rate. They were really comfortable with working in Sprints, organizing refinement sessions, retrospectives, using Jira, and the heartbeat that is Scrum. They flourished in *this* way of working.

Interestingly, the remaining teams, delivering their products in COBOL and Java, didn't really appreciate Scrum at all. At first, I thought that they too wanted to deliver more often, and were hindered by the abundance of ceremonies.

I couldn't have been more wrong.

These teams didn't like Scrum because it went too slowly, as with some of the aforementioned teams. Rather, they didn't dig Scrum because it went too fast for them. They were used to delivering every three months, and not having to deliver a potentially releasable product increment every two to three weeks. They couldn't deal with that speed.

Chapter 13 | The Netherlands

There Is No Single Best Way of Working

Whether or not the software development manager liked it, the different teams in this company were working in very different ways, using different ceremonies and in different cycles. And, not unimportantly, on different technology stacks.

Despite the manager desperately wanting all teams to work in the same way and in the same heartbeat, to his frustration, the teams just didn't do it. Some of his teams found Scrum too slow, other teams really loved Scrum, and again other teams considered Scrum way too fast for their liking.

And although I personally had moved on from Scrum toward much shorter cycled approaches years before, similar to the software development manager, I too was the victim of thinking that there was one way of working that was best for all teams.

There wasn't.

After I spent elaborate time with each of the teams, I slowly changed my single way of working perspective. The teams at this company were not only building different products, based on different technology stacks, the people themselves in the teams were inherently different.

The COBOL and Java teams thrived when working at their own pace, albeit with much longer cycles, and thus less frequent feedback. These people would not be able to work at a faster pace and deal with more frequent feedback. And the people in the teams on the other end of the spectrum would not have been able to work in the longer cycles of the aforementioned teams. It is actually quite simple.

There is no single best way of working.

It's not waterfall, not the Unified Process, and certainly not Scrum. But also not even working in Continuous Delivery or with a DevOps mindset for that matter. There is no framework, Agile or not, that fits everybody, every organization, or even every team at an individual organization.

The good thing, however, is that Agile isn't about following someone's model or framework. It isn't about having Sprint Planning, user stories, estimating in story points, retrospectives, or even stand-up meetings. Yes, all of these elements of all of the Agile frameworks have their use at some point, but still, each team and each team member should be able to work in a way that makes them feel alright – or maybe even, to use this horrible word, the most productive.

Adopting Agile Across Borders

There Is No End-State

Actually, I realized, it had been staring me in the face all along. Agile is about *uncovering better ways of working*, just like the Manifesto for Agile Software Development states in its very first statement, and about continuously delivering value. This literally is what Agile is all about. This is not easy. Being able and willing to improve. From whatever starting state, to whatever still unknown next state. This requires the ability and openness to learn and improve. It also is a never-ending process.

There is no end-state.

Once I accepted what, to me, is the true meaning of agility, I could let go of many things that were always in the back of my mind. I have been evangelizing Agile ways of working since the mid-1990s, always pushing myself to go beyond where I was. But that's just me. Every individual has their own journey, their own pace of improvement. All coming from different starting states, each taking different next steps. And that's fine.

Medan Revisited

Still, you are probably wondering why I started with a description of Medan traffic. I think I've arrived at the point to explain.

When I was working with the teams in this particular company and started to realize that there is no one way of working for everybody, I started to wonder how we could enable the teams to discover their own optimal way of working. Without any need to impose Scrum, Spotify, or SAFe®, or any other framework on the teams, but to let them find out what works best for them. It puzzled me.

How could I encourage them to take the next steps? Any next steps?

And then suddenly, during a dull refinement session, it occurred to me. During this particular refinement session, the full team, including Product Owners, some stakeholders, and all the techies, were discussing the complete list of stories for the Sprint at length. Observing the people in the room, I noticed that nobody of the fifteen people gathered seemed to enjoy this day-long meeting very much. People sighed, doodled in their notebooks, and even dozed off.

So, I asked the team why they were in this session. "Because we have to," said one of the developers unhappily. "It's mandatory. It's how Scrum works. And our manager says we need to do this."

"What would you do if these refinements were not mandatory?" I asked the team.

They laughed and shook their heads. "But it is."

Chapter 13 | The Netherlands

While my driver and I were racing through the mad traffic in Medan – from a European perspective – I was wondering how this traffic worked with hardly any traffic lights, signs, marks on the road, basically without too many rules at all. In my humble opinion, it worked, in general, because participants continuously communicated with each other, and were constantly aware of all the other participants while going through the traffic. There was a constant cacophony of horns, gestures, eye contact, and offering and taking up space. There were *way fewer rules* when compared to the very strictly organized European traffic.

Participants needed to adapt constantly.

I guess that's the biggest difference. Participants need to adapt constantly. Whereas, in European traffic, everything is well-organized and we live by a plethora of rules, with more security, but with very little flexibility to adapt to changing circumstances.

The question is which of these two strategies works best when trying to modernize organizations, where teams face constantly changing circumstances, say technology stacks, frameworks, requirements, and infrastructure. Which of these two strategies works best when you want to encourage teams to take the next steps? Any steps?

Fewer Rules

Back to the refinement session. Again, I challenged the team, asking what they would do if refinement sessions were not mandatory, but optional. And, to take it one step further, what if they would be able to decide what the next steps were in improving their way of working? What if they had fewer rules? What if Scrum wasn't mandatory? How would they adapt?

"Can we really do that?" someone asked.

"Well," I replied, "I am the Chief Technology Officer. So, yes. I guess."

The people in the room looked at me glaringly, and then looked at each other. And for the next thirty minutes an intense and loud discussion took place. And after a while, quite a number of suggestions came out of it. We could discuss stories in smaller groups, only with the people who were actually involved in them. We could discuss stories on the day we would actually pick them up, instead of at the start of a Sprint. Then we could stop estimating story points. Or stop doing Sprints. Or, we could all move our desks to the same location. We could restructure the way stand-up meetings took place. We could use different tools. Or even, place a couch in the office to have better one-on-one conversations.

All useful suggestions. All valid improvements. All valid next steps. For this particular team.

Adopting Agile Across Borders

They turned to me for confirmation. I nodded positively, despite that I didn't really know whether or not I had the mandate to make these changes. But then again, fewer rules, right?

Looking Back

Now, looking back several years later, from a philosophical point of view, this was a defining experience. It taught me the perspective that, in our rapidly and increasingly changing world, each person and each team benefits from following their own learning path, a bumpy path perhaps, but one where we can learn from looking beyond the rules and the generic frameworks, and where we can discover new paths by experimenting.

I do realize that even this, learning by continuous experimentation., is not for everybody. And yes, that is OK too.

> *This post is written in memory of Dick van der Wel, whose inquisitive mind allowed him to challenge the world around him, the people he worked with, and most of all, himself.*
>
> —Sander Hoogendoorn, independent dad, speaker, writer, and traveler. Code philosopher, CTO, software architect, programmer, and beyond-agile coach.

■ **Takeaway** Implementing a particular process is not the goal. We have seen many examples where organizations have adopted Agile with a plan to "be Agile" by a certain date. However, true agility means adapting processes and continuous improvement – there is no end state. Instead of focusing on implementing a particular process, the real goal is to be able to adapt processes so they can meet the needs of those doing the work. Agile is an enabler for this and its adoption is about the implementation of the Agile mindset and values.

Keep retrospectives practical, and use them to address real problems. While acknowledging, celebrating, and learning from what is going well, keep it to a minimum, as some people can see dwelling on these as a waste of time.

Formalities are limited and can even be frowned upon. A little small talk at the start of meetings is about as far as it goes. Formal dress is rare; smart jeans and a shirt are perfectly acceptable at a wedding, so don't expect to see many suits in business settings. Shows of extravagance in appearance or behavior, or acts of superiority will not win hearts or minds. Overall, team members like to deal with others in a straightforward, open, and transparent way, so avoid showing or playing on emotions, covert tactics, and escalating to superiors, for example. People tend to work collaboratively and help each other to

Chapter 13 | The Netherlands

resolve issues without having to refer to superiors. Trust is gained through leading by example, demonstrating competence, providing facts and evidence, and taking a hands-on approach.

Agile Events and Meetups

- Agile Holland: www.meetup.com/agileholland/
- Scrum Facilitators: www.meetup.com/Scrum-Facilitators/
- State of Product Management: www.meetup.com/State-of-Product-Management/
- Liberating Structures User Group: www.meetup.com/liberatingstructures/
- LEGO® Serious Scrum: www.meetup.com/LEGO-SERIOUS-SCRUM/

CHAPTER

14

Poland

Located right in the center of Europe, it can be said that Poland is where West meets East. It is a country that should not be underestimated. It has a land area that is bigger than that of the Netherlands, Belgium, Denmark, Austria, Switzerland, and the Czech Republic *combined* and it is the fifth largest country in the EU by population. The country's economic output is comparable to the sum of that of Hungary, Czech Republic, Bulgaria, Slovakia, and Croatia.

Poland's people are proud, ambitious, courageous, and hardworking, and some form of Agile can be expected to be seen in the companies of the recently established IT industry, much of which functions as an outsourcing destination.

History

Poland has a long history of wars and incursions on its sovereignty. During its history, it was the largest country in Europe at one point, while at another time, it was wiped off of the world map for over one hundred years.

A number of Slavic tribes existed in the area of what is now Poland for thousands of years, but it was in the 10th century when Poland became a state. The realms ruler, Mieszko I embraced Christianity, bringing The Kingdom of Poland into the community of nations with its founding in 1025.

© Glaudia Califano, David Spinks 2021
G. Califano and D. Spinks, *Adopting Agile Across Borders*,
https://doi.org/10.1007/978-1-4842-6948-0_14

Chapter 14 | Poland

Lithuania became a longstanding ally, and they formally became a single state in 1569 with the signing of the Union of Lublin which created the Polish-Lithuanian Commonwealth, one of the largest nations in Europe by population and territory that stretched from the Baltic to the Black Sea. It was mainly run by nobility but featured elected kings as leaders, an early democratic system in contrast to elsewhere in Europe that had monarchies that held absolute power. A period of stability and prosperity followed, with a liberal political system that included acceptance of all faiths. This can be seen as a reflection of the openness of the society which has shown a historical acceptance for cultural and artistic trends from abroad.

A number of uprisings and invasions in the mid-17th century suddenly put an end to what had been known as the Polish Golden Age. Cossacks staged an uprising in the South, other rebels declared themselves subjects of the Russian Tsar. During the Second Northern War between Sweden and a number of adversaries in the region, including the Polish-Lithuanian Commonwealth, Poland suffered a destructive invasion, known as the Swedish Deluge, that devastated the population and infrastructure. Perhaps as damaging as any of the fighting was the liberum veto, a rule that allowed any member of the Sejm (Polish Parliament) to veto decisions. It effectively crippled the Sejm's ability to pass legislation with foreign powers such as Russia and Prussia bribing members to enact their veto rights to weaken the Commonwealth further.

The resulting weakness in the Commonwealth resulted in simultaneous invasions by the Kingdom of Prussia, the Russian Empire, and the House of Habsburg of Austria in 1772. The occupying powers progressively partitioned the country up between them, and the Commonwealth of Poland-Lithuania ceased to exist by 1795.

Despite a number of insurrections, it wasn't for another 123 years, in 1918, that Poland regained its sovereignty with the signing of the Treaty of Versailles after World War I. Poland had at least benefited from industrialization and modernization established by the occupiers. The Second Polish Republic exerted its new authority with a series of conflicts, including a war with the Soviets that stopped the advancement of Communism across Europe.[1]

Any peace was short-lived, however. In September 1939, Nazi-Germany invaded Poland, sparking World War II. An invasion by the Soviet Union followed a matter of days after, and Poland found itself split by foreign occupiers once again. Poland lost the highest percentage of people during the war – around six million fatalities, half of them Polish Jews. Following the war, Joseph Stalin sanctioned a pro-Communist government, ignoring the exiled government that had fled to London. The communist People's Republic of Poland was announced officially in 1952.

---

[1]Moorhouse, R. (2020). *The war that saved Europe from Communism*. Unherd.com. https://unherd.com/2020/01/the-war-that-saved-europe-from-communism/

Adopting Agile Across Borders

In 1980, the independent "Solidarity" trade union was formed. It is widely credited with playing a central role in the end of communist control in Poland, and its leader Lech Wałęsa won the Nobel Peace Prize in 1983 and the presidency in 1990. The country became a republic after the collapse of the Soviet Union in 1989. Like other former communist countries of Eastern Europe, Poland struggled economically, but it was the first to rebound.

There were improvements to human rights. The standard of living grew with a developed education system that included state-provided university education, as well as state-provided welfare and healthcare. It joined the Schengen Area in 2007 allowing freedom of movement of people with the other Schengen countries of Europe. Its economy has grown to be the sixth largest in the European Union as measured by GDP and the population has recovered to be the fifth most populous at the time of writing.[2] It was the only European country not to have fallen into recession as a result of the 2008 financial crisis.

Over the last couple of decades, Poland has strengthened its relationship with the United States, becoming one of its closest allies in Europe. At the same time, it has worked on building strong relationships with its new neighbors such as Ukraine and Belarus. All this while balancing its relations with the other members of the European Union.

The opening up of the European labor market has led to emigration due to the relative higher wages that can be obtained abroad. As such there is a large Polish presence in many countries all around the world, for example, in the United States, Germany, the United Kingdom, and Canada. In 2019, the government passed a law to exempt workers under the age of 26 from income tax to stem the flow of young emigrants and to address the overall population decline.[3] Nevertheless, Poland is now a significant player in Europe and the world stage.

Insights

Following centuries of oppressors threatening their very survival, many Polish people have developed an innate stoicism. When it comes to injustice, people have learned to stand up for themselves and fight for what they believe in. Indeed, assertive behavior is justified if there is unfair criticism, pressure, or insults. It is certainly not a yes culture. This can be seen today in Agile teams, where team members will question the value of work items, push back on

---

[2]*Countries in the EU by population.* Worldometer. www.worldometers.info/population/countries-in-the-eu-by-population/

[3](2019). *Poland to scrap income tax for young workers.* Kafkadesk. https://kafkadesk.org/2019/07/09/poland-to-scrap-income-tax-for-young-workers/

Chapter 14 | Poland

retrospective formats that do not result in concrete actions, and question the value of Scrum Masters if seen not to be effective. Under fair leadership, it can be expected that teams will demonstrate deep levels of courage, commitment, and focus. Polish teams like a challenge and problem solving. They are creative, courageous, flexible, care about quality, and have a great work ethic.

Communication styles vary wildly. A direct communication style is common, which may seem brusque and abrupt to those that believe that it is better to communicate more indirectly to avoid hurting others' feelings or causing embarrassment. In fact, there is a belief that it is more respectful to express opinions openly. At the same time there are those who are very talkative and use a rich array of language. Part of this richness of language can include use of metaphors. There is more consistency in listening skills with Poles careful, sensitive listeners who are quick to pick up on inconsistencies or slurs, however subtle.

Generally speaking, there is a propensity to look to the past in remembrance of their history and to inform present actions. What is in the present is seen as inconsequential in the wider scheme of things and attitudes toward time are relaxed. Yet there is respect for other people's time and so people are largely punctual.

A feature of Polish culture has been that scientific and cultural advancements are seen as important, if not more so, than economic growth. Poles have made considerable contributions to science and technology. Nicolaus Copernicus was the first to place the sun at the center of the solar system. By formulating the quantity theory of money which stated that the general price of goods and services is proportional to the amount of money in circulation, Copernicus was also one of the first economists.[4] Polish physicist and chemist Marie Curie was the first and only person to win two Nobel Prizes for her work on radioactivity and for discovering the elements Polonium and Radium. This is symbolic of Polish creativity and innovation. High standards of education has been a goal for Polish leaders throughout its history, with favorable rankings compared to other OECD countries today.[5] However, we were told that demonstrating experience is just as important, if not more so than formal education and qualifications. Agile certifications in isolation often fail to impress. Given all of this, it is perhaps unsurprising then, that status and advancement in corporations and politics is accorded through merit.

---

[4]Volckart, O. (1997). *Early beginnings of the quantity theory of money and their context in Polish and Prussian monetary policies, c. 1520–1550.* The Economic History Review. Wiley-Blackwell. doi:10.1111/1468-0289.00063. ISSN 0013-0117. JSTOR 2599810

[5]*Poland Overview of the education system.* OECD Education GPS. https://gpseducation.oecd.org/CountryProfile?primaryCountry=POL&treshold=10&topic=EO

Adopting Agile Across Borders

As recently as the early to mid-1990s, there was very little to no IT industry in the country. This has changed very quickly and many companies have grown rapidly. Consequently, technology companies contain few people with very long careers tied to pre-1990s technology, and many people have had to learn their craft very quickly whatever their level of seniority in the company. It wasn't until the 2000s that things began to stabilize, and this included adoption of Agile ways of working. While the levels of skills are good, like most parts of the world, there is a shortage of good developers, but we were told that more and more people are changing careers to become programmers.

While perhaps a little later to the party, agility is now expected as a norm for tech companies. What this means does vary, with many adoptions considered to be "by the book" and following the mechanics only. This is as much a reflection on Polish companies as the fact that a majority of companies are outsource partners or suppliers to clients in Western Europe, the United States, and the Middle East, who are new to the Agile mindset themselves. The level of agility therefore often needs to be limited to what is acceptable to the client. Much like in other parts of the world, the Product Owner role is often misunderstood, and perhaps due to the large outsourcing nature of the industry in Poland, the Product Owner is relegated to order taker unless it is formalized as a role fulfilled on the client side.

All over the world, it seems that human nature is to jump to solutions and requests become tasks to be fulfilled rather than problems to be solved. Commitment from teams can sometimes be lower in these circumstances as teams are treated as a delivery factory. There are of course exceptions, as demonstrated in the following story from Pawel Brodzinski about the level of transparency and empowerment they have achieved at his company, Lunar Logic.

One-Way Street to Transparency

I'd been on a journey to continuously increase autonomy at Lunar Logic for a couple of years already. By that point, we already had what we called the decision-making process. In short, people could make decisions as long as they consulted those who had expertise on the topic and those affected by the decision. The only constraint for what kind of a decision one could make was the financial limit – the total cost of a decision couldn't be bigger than a specified amount. And that limit was going up regularly.

Alas, not all decisions could be made by everyone. Since our payroll wasn't transparent, obviously decisions about salaries weren't subject to the decision-making process. Ultimately, how would you decide what kind of a pay raise your colleague should get when you don't know what they earn?

Chapter 14 | Poland

Lunar Logic is a web development agency, helping startups and established companies develop their web products. In other words, we are a professional services company. We offer our services to our clients and get paid for the time we spend helping them. As you would expect of any such organization, anything between 85% and 90% of our total costs are directly people related, such as salaries, taxes, recruitment, etc. That's where my realization came from. We could get people to decide on everything else, but unless we got them to decide about salaries too, we only enabled them to manage a tiny fraction of the company. And you can't make informed decisions without transparency.

That's how I got the inspiration to make our payroll open. During a town hall meeting, I shared the idea with the whole company. I wanted to ask everyone afterward, "Who's with me? Who thinks it is a great idea?" Fortunately, I was perceptive enough to sense the reaction without voicing the question. Looking at the body language and the looks on the faces of those around, it appeared to me that two-thirds to three-fourths of our folks thought it was a bad idea. My assumption was soon confirmed by many discussions with people who shared their concerns regarding such a move.

One thing is important here. Lunar Logic is based in Poland, and the vast majority of us are Poles. When it comes to openness on finances, we aren't remotely as progressive as Scandinavia. We aren't even close to what would be considered a norm in the United States. Heck, when I talk with Germans, and they say they're conservative on this account, I still believe we are lagging behind.

Poland's cultural norm is not to talk openly about salaries, sometimes not even with a group of friends. The best strategy for an employee is to hone their negotiation skills and get as much as possible from a manager behind closed doors. Managers consider it a norm that salaries are unfairly unbalanced because people were joining their companies at times of different prosperity. In such a culture, telling people that we'd like to have our salaries transparent was a bold move indeed.

Despite the initial resistance I was glad I shared the idea. Throughout the next several months, I spent a lot of time discussing different concerns people had. I confirmed the key assumption I'd made about the change. Transparency alone is not enough. People need to have a way of influencing what's on the payroll. Otherwise, the only expected reaction is frustration. After all, salaries are never ultimately fair. They're filled with biases of people who decided about them in the past. And even if the payroll could somehow be fair, we are only people with subjective opinions. We would still see unfairness only because the salaries aren't exactly what we would set them to be.

**Adopting Agile Across Borders** 273

So the question is whether we have any tools to address such a perceived unfairness. If we have no influence whatsoever over what's on the payroll, it is the equivalent of saying, "You don't like what you see, right? It is what it is, and it won't change. Deal with it." What kind of reaction would you expect? Frustration, obviously.

That's why transparency is not enough. One needs to provide a way to influence how salaries are set or changed in the future. We adapted our decision-making process to help us with that. Since the topic was sensitive, we just wrote down more details about how the discussion and decision happen. The whole thread was supposed to happen in writing, as we wanted to be able to go back to the old discussions as a reference. There was a prescribed format for a decision proposal – who should get a pay raise, how big, and why. The time to speak up was constrained to keep the discussions concise.

However, designing the system was only a part of the effort and only a small part at that. The preparation took ten months. In the discussions, I realized many challenges that I hadn't been aware of. One example: I learned that a couple of people didn't want their salary to be known by everyone. No matter how much we talked and how many others had been convinced, they didn't like the idea.

That's why we ended up designing an opt-out option. Before launching the system, anyone could opt-out. This would mean that their earnings wouldn't be known to anyone and also they wouldn't know anyone else's salary. At the end of the day, no one used that mechanism, yet I believe it was essential to provide such an opportunity.

An important part of the preparations was reformatting myself. Historically, I was the ultimate decision-maker when it came to salaries. I always aimed to pay people what is fair. However, suddenly I started facing a new dilemma. Instead of considering "what I think is fair," it was, "what everyone collectively would think is fair." With that slight change in the problem definition, I started coming to different conclusions. I used the time to make adjustments in the salaries trying to make them better aligned with collective expectations.

Another issue to address was very human. Fear. As a company leader, I was giving up a significant power. I was afraid that the salaries would go through the roof, and with that, we could put the company's future at risk. Fast forward: this has not happened, yet the fear was real. The answer was designing a temporary stage when everything would be happening in a new way, but I would still make the final decisions. Anyone could propose a pay raise for anyone else, or themselves for that matter, and everyone was invited to share their opinion, but at the end of the day, I would call the shots.

While I rationalized it as care of the company finances, now I believe it was more of addressing my own fear of losing control.

Chapter 14 | Poland

Nonetheless, I made an important commitment to myself. I knew that we'd inevitably find ourselves in a situation where the outcome of a discussion would differ from my own opinion. There would be a proposal for a pay raise that I would disagree with. I resolved that I would go with the discussion's outcome and against my judgment in such a situation. That way, I'd show that people had real influence over payroll, and not just a place to voice their opinions, while decisions are made the old way.

With all these things in place, I convinced the vast majority of people that going transparent with salaries was a good idea. We were ready to go.

I had some expectations about what would happen. I hoped people would get involved in setting salaries. I counted on a better collective understanding of how salaries translate to the company's general financial situation. I kept my fingers crossed that the dreaded salary negotiations with me would become a thing of the past. Most importantly though, I wanted to see our payroll become fairer over time.

Was it a quick change? No. Initially, people were reluctant to exploit the new power. Then there was what we called "the raise spree." Suddenly there were multiple pay raises happening all the time. However, instead of limiting the power people had, we started educating how using the new power translates to all sorts of contexts, from a company's financial standing to the collective perception of fairness. However, even if it took longer than I expected, I saw all the changes that I hoped to happen.

There was, however, one effect that I hadn't seen coming. In retrospect, it was the most valuable of all the outcomes.

The new salary system made discussions about salaries transparent, and it distributed the power to start a decision-making process about anyone's salaries to everyone. It meant that I could never know when any specific person's pay raise would be discussed. When it was, however, everyone was invited to share their opinion. If I had feedback about something that had happened several months back, I would be inclined to share it. The salary discussion was happening in the written form, so I would first like to share feedback directly with the person whose pay we would discuss. After all, that's a respectful thing to do. It wasn't that much of a problem when it was supportive feedback. However, when it was a critique, the response I would likely get would be along the lines of "why hadn't you told me that several months ago?" And it would be spot on. Because, seriously, why? What I was encouraged to do then was to share any feedback I had instantly. All the time. With everyone.

We changed our behaviors regarding peer to peer feedback in at least two contexts by introducing open salaries. On the one hand, each time anyone's salary is discussed, they get this avalanche of feedback coming from all around. It became a tradition that once the salary thread is finished, the person thanks

Adopting Agile Across Borders

everyone for their feedback. On the other hand, because we know this feedback avalanche is bound to happen at some point, we tend to be better, more consistent with just-in-time feedback, especially when it's critical.

I couldn't have predicted that.

Some 15 months after the big bang, we made another significant change. Since that point, the final decisions have not been made by people who used to be in power, a.k.a. me, but by people who started the thread. I gave up the illusion of control that I had still kept. Anyone could start a thread to get a pay raise for themselves or give one to a colleague. By starting the discussion, they would claim the right and responsibility to make the final decision. And the best part was that the change of process didn't even feel like something major. It was... meh. It felt more like a formal adjustment to describe what was already happening.

Many might wonder how many people start a thread to discuss their own salary, compared to how many people nominate other people for a raise. In some places, one might expect to see people mainly nominating themselves. In our case, across the first 40 or so salary threads, there was only 1 case where the person raised the thread about themselves. Later, we started seeing more of these occurrences, but they are still just a fraction of all of our salary discussions.

Starting a salary discussion for oneself can make people feel vulnerable. It might be that multiple people voice an opinion against the change, or suggest a smaller unsatisfactory adjustment. People may be concerned that they might be perceived as selfish and their reputation changed as a result. Interestingly, these fears are very rarely justified as the vast majority of salary discussions are not controversial. Whether giving feedback or nominating oneself or others, I cannot deny that the organizational culture of courage and respect that we strive for are needed.

At the end of each year, we make a collective summary of what happened to us that year. Making salaries open was one of the highlights of the year. When I describe it to our potential hires how our salary system works, I often hear that they hardly believe it could work and that it only makes them more likely to be willing to join and experience such an environment themselves. In fact, I get to explain Lunar Logic's open salaries to people in countries with cultures much more open to financial transparency. All that even though Poland is culturally an unlikely place to lead the line on this account.

I teach a management course at a local university, and when we discuss the impact of open salaries, I typically mention that it's a one way street to me. I wouldn't go back to be in a team where salaries are non-transparent. Since the audience often recruits from the corporate world, they often argue how it's

Chapter 14 | Poland

impossible in their case. When we dig deeper around motivations, it's never because there's no way to do so. It's always because there's no will. I totally get that, as the change is most challenging to who is in power – the management.

Open salaries were a huge milestone on our way toward radical self-management. However, I don't try to say that our system is ideal. As a matter of fact, five years down the line and we are dissatisfied with what we have. Initially, in each salary discussion, we could count on at least 7-8 distinct voices. Over time we started expecting more and more structured voices in salary threads. Also, our teams became much more stable, and, on average, we don't have as much of a complete view on some of our colleagues as we used to. We started seeing discussions with just a couple of people speaking up. While some decisions have been uncontested, some others have tended to be challenged, and with fewer voices in play, there is space for resentment.

However, even the system's critics aren't suggesting that we should go back to non-transparent salaries. By now, no one could even imagine that. We voice a need for an iteration of the decision-making process that would be a better fit for our new situation. As I said, once you try it, you're not going back.

It makes me smile even now. I know that almost anyone who experienced the Lunar Logic salary system will hope for, maybe even expect, transparent salaries from their future employers or they will introduce something similar when starting their own company. Through our experiment, we may impact more than just our organization.

—Pawel Brodzinski, Chief Cook and Bottle-Washer at Lunar Logic

---

■ **Takeaway** Transparency by itself is not enough. Creating transparency without the means to inspect and adapt could actually lead to greater frustration. A useful activity that we have used is "circle of concern vs. circle of influence" articulated by Steven Covey.[6] Here team members visualize and share collaboratively with leaders things that are impacting them that they can't control (circle of concern) and things impacting them that they can influence (circle of influence) as shown in the example in Figure 14-1. We often find that following discussion, people discover that they have a lot more influence over things than they realize!

---

[6]Covey, S. R. (2004). *The 7 Habits of Highly Effective People: Powerful Lessons in Personal Change* (15th anniversary edition). The Free Press. ISBN-13: 978-0743269513

Adopting Agile Across Borders

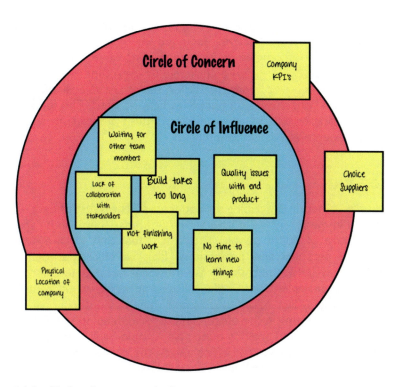

Figure 14-1. Circles of concern and influence example

■ **Takeaway** Avoid managing by exception. We have seen many organizations forming policies such as limiting time working from home or rigid working hours because of the risk of the actions of the very few. This can stifle the sorts of experiments that we saw Pawel undertake and the creation of innovative environments that are great places to work.

Enthusiasm for Agile varies. We heard stories of people in the IT industry that deeply dislike it, others where those involved struggle to understand basic concepts such as limiting batch sizes, and those that struggle to embrace the uncertainty of the complex domain and wish to continue making long-term plans up front.

Getting On and Around

People want a pragmatic approach. Rhetorical and management speak is best avoided. Respect and trust is instead gained through following your words with action and doing what you say you will do. Agile Coaches and Scrum

Chapter 14 | Poland

Masters be warned: retrospectives are seen as a place to be serious to address serious problems. Retrospectives focussed on games and team building without a practical outcome could be seen as of no value, a waste of time, and even childish. In general there is a challenge to overcome skepticism of Agile in many places. This is not to say that Polish teams are all business; other East Europeans often consider Polish people as light-hearted. The following story from Ilona Kędracka, acts as an example of Polish pragmatism and activities that could be perceived as "forced fun."

Forced Fun

I once heard someone describing my country as "The West of East – and East of West" – I immediately fell in love with that phrase, because it captures the complex nature of Polish people just right. I feel that we are not able to separate our personal and professional lives as clearly as our Western neighbors, but we're not necessarily as emotional and people-oriented as our Eastern-Slavic cousins either. We like to focus on work, we try to get straight to the point, to stay fact-based, and do one thing at a time, but, on the other hand, we love socializing in the office, tend to form deep personal connections with our colleagues, and are not quite able to hold back our emotions when conflict sometimes arises in the office. Given the characteristics of a country that doesn't really identify strongly with any dimension of the Lewis Model, it's especially hard to generalize and detect behavioral trends, but one thing kept creeping back in discussions each and every time me and my colleagues debated work-related topics over a glass of beer – and that was our aversion to something we agreed to call "forced fun."

We get it – working in IT requires stretching our collaboration skills to their limits sometimes and it's really crucial that people who spend numerous hours working on a product collaboratively know each other well, possess the skill of resolving problematic issues in a gracious manner, are aware of each other's pet peeves, and, ideally, like each other and enjoy their time at work. Especially during early stages of team forming or while meeting foreign colleagues for the first time, the manager needs to make sure that team members become more and more comfortable with each other's presence – as well as encourage honest and direct communication in the group. However, more often than not, when this goal is trying to be accomplished by activities that are supposed to be fun, energetic, and joyful, instead of becoming more close-knit, team members can sometimes become more irritated and fed up. I've seen these efforts fail multiple times, especially when working with a technical team based in Poland and business stakeholders working from the United States or the United Kingdom. Let me break it down into three categories.

Icebreakers

Even though things are changing rapidly, a very popular model of the team still consists of development team members based in Poland (or other Central European countries) and business stakeholders located overseas. Given these circumstances, business trips (at least during pre-COVID times) weren't unusual and I could often encounter situations when we were supposed to participate in some sort of get-to-know you games before kicking-off project-related discussions. Obviously, you want the team to become more comfortable with each other – but more often than not, if you decide to break the ice using the techniques you remember from college associations or your local volunteering club, it won't work as well in a professional setting as it did in less formal environments. The icebreakers I've either witnessed or heard about from my cringed friends include things such as standing in a circle and making "funny faces" to each other, answering questions like "if you were an animal, what would you be and why?", running around the room and playing "rock, paper and scissors," human knots, remembering facts about one another, coming up with "funny" adjectives that start with the first letter of your name, and all sorts of other jumping, clapping, and dancing activities combined. Don't get me wrong – during business trips people definitely need to have a chance to get to know each other better and I've seen initial tensions between team members disappear while having a casual beer after hours numerous times, but forcing "funny" activities in the office is usually going to make Polish teams cringe at best – and frustrate at worst.

Gamification

Another example of forced-fun-prone moments in the life of a team are Scrum Events. Efficient and direct communication in multinational teams by definition is a lot harder to foster – and I've seen various sorts of ideas tested by Scrum Masters in order to make sure that everyone's opinion is heard. One way to try giving the quieter people a voice that I would also place in a high-risk-of-backfiring category (especially for linear-active-leaning teams) is turning meetings into activities that are supposed to be playful, but can quickly become too abstract for the team to find them valuable. I've noticed that the majority of these activities happen during retrospectives – these include games such as describing your last Sprint with a selected Dixit card, using Harry Potter's artifacts and spells to brainstorm what we want to improve in the next iteration, rose-bud-thorn or sow-grow-harvest to facilitate discussion about ideas to explore, and others. It is true that these might be valuable for people that have troubles with articulating their concerns or are new to the team. From my experience however, this usually happens at the cost of other team members (who are still the majority), as they would rather address the issues or come up with ideas directly.

Chapter 14 | Poland

Art Classes

The last example of forced fun I would sensitize readers to usually occurs during team offsites or workshops – their aim is usually to point people's attention to some issue or waste that is present in the team, but on a similar note as in the "gamification" paragraph, they can easily become too abstract and too frustrating for the team to see value in such exercises. This applies to activities that might be a good idea for a conference or a workshop where people specifically sign up for them, but introducing them in a workplace, when team members have no choice but take part in it, rarely pays off. All sorts of marshmallow challenges, kanban paper plane factories, improv, origami, or other games that require manual or art skills fall under this category – if they aren't closely tied to real-life, specific examples of the issues that teams witness at work. Using them as a tool to help the team members resolve conflicts or spot an ill communication pattern rarely yields positive results. If conducted as a response to a conflict situation in a team, it can also create a feeling of confusion, belittlement, and a waste of time among the participants. If instead of conducting an honest, mature discussion we're spending our time gluing one piece of paper to another, hoping to understand some metaphorical lesson from the exercise, are we not losing the opportunity to strive for more open, honest, and mature communication with each other?

Just to be clear – I do not consider all abstract activities such as games and workshops inherently wrong or doomed to failure. With a skilled facilitator, who makes sure that team members can translate the lessons learnt during the workshop into real-life actions, they can help the team see the "bigger picture," improve their feedback skills, or form a pattern to deal with difficult situations. In that case, I think it's crucial for the leader of such activities to know the team members well, possess a solid skill of empathy, and put a decent amount of effort into shaping the workshop program to make sure the practical – not only "fun" – aspect of all exercises is emphasized.

That being said, when dealing with teams from Poland (and from my experience, the majority of other Central European countries follows similar patterns, too), I would recommend everyone to pay close attention to developing personal connections with as many team members as possible. Make sure the quiet ones are heard, too (as the majority of IT professionals I have worked with tend to lean toward introversion), but don't overcomplicate it. A simple beer and pizza party or a casual discussion over a cup of coffee can go a long way. I've witnessed conflicts and aversions between team members being solved during informal meetings (although obviously, this doesn't apply to really serious matters such as acts of racism or harassment at work). Being able to resolve their own conflicts within the team is also a great sign of maturity, therefore letting the team explore conflict-solving skills themselves should be encouraged. Forcing your teams, however, to experience some "obligatory fun" has a high risk of them becoming even more frustrated with

Adopting Agile Across Borders | 281

each other – and based on my experience, addressing the pain point directly or casually making sure everyone has a moment to get to know each other should make your team happier than any fancy activity they are obliged to participate in.

—Ilona Kędracka, Product Owner/Blogger at Poczatkujaca.pl

■ **Takeaway** Know your audience. Facilitation techniques that work with one group in one context may be completely unsuitable for another group. Facilitators should also focus minds on achieving clear outcomes – clear actions for improvements from retrospectives, for example. Using abstraction to help facilitate discussions is a great technique to get people to open up, but as we saw in Ilona's story, this should be done with a purpose and be translatable to something tangible. Sessions that are fun are all well and good, but are of questionable value if there is no learning or takeaways.

Everything is relative of course. There is a balance of being professional at the right times while not taking things too seriously all of the time, so avoid appearing only results-orientated. Certainly do not use authority for anything that could be seen as unfair or impinge on people's rights, for example, coercion into working extra hours.

Despite what might appear to be a certain level of shyness, Polish people in general are very sociable. We were told one story of someone from Poland on a business trip to the United Kingdom for the first time, describing the time as "such a depressing week." Few British colleagues spoke to her about anything other than work and she was otherwise left alone in the office. In the evenings, everyone else went back to their own family and social lives, while she was left without company in a foreign city. In Poland however, work and social connections are commonly intertwined. Taking time to get to know people on a personal level and socializing with them is appreciated. This social aspect of Polish culture means that teams may be closer knit than in other countries. Combine this with their trait of not being afraid of confrontation, and personal issues may impact work and vice versa.

Meetings and discussions may become long-winded, but it is good etiquette to allow others to go off-topic. There is a delicate balance to be struck with keeping to timeboxes. Overall, it is expected that discussion will result in pragmatic outcomes. Focus more on using pragmatic, direct language instead of using coded speech or expecting people to read between the lines. Avoid sarcasm as it could be seen as disrespectful and cause offense to some. Any offense could be called out. Instead, show respect for others, an attractive quality in Polish culture. Critique is appreciated when made in a constructive way. Eye-contact is important to indicate keen listening.

Chapter 14 | Poland

Agile Community Events and Meetups

- AgileByExample: https://agilebyexample.com/
- Agile Coach Camp: www.accpl.pl/
- Agile Warsaw: https://agilewarsaw.com/
- Kanban Poland: www.meetup.com/Kanban-Poland/
- Management 3.0 Warsaw: www.meetup.com/Management-3-0-Meetup-Warsaw/
- Zwinna Łódź: www.meetup.com/Zwinna-Lodz/

CHAPTER

15

United Kingdom

The United Kingdom was the birthplace of the Industrial Revolution. It also gave rise to the largest empire in the history of the world. Such heights still proudly linger in the national consciousness, despite more than a century having passed since the peak of The British Empire. Tayloristic management styles that were used for managing the cotton mills and coal mines of the past are embedded into the ways things are done. The Agile movement, while widespread, therefore has a challenge of disrupting long held beliefs and the way of doing things as the United Kingdom moves to a knowledge-based economy.

History

The island of Britain was first occupied by people of a Celtic culture known as "Britons" who had originated in mainland Europe. The Romans invaded, bringing with them advancements such as fortified towns, aqueducts, and roads. They enlisted the help of Germanic mercenaries to help protect their lands, including the Angles and Saxons. Once the Roman Empire collapsed, the Anglo-Saxons invaded while the Gaelic speakers in the North united to create the Kingdom of Scotland during the 9th century. English kingdoms became established, but these came under a new threat originating from Scandinavia – the Vikings of Denmark and Norway. The Vikings plundered areas along the British coastline and occupied large areas of the North and East of the island.

© Glaudia Califano, David Spinks 2021
G. Califano and D. Spinks, *Adopting Agile Across Borders*,
https://doi.org/10.1007/978-1-4842-6948-0_15

Chapter 15 | United Kingdom

The English kings reconquered and reunited the lands into the Kingdom of England in the 10th century. When the king, Edward the Confessor, died without an heir, his brother Harold was crowned king. However, Harold's cousin, William the Duke of Normandy, declared the throne for himself. William and the Normans invaded in 1066, conquering England and large parts of Wales and Ireland.

Tensions with the French monarchs grew, culminating in the Hundred Years War between England and France from 1337 to 1453, only formally ending when Edward IV of England renounced claims to the French crown. The English continued fighting among themselves for the English throne in the Wars of the Roses in the 15th century. In the 16th century Wales was brought into the Kingdom of England and the king of England was declared King of Ireland by the Irish parliament. When the monarch Elizabeth I died without an heir, her cousin, James VI of Scotland simultaneously become James I of England and Ireland in 1603 in a dynastic union called "The Union of the Crowns."

The English civil war broke out in 1642 between the Parliamentarians, led by Oliver Cromwell, and the Royalists, resulting in victory for Cromwell and the overthrow of the monarchy. Though the monarchy was restored after the death of Cromwell, a parliamentary system was established, where monarchs no longer had absolute power.

In the 17th century the union, along with other European powers, began colonizing territories overseas. In the 18th century, acts were passed in the parliaments of England and Scotland in an Act of Union to form the Kingdom of Great Britain. Development accelerated in the mid- to late 18th century with the start of the Industrial Revolution, initially driven by manufacturing methods with machines and the use of steam power. By the end of the century, Great Britain controlled a global trading empire stretching from colonies in North America and the Caribbean to the Indian subcontinent, though some of the American colonies were to break away in the American War of Independence to become the United States of America.

In 1801, further Acts of Union created the United Kingdom of Great Britain and Ireland. The United Kingdom and her allies defeated France in the Napoleonic wars, resulting in a redefining of the borders across Europe and leaving Britain as the main world power as the Spanish (under pressure from Latin American independence movements) and Portuguese empires collapsed.

The British Empire expanded to include most of India, parts of Africa and the Middle East, Canada, Australia, and New Zealand. Victory for the allies in World War I allowed Britain a mandate over a number of German and Ottoman colonies, extending the British Empire further to cover almost a quarter of the world's land area and population. However, the war left it with a huge national debt and a sense of nationalism in the colonies that would go

Adopting Agile Across Borders

on to spark a number of independence uprisings, though many remained part of what was to be called the Commonwealth of Nations with the British monarch remaining as their head of state. Ireland was partitioned in 1921, resulting in the renaming of the union to The United Kingdom of Great Britain and Northern Ireland, which remains to the present day.

The United Kingdom was still recovering from World War I when it was hit hard by the Great Depression that was sparked in 1929, and then it entered World War II when it declared war on Nazi Germany after its invasion of Poland in 1939. After the allied victory, the United Kingdom was economically ruined. A shortage of workers led the government to encourage immigration from the other Commonwealth countries, making the United Kingdom a much more diverse country. Guerilla warfare and civil unrest continued over Northern Ireland, with Unionists opposing the nationalists who wanted a united Ireland. The Good Friday Agreement of 1998 devolved powers to Northern Ireland, and included agreements on a number of issues surrounding sovereignty and civil rights. Scotland and Wales also became devolved administrations with each country granted greater autonomy, though, in 2014, full Scottish independence was rejected in a referendum.

The United Kingdom was one of the founding members of the European Union. Freedom of movement within the EU combined with a high number of migrants into the EU in the mid-2010s contributed to more population growth and further multi-ethnicity. With a long period of austerity following the 2008 financial crisis, widening inequality, and divisions in the United Kingdom, political unrest was demonstrated when the United Kingdom voted by a slim majority to leave the EU. The United Kingdom left the EU on January 31, 2020, and, at the time of writing, is working to define its place in the world as the coronavirus pandemic has gripped the world, a crisis during which the United Kingdom has been one of the most badly affected countries so far.

Insights

As of 2020, the United Kingdom has the sixth largest economy by GDP in the world. Despite its falling down in the order, it still has a large economy. That, and its lofty historical place in the world has perhaps led to a certain amount of complacency and a reluctance to "move on." Old factories and coal mines are examples of British industry that were kept going well beyond the time it made financial sense. Many of the pro-Brexit arguments in 2016 focused on how Britain was better off by itself outside of the EU. Certain aspects of society still believe that the ways of the old Empire should be continued indefinitely – which had its conveniences of having one set of rules and a common way of doing business that was all centered around a single language.

Chapter 15 | United Kingdom

Since English became the de facto language of the world, Brits generally lack – and do not expect to need – foreign language skills. This linguistic complacency and has led to a lack of cross-cultural awareness to a certain degree. British insularity is perhaps best demonstrated by observing British people vacationing in other countries. Spain's Costa del Sol, for example, has been transformed over the years. Cafés serve English breakfasts and British-themed pubs cater for tourists that have been coming from the United Kingdom in droves.

The English language itself is rich, though the British use it in subtle ways that goes beyond the vocabulary and grammar. British coded-speech is real. Instructions, critique, or praise may be hidden among the obligatory small talk. Use of humor is prevalent and is dry, or littered with irony. It also includes what is perhaps the unique trait of deep self-deprecation; many other cultures struggle to understand the way the British mock themselves. People in the United Kingdom generally are a mix of those that are prepared to speak out (though never to strangers when travelling on the London underground) or give an opinion, and those that will be quietly complicit with what others decide.

Paradoxically, while in organizations we saw a very linear approach to work, with step-by-step plans and desire to do things one thing at a time according to schedules, the reality is often much more chaotic with the common result of people "muddling through" to get things done. People often go to great lengths to appear to be laid back about work, though in actuality they are often far from relaxed. Negotiations and demands can be as ruthless as in any other part of the world – people are just far less explicit about it. While open debate and seeking agreement is common, status and people's place in the hierarchy wins out with people often deferring decisions to superiors. Embedding self-organization is often a struggle in a culture where escalating issues to managers is normal, and where those managers then duly step in to make a definitive ruling. Leaders generally keep a certain level of power-distance, yet it is common for many to attempt to be seen to be "part of the team."

While teamwork is encouraged and we ourselves have experienced working with teams that were excellent collaborators, people are often inevitably forced to "act in competition" with others by the organizational policies around them. Company cultures include the "annual appraisal" of individuals, with salary increases and bonuses based on individual performance. People look to how they can progress their career in what can be fiercely competitive environments. Employees will often keep their eye open for positions that come with more money, benefits, or power, and unless it involves a long commute, will think little of moving company. House prices are a common subject of discussion in daily lives and "climbing the property ladder" is a national obsession. Taking out mortgages and financing high standards of living

Adopting Agile Across Borders

via credit is common, making it a necessity in many cases for people to progress their careers as fast as possible. Over the last few decades, the number of people choosing to work as contractors and freelancers rather than as permanent employees has increased, the perceived "freedom" often cited as preferable to security.[1] As a consequence, building stable, long-lived teams is difficult, compounded by a common perception of seeing people as interchangeable "resources" (and in many organizations it is still common for workers to actually be referred to as "resources"). On the flipside, a positive of all of this is that many people have built up a rich set of experiences and skills, including getting up to speed and being able to soon make a contribution quickly when joining a new team.

Considering the above, it is no surprise then that the United Kingdom is one of the cultures with the clearest distinction between people's professional and social lives. While it is common for colleagues to have a drink (usually alcoholic!) together after work, it is rarer for people to form the same bonds with colleagues as seen in other cultures. People value their own and other's privacy, which may leave some visiting outsiders perplexed when they are left to their own devices.

The United Kingdom has a history of innovation and scientific discovery. Its scientists and engineers were instrumental in leading the Industrial Revolution. Isaac Newton, who made breakthroughs in the laws of gravity and motion in the 17th and 18th centuries, is considered by many as the father of modern science. Charles Darwin created the theory of evolution in the 19th century. It was another Brit, Alan Turing, who was a key figure in developing modern computers. Tim Berners-Lee was the inventor of the World Wide Web. The list goes on of innovators and creative thinkers from the United Kingdom. The recognition that knowledge should be verified by experience was so central to British science that there was a philosophical movement known as "British Empiricism,"[2] perhaps making those involved in it in the 17th and 18th centuries the first agilists.

An example of someone taking an empirical approach to starting up a new business in the United Kingdom comes from Futhi Mthupha, founder of The Afro Hair Plug.

---

[1]Chesworth, N. (2016). *Freelancing an increasingly attractive option for UK workers*. raconteur. net. www.raconteur.net/freelancing-an-increasingly-attractive-option-for-uk-workers/

[2]The Basics of Philosophy. *British Empiricism*. www.philosophybasics.com/movements_british_empiricism.html

Chapter 15 | United Kingdom

User-Centered Research to Plug the Afro Hair Problem

The Afro Hair Plug stemmed from a simple question, "Where can I get my hair done right?"

I was living in Plymouth and unable to find the answer to this question. My only option was to travel all the way to London to a hairdresser I knew and trusted, a journey of five hours. This might seem unnecessary, but having confidence in our hair is integral to many people like me in the Afro-Caribbean community.

I was born and raised in Swaziland, but moved to the United Kingdom when I was 16. My professional background is in Business Analysis, and I have been working in Agile teams in large financial organizations for a number of years now. I see it as my job to understand, create, and improve how processes and services are working to make people's lives better.

My lengthy journey between Plymouth and London got me thinking if I was the only person who had experienced this problem. The best line up or bantu knots could have been right on my doorstep, but not knowing where to find a trusted stylist was a problem for me. The more I looked, the more I noticed how little visibility there seemed to be for afro hair services, and the whole BLM movement has highlighted the lack of diversity and inclusivity in the hair and beauty industry. I made it my mission to "further the movement of afro hair positivity."

However, all I had was the perception of one person, namely, me. I teamed up with a user research expert, and together, we took a User-Centered Design approach to learn about others with afro hair. We invited people via social media to complete a survey and had approximately 50 responses. The answers gave me greater confidence that I was onto something.

We believed the simplest solution to the problem would be to create a directory that would enable people with afro hair to connect with stylists. The idea was that stylists can list their business and build a profile of their work to show what they offer, while customers can find professionals that provide what they need. We brought in a developer to help create a simple website, just enough to launch and test if anyone would use it. The Afro Hair Plug was born!

Our user research continued, and we carried out interviews with stylists and salons. A key issue seemed to be how people viewed their own business. We found some salons provide afro hair services, but you would never know by looking at their website or shop window. Images were of people with long, straight hair only, for example. Or there were those that saw an opportunity to diversify, without understanding what it really means. It was clear that in

Adopting Agile Across Borders 289

some cases, hairdressers would need further specific training to be able to properly style afro hair as well as make themselves more visible to customers looking for those services. We have found ourselves giving advice, and I can see The Afro Hair Plug evolving to provide services such as marketing and guidance in setting up a business to provide services for afro hair.

The Afro Hair Plug has only been operating for six months, and those of us involved are developing it alongside our day jobs. When I look back, I am surprised at what we have achieved in such a short time. I am used to having to go through organizational red tape to get anything done in my roles as a Business Analyst, but we have shown what can be done when decisions are made quickly and there is focus.

What has helped us progress is really understanding our user, both people searching for afro hair stylists and the professional stylists themselves. By talking to all of the users of our service we are learning to design solutions suitable for them. As a BA in large organizations, it is rare that I have actually been able to talk to the end customer. Usually I am given second-hand information, or at best, get to do some call listening with customer services. Our Human-Centered Design approach at the Afro Hair Plug puts us closer to people's real problems. This for me is the most important thing we can do to come up with the best solution.

—Futhi Mthupha, Business Analyst and Founder of The Afro Hair Plug

---

Takeaway Just the right amount of research. In her story, Futhi is a prime example of taking the Lean Startup approach. She put the user at the center of everything and progressed iteratively through validated learning with just the right amount of effort to take her business to the next level at each stage. For example, she started with surveys to confirm her hypothesis that there was a problem to be solved. Then she and her team came up with a simple solution to the immediate problem by providing a portal to connect customers with stylists. She has continued to iterate, evolving the business to provide marketing and specialist afro hair advice as they better understood professional stylist's needs.

The United Kingdom has an almost unique class system, where historically people would identify as "working class," "middle class," or "upper class." Traditionally, positions of power, be it in politics or in organizations, were based on class, hereditary rights, and longevity. Though taking longer than perhaps other European countries and there is still some way to go in many places, meritocratic systems are becoming more of the norm. While the United Kingdom is regarded as a rich country, there are distinctions to be

Chapter 15 | United Kingdom

made based on wealth, education, profession, and family background. In recent decades, the United Kingdom has seen an expansion of the middle classes, yet also growing levels of inequality[3, 4] in another hint of individualism.

Agile is widely established, with most software development companies and departments adopting some form of agility. XP and DevOps practices are widespread and at the stage where they could be considered as industry standard. And Agile is spreading beyond IT departments with many organizations seeking business agility.

The true Agile mindset is a major culture shift from the management methods borne out of the Industrial Revolution that have become ingrained into the culture. The United Kingdom and many other economies built on the Industrial Revolution are made up of many organizations that have been established for decades, if not centuries. Some of these have grown to become massive in scale. Even here, it is common for these historically successful companies to be attempting Agile adoptions. The transition in-progress in many cases results in adoptions where there are anti-patterns to be ironed out. Product Owners and teams that are not truly empowered and trusted, command and control management, insistence on making long-term plans, treating estimates and forecasts as promises. It could take time, years, or even decades for these sorts of organizations to move on from methods that have been the way to do things for centuries. The danger is that in the meantime more nimble competitors take an unassailable lead.

■ **Takeaway** Trust and empower Product Owners. One of the most common anti-Agile patterns that we saw on our journey is when people are made Product Owner, but not given the proper autonomy that the role demands. The intent behind the role is lost when Product Owners are treated as proxy order takers and have no decision-making power. Agile teams, including the accountabilities of the Product Owner, are most effective when they are trusted and the right level of autonomy given to them.

In the following story, Jon Pheasey, a Senior Software Test Engineer, shares his experience in busting the silos that are commonly seen in many UK companies.

---

[3]*The Scale of Economic Inequality in the UK.* The Equality Trust. www.equalitytrust.org.uk/scale-economic-inequality-uk#:~:text=Compared%20to%20other%20developed%20countries%20the%20UK%20has%20a%20very,fourth%20most%20unequal%20in%20Europe

[4]Barnard, H. (2017). *UK Poverty 2017.* Joseph Rowntree Foundation. www.jrf.org.uk/report/uk-poverty-2017

Busting Silos

Functional silos exist when building software – there is no getting away from it!

When I started as a software tester, I worked in a very large organization using something called the V-model which seems to have very much gone the way of waterfall in recent years. Though it is now quite rare to find people that have used it, there are a few organizations that still seem to follow the V-model, where a "verification" stage follows each development phase, and only when the development phase is complete.

During this first testing role, I found it incredibly difficult to get anything from development teams. My requests for information were almost always denied and I was instead asked constantly to raise tickets, bugs, defects, etc. when all I wanted was to get answers to a couple of questions. I remember one occasion, when digging through a particularly complicated functional specification and finding that the software I was testing simply did not conform to all of the user requirements, an idea like a bolt of lightning came to me: I could go and speak to the developer.

Working my way down through the office felt like being in a scene from a Western when a stranger has just walked into town. As I passed the software development manager, all eyes seemed to look in my direction. Passing developer after developer, I found the person that I needed to speak with. But rather than ending in a Mexican standoff, he was actually delighted that for once, somebody had come to him, proactively asking questions about a piece of software. We soon agreed the documentation did not make sense. It turned out that he was also in a cycle of hand-offs and had not felt able to go and talk to the author of the document. Within a few minutes, another silo was broken when we did just that.

Over the next few years this developer and I built up a great relationship where we would review the specification documents we received together. We would also review test scripts so that I could get feedback form the developer before running them. This level of collaboration was fairly revolutionary for such a large organization, and what we were doing seemed to inspire others to do the same. What were called "daily catch-ups" started happening, where developers, testers, and analysts came together to talk about what had been done in the last 24 hours, and what to do next. Although, at first we sat in a meeting room for this, what we were doing later became known to us as a "stand-up."

We had system testers and developers working much closer together. The next hurdle was UAT!

Chapter 15 | United Kingdom

User acceptance testing was handled by an offsite team where the end customer was based. At the time, the only interactions between the UAT team and us was in a once-a-week call, and of course when there were bugs to be reported. So, a Project Manager started including them in our daily meetings so we could assess the progress of the software that we had sent to them. Later, this was expanded to include the live support team.

I later found out that the UAT team were unable to see all defects which were being raised within other parts of the development process. This seemed very wrong to me, I believed that all people involved should be able to see all issues which had been raised and so it was ensured that everyone had access to the bug tracking software.

These simple steps gave greater transparency and allowed us to maintain openness with all of the stakeholders. We also had a wall covered in "post-it" notes in our area of the office to visualize the flow of work through the testing process. "Waiting," "Doing," and "Done" columns was all that was needed, but it ensured that all items for a release from Development were tested before being ready for UAT and progress that we were making toward each release was easily understood by taking a look at the wall. The system had such great ease of use that the wall became the master artifact for understanding what was going on, with our tracking software relegated to a supplementary tool.

The new ways of working led to us completing our testing quicker than anybody else had in the organization's history, helping the project to be completed earlier than planned. Our team became known as "The Silo Busters." It was a great name to have to recognize how we had brought different functions closer together, but I remember thinking at the time, "Why are people not already doing this? Why is this something seen to be so different?"

When it became time for me to change organizations, I thought this way of working, where functional silos no longer exist, would be the norm. I looked forward to starting afresh and working directly with developers and business analysts. The truth however, was that I have found many organizations continuing to very much have silos between testing and development where never the twain shall meet.

I have made it a goal of mine to try remove such silos where they exist. This has sometimes led to conflict with some managers, but when siloes are broken down, the benefits are there to see.

Functional silos exist when building software – there is no getting away from it, unless you make an effort to remove them!

The transparency, free flow of information and quick decision making that comes with busting siloes is a true must-have for an Agile environment.

—Jon Pheasey, Senior Software Test Engineer

Adopting Agile Across Borders

■ **Takeaway** Break down silos. Jon's story is not unique. Many organizations, whether formally adopting Agile or not, have silos of different functions, teams, and individuals leading to bottlenecks, increased lead-times, waste, lack of collaboration, and frustration. Agile methods encourage breaking silos down and having cross-functional teams that have all the skills on the team needed so that the team can work independently. Many organizations focus improvement efforts on making individual functions more efficient. The real gains can be made by reducing the waste and inefficiencies caused by hand-offs and communication between functions.

David Leach, an experienced Agile ways of working coach, shares a story of one company in the United Kingdom experimenting with their ways of working to come up with new innovative ideas and products.

Helping a Business to Innovate and Inspire

I'm sure we have all heard strategies that talk about leading markets, sustainable profit growth, and shareholder value but what does that actually mean to our teams? At reed.co.uk we asked ourselves this same question. In 2014, after many years of trialing different methodologies to support creating valuable timely software changes for customers, we realized that many of the inefficiencies ran deeper than just how software was designed, built, and released to customers.

Teams around the building were siloed, they had contradicting objectives and separate budgets. The products we built and sold access to (subscriptions) were nearing the end of life or growth was slowing. We were increasing turnover by charging our current customers more which wasn't going to be sustainable. So off the back of the move to Scrum for our development teams we looked to make some other deeper changes across the rest of the business and trial new ways of working.

The moment was Halloween 2014, our bi-annual hackathon. We had been doing hackathons for a few years, but this year would be very different. Traditionally hackathons were a software thing and traditionally to build digital features. This year we instead invited the whole organization and encouraged teams to consider new markets we could enter and new business models. We hoped to be creating completely new businesses and not just new features.

Our Technology Director at the time had the view that a great team could build any product, learn any new technology, and test the waters in any market. So we put this hypothesis to the test. We sold the idea successfully to our Strategic Board that the output of the hackathon shouldn't be shiny new features (most of which never actually made it to customers) but instead new business and product ideas that the board would vote on to determine if we wanted to form some internal startups.

Chapter 15 | United Kingdom

The idea quickly went further, the winning teams would not only be given more time after the hackathon to formulate a business plan but also the potential to move to an entirely different location and work on developing the proposition.

So off we went with planning the hackathon; our Scrum Masters had all read Eric Ries' book *The Lean Startup*,[5] and we familiarized ourselves with the Lean Canvas,[6] MIT Disciplined Entrepreneurship,[7] and New Product Development.[8] This was to train teams to have the best chance to formulate successful propositions, target markets, develop personas and MVPs, to reinforce that MVP was a chance to learn, not about releasing code, and to try and earn money immediately.

We already had 10% learning time in place on a Friday afternoon so we could use this time to train the theory and ideas.

We already had a research and development team but the ideas generated were seemingly either so leading edge that we didn't know how to integrate them into the customer experience or seemed like duplication of what the feature teams were already doing. This hackathon was the chance to get everyone thinking about disruptive innovation.

We had also recently visited Toyota at their Derbyshire-based plant where we got to see TPS (Toyota Production System) in action. The thing we really noticed was the efficiency of the production line and all the things we had tried to bring to the teams following in the footsteps of the great work of Jeremy Liker[9] and Mary and Tom Poppendieck[10] such as removing waste and increasing customer focus and value. However, what became clear was that at Toyota, improvements came from an element of certainty that what was being built had customer value, and the encouragement of kaizen – a series of small improvements.

---

[5]Ries, E. (2011). The Lean Startup: How Constant Innovation Creates Radically Successful Businesses. Portfolio Penguin. ISBN-13: 978-0670921607

[6]Lean Canvas. LeanStack. https://leanstack.com/leancanvas

[7]Disciplined Entrepreneurship www.d-eship.com/

[8]Adams, M. (2015). *Step-by-step guide to bootstrapping your new product development – Part 1, Principles*. Endjin. https://endjin.com/blog/2015/03/step-by-step-guide-to-bootstrapping-your-new-product-development-part-1-principles

[9]Liker, J. (2004). *The Toyota Way: 14 Management Principles from the World's Greatest Manufacturer*. McGraw-Hill Education; Reissue edition (16 Jan. 2004). ISBN-13: 978-0071392310

[10]Poppendieck, Mary and Tom. (2003). *Lean Software Development: An Agile Toolkit*. Addison-Wesley Professional. ISBN-13: 978-0321150783

Adopting Agile Across Borders 295

What we craved was some disruptive innovation. At Toyota they had a completely separate area for proof of concepts, so we also wanted to try this separation between the growing and mature products and these conceptual propositions. Our board was at a point where they were comfortable for a small percentage of the year's investment in change being allocated to this experimental work. So we grabbed the opportunity to truly innovate, not just in generating the ideas themselves but also the way we generated, articulated, and validated the ideas.

The time for the hackathon arrived. The format was for a 36-hour hackathon, split into two elements. The first 12 hours was idea generation and team formation, then 24 hours to create the business model/proposition. After the initial 12 hours we had 20+ ideas ranging from small pivots of current products to completely different propositions to be tested in new markets in new regions. After an afternoon of discussion, 10 teams formed to spend 24 hours working through creating new propositions. My team, for example, had the idea of a business like Goodreads where like-minded people could create book clubs and knowledge share. Sadly we finished 4th (against the judging criteria – see Table 15-1) as our route to profit was via an Amazon buyout. We had relatively low confidence that was possible. Confidence and uncertainty were words we were getting more comfortable with.

Table 15-1. Example Judges criteria

Criteria	Score (out of 10)	Comments
Proposition	8	Able to clearly articulate the need being met
Customer personas	7	Understands the different potential customer types and which will be targeted for an MVP
Beachhead (initial target) market	10	Target market very clear with a marketing and sales plan
Understanding of how to make money	5	Not entirely clear yet other than creating an engaged community
Stated needs/resources for next stage	8	Identified needs across dev, test, marketing, and sales
Customer journey	7	Wireframes and prototypes created as part of the hackathon

I was so proud of what was achieved, the team really took to it, they used the training and canvases to embrace the approach and language. We had ten pretty robust propositions and well-thought-through customer value and target markets. For many propositions, we were not completely sure how to make money, but that was where the learning started.

Chapter 15 | United Kingdom

Then the next hurdle. The top 3 as scored by the board of directors were given another week to work together on the business plan. We sat down as a team to ensure the winning teams had some time each day to commit to the task, as well as also using their 10% time. They all had day jobs, ranging from people in sales to our Head of Service Delivery, so we needed to ensure they were supported and given a fair opportunity.

A week later, the winning cross-functional teams from the hackathon met with our Chairman and walked through their business plan. He loved all of them and he was happy for them to spend an initial three months exploring with target customers the potential value of the product/service.

At this point we took the outcome to our Operations Board. The Operations Board differs from the Strategic Board that judged the winning hackathon propositions. They are a group ensuring the successful execution of the strategy and day-to-day effectiveness of the business and we had a lot of pushback to disrupting the current teams and resource commitments.

We spent time discussing that innovation, skills development, and growth in new and existing markets was core to our strategy and then how we could cover and backfill roles. It gave development opportunities and promotion opportunities to other team members. Some roles could be filled in a matter of weeks, others would require cover and take a bit longer, and some we wouldn't cover as we would review if the person was in a team where the startup went beyond six months. A sensible and pragmatic approach, the Operations Board was convinced and we were given the green light to proceed.

After a few months of planning, preparation, and handovers, we were ready. We also secured a small space above a Reed recruitment office, redesigned it, and then moved the teams in in early 2015. Figure 15-1 shows one of the teams as they moved into the new office space.

Adopting Agile Across Borders

Figure 15-1. One of our internal startup teams when they moved into their new office space

In one example, the team in charge of the initiative called "Startup Startup" (also known as Startup2) moved into the office in March 2015 and a product was launched to market after a lot of research in June 2015. The landing page is shown in Figure 15-2. Startup Startup aspired to be the platform where talent connected in order to create awesome startups. The vision was for a platform that would attract and build a startup community.

Chapter 15 | United Kingdom

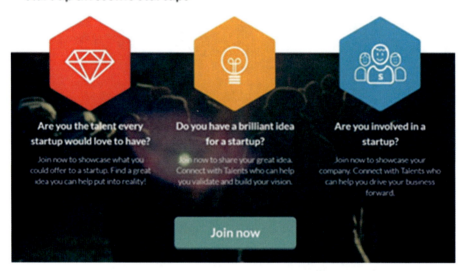

Figure 15-2. Startup Startup website landing page

The small team embraced the idea that they were the whole team; while they didn't have the same financial reality of other startups, that is, a small runway of funds that if not replenished would mean bankruptcy, they did have to learn to be self-sufficient in all other aspects. There were no specialist teams from reed.co.uk to lean on for support, from marketing to sales to financial modelling to development and testing. The four people in the team were the entire business.

At the first of the gates the team were very honest about the fact that they had a lot of interest from the huge startup community in London (150,000 users had spent 10,000 hours engaging) but they had no real idea how money could be made. The goal of the first gate was to determine market size, confirm personas, and engage with an initial community, so success thus far.

However, the question mark remained over how the growing and engaged community could lead to a product that had a growing and sustainable revenue stream. This made the Strategic Board nervous, and with each stage gate the confidence dropped until the point in late 2015 at the third gate when the decision was taken to stop active development and reduce the team. The product was then taken offline in May 2016.

Adopting Agile Across Borders

It was a disappointment as the community that was created met regularly and offered genuine support for helping shape ideas and provide skills needed within the London, wider UK, and international startup community. Sadly it seemed to fall somewhere between a job board and meetup.com so in itself didn't articulate enough value to mean people would subscribe to a service to access the community.

A pretty awesome failure. So you might think anyway. But the team learned so much about our customer base and successfully invalidated many of the hypotheses from the original hackathon.

These could have been expensive failures had we chosen to invest in developing them in the way we always had with traditional products and projects. While we talked about MVP, our solution often was many weeks of software development to validate a hypothesis and often resulted in unused features that remained customer facing or at best with feature flags switched off, which still adds cost and complexity to the product.

We had failed, but had failed with greater ambition, faster and cheaper than ever before.

What happened to the team you ask? They have all gone on to great things. One is the founder of lovethesales.com and another is now the Head of Product at another global job board, after three years back at reed.co.uk growing sales. All the team members loved the experience of working in the internal startups, and they all brought knowledge and a new mindset back into the teams they rejoined.

Of the other two ideas, one was metrodesk.com (renting out spare desks in London, which may have given WeWork a run for its money) which ceased after the second gate due to an inability to either grow a user base or have a solid plan for how the commission model would be profitable and sustainable. There was also a challenge over insurance and liability of renting space within an existing business. We were so far away from our main recruitment business model that these types of conversations again made our Strategic Board a little uncomfortable.

The third startup was another platform focused on matching people with franchises, in financial terms this was the most successful, due to it leaning on an existing reed.co.uk customer group and reusing some elements of existing products. It became more about the sales and marketing channels and pricing of the solution, so we had greater confidence in the outcome.

The product quickly became Reed Commercial, so the team moved back to the main office and as a product offering sat alongside our main activity and over time is now back as a feature of the flagship mature product website reed.co.uk given the growing and sustainable nature of the proposition.

Chapter 15 | United Kingdom

The original problem statement for Reed Commercial was that customers looking for franchises lacked sufficient signposting for where to find information on the broader questions around taking on a franchise and then once they were comfortable being matched to a franchise. The user experience findings from the startup activity allowed the journeys, information architecture, and signposting within the main product to be changed. Without the focus of the startup this would have been activity that was unlikely to occur so Reed's growth in the franchise market may never have occurred.

The team learnt a lot and the business even more. We put all our theory into practice, we helped the business understand the markets in which it thrived and the product that it wanted to strategically invest in for the year to come. The experience helped Reed to understand its own tolerance of risk. While the idea of investing in startups was attractive, it helped everyone discover where the limits lay. This was a great lesson to learn as it fed into the overall strategic view of the business as a whole for the future.

I remain extremely proud of the fact that we were able to execute a hackathon and training, then fed into the creation of startups. I am grateful to the board of directors for being open to trying something new and supporting it through to a conclusion. The board of directors talked a lot about a culture of diversity, learning, curiosity, and creativity and we really put that to the test.

If you don't fail at least 90% of the time, you aren't aiming high enough.

—Alan Kay, Computer Scientist
—David Leach, Ways of Working Coach

■ **Takeaway** Come to the team with problems to be solved. Professional people that carry out knowledge work are problem solvers. We should be hiring people and building teams of smart people capable of solving complex problems. If we create teams to carry out tasks assigned to them, to implement solutions that have been designed from outside the team, we lose the opportunity to tap into the team's creativity and find the best solution. So hire smart people and unleash them on problems to be solved and goals to be achieved.

Getting On and Around

The United Kingdom's parliamentary system where decisions are arrived at through open debate has been imitated all around the world, and is a reflection of a culture valuing fairness and giving everyone a voice. Sharing views is generally respected, but ensure that it is done with diplomacy and sensitivity.

Adopting Agile Across Borders

The communication style may appear to others as vague and people do not say what they really mean. This may be frustrating and may seem as if people are being untruthful. The reality is that on many occasions, they are simply trying to be diplomatic and are trying to avoid direct confrontation. Criticism is often veiled and recipients unused to the communication pattern may miss it completely. The same applies for praise or celebration, with responses generally understated (unless it involves soccer!). A default demeanor is to appear to be casual and laid back, but be aware that beneath the surface the reality may be very different.

Be aware that most business and interactions are conducted in a transactional way so that results can be achieved and actions identified, while relationship building is a secondary concern.

The use of humor is endemic and can be cutting. The best approach is to accept it "in good humor" and meet people well stocked with your own jokes and anecdotes. Humor is used for multiple purposes: as a tactic to relieve tension, to disguise criticism, introduce ideas, and as a form of relationship building.

"Small talk" may also appear to be a form of relationship building. This is an almost unwritten rule where any meeting, formal or not, starts with a discussion on anything from the weather, sports, family, or TV. This continues for a few minutes before formalities begin. For formal meetings, this also serves the purpose of filling the time and silence while waiting for some of the attendees that arrive a few minutes late – something that happens commonly. With a desire for fair debate and risk aversion, don't be surprised if meetings result in inaction and instead there needs to be a period of reflection or further analysis before decisions can be made. Spontaneous decision making is a rare occurrence, and it is common to be invited to a meeting where the agenda is to prepare for another meeting.

The United Kingdom is an open-minded country and many of its people could be described as non-conformist. Eccentricities are common and tolerated. A casual appearance that brings with it creativity and inventiveness in the likes of professors, scientists, and computer programmers is a stereotype that stands up in actuality. Few are the organizations that now insist on IT people wearing smart business dress.

While true of just about every country, there is a rich diversity of subcultures in the United Kingdom, perhaps richer than expected given its size. As well as differences between the countries within a country – England, Scotland, Wales, and Northern Ireland – the people of London have a culture all of their own that is quite incomparable with the cultures found in the North of England, for example.

Chapter 15 | United Kingdom

Agile Community Events and Meetups

- Kanban Coaching Exchange: www.meetup.com/Kanban CoachingExchangeKCE/

- Agile Coaching Exchange: www.meetup.com/ACE-Agile-Coaching-Exchange/

- Aginext Community: www.aginext.io/

- Agile on the Beach: https://agileonthebeach.com/

- Agile for Agencies: www.meetup.com/agileforagencies/

- Women in Agile London: www.meetup.com/Women-in-Agile-London-UK/

- Red Tangerine Across Borders: www.meetup.com/meetup-group-redtangerine-org/

PART

V

Africa

The continent of Africa is made up of 54 countries at the time of writing,[1] more than any other. It is also the most culturally diverse,[2] with the number of languages spoken estimated to be up to 2,000,[3] and the second most populous after Asia.

A history of repression and political unrest has left the majority of the continent underdeveloped in comparison with most of the rest of the world and a legacy of problems to solve. After centuries of damaging occupation by foreign powers, there can be a general distrust of anything from overseas, with a widespread belief that African problems need African solutions. Agile then, faces a challenge of gaining acceptance. And yet we still discovered pockets of Agile alongside a growing technology industry, with some people seeing Agile as one way of solving their complex problems.

Africa's people are known to be warm, hospitable, and optimistic, and they have a great sense of humor. There are signs that values aligned with agility such as transparency, continuous learning and collaboration are being embraced, which could contribute to the continent's vast potential being unleashed.

Agile Community Events and Meetups

- Agile in Africa: https://agileinafrica.com/

---

[1]*How many countries in Africa.* Worldometer. www.worldometers.info/geography/how-many-countries-in-africa/

[2]Morin, R. (2013). *The most (and least) culturally diverse countries in the world.* Pew Research Center. www.pewresearch.org/fact-tank/2013/07/18/the-most-and-least-culturally-diverse-countries-in-the-world/#:~:text=A%20comparison%20of%20the%20Harvard,more%20diverse%20than%20the%20US

[3]*Introduction to African Languages.* Harvard University. https://alp.fas.harvard.edu/introduction-african-languages

CHAPTER

16

South Africa

The early 21st century is seeing South Africa emerging as a leading light for Africa. It is one of the most multicultural nations on earth, with a mix of indigenous groups such as the Zulu and Xhosa, and a number of communities heralding from overseas from the likes of Britain, the Netherlands, and India. These separate cultural forces have been a source of tension and troubles in the past, but as the society learns to integrate with one another and with a growing Agile movement, there is vast potential to be unleashed.

History

An area dubbed "The Cradle of Humankind" to the Northwest of Johannesburg is the archaeological site where some of the oldest human fossils in the world have been found. These and other finds provide evidence of hominid existence in South Africa from at least 2.5 million years ago, with modern humans having formed settlements around 125,000 years or so ago. The DNA of these people has been traced to still be present in the indigenous Khoisan people today. Expansion by people from the Congo basin reached South Africa in the 4th century, conquering and dispersing further afield many of the original tribes.

The Cape of Good Hope got its name from the Portuguese king, John II, as the route led to the riches of the East Indies. The Portuguese explorer, Bartolomeu Dias, was the first to sail around the southern tip of Africa in the late 15th century, but by the early 17th century, it was the British and Dutch that dominated the seas. A shipwreck resulted in two employees of the Dutch East Company surviving on the Cape for months courtesy of the indigenous

© Glaudia Califano, David Spinks 2021
G. Califano and D. Spinks, *Adopting Agile Across Borders*,
https://doi.org/10.1007/978-1-4842-6948-0_16

Chapter 16 | South Africa

people and the fertile land. On their return, they reported back on the area's potential and the Dutch East India Company established a station at what became Cape Town.[1]

Many Dutch people settled in the area, with many others brought in from the colonies of Indonesia and other parts of Africa, adding to the cultural mix. As they expanded eastward, the Dutch colonists fought a series of wars with the Xhosa people, a group of several indigenous tribes.

In the late 18th century, in the name of preventing it falling under the control of the French, the British invaded the Cape colony. After control switched between the British and Dutch a couple of times, it formally became part of the British Empire after the end of the Napoleonic Wars. British colonists began settling from around 1820 and many of the Dutch migrated to the North and East.

Meanwhile, Shaka Zulu, originally exiled as an illegitimate son of Senzangakona, King of the Zulus, had returned to become chief after Senzangakona's death. Shaka introduced important military and political reforms, reorganizing the Zulu clan into a well-organized state. Under Shaka, the Zulu empire aggressively grew and expanded its territories.

The discovery of gold and diamonds later in the century swung British interest inland and their efforts at gaining control over the entire region. In 1879, the Anglo-Zulu war was fought between the British and the Zulu, resulting in British victory and annexation of the Zulu kingdoms. *Vrijburgers*, ex-Dutch East Company employees and their descendants that also became known as *Boers*, had settled into their own independent republics. They formed their own militias and used guerrilla warfare tactics to repel the British in the first Boer War in 1880 to 1881, but were overcome in the Second Boer War between 1899 and 1902. A few years later, in 1910, the British negotiated the combination of the various colonies, creating a new self-governing country and dominion of the British Empire, the Union of South Africa. In 1931, the Statute of Westminster 1931 was passed in the United Kingdom, effectively giving immediate, or on ratification, legislative independence to South Africa as well as the likes of Australia, New Zealand, Canada, and others.

The ownership of land by indigenous people was mostly inhibited and black people were denied the right to vote. The ruling National Party classified people by law according to one of three races, Black, White, and Colored, with legal rights developed for each. A classification of Asian was added as another group later. The system of racial segregation became known as *apartheid* ("apartness" in the language of Afrikaans). The black majority were disadvantaged in just about every element of life. Opposition organizations

---

[1]Wilmot, A. and John Chase, J. C. *History of the Colony of the Cape of Good Hope: From Its Discovery to the Year 1819*. Nabu Press; (2010 edition). ISBN-13: 978-1144830159

Adopting Agile Across Borders

such as the African National Congress (ANC) emerged and South Africa came under international pressure because of its policies. In a referendum open to whites only in 1961, the country voted to become a republic. The new Republic of South Africa withdrew from the Commonwealth group of countries. The Constitution Act of 1983 removed the office of Prime Minister, making the President head of government as well as the head of state.

What was to be a remarkable political transition started in 1974 when the Mahlabatini Declaration of Faith was signed by Zulu tribal leader, Mangosuthu Buthelezi, and Harry Schwarz, a political opposition leader against apartheid. The declaration acted as a foundation for the future development of the country. It laid out a set of principles that included change without the use of violence, giving opportunity for all and the creation of a Bill of Rights. It was in 1990 that the ban on the ANC and other opposition political organizations was lifted. In the same year, Nelson Mandela, an anti-apartheid leader who had been sentenced to life in 1962 for leading a campaign to oppose apartheid rule, was released from prison. Following negotiations between the political parties and approval from the white population in a referendum to end apartheid, South Africa's first elections, where all adult citizens had the right to vote, were held in 1994, which the ANC with Nelson Mandela as its leader won comprehensively.

Mandela's government set about facilitating the end of racial conflict. The country rejoined the international community. It became part of the commonwealth and joined the Southern African Development Community. Mandela elaborated on a phrase first used by Archbishop Desmond Tutu to describe post-apartheid South Africa, and the country came to be referred to as "The Rainbow Nation" in reference to its cultural diversity.

Progress was made in giving millions access to electricity, water, housing, healthcare, and education for children. Nevertheless, Mandela's and successive administrations have continued to grapple with huge inequality. While some black people could be said to have risen into the middle classes, unemployment has remained high. A set of policies called Black Economic Empowerment (BEE) was created with the aim of addressing inequality, but there were many criticisms of it, including that its benefits were too narrow. In 2003, the government introduced the Broad Based Black Economic Empowerment (BBBE) program, with a Code of Good Practice published in 2007. This was then updated in 2015, and debate continues as the government continues to grapple with policies that are fair and meets the goals of reversing the effects of apartheid. The following story comes from Khwezi Mputa, a Scrum Master who shares a story demonstrating the courage needed to speak out on the subject as a black woman working in South Africa.

Chapter 16 | South Africa

Finding My Voice

I have worked as an IT professional since 2008 and throughout my journey as a black female in the IT industry working mostly in the private sector, I observed a certain common trait that some of my black female counterparts had. I noticed that when among each other we were boisterous, opinionated, confident, and had great ideas, but this was somehow silenced when in the presence of our white colleagues. Having been a drama student in high school that starred in school plays, self-confidence was always something that I had.

One day, while sitting in a meeting, I remember the CEO of the company I worked for at the time posed a challenge that he asked the attendees to assist in solving. I remember having a great idea but strangely not having the ability to raise my hand and share it with the audience. It was then that I realized that I too had been silenced. I asked myself what had brought upon me this silence, what was holding me back from sharing my thoughts and opinion? It dawned on me that although my direct line manager was also a person of color, an Indian female, I had never seen her challenge her white counterpart or seniors, she would always just agree with them. In the company that I worked for, I had never seen any black woman or person of color challenging any senior (who were all white) even if their idea would be more beneficial. I started having conversations with other black females and they shared a similar sentiment. In corporate South Africa, the reality is that most black females are quota hires to satisfy a BEE rating (Black Economic Empowerment, also known as affirmative action) and because of this, there is an unspoken sad truth that had it not been for BEE, we would probably not have been hired in a predominantly white workspace.

As black women, we diminish our authenticity in fear of making others uncomfortable and limit our professional growth. We have been conditioned to believe that our opinion has no weight as a result of being quota hires, even if it is the same opinion as our white female or male counterparts. It is this conditioning that silences us. In my own journey I have witnessed black females that were vocal in the workplace being labelled loud and too aggressive, and they were not taken seriously because of this labelling. In one company I have also witnessed a female of color being demoted after challenging her seniors with a suggestion that could have been beneficial but because it was different, or went against that of the dominant majority, she was even eventually pushed out of the company. Then a week later, a white male suggested the same idea as his own and it was accepted. Was this the reason why so many of us were silent and how long would our silence last? Far too many of us were opting to be victims instead of victors, I realized that my silence would not help this problem. As a mother of two black girls, into who I try to instill the value of self-worth every day, what example would I be setting if I was not a model of this in my day-to-day life? I knew I had to be the leader that I needed to learn from, and this gave me the courage to find my voice in the workplace. From that day forward I made a conscious decision to never be silenced and to lead by example even if by doing so, I would limit my professional growth.

> *Make sure you don't start seeing yourself through the eyes of those who do not value you nor your opinion. Know your worth even if they don't.*

> —Dr. Thema Bryant Davis, psychologist, ordained minister, and sacred artist

I hope to inspire other black females to find their voices if they have been silenced, in the hope of changing corporate South Africa and also influence the corporate culture round the world to one day hire black females on merit and not because the company had to satisfy a BEE rating.

> —Khwezi Mputa, Certified Scrum Master/Agile PM Practitioner

Continued immigration from other parts of Africa, much of which has been illegal, has been another cause of further racial unrest.[2] Other challenges that are being tackled include reducing crime and corruption, addressing infrastructure and transport issues, and dealing with the HIV/AIDS epidemic. This is before the impact of the coronavirus pandemic.

At the time of writing, South Africa has the second largest economy in Africa after Nigeria when measured by GDP.[3] The economy is highly developed with established financial, legal, energy, communications, and transport sectors as well as being one of the world's biggest exporters of gold, platinum, diamonds, and other natural resources. The state is promoting entrepreneurship and an economy based more on digital technology. In a speech in 2019 at the South African Digital Economy Summit, president Cyril Ramaphosa spoke about the government's ambitious plans that included broadband connection for all, teaching coding and data analytics from primary school, pioneering new technologies with the advent of the Fourth Industrial Revolution.[4,5]

---

[2]Crush, J. (editor). (2008). *The perfect storm: the realities of xenophobia in contemporary South Africa.* Southern African Migration Project; Queen's University. ISBN-13: 978-1920118716

[3]Varrella, S. (2019). *African countries with the highest Gross Domestic Product (GDP) in 2019.* www.statista.com/statistics/1120999/gdp-of-african-countries-by-country/#:~:text=GDP%20of%20African%20countries%202019%2C%20by%20country&text=Nigeria's%20GDP%20amounted%20to%20410,second%20highest%20on%20the%20continent

[4](2019). *President Cyril Ramaphosa: South African Digital Economy Summit.* www.gov.za/speeches/president-cyril-ramaphosa-south-african-digital-economy-summit-5-jul-2019-0000

[5](2019). *Ramaphosa at Digital Economy Summit: "SA will retain human capital in 4IR."* The SouthAfrican.www.thesouthafrican.com/news/ramaphosa-digital-economy-summit-sa-retain-human-capital-4ir/

Chapter 16 | South Africa

Insights

The people of South Africa have a wide range of origins, and so there is a great diversity of cultures. The Black African majority can be divided up into various ethnic groups, and people strongly identify with their tribal affiliation, though there has been a decline in cultural traditions in the few that have become more economically mobile compared to the more impoverished that strongly hold on to their traditions. Each tribe has a rich tapestry of beliefs and behaviors of their own. For example, women may be regarded in different ways: in some they would be seen as equal to men, in others much more subservient and certainly discouraged from going into a career in technology.

The rest of the South African population is of European or Asian descent. The country's diversity is demonstrated by the fact that the Constitution names 11 official languages,[6] including English, which is considered a common or "bridging" language.

The "Afrikaners," a group descended from the 17th-century Dutch, German, and French settlers and that slowly developed a culture of their own as they mixed with Africans and Asians, have inherited a communication style that is direct. This is in contrast to the communication style of British descendants, who try to avoid conflict. A history of warfare has left some residual tension between the two groups. Either way, both Afrikaners and British descendants have learned to be inventive, flexible, and decisive, having developed great skill and empathy when negotiating with other cultures at home and internationally.

Other significant groups are the Indian community whose culture has been influenced by exposure to the other groups in the country, and a category classified by the South African government as "Coloured South Africans" which includes people of mixed ethnicity. They belong to socioeconomic groups that are generally relatively affluent, well educated, and highly skilled.

Like many countries, there are regional variations and what could be seen as local cultures. The Southwest, including Cape Town, site of the first overseas settlers, is regarded as more traditional and conservative with a more laid back pace of life, compared to the economic hub of hip, cosmopolitan Johannesburg to the Northeast of the country.

While the spectrum of different cultural groups is wide, there are traits that can be seen widely in South Africa as a whole. There is a sense of looking to the future with optimism, a preparedness to be cooperative, empathetic and sensitive to other cultures, and a willingness to take risks and experiment. People in South Africa can be described as being warm, they love to socialize, and build communities.

---

[6](1966). *Constitution of the RSA, relevant sections.* https://web.archive.org/web/20121113225722/http://www.fs.gov.za/Departments/SAC/Library/DEPART/lang_legislation1.htm

Adopting Agile Across Borders | 311

There is a growing realization that much of the success of the nation depends on the Black majority. There is a recognition of the growing black middle classes and their purchasing power, with brands such as Black Like Me catering specifically for this market. In a part of the world where there is great cultural sensitivity, _respect_ is a watch-word that people are trying their best with: respect for people, not just for their heritage but generation, socioeconomic background, gender, etc. Natural warmth, tolerance, patience, an expressive communication style, and a great sense of humor are behaviors that can help to bridge the differences.

A bigger issue perhaps is actually respect from senior leaders, respect for teams and individuals as professional and competent that should be empowered and not micro-managed. Like in many other parts of the world, it is an unnatural trait to give up control. Instructions are passed down through a hierarchy. Projects are given up-front approval, and run with a planned scope to be delivered to a planned budget and timeline. From our discussions with Scrum Masters in South Africa we found that it is very common for Scrum Masters to be acting as Project Managers, and Product Owners that are simply order takers. Despite a strong social inclination outside of work, the work environment is a competitive place, with a high turnaround of people regularly moving companies to progress their own career. With lots of competition for jobs, rewards and recognition are given to individuals. The shift in thinking that comes from Agile: collective success or failure, empowerment, trust, seeing progress toward goals ahead of keeping people busy, challenges embedded thinking that is creating tension. It is perhaps an individualistic mindset in the workplace more than anything that hampers true agility in many cases.

Agile, and in particular Scrum, has been around for a number of years and there is a general acceptance that it is not an option to not adopt Agile in order to stay competitive. We heard a number of stories of organizations going through a second or third Agile transformation driven by large consultancies, and working out which framework or technique to achieve agility at the enterprise level. Coaches and Scrum Masters that we spoke to were largely positive when it came to people understanding Agile at the team level. SAFe has been a popular technique with the perception of control it still affords managers and more comforting structure to follow.

There are some highly compatible traits for agility. Whatever their background, team members are great communicators and natural storytellers, using visualizations which makes for great collaboration. Given the diverse backdrop of the nation as a whole, people are skilled at understanding and having empathy for one another, be it a teammate or customer. Life in South Africa is challenging and unpredictable – when things such as power outages are common, people have built up an innate ability to adapt to changing circumstances quickly. There is a positivity in the mindset and we heard

Chapter 16 | South Africa

many proverbs all equating to something like "no challenge cannot be overcome." The new generation of employees in particular are showing more of an Agile mindset with courage in spades, developing an attitude to push back, question things, and a desire to work with more autonomy. Transparency is becoming of growing importance and relevance. Many problems, for example, corruption, so long hidden or ignored are now becoming more openly acknowledged and discussed.

■ **Takeaway** Tell stories. We find that some aspects of Agile may appear abstract and hard for people to relate to their everyday working life. This is where storytelling can help. As human beings, our minds connect with stories, they help us to relate to and engage with concepts, bringing them to life so they have applicable meaning. Great Change Agents, Agile Coaches and Scrum Masters are great and inspirational storytellers. Good stories have a beginning, middle, and an end, a protagonist/hero who goes through the story arc of facing a challenge, going on a journey of discovery, through to resolution.

Getting On and Around

South Africa is a relatively masculine society. Women, and especially younger women in roles such as Scrum Master or Product Owner have to prove that they can stand their ground, almost as a right of passage, else be bulldozed by men. While overall people in teams and organizations have good cross-cultural understanding, certain aspects of the idea of openness may be challenging for some with regard to revealing true feelings and emotions, though we have been told that this is less prominent in younger generations. Teams need time to grow comfortable with each other to really open up. Activities that allow the team to socialize together will help here. This is likely to happen naturally anyway.

The competitive nature of the workplace and general challenges of life make for a stressful state of being. Change initiatives such as adopting Agile can only add to this. Humor is a commonly used tool for relieving tensions. It is common for meetings to be started with light-heartedness. Facilitators are advised to try and keep proceedings light and fun in meetings and events as much as possible.

Negotiating the different tribal systems may be daunting, especially to foreigners. But it is important to recognize that there are differences, including what can be age-old rivalries between tribes. As we will discuss later, by leveraging these differences, great gains can be had. Build a true understanding of each other and adapt, while avoiding the formation of old-fashioned alliances, language, and attitudes associated with the apartheid era. It is important to be even-handed and fair to all. Seek out the commonalities that all in a group will share. Scrum Masters, Agile Coaches, and facilitators are advised to listen more than they speak.

In the following stories, we hear from Suwilo Simwanza, a Scrum Master, and Agilist Nono Donsa. Both are experienced practitioners in South Africa, and they each discuss their experiences with the cultural diversity of teams in the country.

Navigating Cultural Differences in the South African Context

One of the most important things that I have learned while being a Scrum Master is never to ignore history, but also don't try and tackle it head on at the same time. It is a very sensitive topic to navigate.

South Africa has had a very recent history of apartheid and it cannot be ignored. I have found that it is easier to work with a diverse younger generation team than a non- or semi-diverse older-generation team. Older people have more experience and may feel like they know better. Younger people are less formal and more eager to try new things. However, my age, 27, makes it easier for me to relate to the younger generations. While someone older might take offense to someone younger guiding them.

What has helped with the teams that I've worked in creating good inter-team relationships is to overcome our cultural differences by establishing a team culture. This is done by:

- **Rules of engagement/Working Agreement**: Allow the team to create the rules by which they will follow. This gives us something that we can reference when things go south. It allows the team to solve whatever issue that they have, cultural or not, based on the rules that they themselves have set. It creates ownership and helps mitigate resentment when some "black" or "white" decides on rules and pushes them down onto the team.

  We do this by gathering the team together to answer the following:

  - What values would they like their teams to follow?

  - How would they like to handle cultural differences?

  - How would they like to deal with conflict?

  - How would they like to communicate?

Chapter 16 | South Africa

- Round robin question: What do you need your team members to do that would enable you to do your work well?

We then base the working agreement content on the answers provided. We also have a run-through of all the rules to make sure that the team asks for clarification where needed.

- **Help the team see each other as humans**: Retros come in super handy here. Retros focused on team appreciation and collaboration go a long way in creating a safe space.

- Retros must focus on problems experienced on the project at first and not on cultural differences. I use self reflection techniques to help the team introspect before they retrospect.

- For example, ask team members to individually reflect on questions such as "**What problem did I face in the Sprint and what could I have done differently?**" It is so easy for team members to speak about how they did not receive help and have resentments. Therefore, having self-reflective questions gives them the opportunity to look at how they can help themselves. When they provide these, the rest of the team learns.

- After this, we can then ask, "How can we as a team work together next time one of us faces this issue?" **A little introspection goes a long way**.

- **No one likes a know it all**: I have learnt to be more humble in inquiry rather than assumption when it comes to culture. Team members in my experience, have been more receptive when I have asked them to teach me. This makes it easier to establish relationships and has made necessary interventions on my part easier to accept by the team. I am as much a part of the team as any other team member, learning and sharing in the same culture that they are a part of. We are all experts in our own right that come together to achieve goals, BAs, Product Owners, Designers, Testers, Scrum Master alike. Therefore we all work to follow the rules we set out ourselves and respect each other's expertise.

—Suwilo Simwanza, Scrum Master

The Impact of Cultural Traits on Agile Adoption

Being an Agile Coach in my country is a very colorful experience. We have a very diverse and multicultural population. This, at times, is reflected in the composition of the teams.

South Africa has a deep and complex history of colonization and racial injustice. The migrant labor system that was put in place by the apartheid government meant that people (mostly black men) had to leave their homelands, to seek employment in the cities (this was in the form of cheap labor in the mines and factories). This migrant labor system led to a dispersion of the various people groups. This remains evident to this day.

I am a black Xhosa woman from the AbaThembu tribe. My ancestors migrated from Central Africa along the east coast before settling in KwaZulu-Natal. With further migrations, our tribe is now mainly concentrated in the Eastern Cape. I studied in the Western Cape and currently work in Gauteng.

This goes to show how the Agile team I am part of in Gauteng, Johannesburg can easily be made up of a rural umThembu lady from the Eastern Cape, an Afrikaans man from a Free State farm, a traditional Indian man from KwaZulu-Natal, a few Zulu-speaking locals from Gauteng, and one person from a neighboring country.

The speedup of movements and exchanges, all over the world (globalization), as well as the improvements in technology also promotes an increase in interactions and exposure to even more cultures and people groups. All this rich diversity comes with ingrained biases which affect the way we consciously or subconsciously interact with one another in our personal lives, as well as our places of work.

The first core value statement within the Manifesto for Agile Software Development states:

Individuals and interactions over processes and tools.

This means allowing each individual the space, opportunity, and time to make their unique contribution. This also means as an Agile Coach, one needs to, as a bare minimum, have some awareness of the cultural diversity that almost certainly always exists within the teams. I believe a good Agile Coach takes the time to understand some of the obvious biases that could exist in the team and the impact that these biases could have. Similarly I believe an excellent Agile Coach gets well versed on the stereotypes that have been projected onto the different people groups and points these out to the team, at the appropriate time, with the necessary sensitivity.

My Agile coaching journey was not without its challenges. Whose is, right?

Chapter 16 | South Africa

I arrived at a new job, excited and starry eyed. "You will be thrown into the deep end" – I was told. I love a challenge and this was exactly what I was hoping to hear.

I was the first team member to arrive and I was escorted to my desk. My plan of action for that day was to observe, nothing more. When the whole team had arrived the Scrum Master mentioned that it was retrospective day and, with my experience as the incoming team coach, he was confident that I would be able to facilitate the session objectively. This was especially important to him because he wanted to participate in the session. His facilitator hat was off.

How hard could it be, right?

I prepared myself and got my mental retro template ready:

1. Set stage
2. Gather data
3. Generate insights
4. Create actions
5. Wrap up

The meeting had been booked, the venue was confirmed, and the Scrum Team arrived.

The setting of the stage went well. The data gathering is when things started to get interesting.

The team was as diverse as they come. We had men and women, all five racial groups as defined by Statistics South Africa (Black, White, Colored, Indian, and Other) and a mixture of tribes within two of the five racial population groups (UmXhosa and UmZulu from the Black population and Telugu and Tamil from the Indian population).

One interaction that is etched in my memory is one between myself and a male team member. He had made a statement and in my quest to get to the "why," I asked some clarifying questions. I was looking him in the eye, as a sign of focused listening and respect. He seemed to get more and more irritated and brash with every second.

It was only a couple of weeks later, after getting better acquainted with the team, that I came to the insight that in his tribe, making eye contact is a sign of a challenge. The fact that I am a woman and I was standing (thus making myself bigger), while he was sitting (making him physically appear yielding), made things difficult for him.

Adopting Agile Across Borders

After I had come to that realization, a tool that assisted me in coaching this diverse team to high performance was the use of the Scrum values. The team had a look at each value and were explicit in terms of what each of these values meant to them. For example, **courage** in action would be that each team member would have the courage to speak up when they felt uncomfortable during a discussion or activity. The team also decided that all of their actions and interactions would be based on a foundation of **respect**. The team was **committed** to creating an environment where all team members were equal and this would foster an environment where everyone could be **open**. The team's intentions were to **focus** not only on the deliverables alone, but working toward a healthy team dynamic.

The interpretation and definition of these values was reviewed regularly, and updated as needed.

My experience has taught me that

1. An Agile Coach needs to, as a bare minimum, have some **awareness of the cultural diversity** that exists, within the teams. Even if it is outside of your experience – get curious about learning more.

2. A good Agile Coach should take the time to **understand some of the obvious biases** that could exist in the team and the impact that these biases could have.

3. An excellent Agile Coach should **get well versed on the stereotypes** that could be projected onto the different people groups and coach the team to recognize and deal with these.

Finally, there was a lot that this team needed to align on, and having an up-front awareness of the diversity and dynamics within the team would perhaps have changed the outcomes of the session.

—Nono Donsa, Agilist

There is unity to be had, after all no one wants to do a bad job and all South Africans want to see their country prosper. There is a South African philosophy called "Ubuntu" translating to "I am, because you are." It derives from the Zulu and Xhosa languages and was popularized in South Africa after apartheid as a founding principle of the new republic of South Africa. Ubuntu is a belief that there is a universal bind of sharing that connects all humanity. Therefore, with this optimism and hope for the future, short-termism or dwelling on the past should be avoided.

Chapter 16 | South Africa

■ **Takeaway** Acknowledge sensitive topics. There will be sensitivities to navigate when any group of people are brought together. This is particularly highlighted in the stories of Khwezi, Suwilo, and Nono in this chapter. Ignoring them, we believe, will do more harm than good. It takes courage and openness, but acknowledging topics of sensitivity with compassion and creating inclusivity is important in an Agile environment where we strive to leverage the diversity available to create high performing teams.

Agile Community Events and Meetups

- Agile Equity South Africa: www.agileequitysa.com/
- New African Voices in Agile: www.meetup.com/new-voices-of-colour/
- Scrum User Group Cape Town – SUGSA: www.meetup.com/Cape-Town-Scrum-User-Group-SUGSA/
- Scrum User Group Johannesburg – SUGSA: www.meetup.com/Scrum-User-Group-Johannesburg/
- Scrum Master Meetup: www.meetup.com/Cape-Town-Scrum-Master-Meetup/
- Durban Agile and Developer User Group Meetup: www.meetup.com/Durban-Agile-User-Group-Meetup/
- Think Agile Neighbourhood: www.meetup.com/Think-Agile-Neighbourhood/
- Women in Agile South Africa: www.meetup.com/Women-in-Agile-South-Africa/
- Flow-ZA: www.meetup.com/Flow-ZA/
- Developer User Group: www.meetup.com/DeveloperUG/

CHAPTER
17

West Africa

In a region on the west side of the continent of Africa, bordered by the Atlantic Ocean to the west and south, and the Sahara Desert to the north, are a number of nation states that include Senegal, Gambia, Guinea, Sierra Leone, Ivory Coast, Ghana, Nigeria, Niger, and Mali. The borders of these countries meant nothing until very recently when they were arbitrarily – at least as far as the indigenous people were concerned – drawn by European colonizers.

Free from foreign rule, the people in this part of the world are still living with past and present exploitation. Despite adversity being part of life for many in West Africa, people are full of warmth, kindness, optimism, and potential. Nigeria is a potential economic powerhouse of the future. Ghana, a soon-to-be major tech hub. And here too, Agile is emerging as a driving force.

History

Archeological evidence found in Mali suggests that people were using pottery and fire for cooking by the 10th millennium BCE.[1] Farming and the keeping of cattle began around the 5th millennium BCE, with the development of iron

---

[1]Bellwood, P. (2014). *The Global Prehistory of Human Migration.* John Wiley & Sons. ISBN-13: 978-1118970591

© Glaudia Califano, David Spinks 2021
G. Califano and D. Spinks, *Adopting Agile Across Borders,*
https://doi.org/10.1007/978-1-4842-6948-0_17

Chapter 17 | West Africa

tools allowing agricultural development and the emergence of tribal settlements. Domestication of the camel enabled trade across regions, including across the Sahara, though the desertification of the Sahara at the time impeded progress.

A succession of early empires came and went, perhaps the most significant of which was the Oyo Empire whose influence between the 15th and the 18th centuries covered modern-day Western and Northern Nigeria, Togo, Benin, and beyond. Much of its success is credited to the organizational skills of the Yoruba ethnic group of the area.

The Portuguese were the first of the European powers to arrive in the region in the 15th century, and they started establishing settlements along the coast, as well as taking hundreds of people back to Portugal as slaves. The Portuguese were soon joined by the French, British, Spanish, and the Dutch. Following Columbus's discovery of the Americas, demand for labor skyrocketed with the trade in African slaves formally legalized by first the Spanish and then the British in the 16th century, leading to centuries of destabilization of West Africa's population and economy. The true number of people enslaved may never be known, but estimates of the Atlantic slave trade alone puts the number at 12.8 million between 1450 and 1900.[2] Due to the large numbers involved, it is believed that most African-Americans have West African heritage.

Growing rivalries between the European powers and the discovery of natural resources further inland, alongside technological advances such as the railway, the telegraph, and medicines for tropical diseases led to what became known as the "scramble for Africa" in the late 19th century. The "Berlin Conference" of 1884, is seen as the starting point of the partition of Africa, though the resultant "General Act" that was agreed did include a clause to end slavery. In just a few short decades, the whole of the continent, apart from Liberia and Ethiopia, was under European control. The British and the French had most influence. Britain had control of the likes of Nigeria and Ghana in the west, Kenya in the east, as well as South Africa. The French largely claimed Central and other Western areas such as Chad and Senegal, with the remaining areas divided up between Portugal, Spain, Italy, Germany, and Belgium.

The dividing lines of the new colonies meant nothing to the indigenous populations. The map had little in common to preexisting tribal and cultural lines. During World War II, in 1941, the British and Americans set out their goals in the Atlantic Charter, which included the declaration to, "respect the right of all peoples to choose the form of government under which they live; and they wish to see sovereign rights and self-government restored to those

---

[2]Lovejoy, P. E. (2012). *Transformations of Slavery: A History of Slavery in Africa.* Cambridge University Press. ISBN-13: 978-0521176187

Adopting Agile Across Borders 321

who have been forcibly deprived of them."[3] The European powers were heavily indebted following the war and keeping control of their colonies was unsustainable. A period of rapid decolonization took place. By 1974, all of the nations of West Africa were independent, with the rest of the continent following suit in the following years.

Though decolonization occurred with little conflict between the occupiers and the indigenous peoples, the damage had already been done. The new countries of West Africa were unprepared for independence. Education for Africans had never been a priority for the colonists and the country's new leaders were ill-prepared to deal with the challenges. Economies were fragile as they were based on crops that were prone to fluctuations in price. The artificial boundaries favored some ethnic groups over others, and the growing tension this caused resulted in a series of brutal and disastrous civil wars and military coups in the likes of Nigeria, Ghana, Liberia, Guinea-Bissau, Côte d'Ivoire, and Sierra Leone. European hunters had decimated the wildlife of West Africa, natural resources that had been tied to the region's cultural identity. Over 90% of West Africa's original rainforests have been destroyed[4] for the logging industry, agriculture, and fuel. West African waters are continuing to be overfished, largely by foreigners who pay meager taxes to do so, or by illegal trawlers.[5] Corruption in politics remains a reality.

There are causes for optimism. Ghana itself has ambitions to become the information technology hub of West Africa.[6] It was the first country in sub-Saharan Africa to launch a mobile phone network in 1992 and one of the first to be connected to the Internet. Education policy is that ICT is to be integrated in teaching and learning at all levels of education.[7] Nigeria, one of the world's largest oil producers, is the largest economy of the region and has been

---

[3](1941). *The Atlantic Charter.* NATO. www.nato.int/cps/en/natohq/official_texts_16912.htm

[4]Nix, S. (2019). *The Territory and Current Status of the African Rainforest.* ThoughtCo. www.thoughtco.com/african-rainforest-1341794

[5]Ighobor, K. (2017). *Overfishing destroying livelihoods.* Africa Renewal. www.un.org/africarenewal/magazine/may-july-2017/overfishing-destroying-livelihoods

[6]Rogers, P. (2019). *Technology evolution helping Ghana become the hub of West Africa.* Intelligent CIO. www.intelligentcio.com/africa/2019/03/26/technology-evolution-helping-ghana-become-the-hub-of-west-africa/

[7]Mereku, D. K., Yidana, I, Hordzi, W., Tete-Mensah, I., Tete-Mensah, W., and Williams, J. B. (2009). *Pan-African Agenda on Pedagogical Integration of ICT Ghana Report.* University of Education, Winneba, Ghana. https://web.archive.org/web/20140808202336/http://www.ernwaca.org/panaf/pdf/phase-1/Ghana-PanAf_Report.pdf

Chapter 17 | West Africa

described as an emerging global power.[8] The Economic Community of West African States (ECOWAS) was created in 1975 to promote economic integration across the region and as a peacekeeping force. Its achievements include overseeing major road construction between the big cities, installing a telephone network between states, stabilizing relationships between former British and French colonies, and introducing policies allowing a smoother and freer movement of people between member states.[9]

Women, largely repressed, are playing a major part in trying to turn the region's fortunes around. The "Women of Liberia Mass Action for Peace"[10], "Women in Peacebuilding Network" (WIPNET) (part of the West Africa Network For Peacebuilding[11]) and "Women Peace and Security Network" (WIPSEN)[12] are women-led organizations focused on bringing peace, rebuilding Africa, and empowering women to have a political role in Africa's future. Figure 17-1 is an illustration in tribute to the work of these women.

---

[8]Maliki, A. (2018). *Nigeria as a nation of influence.* Lowy Institute. www.lowyinstitute.org/the-interpreter/nigeria-nation-influence#:~:text=of%20influence,-Anthony%20Maliki&text=dubbed%20an%20'emerging%20power'.&text=The%20strength%20of%20Nigeria%20in,growing%20weight%20in%20international%20affairs'

[9]Ademola, D. (2018). *Achievements of ECOWAS since its establishment.* Legit. www.legit.ng/1165636-achievements-ecowas-establishment.html

[10]Kuwonu, F. (2018). *Women: Liberia's guardians of peace.* Africa Renewal. www.un.org/africarenewal/magazine/april-2018-july-2018/women-liberia%E2%80%99s-guardians-peace

[11]*Women in Peacebuilding (WIPNET).* West Africa Network For Peacebuilding (WANEP). www.wanep.org/wanep/index.php?option=com_content&view=article&id=8:women-in-peacebuilding-wipnet&catid=10:wipnet&Itemid=20#:~:text=The%20Women%20in%20Peacebuilding%20Network,conflict%20reconstruction%20in%20West%20Africa

[12]The Women Peace and Security Network Africa (WIPSEN-Africa). www.wipsen-africa.org/wipsen/about/?lang=en-us

Adopting Agile Across Borders

Figure 17-1. Faces of African women, who are playing a major part in turning around the fortunes in West Africa (image courtesy of Tasia Graham)

Insights

Definitions of "West Africa" vary, from anything from the 15 current nations of ECOWAS, to counts that include the likes of Chad further to the east, which can take the total up to 19 countries.[13, 14] Such arguments could be seen as arbitrary when in reality, each of these states are made up of hundreds of different ethnic groups and cultures. The complexity of Africa would seem to have no bounds.

---

[13]*African Studies and African Country Resources @ Pitt: West African Countries.* University of Pittsburgh Library System https://pitt.libguides.com/c.php?g=12378&p=65818
[14]Western Africa. Britannica. www.britannica.com/place/western-Africa

Chapter 17 | West Africa

That is not to say that there are no parallels to be drawn, not just within the region, but in the many commonalities that can be seen with people in other parts of the world. We found people to be warm, laid-back, humorous, and full of joy despite the backdrop of their history and current challenges.

The main common challenges to Agile adoption that we came across included being the first to dare to adopt it. We were told that people will wait for others to try something and only when they see things are successful will people follow. The Agile movement is in its infancy in the region, and we were told stories where practitioners themselves acknowledged that Agile is often misunderstood.

Where trust is low and competition fierce, the notion of transparency is met with resistance. Influencers and those with authority need to be on board to really spark progress. This is quite a barrier in cultures when control is from the top downward and it is inherent that "grey beards know best" – meaning people give great respect and defer decisions to elders. Leaders have traditionally used coercion and displays of power based on their status, and to challenge them is disrespectful. Another traditional aspect of leadership is to protect ingrained beliefs of the tribe. The Agile Coaches in the region we spoke to were under no illusion that progress will take time to fully embrace Agile values and baby-steps are needed.

It may be seen as fatalistic, but people have traditionally learned how to be adaptive to their circumstances and live with them. The status quo is being challenged though. Protests in 2020 in Nigeria against the police and the government are a sign of people being ready to stand up for themselves and make change happen.[15] This is being driven by the young majority; 60% of Nigeria's 200 million people are under the age of 24. In 2017, the former President of Nigeria, Olusegun Obasanjo said, "we are all sitting on a keg of gunpowder," referring to the continent's young people.[16] Courage is a value that is not in short supply in the culture of the region.

More startup companies are emerging in the region that are using Agile to drive their progress. The key to long-term success would seem to be in creating a solid foundation. We heard stories of attitudes of shortism, this is where any success is celebrated and taken advantage of while people still can. Consequently, when money is made, it is soon taken out of companies in order to finance people's personal lives rather than being reinvested in the company for the long term. Money is a prime motivator however it is obtained, mainly in order for people to be able to provide for and look after their family.

---

[15]Abaga, J. (2020). *Nigerian protests: A once-in-a-generation moment for change.* www.aljazeera.com/opinions/2020/11/11/nigerian-protests-a-once-in-a-generation-moment-for-change

[16](2020). *How the End Sars protests have changed Nigeria forever.* BBC. www.bbc.co.uk/news/world-africa-54662986

Family is where people's loyalties lay. Corporate loyalty, outside of the government and the military, is another matter. People move companies readily or can just as easily be made redundant by their employer in what is a competitive environment. It is not uncommon for people or companies to embellish what they can offer in order to compete with everyone else who are using the same tactics.

While in Agile we promote self-organization, empowerment of people, and sharing accountabilities, it is difficult for people to take on roles such as the Scrum Master or Product Owner because of a stigma being attached to anything that makes an individual "known." We heard stories that there can be a distrust and a perception that you must be a problem if everyone knows who you are.

It can be unsurprising that distrust and a lack of transparency runs deep following years of exploitation. Billions of dollars that could have been spent on vaccinations, infrastructure, schools, hospitals, and water treatment were – and continue to be – lost to corruption, which in turn deters foreign investment.

People have stuck together through a sense of tribal kinship. Many identify themselves through their tribal heritage ahead and above of their nationality. Life is still enjoyed through things like family, song, dance and food. Extended families are what provide people with security and a feature of life is to look after and care for the more vulnerable in the community. Children look after their elders in old age.

Women's place in West African society varies depending on factors such as geographic, religious, and cultural aspects, though they are generally at a disadvantage, with women often seen as mothers and wives. The high birth rates in most West Africa countries places an extra burden on women, as well as women generally receiving less schooling. Few women get to occupy high positions in organizations or politics. However, African women show levels of reliability, integrity, charisma, and drive, and this is helping them to have greater influence to the benefit of the region and the continent as a whole. The following story from Mercy George-Agbafe, founder of Learntor is just one story of one African woman driving change for the betterment of Africa.

Learntor: On a Mission to Create a Level Playing Field for Nigerians

I have always had a collaborative, problem-solving, value-driven, and learning-fast mindset, even before I had heard about Agile. I guess Agile has helped me articulate these things into words. Since learning about Agile, and applying the practices in my day-to-day life, it has helped me uncover better ways of planning and executing everything I do.

Chapter 17 | West Africa

My journey has not been a walk in the park; at the age of 13, I was a rape survivor and mother. I had no support from my immediate family or friends. With the untimely death of my mother as a teenager, I had to quickly adapt, embracing my challenges and assuming responsibilities for my daughter and siblings, which led me into immense poverty. I started working at the age of 14, alongside going to school and caring for my one-year-old daughter. However, my determination to never quit propelled me to continually improve and kept me motivated and focused. Deep down I also believed I was destined to help others like me to circumvent my kind of suffering. I have a saying that, "True greatness is not in being great but in the ability to make others great."

I had decided that my best option was never to give up on my own education. Despite countless rejections, disappointments, failures, and setbacks, I graduated with a BSc in Business Administration from the University of Lagos in 2010. I gained work experience across various sectors, including seven years in the banking sector. I worked as a Project Manager for a London-based company in the United Kingdom where I earned a nomination for "most outstanding Project Manager" at my company, simply because of my natural Agile mindset fostering collaboration with the team members. But in 2017, I suffered a midlife crisis, overwhelmed with uncertainty about my career path and how to navigate the next stage of my life. My big sister Olive Iluyomade saw my drive and passion for learning, and she encouraged me to enroll in further training in Agile with an internationally sought certification. I earned a Scrum certification, and I also enrolled in a training course in digital transformation, where I gained hands-on experience working as a Business Analyst and as a Project Manager. I fell in love with digital marketing and I earned a Professional Diploma in digital marketing from the Digital Marketing Institute.

All my life, I never knew there was something called a "grant." Suddenly, one day I saw an advert for the Tony Elumelu Foundation on TV. The Tony Elumelu[17] Foundation promotes entrepreneurship in Africa. With support from my childhood friend Yo Abiodun Iroha (Joy) who reviewed my application with a keen focus on the financials, I applied. In March 2020 I got a call from Joy, screaming with excitement that my name was on the list of the 3,050 out of the 256,000 applicants from across Africa to be awarded a grant. After the completion of the program, I was awarded $5,000 seed capital.

This grant facilitated the birth of Learntor. The aspiration is to become the No. 1 Nigerian comprehensive Agile Digital Transformation Training and Consultancy company, offering Agile Digital Transformation, Data Analytics, Digital Marketing, Business Analysis, and Capacity Development, with

---

[17]The Tony Elumelu Foundation. www.tonyelumelufoundation.org/

Adopting Agile Across Borders

hands-on practical learning, one-to-one mentoring, and internationally sought after certifications. The overall goal is to bridge the digital skills gap for Africans with an emphasis on women.

Fast-forward to 2020. Data has helped me to quickly learn not to focus on digital marketing for the West Africa market because it would not help me achieve my vision of bridging the digital skills gap for Nigerians and Africans as many people have the title of Digital Marketer, but have limited knowledge and expertise. Again I struggled, feeling helpless and unsure which direction to go while the world was crippled by the impact of coronavirus. Thankfully, Agile has helped me with Learntor with the application of Agile values and principles to the company. The more I learned about Agile, the more motivated I became to learn and practice it more.

Along the way, I met John Kiama on LinkedIn. John is a seasoned digital marketing professional based in Australia. He helped me to discover how I could base my services on Agile Digital Transformation. I reached out to find people at the top of their profession to build a great team of learning facilitators. Ayodeji Folarin, Data Analyst in PowerBI and Microsoft Most Valuable Professional. Adekunle Adetokunbo Talabi, a seasoned Agile Coach and Trainer in Scrum. Harry Boje, Data Protection Officer in GDPR/NDPR. Iyabo Okwuraiwe, Solution Architect and Project Portfolio Manager. Our goals are to produce comb-shaped people, with a broad range of knowledge and multiple areas of expertise to give them a global competitive edge. It should be simple to learn, meaning learning should be accessible for everyone. One of Africa's biggest problems is the high barrier of entry. In other words, the cost. We want to level the playing field, yet not compromise on quality, so we only work with trainers that are experts.

Learntor became a registered company in May 2019 and won its first client in November 2019. We have provided free training as part of our mission, with over 1000 people trained in digital marketing. Our first cohort of paying students on the Agile Digital Transformation training program of three months were a group of 19 students. Our facilitators were simply excellent. They were patient with the students – 80% of them did not know about Agile before the start of the program, but they were hungry to learn. One hundred percent of people that joined the program passed their Scrum.org Professional Scrum Master (PSM I) assessment. Student feedback did reveal that the program was overwhelming. As an Agile organization, we inspected our programs and, based on the feedback, we made adaptations ready for the next cohort.

We want to spread Agile to every nook and cranny of Nigeria, to create an enabling learning environment, all while aiming to be the No. I Agile Digital Transformation training company in Nigeria and Africa. Our learning programs are true learning experiences designed to make people job-ready and include giving people hands-on practical experience through internships, so we look for companies that offer the chance for our students to work with them.

Chapter 17 | West Africa

Once people graduate from the program, they stay part of the Learntor alumni community for ongoing support. All of this while being affordable to the people whose lives we are helping to change.

I am aware this is not a sprint, but a marathon of inspecting and adapting for continuous learning and improvement. I am incapable of bridging the digital skill gap and moving Nigeria and Africa forward digitally alone. I am therefore continuously seeking strategic partners to support the vision and provide scholarship funding for students seeking the Agile path, mentors to offer their expertise to our mentees, and organizations interested in absorbing our students as volunteers for internship opportunities.

My deepest sincere appreciation is to God for the grace to be tenacious and resilient. My darling husband Prince George Igbafe and my beautiful daughter Vivian Ekpo for their support. My faculty and the entire group of students. Most importantly, connections like Martin Hinshelwood of naked Agility, who contributed greatly because of his connection with Daphne Harris, Director of the Professional Scrum Trainer Program at Scrum.org, and contributing to the success of cohort 1 by facilitating PSM 1 training along with Professional Scrum Trainer Glaudia Califano. Lizzy Morris for connecting me with Howard Sublett, Co-CEO/Chief Product Owner of Scrum Alliance, and for facilitating a Certified Scrum Master class with Aanu Gopald. My profound gratitude goes to Glaudia Califano and David Spinks for sharing their platform, and for connecting with Kanban University to facilitate a Kanban System Design (KSD) with us. I appreciate Alexandre Gbaguidi and Erin Randall for their mentorship and the Agile20reflect team, Scott Seivwright, Karl Smith, Sabrina C E Bruce. Myles Hopkins, for the freedom to express her creativity as one of the Trustees and members of the digital marketing team.

—Mercy George-Igbafe, Digital Strategist, Agile and Data Enthusiast,
and Founder of Learntor

■ **Takeaway**   Be prepared to pivot from your first idea. As Mercy showed in her story, she started with the goal of creating a Digital Marketing agency, but through data and feedback, she realized that she needed to pivot and provide a different service to meet people's needs and stand out in the market. Business agility is all about setting a strategic goal, but being prepared to adapt it based on iterative learning. The key is understanding the relevant measures toward your goals, for example the Evidence Based Management framework from Scrum.org[18] provides guidance on Key Value Areas such as measuring an organization's current value, unrealized vale, ability to innovate, and time to market as a way to enable improvement and agility.

---

[18]www.scrum.org/resources/evidence-based-management

Adopting Agile Across Borders

The hot climates of West Africa are not conducive to rushing; punctuality or a sense of urgency is generally not at the forefront of people's minds. This and unreliable infrastructure make people inherently patient. Meeting's start times are more determined by when enough people, or those that are seen as most important, arrive. When people do meet, they afford each other plenty of time. Relationships and trust is built on communication styles that are very open, warm, and charming, with physical contact that might be uncomfortable to outsiders. Body language is such a big part of communication that it is much better done face-to-face than by telephone or electronic message. Humor is also frequently used and an important part of communication and relationship building. Meetings themselves may seem to be noisy and chaotic for an outsider, yet is absent of the aggression seen in meeting rooms in some other parts of the world.

Getting On and Around

Recognize that religion plays a major part in many people's lives. The spread of Christianity and Islam in different parts of the continent supported underlying traditional beliefs in a God and the supernatural, and this influences people's values, morals, and ethics. Some people seek to uphold the beliefs of the past. When past words and deeds have such an influence on the present, culture changes slowly, and that includes adopting an Agile culture. Understanding and recognizing what you can of the history and traditions of the tribe can help in understanding behaviors, building empathy, and gaining trust.

People tend to come to work or meetings smartly dressed, especially more so in the ex-British colonies, though meetings are generally expected to start with friendly small talk that might include checking on the health of others' well-being and that of their relatives. This is all important for trust and relationship building. How many, and which people turn up is a factor in determining the start time. Team discussions are conducted in an unhurried and seemingly random way. Agendas are not often followed, with whatever is seemingly most important brought up. Team members may voice disagreement through silence, or issues may be talked around to test finding mutually agreeable solutions, but teams find it important to try to seek a level of consensus before moving on. Decision making can be a long drawn out process. The point at which to move on is again determined by the most senior person present. All of this means that in general, facilitators should be relaxed about following strict agendas and balancing collaborative discussions with any sensitivities around status, being mindful of any explicit or hidden hierarchies. Above all, they should expect and allow discussions to be conducted on a very human and personal level.

Chapter 17 | West Africa

If there are major differences of opinion, it is best to facilitate discussions between the different sides privately, sometimes with a third-party mediator. Displaying major differences of opinion in public is regarded as abhorrent as people must not lose face. In general, such instances are likely to be rare. In a nod to tribal traditions, people think and act collectively. Agile teams may therefore need coaching and time to learn to critique one another openly and learn that this is for the greater good of the team. Recognizing teams as a whole rather than individuals is much more motivating.

■ **Takeaway** Center retrospectives on the Prime Directive. The Retrospective Prime Directive was created by Norman L. Kerth to encourage the right culture so that retrospectives are positive and results in teams learning and finding ways to improve. It states

Regardless of what we discover, we understand and truly believe that everyone did the best job they could, given what they knew at the time, their skills and abilities, the resources available, and the situation at hand.

—Norman L. Kerth, *Project Retrospectives: A Handbook for Team Reviews*[19]

With all new teams that we coach, we always set the scene at the start of the first retrospective with the Retrospective Prime Directive.

Friends are easily made, and are quickly protected and treated with generosity. When acquaintances are made, introverts beware: you'll need to accept physical closeness, privacy does not mean much and you are unlikely to be left alone for fear that you might get lonely. The propensity is to share, so respond in kind. Gift giving is a custom in many African countries, and any gains are quickly shared with the extended family or tribe. An individual prize in any friendly team competition is largely irrelevant as it is likely to be shared among the rest of the team members whatever the outcome. Against a background of a disparity of income relative to the rest of the world, anything acquired is quickly consumed due to this obligation to share, meaning that many individuals and companies are unable to accumulate savings or capital. This should be seen as people taking a rare opportunity to celebrate and enjoy life with loved ones rather than any sort of weakness. Lack of long-term planning may appear as a deficiency, but makes sense when most people's immediate concern is survival. We did find a real eagerness in many people to learn especially in the young; perhaps traditional fatalism is giving way to people wanting to take control of their own destinies.

---

[19]Kerth, N. L. (2001). Dorset House Publishing Co Inc., US. ISBN-13: 978-0932633446

Adopting Agile Across Borders

All in all, the people of West Africa, and the rest of the continent for that matter, are warm and kind. How they treat others in this part of the world is how the rest of the world needs to be treating them. The need is for practical help. Recognition and pay should be given where it is due. Companies looking to Africa for outsourcing should look past short-term gain in terms of taking advantage of cheap labor, to developing long-term and sustainable relationships. The region's current shortcomings, the causes of which are rooted in the acts of outside oppressors, should also be seen past. Instead, with appropriate openness, commitment, courage, focus, and respect, we can look to the strengths of the people and the great potential that the region has.

Agile Community Events and Meetups

- Women in Agile Nigeria: www.meetup.com/Women-in-Agile-Nigeria/

- Agile Nigeria Meetup: www.meetup.com/Agile-Nigeria-Meetup/

- Design Thinking Ghana Meetup: www.meetup.com/Design-Thinking-Ghana-Meetup/

PART
VI

Survival Guide

When the power of love overcomes the love of power, the world will know peace.

—Jimi Hendrix

CHAPTER
18

The State of the World

The Industrial Revolution had a tremendous impact on the world. One invention led to another. Capitalism and Frederick Taylor's scientific management theory emerged to organize our financial, labor, and production techniques. These techniques have become embedded into our cultures over the last couple of centuries. Times are changing though, and a new revolution is taking place. We are now in the information age and the old tools that worked so well since the Industrial Revolution are no longer fit for purpose. Agile may be just one of the techniques to help lead us in the new world.

Power to the People

In the following contribution, Martin Hinshelwood, Professional Scrum Trainer and Microsoft MVP discusses the trouble with Taylorism.

© Glaudia Califano, David Spinks 2021
G. Califano and D. Spinks, *Adopting Agile Across Borders*,
https://doi.org/10.1007/978-1-4842-6948-0_18

Chapter 18 | The State of the World

Taylorism, and Why Waterfall Is Just the Tip of the Iceberg![1]

Prior to the Industrial Revolution, goods were made in small cottage industries and people worked close to their homes. Customers were local, and both the producer and the consumer knew each other well. Mastery in one's chosen profession was paramount and rewards for the master craftsman were earned through increased money, or more time to pursue other interests.

When the Industrial Revolution came along, massive mechanization was needed to produce goods at scale. However, the technology of the time was unable to automate at that scale, so the only available "machines" were people. When, in pursuit of higher production volumes, you take away from people their autonomy, mastery, and purpose in your pursuit, you take away their soul. When you take away the essential elements of rewarding work, people become mindless automatons.

> *Frederick Winslow Taylor is a controversial figure in management history. His innovations in industrial engineering, particularly in time and motion studies, paid off in dramatic improvements in productivity. At the same time, he has been credited with destroying the soul of work, of dehumanizing factories, making men into automatons.*
>
> —Vincenzo Sandrone

Traditional management practices were born out of the disengagement of the workforce. With the outcome controlled and repeatable, management focuses on best practices and incentivizing people to work faster and harder. They wanted to remove thinking from the work since thinking creates ideas, and ideas create deviations from the pre-defined optimal way of working.

The thinking goes like this: ideas and innovation from your workers were a risk to your business and thus must be eliminated. We need to remove thinking!

When you remove thinking from work and turn people into automatons:

- People don't care about the work: your workforce disengages, so their interest in the work and empathy for the customer also wanes. Your workforce doesn't care about the work, and workers' primary concern is no longer the success of the company. They are instead concerned mainly with the output of their repetitive operation and maintaining or increasing their levels of remuneration.

---

[1] Contribution based on the blog post at https://nkdagility.com/blog/what-is-taylorism-and-why-waterfall-is-just-the-tip-of-the-iceberg/

Adopting Agile Across Borders

- People become replaceable cogs: Indeed the company comes to see an uneducated workforce who just do as they are told as easily replaceable resources. They don't have any discernible skills and the company has many people waiting for those jobs that can be easily slotted in. The company now no longer cares about the individual and they become resources to be allocated and replaced.

These two outcomes result in an erosion of trust between the workers and the company.

These working practices have:

- Put people in competency-based groups: This has not only resulted in isolated silos but also hierarchies within organizations.

- Created standard practices: The idea that best practices can be created and the best outcomes will result from the use of these practices.

- Reduced wages based on expected low performance and offered bonuses for increased output: In the output-driven world, we need our employees to be competing for the jobs so that they toe the line or lose their jobs and the benefits that come with them.

This was the advent of the age of bureaucracy.

Is Taylorism Ingrained in the Way We Work Today?

If you are lucky enough to work in one of the small numbers of companies that have already transitioned away from departments, hierarchies, headcount, work breakdown, best practices, and individual bonus systems, then you are fortunate, or maybe selective.

Most people are not so lucky.

The Trouble with Departments and Hierarchies

In the days of the Industrial Revolution, employees were perceived as untrustworthy. Managers were needed to tell workers what to do and how to do it. As our organizations grew, we needed managers to manage the growing number of managers and incentivize those managers to increase productivity in our employees through any means that they could.

Chapter 18 | The State of the World

Using the scientific management method, business owners identify each problem domain (e.g., Sales, HR, Marketing, Engineering, Testing) and come up with the "one true way" to do that work within the domain. The business owners can then hire managers and workers that will be trained in the "one true way" of doing that work, and minimize deviation from the business owners' control.

And so we created departments so we could centralize training and knowledge on a single topic, such as those shown in Figure 18-1. If you were hired for sales, you ended up in the sales department: completely disconnected from the makers, the designers, and the implementers. There would be no need for communications between sales and the other departments since we have planned all of their work methods and need only follow the script.

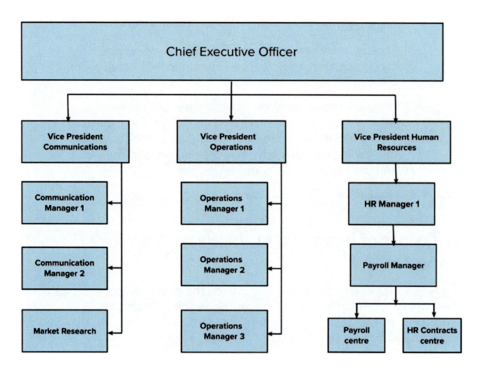

Figure 18-1. Put people into ability-based groups

As the world became more complex and sales became a creative endeavor, the imposed departmental isolation model became a negative impact. Sales personnel started making decisions in the complex world only taking sales concerns into account; that, by design, was all they knew. Creation and delivery had no bearing on closing deals, so they were ignored except in the most general terms. To close the deal and get one's bonus, sales personnel only needed to get the customer to sign, it mattered not if you could actually deliver.

Adopting Agile Across Borders 339

Often the result of this relationship was animosity between the departments, and unhappy customers when either quality, money, time, or features had to suffer.

An example of this was the Microsoft Azure Platform. Salespeople were measured and had bonuses paid based on the amount of Azure that customers bought. This measure resulted in salespeople pushing output over the outcome. They sold millions of dollars of Azure to companies that never used it. This resulted in unhappy customers and declining sales. Customers failed to see the value in what they were buying.

Then Satya Nadella (CEO of Microsoft) changed the measure for sales from the output-based measure to one based on the customer's outcome. Salespeople were no longer bonused based on how much they sold, but instead on how much a customer used. This change was revolutionary for sales of Azure. They were no longer focused on the short term (to get executives to sign) but on a much longer engagement model with customers. It became critical to encourage customers, with direct help, to move toward DevOps practices. Microsoft provided (and continued to provide) consultants and coaches to help create better outcomes for customers. This has paid off hugely for Microsoft as they are now the largest cloud computing provider despite starting late.

This seemingly small change in how people are measured changed behaviors greatly. Many salespeople left Microsoft as a direct result as they were only interested in the short-term and not the long-term investment in customer success.

Microsoft also restructured how sales personnel work so rather than it being one huge department, each product was responsible for their own sales, marketing, engineering, and support. With sales now a skill within the product teams instead of a separate organization, product groups can leverage the combined knowledge of all disciplines to encourage customers to use more Azure.

The Trouble with Best Practices

In the days of the Industrial Revolution, standard operating procedures were created to complete repeatable tasks and work that may be categorized as "simple." Repeatable work in low variance environments allowed mass production and output correlated directly to profitability.

With reference to the Stacey Model in Figure 18-2, as the world became more complicated (work required more skills, but was still repeatable given the right expertise), the simple and some of the complicated low variance work could be automated using machinery with software to control it. This

Chapter 18 | The State of the World

allowed workers to focus on more complex cognitive tasks (where work requires originality and innovation), but the management practices more suited to repetitive, low-variance work persisted.

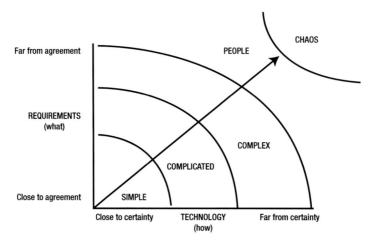

Figure 18-2. The Stacey Model[2]

Although the work had changed, the belief in predictive planning prevailed. There was a belief that if people just followed the detailed work breakdown and Gantt chart, then everything would be fine.

Best practices, centers of excellence, and innovation labs are all constructs of the Tayloristic practices designed for simple, low-variance work. These practices seek to exert more control over the new complex modern world of work.

Even in the simple, low-variance domain, the old Tayloristic practices based on the scientific management method destroy the soul of work. These practices create workers that hate the work, their managers, and the company.

We Need a New Way!

The Toyota Production System is the poster child of innovation and discovering new ways of working. Optimizing the workspace and creating good practices became the job of the employee and they were encouraged to periodically stop and reflect on how to do things better.

---

[2]Stacey, R. D. (2002). *Strategic management and organisational dynamics: the challenge of complexity.* 3rd ed. Harlow: Prentice Hall. ISBN-13: 978-1292078748

Adopting Agile Across Borders

In the complex world of sales, marketing, and software development we also needed new ways of thinking that would power the same ideas from Toyota and Lean into the high variance world of complex cognitive work. This was the birth of the Agile movement with the Scrum Framework (1993), the Agile Manifesto (2001), and later Kanban (2004).

Instead of coming up with best practices, we realize that there are only good practices for the situation at hand. A good practice today might not be quite so good tomorrow, and thus we need to be a lot more flexible. No longer is the business owner (or manager) the best person to define these practices since they are no longer close to the problem.

The best people to make decisions and define practices are those with the most information. Today, that is the people doing the complex cognitive work.

We need to accept that our practices are imperfectly defined. With this in mind, we need to push responsibility for defining those practices down to the people doing the work: they have the information required to make better decisions about which actions are more likely to yield the desired outcomes.

The Trouble with Task and Bonus Systems

In the days of the Industrial Revolution, it was perceived that revenue was lost due to a lazy, malingering workforce and so business owners needed to figure out how to minimize downtime and maximize output. Since managers were keeping people with the same ability in the same group and planning everyone's work, the one remaining thing to be controlled was the worker's focus.

Managers used various methods to incentivize workers to work harder and faster:

- Taylor differential piece work system: This system provides for higher rewards to more efficient workers. For different levels of output below and above the standard, different piece rates are applicable.

- Gantt task and bonus system: The system consists of paying a worker on a time basis if they do not attain the standard and on piece basis (high rate) if they do.

- Emerson's efficiency system: Under this system minimum time wages are guaranteed, but beyond a certain efficiency level, a bonus in addition to minimum day wages is given.

The task and bonus system is by far the most prevailing practice today; however, all of these systems were designed to create the same outcome and have a similar negative impact on workers.

Chapter 18 | The State of the World

Developed by Henry Gantt, the task and bonus system is an augmentation to the Taylor differential piece work system and was intended to pay workers a low wage, since we expect them to have low performance, and then have a bonus that takes them to a potential high wage.

Taylor, Gantt, and Emerson all created different "carrot and stick" approaches to management.

There are other ways to try and incentivize people, rather than just how they are remunerated:

- Employee of the Month: The Employee of the Month (EOM) is a type of reward program given out by companies (often to encourage the staff to work harder and more productively).

- Performance Appraisals: A performance appraisal, also referred to as a performance review, performance evaluation, (career) development discussion, or employee appraisal is a method by which the job performance of an employee is documented and evaluated. Performance appraisals are a part of career development and consist of regular reviews of employee performance within organizations.

- Hierarchy Progression: The idea that job title in some way related to reward, success, or expertise.

The idea that you need to dangle a carrot in front of the employees in order to get them to work more efficiently is a logical outcome of the practices we have been discussing throughout this contribution.

There have been many studies done at universities around the world on financial incentives for employees. All of them agree that higher pay and bonuses only resulted in better performance when the tasks were basic mechanical tasks. More money works for tasks that have a pre-defined set of steps with a single answer.

If a task involved even a small amount of cognitive skills, decision making, or creativity then more money resulted in lower performance. This is contrary to the common understanding of wage incentives.

If you are managing people you should pay them enough so that they feel that they are compensated fairly and not struggling to meet their basic needs. You should pay them enough to take the issue of money off the table.

Adopting Agile Across Borders ｜343

There are three key areas[3] that leaders need to focus on that will increase the performance of your workforce:

- Autonomy: Employees desire to be self-directed. Autonomy increases engagement.

- Mastery: The urge to get better at a skill, craft, or discipline.

- Purpose: The desire to do something that has meaning and is important.

Clients do not come first. Employees come first.

If you and your business only focus on profits without valuing your employees' need for autonomy, mastery, and purpose, then you may end up with unhappy employees and poor customer service. I don't know about you, but I do not do my best work when I am unhappy!

The Trouble with Taylorism

These Tayloristic practices worked well for employers during the Industrial Revolution. However, even factory work has progressed in the shadow of the Toyota Production System and the Lean movement. People are no longer cogs in a machine that can be replaced at a moment's notice. Each employee brings a unique skill or ability to your product discovery and product development story. That story will be unique because of it. These Tayloristic practices kill ingenuity, focus, and enthusiasm.

Foster ingenuity, focus, and enthusiasm and stop killing it with Taylorism. Bring the soul back to the work.

—Martin Hinshelwood, Professional Scrum Trainer, Microsoft MVP

To say that some of the Tayloristic organizational policies discussed in Martin's contribution is harmful to a company's ability to innovate is an understatement. Organizations that purely focus on producing as cheaply as possible and treat people as resources for churning out work as fast as possible lose out on these same people's potential for innovation. Those that are not inclusive and do not focus on accessibility to the extent that people with health conditions or impairments are not invited to contribute miss out further still.

---

[3]Pink, D. (2011) *Drive*. Canongate Books Ltd; Main edition (13 Jan. 2011). ISBN-13: 978-1847677693

Chapter 18 | The State of the World

Two generations ago, advantage was gained by the accumulation and absorption of knowledge. Some decades later, advantage came to those who could most efficiently find knowledge. We are now in a place where the advantage is in filtering knowledge. Too much information is available to us, at too great a speed, from too many sources. We have faster access to more information than ever before, but by the time it has been processed and analyzed, by the time managers have decided on its impact and a strategy formed in reaction to it, the data is often already obsolete. Our systems for managing information are frequently too slow. In addition, information coming from the media, customers, and our own analysis may be biased, fickle, contradictory, or incomplete. Those running companies, the decision-makers at the top of our organizations, don't really understand what the reality is of what is happening. They do not get the information they need when they need it, and it is usually wrong when they do. They get a relative, and never a complete, view.

For organizations and individuals to be successful in the modern world, a culture of continuous learning should be adopted. Sarah Toogood, an Agile Coach based in the United Kingdom, shares her perspective on learning cultures.

The Learning Culture of Humans
The Inspiration of David Attenborough

I am a person with a passion for learning and I have a huge curiosity about the world around me. As such, I love watching nature programs, especially any featuring Sir David Attenborough.

One Sunday Afternoon, I was satisfying my curiosity, watching Sir David as he descended through the spectacular history of the Grand Canyon.[4] As he proceeded, he was explaining the diversity and evolution of life through each layer of rock. That is, the rocks themselves gave incredible insights into what was happening at each stage of the world's history by showing how cataclysmic events accompanied dramatic change in the evolution of species. This got me thinking about human evolution.

The dramatic changes of thoughts and ideas, especially in technology and business, has made our society and culture the way they are today.

If we imagine the layers of rock of the Grand Canyon representing human history as we climb back up to our current moment in time, Agile is just one evolution[5] of human society.

---

[4]Episode 1, *Life on Earth*.
[5]Thanks to Simon Powers for introducing me to this idea.

Adopting Agile Across Borders

As we ascend our metaphorical Grand Canyon of human history, each step we make takes what worked before and incorporates it to provide a foundation for the success of the next. It incorporates the learning – the empiricism if you will – of an evolving capability of people to get to where we are now.

Standing at the top of the Grand Canyon and looking out across the landscape of Arizona, it's very easy to forget we are standing on the collective learnings of our society. We all too easily forget that history has demonstrated that we should expect to change and learn. Instead, both at companies and in wider society, we resist the change and learning opportunities open to us.

This mindset of only focusing on our immediate surroundings can lead us to some potentially limiting ideas about learning, such as:

1. Education and learning only occurs during the early stages of a human's life

2. Learning takes place in formal environments, such as in classrooms and training and at set times

3. Learning always requires a significant investment, such as taking a university loan, time, etc.

4. When you've completed your education you are an *Expert*, and you are *now ready* to do the *job*, and you'll be an *Expert* forever more

The attention on learning stands in the Agile Manifesto as unmistakably as the Grand Canyon: "We are uncovering better ways...."

If humans weren't a learning species, we wouldn't have evolved from the nomadic lifestyle of our ancient ancestors. We would not have evolved new technologies, structures, philosophies, or businesses to overcome challenges and take advantage of opportunities. We'd still be sitting around a campfire in the depths of our caves, hunting animals and painting art onto cave walls like those in the pre-historic caves of Lascaux in France.

Like society, we as individuals need to learn continuously. When we recognize that the world is evolving, we recognize that we need to keep pace and learn with it. Otherwise, if we rest too long during our ascent up our metaphorical Grand Canyon, the world will progress without us and all too quickly we will end up lagging far behind.

Chapter 18 | The State of the World

Learning then, is fundamental to the success of human society and individuals within it. It is the key to successfully navigating a complex world where the nature of events and opportunities are unpredictable.

Just like human society, organizations need continuous learning to adapt and survive – this is business agility.

> *Businesses do not transform, people do.*
>
> —William A. Adams and Robert J. Anderson,
> *Mastering Leadership: An Integrated Framework for Breakthrough Performance and Extraordinary Business Results*[6]

A Learning Culture

Why is a company's learning culture like an iceberg? Roughly only 10% of an iceberg is visible above the water surface, and a company's formal training should be just like that: a small section of easily visible, formal learning with a much larger mass of learning going on beneath the surface. This idea is illustrated in Figure 18-3. Formal learning and qualifications are supported by informal learning. Certifications are simply an output of training to show that minimum standards of capability, skill, and knowledge have been met. Certifications are not the goal.

Figure 18-3. The learning iceberg

---

[6]Adams, W. A. and Anderson, R. J. (2015). *Mastering Leadership: An Integrated Framework for Breakthrough Performance and Extraordinary Business Results*, page xxix. Wiley. ISBN-13: 978-1119147190

Just like an iceberg, with its mass hidden beneath the surface, a learning culture should have a large volume of regular informal learning which constitutes most of the learning going on. Below the surface, within a team and company, we have a complex series of connections: networks of influence, opportunities, events, and moments of learning for people, teams, and groups to draw upon. Just like our iceberg is influenced by the waves it floats in, our specific learning is influenced by the environment in which we live and work.

Next, let's explore this informal learning below the surface of our learning iceberg.

Exploring the Informal Mass of Opportunities in a Learning Culture

I'm a lover of mental models.

> *Models help explain how things work. Once a good model gets inside you, it can inform and guide you throughout a lifetime.*
>
> —William A. Adams and Robert J. Anderson,
> *Mastering Leadership: An Integrated Framework for Breakthrough Performance and Extraordinary Business Results*[7]

Figure 18-4 shows my mental model for the informal learning opportunities that sit within a strong learning culture.

---

[7]Adams, W. A. and Anderson, R. J. (2015). *Mastering Leadership: An Integrated Framework for Breakthrough Performance and Extraordinary Business Results,* page xxvi. Wiley. ISBN-13: 978-1119147190

Chapter 18 | The State of the World

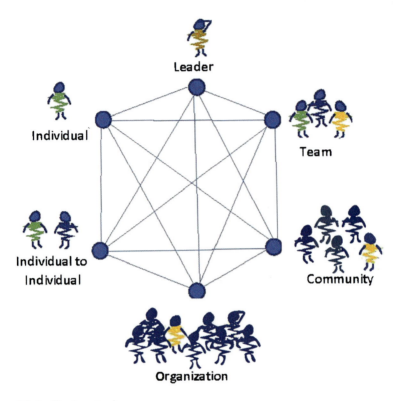

Figure 18-4. The learning hexagon.

Category	Brief Explanation	Examples of learning types
Individual	The individual focusing on learning by themselves, and their personal experiences and understanding.	• Personal knowledge • Personal experiences • Self-reflection • Self-realization
Individual to Individual	The connection of one individual to another either synchronously through conversation or asynchronously, e.g., the written word. This is usually focused on one individual sharing learnings with another.	• Blogs, vlogs • Conference presentation • Books • Coaching • Mentoring • Shadowing

(continued)

Adopting Agile Across Borders

Category	Brief Explanation	Examples of learning types
Team	The shared learning of a team working on a common purpose, creating partnerships and connections within the group for a bigger benefit. This often involves the building of ideas and learnings together, to create new learnings that couldn't be achieved by a single individual.	• Shared experience • Working together to learn either in a targeted fashion such as spikes or hackathons • Daily learning through doing work together • Sharing knowledge • Apprenticeship • Skills matrices • Pairing
Leadership	Leaders set direction and align people within a company around purpose. Through this meaning they provide expectations, accountability, and instructions. This provides insights and opportunities for anyone connected with the leader to learn concerning what is important.	• Intent • Goals • People performance measures • Guardrails • Policies and business rules • Business performance
Organization	Organizations are groups of people with a shared purpose and outcome (whether this is explicit and transparent can depend upon the culture of the organization). Organizations are ultimately looking to provide products and services to a customer for an exchange – this is usually monetary, but in the case of charities can also have other intangible exchanges.	• Market research • Competitor analysis • Customer feedback • Return on investment • Market share • Business measures, e.g., key results
Community	This is the connection beyond the individuals and teams to people outside of their context. This is a great opportunity to learn challenging ideas that can dramatically influence how you work, and how you view work. Communities are focused on a purpose, a shared passion. Choosing communities is therefore about the areas that most interest an individual.	• Agile communities and meetups • Networks of like-minded individuals sharing ideas and challenges • Book clubs

Let's explore an example of learning within each area.

Chapter 18 | The State of the World

Individual – Self-Reflection and Awareness

There's growing research which demonstrates the importance and effectiveness of learning through personal experience.[8] While we learn from doing, it helps to learn faster if we evaluate and reflect on our experiences so we can better identify patterns. Humans are pattern-orientated,[9] so identifying patterns helps us change behaviors and outcomes. A good example of this for me was a repeating situation when the team I was working with would develop a highly performing Agile culture at a pace ahead of the rest of the organization. There were tensions in managing the pressure of the different cultures of the team and the wider organization. After I left the team, the bubble of team culture and performance often collapsed under the pressure of the wider organizational culture, impacting the team behaviors and ways of working. After seeing this happen three times, I took time for personal reflection to think about what I could do differently next time.

Some of my key learnings:

1. By knowing the pattern, I could make conscious choices and experiment to create different outcomes, with greater success.

2. I was then able to consider how I view and work with people, teams, and especially leadership outside the team.

3. With my new awareness, I had an opportunity to gain a greater appreciation of systems thinking, other potential practices, and explore new mental models.

Individual to Individual – Inspiration

I love being inspired by people, it's one of the reasons I love personal coaching: I'm invited into someone's journey and I'm blessed with the privilege of seeing where they go, what they do, and what they achieve as they use more and more of their potential.

It took me a frankly embarrassingly long period of time to realize that surrounding myself with people who inspire me is one of the quickest and most effective ways for me to learn. I firmly believe that every individual I meet can teach me something. This means I need to be open and looking for

---

[8](2019). *The benefits of Experiential Learning and Kolb's Learning Cycle for Training.* ISC Medical. www.medical-interviews.co.uk/blog/benefits-experiential-learning-kolbs-learning-cycle-training

[9]Mattson, M. P. (2014). *Superior pattern processing is the essence of the evolved human brain.* Front Neurosci, 8: 265. doi: 10.3389/fnins.2014.00265. www.ncbi.nlm.nih.gov/pmc/articles/PMC4141622/

that moment of learning. It can be from something simple, like finding out about a great facilitation technique, to acquiring complex knowledge and skills, like learning an approach to managing resistance or conflict. By opening up and looking for learning through observation, you can learn effective new techniques and approaches multiple times a day from anyone around you, be it in a discussion with a stranger on a train to being at a three-day facilitated event. The number of things I've learnt from people is too numerous to mention: some small, some powerful, some positive, some negative; yet each one has sculpted the person I've developed myself into today, and who I will be tomorrow. I thank each person who has inspired me, and all I had to do was to watch, listen, and self-reflect while I live my life.

Team

Many times in my career I've been lucky enough to be part of a wonderful, powerful team of connected individuals. I'm a strong advocate of the power of teams for success, they are the building block and critical fertilizer in enabling achievements to be reached. Teams are a cauldron of magic just waiting to happen.

The main power of teams is not just the combined skills that they bring, it's in the developing of ideas and the shared learning that happens when aligned with a shared purpose and goal. It's the moment when you complete a discussion and you have no clue how an idea was created, because the result is more than you thought possible.

A good example of this in my career was when I joined a company where the team I was working with had built up a huge backlog of work. It had been estimated that it would take six months to clear it. Instead, through focused team discussions, we challenged each other to really understand what we were trying to achieve, what was important, what we could let go of, how we could solve this or that problem, how we could improve, where we could add automation, and how we could provide support to each other. Ultimately, we learned together.

Some of our key shared learnings:

1. Agreeing high code quality, and building quality in from the beginning of the flow.

2. Creating a culture of whole team effort, with focus on the same goal; rather than optimizing and prioritizing work to keep people productive, we focused instead on the value being delivered and iteratively improving our flow to achieve this result.

Chapter 18 | The State of the World

3. Providing clear transparency and prioritization of outcomes.

4. Accepting some work developed was no longer a priority and could be removed.

Though hugely challenging, within seven weeks we had turned things around; we started delivering value, and dramatically improved how we worked and delivered value as a team, with higher build and quality standards. I watched the seemingly improbable (or even the impossible) become a reality through the power of a team working and learning together.

Leadership – Intent

Leaders provide learning in several ways. David Marquet's intent-based leadership[10] provides leadership learning through asking intent-based questions. Rather than managing an individual and controlling what they do through instruction, the individual seeks confirmation of an action instead. During a conversation, the leader asks questions regarding the key decision influences. Over time the individual quickly learns to predict what the questions will be, and answers them before they are asked.

This is a technique I like to use a lot as a leader. I've recently been using this with a group of 14 teams on a client site. We've been discussing how we plan to ensure quality. I'd ask a team a question on aspects they may or may not have thought about, for example, "How will you collaborate with other teams?", "What key risks do you have?", and "How are you going to handle them?"

Organization – Customer Focus

Organizations, from my perspective, are there to provide products and services to people. A common focus of learning within a company, therefore, is learning from the customer. I was lucky enough to experience the importance of this type of learning early on in my career while working as Product Owner for an online company. As part of my role, I travelled to multiple European countries, interacting with and learning about both the customers and the operational teams who would use and support our products and services. The learnings we gained as a company and product team were revolutionary to the decisions we made for the product we created. They enabled a dramatic

---

[10]Marquet, D. (2013). *Turn the Ship Around!: A True Story of Building Leaders by Breaking the Rules.* Portfolio Penguin. ISBN-13: 978-1591846406

Adopting Agile Across Borders

change in the success of the product with great feedback, and drove new sales and a higher-quality, more-valuable product for both our customers and our organization. Fifteen years later, and I'm still proud of what we created, and how we achieved our successes.

Community – Connection and Passion

One of my favorite approaches to learning is through communities. They hold the fourfold benefit of connecting with others, sharing passion and interest, challenging and learning with peers, and providing support and advice.

Communities are an excellent place to uncover new ideas on topics you hadn't considered, to seek advice tailored to your passions, and to connect with people who excite and interest you. When you find a great community you can connect with, you often go on a journey together. Finding a community which works well for you can often be a challenge, but my advice is to keep looking until you find one that embraces, nurtures, and challenges you – and that you can provide opportunities for growth in others.

Looking back, I can clearly see periods of time in my life when I have dramatically increased my skills, confidence, knowledge, and positive behaviors. These have often coincided with the times I felt my greatest connection and engagement with a community.

In Conclusion

I hope that I've shared some of the passion and joy that I have for all of the learning types possible to you, your teams, and your organizations. I'll leave you with one final story.

I often get asked, "When will you have learnt enough?"

"Enough for what?" I usually respond, "I learn for myself, for my teams, and for my organization. I know enough for today, imagine what I can learn tomorrow!"

—Sarah Toogood, Agile Coach

The role of software is changing from supporting the core business to becoming THE core business. Many companies are adapting to make IT the center of their operations. Those that are not doing so are at risk of a young, lean startup company discovering the needs of the customers of their core business first and taking their market. Recent history is already littered with casualties: Blockbuster, Kodak, Borders to name but a few of the more high-profile examples.

Chapter 18 | The State of the World

We believe that our leaders deserve some sympathy, not scorn. There is much to fear for our CEOs and CTOs. Keeping up with the pace of change and the competition. Competing for, and keeping the best talent from the new generation who have different life motivations than them and which they cannot understand. Company's reputations are fragile, where one post that goes viral on social media can tarnish the whole organization. And then there is the worry of falling victim to data breaches and cyber-attacks.

Agile adoption is something else to be feared. The paradigm shift involves devolving power, trusting employees, and admitting that the person at the top does not know everything. In all of our travels around the world, the most common barrier to Agile adoption was that of the old models in place where leaders use command and control tactics down through a hierarchical structure. These models worked brilliantly in the past, but they no longer make sense in a complex world where it is impossible to have up-to-date information, and where it is an illusion to believe that we can control and predict things like customer behavior and market dynamics in advance.

■ **Takeaway** Organizational hierarchies have a significant impact on Agile adoption in different ways. Before our journey, we naturally associated hierarchy with top down decision making and autocratic leadership.

We now know that the reality is much more complex with differing leadership styles, meaning that decision making and authority within hierarchies works differently in different parts of the world.[11]

Organizations in Japan, for example, are structured very hierarchically; however, building consensus for a decision is essential and is done through the practice of Nemawashi as we discussed in the chapter on Japan. Organizations in the Netherlands are known to have flat structures, but just like in Japan, consensus building in the decision-making process is essential. The Dutch too have a name for this practice – the Polder Model. These styles may slow things down at first, but can mean more collective buy-in and faster progress later.

In the United Kingdom, the business culture has become more egalitarian over time; however, consensual decision making is not the norm. Quick and flexible decision making is preferred. And though a leader will ask for input from teams, in the end it is still generally the case that leaders are the ones that make and are accountable for decisions. This style would be perceived as autocratic to many Japanese and Dutch people.

---

[11]Meyer, E. (2017). *Being the Boss in Brussels, Boston, and Beijing.* Harvard Business Review. https://hbr.org/2017/07/being-the-boss-in-brussels-boston-and-beijing

Adopting Agile Across Borders

This all has an impact on the effectiveness on the role of Product Owner, who, according to Agile theory, should be empowered by the organization to be the final decision-maker for the products they own. We saw many cases of Product Owners not properly empowered, or trying to balance the opinions of many people to build consensus. All this impacts the ability of a Product Owner and an organization to pivot and adapt to change, which is what business agility is really all about.

When adopting Agile, it is important to understand the organizational structure, how decisions are made, and how to evolve these to be aligned with the Agile mindset.

The sin is not in a distrust of Agile, but in clinging to old methods that are no longer producing results. Many of the coaches that we met across the world expressed a frustration in people's unwillingness to see beyond the practices to the real intention of Agile. For example, we heard stories about companies adopting "The Spotify Model" in their organization with these implementations often going only as far as introducing terminology such as "squads," "tribes," and "chapters," and perhaps the introduction of some of the mechanics. But a common outcome is little actual change or improvement in how teams actually work, no real improvement in the delivery of value, and little understanding of the underlying Agile values.

Einstein defined insanity *"is doing the same thing over and over again and expecting a different result."* Darwin once said *"It is not the strongest of the species that survives, nor the most intelligent that survives. It is the one that is most adaptable to change."* It takes courage, but the motivation is for survival. And this is only achieved by the ability to change, through experiment, but most of all, by empowering the people that are closest to the work to decide the best way to carry out the work. The leader's role is in serving the people and creating an environment that allows them to do their best work.

This in itself, requires a huge cultural shift. To make any transition, we first of all need to understand where we are transitioning from. This is why we believe understanding ourselves and others culturally is key. If Agile is going to be fundamental to the future of our companies' success and sustainability, then we need to embrace the "Agile culture," such as putting teamwork before individualism, and collaboration before competition. And to do these things, people need to understand and empathize with each other where they are now.

Cultural models such as the Lewis Model, gives us insights into potential cultural barriers of adoption. For example, Linear-active leaning organizations may be uncomfortable starting projects without a detailed up-front plan, and may insist on output based metrics to measure progress, which actually ends up obscuring transparency and reducing trust. Multi-active dominated organizations may need to learn to make decisions, based not on emotions,

Chapter 18 | The State of the World

but on hypotheses and validated learning. Reactive organizations need their people to get over their reserved nature and have the courage to risk losing face by speaking out. Can they also build on their consensus-building approach to validate ideas with faster feedback loops and empower a single person to make decisions?

We were perhaps most surprised, not by anything that we saw on our journey, but by how well the behaviors that we were expecting to see in Agile teams were born out as described by the Lewis Model. An awareness of different behaviors can be gained by looking at these types of cultural models. Having done so, we feel that we now have a better understanding and empathy for people from a wider range of backgrounds. That can only be a positive for us as Agile practitioners.

Where in the World

Large global companies from the likes of the United States and Europe have become so dominant that they have not just invaded all parts of the globe, but they have also imposed their own corporate cultures across the world. At the same time, Toyota has shown that ideals from Japan can lead to global success and lead to companies in other countries attempting to replicate their practices for themselves. Perhaps, in an age where teamwork and collaboration are essential for innovation and efficiency of outcomes, where successful companies have managers that are servant-leaders, we will begin to see a shift from Western to Eastern standards in our global companies' culture. This vision would fit in well with the view of agilists that advocate collaboration, feedback, adaptability, and building relationships based on trust – characteristics that are part of Eastern philosophies.

Countries in Asia have demonstrated an ability to develop a cross-cultural understanding for overseas customers' wants and needs. They have a global presence, with people from the likes of China, India, and the Philippines working in other countries throughout the world, allowing them to build cross-cultural understanding of others. The language skills of the people of the Philippines and India combined with low labor costs has allowed them to become outsourcing centers of the world. Korean and Japanese companies have penetrated US and European markets. China's pace of economical and technological growth has closed the gap between them and the traditional big five countries of the United States, Japan, Germany, the United Kingdom, and France.

In contrast, the likes of the Americans and the British have more to do to suspend their judgement and develop cultural empathy in order to continue to develop their successes in a globalized world. Canada, one of the most

**Adopting Agile Across Borders** | 357 |

culturally accepting and diverse countries in the world, is placed to do well. Scandinavian countries have people that have developed great intercultural skills and organizations with flat structures, making Agile a natural fit to them. The success of companies such as Spotify shows the region's potential.

In parallel to this, South American countries, perhaps a forgotten part of the world, are starting to see some kind of stability that has historically been largely elusive on the continent. Their people's relationship-driven approach, their curiosity and willingness to experiment could see them rise to become leading players in the new technological world.

Where then, does this leave those traditionally leading countries in Europe and the United States? Their need for certainty and discomfort with ambiguity, their individualistic mindset, the desire for step-by-step plans seem most at odds with Agile. Perhaps becoming aware of their own cultural barriers and embracing Agile fully could allow them to evolve with the times. Presently, they have a headstart in their industrial and economic development, but if they don't adapt, their complacency risks them getting stuck and being left behind as the rest of the world moves on. It does seem that an insular mindset has set in. We've often felt that one of the problems with big companies and rich nations is that they have too much money. Waste can be afforded, even tolerated, while the rest of the world is lean and hungry.

A Changing World

At the same time companies operate on an international scale with multiple locations all over the world. Humanity's priorities have got to, and are, changing. Climate change is a major concern for us all and an increasing number of organizations are adopting climate-friendly travel policies alongside other actions aimed at being environmentally friendly. There is an increased focus on creating equal opportunities, diversity, and inclusion. Technological advances have continued to accelerate, with more and more advanced remote collaboration tools available to teams who are trying to bridge the distance between physical locations. The illustration in Figure 18-5 represents people from different cultures coming together with different perspectives – today's global economy increasingly requires people to collaborate in teams that

Chapter 18 | The State of the World

Figure 18-5. People from different cultures bring different perspectives (image courtesy of Tasia Graham)

cross cultural and geographical boundaries. And the world continues to prove that the future is unpredictable.

In 2020, just as we were completing the first draft of this book, the world changed for us all on a global scale with the arrival of the coronavirus pandemic. At the time of writing, just about every country in the world has been affected, with lockdowns common, and terms such as "social-distancing" and "furlough" entering our everyday vocabulary. New ways of working and collaborating together has been forced upon us. Some have adapted better than others. Many businesses will not survive.

Every threat brings opportunity. Technology that had been a convenience to ease the need for travel has become a necessity. Teams all over the world have had to learn to work together remotely. As we complete this book, we hear and

Adopting Agile Across Borders

see stories where some are adapting better to this than others. We are reminded of the Manifesto for Agile Software Development value, *"Responding to change over following a plan."* Organizations have had a range of policies on what to do practically in responding to the crisis. There are no easy answers, but we come back again to the Agile Manifesto and look to the principle of, *"The best architectures, requirements, and designs emerge from **self-organizing teams**."* Even in this time of crisis, the Agile Manifesto guides us. We are confident that the organizations that adapt the best are those that support the people doing the work in deciding for themselves how best to organize how they work. Leadership's role in an Agile environment has always been to ensure that teams have a clear purpose and to create the boundaries within which they can self-organize.

Another of the Manifesto principles states, *"The most efficient and effective method of conveying information to and within a development team is face-to-face conversation."* If "face-to-face" is to be taken literally, then at what cost? The idea of insistence of co-located teams while coronavirus disrupts the world is absurd. As Agile practitioners ourselves, we have a preference for having co-located teams, but teams are proving that collaboration is possible remotely. Organizations that have reacted swiftly to offer digital services when before the crisis they may have only had traditional physical offerings are evidence of this.

Regardless of coronavirus, we are not being inclusive or encouraging diversity in our teams and organizations with policies that exclude people. Policies of co-located only teams reject people that cannot come to the same location every day, whether it is because of geography, family commitments, or because of requiring special assistance. Such an approach would mean potentially missing out on having highly collaborative and talented individuals on the team. Do we then value "face-to-face communication" more than having diverse and inclusive teams? Perhaps "face-to-face" requires a recontextualization. In our view, technology is enabling face-to-face communication regardless of whether people are in different rooms, buildings, regions, countries, or continents.

Reality shows that, over the years, numerous organizations have already shifted to more "flexible" working arrangements. Since its inception in 2006, the Annual State of Agile report[12] has included questions about distributed Agile teams. The version of the report published in 2020 clearly states, *"While working together face-to-face can be desirable for Agile practices, survey respondents indicated that organizations are supporting distributed teams and team members... 81% of respondents said their organization has Agile teams where the members of the same team do not all work in the same location (i.e. not co-located)."* The report goes on to say, *"There is no evidence of a trend toward increased co-location,"*

---

[12]*Annual State of Agile report.* VersionOne. https://stateofagile.com/

Chapter 18 | The State of the World

and, *"71% of respondents said their organization practices Agile with multiple co-located teams collaborating across geographic boundaries."* Note that the data for this version of the report was gathered before the 2020 pandemic, the surveys having been conducted between August and December 2019.

Remote working was already becoming more normal. It opens up possibilities and opportunities to build teams of highly diverse people, allowing organizations to select talent from a wider pool than before. However, this brings a new set of challenges with it, least of which – in our opinion – is how well the technology works.

Takeaway   Tips for building a collaborative and productive remote office environment:

1. Create a remote office environment that allows and encourages active participation and communication from everyone. This can range from choosing tools that are accessible and usable to everyone involved, to making sure a person in another part of the world does not go bankrupt from Internet data usage.

2. Make deliberate investments in team building. When a team are all working remotely, put extra effort in to allow everyone to get to know each other. Arrange casual end-of-week calls, virtual coffees, regular virtual games, or any other type of regular unstructured virtual meet up. Just keep these sessions casual and not about work!

3. Work with teams to help them choose remote collaboration tools and equipment that are best for them ahead of sticking to tools that were chosen to meet organizational policies that were made in the past. If there are security concerns and firewalls in place, for example, work with the relevant people to agree shared goals for collaboration and find the best tools and approach that will still be compliant and secure.

4. Transparency is always important, even more so in a remote setting. Ensure that information is accessible and visible to everyone involved, and create a shared understanding of this information through conversation. There are many tools out there such as Mural, Trello, Jira, Miro, Zoom, Teams, and Group Chats to enable transparency.

5. Respect others. Just as you would not interrupt another team member when they are in the middle of something if you were in the same office (unless it is something urgent), respect the fact that other people might not reply immediately. It is easy to get distracted by numerous messages that come in, make it visible when you need to focus. Agree with the team an approach that allows people enough space to focus when they need to.

Adopting Agile Across Borders

6. Working remotely does not mean having to only work from home. If you are someone who gets distracted by day-to-day stuff at home, or you just need some buzz around you, change the scenery. A great little book to explore some great stories of working where you like to achieve more is *Out of Office* by Chris Ward.[13]

7. Plan face-to-face time. Even if it is just once a year, find a way to bring the team together so that people get to know one another face-to-face.

8. Build a virtual team wall. Include pictures and Personal Maps[14] of all of your fellow team members.

9. Working collaboratively remotely without good tools is virtually impossible. Fortunately, the tooling is getting better all the time. Check out *Collaboration Super Powers* at `www.collaborationsuperpowers.com/tools/` which is full of tips for remote working and has a comprehensive list of remote collaboration tools.

10. Chat tools and emails can only go so far. Some discussions are always better done directly, whether via video conferencing or by telephone. Keep talking to your colleagues!

Beans Before Beanbags

We can see an argument that Agile is a movement for solving first world problems. Many people in developing countries struggle to make a living for themselves and their families. Across, but also within countries, there are big disparities. Professional office workers in Jakarta or Manila have a very different life to the ubiquitous motor-scooter taxi drivers on the streets of these mega-cities who are just trying to earn enough money to provide for their families. The contrasts go further when considering these mammoth countries as a whole, for example, the remote tribal people in the far East of Indonesia could be from another time when compared to someone living in Jakarta or Bandung. As we have seen for ourselves, people living in countries such as these – a majority of the world's population – are preoccupied with dealing with the basics of life.

In contrast to more individualistic cultures such as the United Kingdom and the United States, in many parts of the world, family and group considerations come first. People work to feed, clothe, and put a roof over the heads of their

---

[13]Ward, C. (2013). *Out of Office: work where you like & achieve more.* Blue Dot World. ISBN-13: 978-0-9576123-0-3

[14]*Personal Maps.* Management 3.0. `https://management30.com/practice/personal-maps/`

Chapter 18 | The State of the World

families. Job security is a priority, especially in countries where there is little or no welfare state to catch people that fall on hard luck. Discussions about motivation, about achieving autonomy, mastery and purpose or ideas from the upper echelons of Maslow's hierarchy of needs[15] are irrelevant for a majority of people around the world who are mainly concerned with meeting the basic needs of food and shelter. The Scrum values of openness and courage may be hard to swallow for people whose lives and those of their family depend on their job security. Agile then, encouraging people to speak out, to critique working processes, for people to self-organize and take responsibility can no doubt be seen as a destabilizing force. This is especially the case in a majority of corporate organizations that have not yet created safe-to-fail environments and embraced a true Agile mindset.

We have seen and experienced a trend for CEOs to create cool, modern offices that are inviting places to work to the new generations of developers. Their office space is open-plan with desks laid out for teams to collaborate with each other, and break-out areas for people to go and have deeper conversations. More and more offices in developed countries are furnished with the likes of pool tables, table tennis tables, and bean bags. And yet the Agile mindset is missing. People are not empowered. It is not safe-to-fail. People are not free to experiment or innovate. Corporate processes must still be followed. Project scope must be completed on time and on budget. Or else.

Whether analyst, programmer, tester, or any other professional software development role, in many parts of the world, people aspire for security and a basic standard of living before all else. They need to feed their family, and beanbags in the office are superfluous to their immediate needs. Another principle from the Manifesto for Agile Software Development comes to mind: *"Build projects around motivated individuals. Give them the environment and support they need, and trust them to get the job done."* For us, this is about creating environments where people can feel safe and secure to do their best work, knowing as much as possible their – and their family's – immediate life needs are going to be met.

■ **Takeaway** Recognize that we are not all the same. What motivates each of us is going to be different. It is easy to be judgmental and jump to conclusions based on our own perceptions, but we are likely to be missing context and background when transposing our views of the world onto others. Just as we advise understanding our customers' needs and expectations, we advise investment in understanding what team members' goals are and what really matters to them.

---

[15]Maslow, A. H. (1943). *A Theory of Human Motivation.* Originally Published in Psychological Review, 50, 370–396. https://psycnet.apa.org/record/1943-03751-001

CHAPTER
19

Unite and Move Forward

We started the journey that led to this book with the aim to better understand the impact that culture has on Agile adoption. During our journey we were not only exposed to Agile practices that were new to us, but also to different perspectives of viewing the world. Our own journey and thinking has evolved beyond the impact that culture has on Agile adoption, to the individuals and interactions of diverse Agile teams. Diversity goes beyond differences such as gender, race, and ethnicity. It includes different abilities, learning styles, specialties, and experiences to name just a few. In a world where teams and organizations are more diverse than ever, there are great opportunities in leveraging this diversity, but diversity without true inclusion gives little benefit and could even be detrimental.

Strength in Diversity

Dubai is an example of a place that has become a multi-national melting pot, with people attracted to the city from all over the world. We saw for ourselves that it is a place that is seemingly lacking an identity of its own. Instead, it tries to please all of those that have come there, through wealth and excess.

© Glaudia Califano, David Spinks 2021
G. Califano and D. Spinks, *Adopting Agile Across Borders*,
https://doi.org/10.1007/978-1-4842-6948-0_19

Chapter 19 | Unite and Move Forward

Consequently, in some instances, the corporate culture of the multinational companies that people work for has more of an influence on people's behavior than their own national culture.

With such a mix of nationalities and backgrounds such as those found in Dubai, there are dangers when diversity is not managed well. Teams may not have their own identity. Misunderstandings can arise, trust breaks down, and teams become dysfunctional. Today's demographics mean that some level of diversity in teams and organizations is inevitable in most parts of the world. This is actually a good thing, as we will come to discuss, there is a lot of evidence that shows greater diversity can give a competitive advantage and leads to greater performance. However, there can be no strength in diversity without inclusivity.

People have their own experiences and expectations in different scenarios. For example, meetings serve different purposes in different contexts. Typically American organizations and teams use meetings for a group of people involved in an initiative to come together, discuss, and make decisions. Contrast this to the Japanese whose culture of Nemawashi that was discussed earlier see meetings as largely ceremonial where decisions are formally unveiled. In Dutch organizations and teams, it is common that meetings are used to give feedback on proposals and to look for problems. Positives are generally ignored – behavior which could be seen as pessimistic in other cultures is for them an efficient way of working, since spending time on items that are already in a good state is seen as a waste of everybody's time. Most South American, Spanish, Italian, and French teams see meetings as an opportunity to get to know other people and build relationships. Whatever the scenario, mutual understanding of purpose and clear communication is key.

■ **Takeaway** Make desired outcomes of meetings clear. Let's face it, most of us have sat in some meetings, feeling as if we are wasting our time. A common policy is to have a meeting agenda created beforehand so it is clear what will be discussed, but this stifles creativity and is output focused – that is, achievement is perceived by getting through the agenda items. We think a better approach is to make it clear what the objective of the meeting is. Having clear objectives for meetings encourages greater self-organization in how to achieve the objectives by the attendees. This does require a good facilitator and some practice, but the results are worth it in terms of productivity and reduction of waste.

A big differentiator between people is in individual's communication styles. Speech is used for a diverse range of reasons: sharing information, influencing, negotiating, persuading, controlling, inspiring, showing solidarity. For some, talking is even shied away from and can be uncomfortable. Different cultures use speech in different ways, and these ways are engrained. In addition, the very nature of how different languages are constructed will also be an influence in the resultant pattern of communication.

In his book *Cross-Cultural Communication: A Visual Approach*,[1] Richard D. Lewis visualizes different communication patterns that he has studied in different parts of the world. According to Lewis, *"In each culture the patterns of communication, listening and manipulation are remarkably consistent."* His stated aim is to provide a visual reference guide to set expectations on how people of different countries can be expected to communicate. This can allow interlocutors a better understanding of the communication processes at work.

We will take a look at some of the visualizations from the work of Lewis. The setting here is communication patterns in meetings. In this context, we will see how communication patterns differ and this is in large part because of the reasons given earlier.

Take for example the Finnish communication pattern as shown in Figure 19-1. Finnish people on the global stage are sometimes seen as eccentric, and even mocked[2] for being blunt. Lewis's visualization shows us that use of a narrow word base and minimal speech is actually typical of the Finnish communication style.

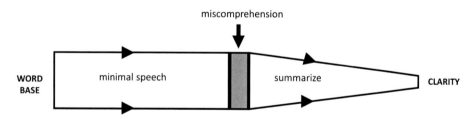

Figure 19-1. Finnish communication style (based on image from Cross-Cultural Communication: A Visual Approach, copyright of Richard D. Lewis)

When they hit a period of miscomprehension, Finnish people actually seek clarity by narrowing their speech even more to summarize what they are trying to say as succinctly as possible.

Contrast this to the communication pattern of the Spanish that is shown in Figure 19-2. According to Lewis, Spanish people have a much broader word base.

---

[1] Lewis, R. D. (2008). *Cross-Cultural Communication: A Visual Approach* (Second Edition). First published by Transcreen Publications in 1999. ISBN-13: 978-0-9534398-3-6r
[2] *Mika Häkkinen in Have I got News for you* https://youtu.be/aK3Eaoda9v8

Chapter 19 | Unite and Move Forward

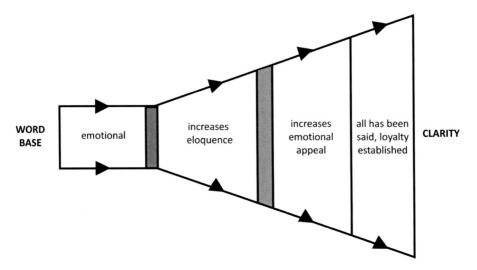

Figure 19-2. Spanish communication style (based on image from Cross-Cultural Communication: A Visual Approach, copyright of Richard D. Lewis)

The language is richer in emotion and eloquence. If Spaniards have moments of misunderstanding or miscomprehension, their use of language actually becomes richer still in their attempts to get to understanding and clarity. Spaniards also become more verbose as they form relationships and the emotional appeal with others grows.

Now if we take a look at the English communication pattern shown in Figure 19-3, we see yet another contrast.

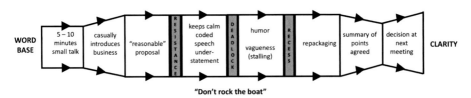

Figure 19-3. English communication style (based on image from Cross-Cultural Communication: A Visual Approach, copyright of Richard D. Lewis)

Anyone that has been in meetings dominated with English people will recognize this pattern. It is undesirable in meetings in England for people to "rock the boat." Meetings begin with a few minutes of small talk; it can be about the weather, movies, sports, or something along those lines. Business is introduced, almost as if it is an imposition. When there is a period of miscomprehension, the reaction is to keep calm and be understated. The English are masters at using coded speech. Examples of this include saying things like "Hmm… that's interesting," which can be translated to "that's a bad idea," or "I hear you, but

Adopting Agile Across Borders

I'm not interested." Or they say things like, "I'll get back to you on that," which basically means they have already rejected the suggestion and have no intention of giving it any further attention. This can cause huge miscommunication problems with those that do not understand the coded speech, such as the Finnish or the Dutch who are used to being much more direct for example, and will take what is said at face value.

When deadlock ensures, it is common for people to continue to maintain their calm. Humor is commonly used to ease tension. Taking breaks is popular (after all, the English love their tea!), where they may talk among themselves, come back to re-package what has been said, summarize it, and agree that decisions will be postponed until the next meeting.

Considering these contrasting communication patterns – and we have briefly discussed only three – it is a wonder that we can comprehend one another cross-culturally at all. In these examples, we have only talked about speech. Of equal importance is what is not said. Use of silence is a major part of many cultures. We heard earlier about "reading the air" in Japan, something that is almost impossible to do as an outsider and ingrained with the subtleties of the culture.

This potential for miscommunication applies much more widely as well. We have spoken about national communication patterns, but we see differences in other areas of diversity. People of different generations, socioeconomic class, across regions, even gender have different communication patterns. Understanding each other is much more than information being conveyed from speaker to listener. Assuming people understand each other is not a given when people have any type of different background.

Good communication is essential for Agile teams to work well. If our teams and organizations are to navigate a complex world where more is unknown than is known, where the best way to navigate this complexity is through collaboration and dialogue, if Agile teams are to perform at anything like their potential, then it makes sense to invest some time and effort into understanding one another culturally, so that our communication is effective.

Good Agile teams welcome participation and a wide spectrum of inputs, believing that a range of ideas helps to triangulate the team toward the best solution. Over the years, studies have shown that diversity in organizations and teams can lead to higher performance and innovation because of the wider range of viewpoints it can bring.[3] However, we also need to recognize that many organizations and teams don't take advantage of their diversity. In some cases, it can result in a drop in performance.

---

[3]Rock, D. and Grant, H. (2016). Why Diverse Teams are Smarter. Harvard Business Review. https://hbr.org/2016/11/why-diverse-teams-are-smarter

Chapter 19 | Unite and Move Forward

According to a paper[4] from Joseph J. Distefano (professor of organizational behavior and international management at the International Institute for Management Development (IMD) in Lausanne) and Martha L. Maznevski (assistant professor of organizational behavior and international management at the McIntire School of Commerce, University of Virginia), cultural differences, *"provide the greatest potential for creating value,"* by virtue of a greater range of perspectives that the team can draw from, which leads to greater innovation. In addition, if the effort to understand other people's ways of thinking and character traits is made, then people's own perceptions are expanded, giving rise to a greater range of thought, innovation, and views of possibilities through team interactions. This is illustrated in Figure 19-4. However, Distefano and Maznevski also recognize that, *"cultural differences provide the greatest potential to hinder effective interaction within teams... Furthermore, cultural values and norms are deeply held, and almost always implicit and taken for granted. Their deepest effects on behavior and interaction are usually hidden, and extremely difficult to identify and address."*

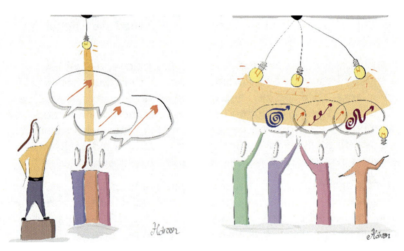

Figure 19-4. Broader spectrum of views leads to greater innovation (image courtesy of Haroon Khalil)

Distefano and Maznevski noticed three main patterns that they coined:

- The *destroyers*: Teams where members distrust and have little or no understanding of each other, with decisions having to be made through a manager or formal leader without genuine discussion in the team

---

[4]Distefano, J. J. and Maznevski, M. L. (2000). *Creating Value with Diverse Teams in Global Management.* www.sciencedirect.com/science/article/abs/pii/S0090261600000127

Adopting Agile Across Borders

- *The equalizers*: Mediocre teams that have compromised, with little or no leveraging of the differences that the different team members can bring

- *The creators*: Teams where differences are explicitly recognized and the implications are integrated into their working processes

In the most successful teams, differences are explicitly called out and discussed, and a conscious effort made by the team to evolve their working practices to incorporate them. This goes further than simply acknowledging different mindsets, or smoothing over and tolerating the differences. Focusing on areas that people do have in common and assuming this translates as successful cultural integration risks losing out on possible improvements from building empathy and understanding of the differences. Great teams use their different world views as a base for discussions and evaluation for improvement.

To get the best out of our diverse teams we need to be inclusive and allow teams to develop their own strategies unique to their context. Team member's good ideas will not surface if there is no environment of active participation for everyone.

Distefano and Maznevski describe the three steps for diverse teams to integrate for creating value: *map*, *bridge*, and *integrate*. Mapping involves the team coming together, and describing their differences objectively and in measurable ways. Equalizer teams tend to focus only on similarities, but to reach the creator state, teams start with an assumption that there are differences which need to be identified and talked about. Bridging involves identifying communication techniques that explicitly take these differences into account. Integrating involves putting these into practice, monitoring participation, active conflict management and building on ideas as a team with the view of considering everybody's perspectives.

These ideas are something that we have begun experimenting with ourselves, as discussed in the following story.

Using Design Thinking to Map, Bridge, and Integrate Cultural Diversity

I worked in a diverse team where we failed to consider our fundamental cultural differences which led us to unhealthy conflict and frustration. I have also fallen into the trap of hiring new team members because I thought they would be a great cultural fit, in that they were similar to my colleagues and to me. In my experience this is easy to do, after all we want to have colleagues that we can easily get along with, who we click with, and who we have interests

Chapter 19 | Unite and Move Forward

in common to help us bond quickly. The problem is that we then often end up with homogeneous teams. Teams that are harmonious and fun to be part of yes, but when it comes to doing groundbreaking work, likely not.

Over the years, I have learned that having a group of people with diverse thinking styles, abilities, experiences, and backgrounds means that there is a wealth of available perspectives. Regardless if we agree with each other's perspectives or not, it is in this diversity of views that there is the greatest potential for us to have a greater range of ideas, leading us to be more innovative. However, having diversity without being inclusive is not taking advantage of the potential. It is like sitting on a goldmine without extracting a single gold nugget.

I see organizations and teams employing policies and ways of working that encourages groupthink. Standard ways of approaching problems are used. This is done with good intentions. Some believe the answer to conflicting ideas and behaviors is to find compromise. Others arrange team-building workshops focused on people creating better awareness, understanding, and empathy between participants. Approaches such as these are a great start, but in my opinion, they are not by themselves enough to dig deep enough to get to those precious nuggets of gold.

I always felt there was something missing to guide us. And then I was introduced to Design Thinking.

At its core, Design Thinking is a mindset of approaching every problem in a human-centered way, encouraging us to focus on the people we are creating for, which leads to better products, services, and internal processes.

Given this definition, I figured a Design Thinking approach would work very well for a team to explore the opportunities that diversity and inclusion could give them. Since I made this link a few years ago, I have been experimenting with applying Design Thinking and the approach of map, bridge, and integrate of cultural diversity in my work coaching teams, helping with changing organizational structures, and in change management.

One description of Design Thinking that resonates most succinctly with me and is most relevant here comes from the Interactive Design Foundation:

> Design Thinking is a design methodology that provides a solution-based approach to solving problems. It's extremely useful in tackling complex problems that are ill-defined or unknown, by understanding the human needs involved, by re-framing the problem in human-centric ways, by creating many ideas in brainstorming sessions, and by adopting a hands-on approach in prototyping and testing. Understanding these five stages of Design Thinking

Adopting Agile Across Borders 371

> will empower anyone to apply the Design Thinking methods in order to solve
> complex problems that occur around us – in our companies, in our countries,
> and even on the scale of our planet.[5]

Looking closely at this description, you can see that the focus is not solely on product design, but on how Design Thinking can be used to help solve complex problems around us, in a human centric way. Design Thinking is a non-linear iterative approach that I believe fits perfectly well for a team to solve the problem of how to leverage their cultural diversity. The Design Thinking process is shown in Figure 19-5.

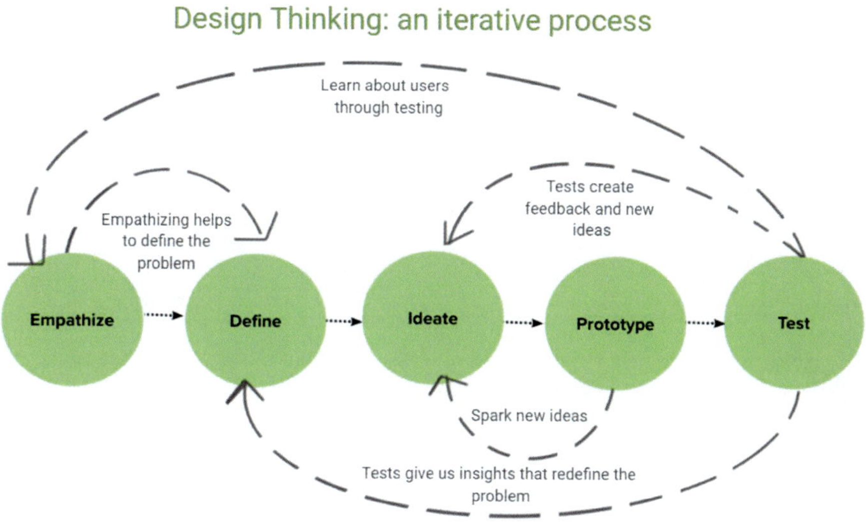

Design Thinking: an iterative process

Learn about users through testing

Empathizing helps to define the problem

Tests create feedback and new ideas

Empathize → Define → Ideate → Prototype → Test

Spark new ideas

Tests give us insights that redefine the problem

Figure 19-5. The Design Thinking process

So how has Design Thinking helped me with leveraging diversity with teams that I have worked with? I will give an example.

I was part of a small distributed team that was made up of six people from five different countries. We had a mixture of team members that identified themselves as either male or female. Our professional backgrounds spanned software development, design and UX, QA, marketing, and communications. We had each worked with at least one of the other team members in some

---

[5]Friis Dam, R. and Yu Siang, T. *5 Stages in the Design Thinking Process.* Interaction Design Foundation. www.interaction-design.org/literature/article/5-stages-in-the-design-thinking-process

Chapter 19 | Unite and Move Forward

form previously, the team coming together in this instance through us making recommendations of each other. However, having this team form organically in this way does not mean that we always agreed and never clashed. And, many of these clashes were down to misunderstandings due to cultural differences.

This was apparent, for example, in the way we gave feedback to each other, in the things that were said and not said, the way different team members preferred to work on a daily basis and conduct meetings, and so on.

To start with, we made compromises and accepted each other's traits, muddling through, as we did appreciate that we are all different after all. We ran regular retrospectives to improve ourselves as a team and our ways of working. Still, frustrations were bubbling underneath the surface, and there was one thing we all agreed on: we could be doing better than we were! But it was hard for us to express ourselves in ways that others in the team would fully understand.

So we decided to experiment with the map, bridge, and integrate concept with a Design Thinking approach.

Map

Empathize

To begin the process of mapping our differences and empathizing with each other, we had all agreed to take the CultureActive online assessment. It is short and has straightforward questions. It has been taken by over 150,000 people worldwide. This cultural platform, originally launched in 2001, uses the LMR Model, based on the three categories of Linear-active, Multi-active, and Reactive. Many leading cross-culturalists consider this model to be the most practical and intuitive cultural framework. Over twenty years, experts from academia, corporate clients, and intercultural trainers have used CultureActive in a wide variety of pedagogical contexts.

The CultureActive assessment is not a personality test. The result does not place people into a single category or label someone as one personality type. The LMR Model is relative; the results show where an individual sits on the model relative to how strongly they display behaviors associated with the three categories of Linear-active, Multi-active, and Reactive that Lewis defines. It is highly unlikely that anyone fits purely into only one of the categories. The assessment questions are purely based on behavior and values. There are no abstract questions with complex algorithms behind the scenes subjectively judging where you belong.

Adopting Agile Across Borders 373

Aside from giving us great insights and discussion points, we had many other reasons why we chose to use CultureActive to kick off our journey, such as:

- The LMR model is very pragmatic and over time it has gone way beyond the original focus on national culture. The LMR methodology is now widely used in all forms of professional development, including coaching, communication skills, team-building exercises, and more, which suited us perfectly within the context of our team.

- The great analysis tools such as charts and graph results that we could use as part of our discussions and debrief from the self-assessments we took. The platform also incorporates a 360° feedback system.

- As we as a team work virtually, it was important for us to use a platform that fits well within the virtual environment and still gave us the high level of engagement, interaction, and connection that we would have if we would have been in a physical environment.

With the help of the CultureActive assessment we identified our individual behaviors and then this was plotted on a visualization that gave an overview of the whole team. The results are shown in Figure 19-6. This allowed us to get some good initial insights, discuss our common behaviors and values, and our differences in behaviors and values.

A few things to note:

- The CultureActive assessment is not a silver bullet, it is just a starting point to raise awareness, initiate discussion, deepen understanding, and create more transparency.

- It needs to be facilitated carefully in a safe space.

- Participants should avoid judging findings from the assessments as "good" or "bad." There is no notion of a good or bad result in this assessment.

Chapter 19 | Unite and Move Forward

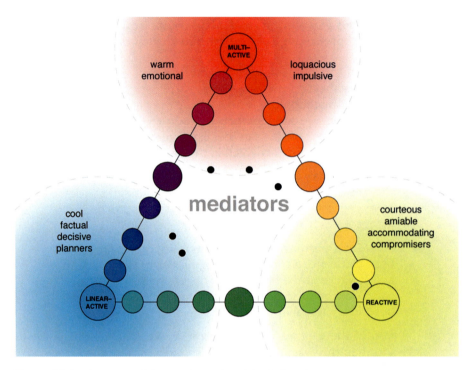

Figure 19-6. Overview of the team's results of the CultureActive assessment

Included in the assessment was an overview of the team in areas such as our approach to problem solving, risks, how each of us expresses disagreement, plan and approach our daily work, sees making mistakes, at what costs each of us want to achieve things and more, as shown in Figure 19-7.

Adopting Agile Across Borders

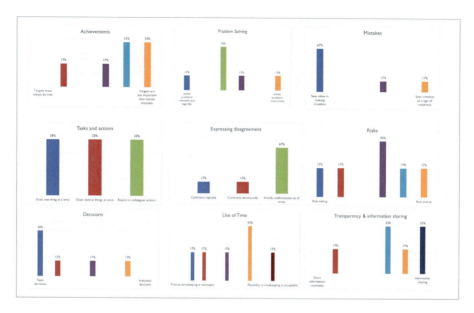

Figure 19-7. A few examples of the team's results of the CultureActive assessment

It is not enough to be aware of each other's behaviors, we need to find a way to put ourselves into other people's shoes. We needed to build empathy.

A common way to build empathy in Design Thinking is by building an Empathy Map.[6] Another great alternative to Empathy Maps that we used in our context is to build a Personal Map.[7] A Personal Map is a Management 3.0 technique to get to know and understand our colleagues better. You can see it as a mental map of a person. And by building a Personal Map of our colleagues, capturing what we know about them, we can make an effort to better understand each person. Thanks to all the insights we had gathered from our research and discussions we could expand the Personal Maps we built for each other with the cultural aspects we identified earlier. Figure 19-8 shows an example of a Personal Map for one of our team members.

---

[6]*Empathy Map.* GameStorming. https://gamestorming.com/empathy-mapping/
[7]*Personal Maps.* Management 3.0. https://management30.com/practice/personal-maps/

Chapter 19 | Unite and Move Forward

Figure 19-8. An example of a Personal Map

Defining the Problem

Using all the insights, our next objective was to analyze our cultural similarities and differences that were having the most impact, positive or negative, on how we were working. We could then see what stood in the way of us leveraging our different perspectives to achieve greater creativity and innovation.

Based on this we created Problem Statements that we wanted to explore further. We phrased these as "How Might We" questions.

One problem area we had was with idea generation. Analyzing the problem we seemed to be:

- Reluctantly compromising
- Generating too many ideas, with potentially good ideas getting lost in all the noise
- Having dominant personalities whose ideas would usually win

We rephrased this problem as the following How Might We question:

"How Might We surface and actively discuss a range of ideas from different perspectives?"

Adopting Agile Across Borders

How Might We is a great technique for ideation or brainstorming sessions. By rephrasing problems into How Might We questions, we open up a safe space for new ideas. We admit that we do not know the answer yet (How). It enables us to come up with more than one solution (Might) and it encourages a collaborative approach to solve the problem (We).

Bridge

Ideate

To brainstorm on potential solutions that would be an answer to our How Might We questions we used three techniques:

1. Worst possible idea

   In this activity, individuals purposely come up with the worst possible solutions to our How Might We question. The worse the better! This is a great way to get everyone relaxed, boost confidence, and unlock people's creativity. We all worry if our ideas are not seen as good and of losing face, of being embarrassed that our ideas might make us look silly. These feelings hold us back from putting forward ideas that might actually be great. By purposely getting everyone to come up with their worst possible ideas, we can break the ice, get people to relax and make everyone feel that their actual ideas may not actually be that bad. It gets the creative juices going, and discussions about why the ideas are actually so bad might even unlock an insight that leads to some good ideas. The Worst Possible Ideas that we generated for our How Might We question is shown in Figure 19-9.

Chapter 19 | Unite and Move Forward

Worst possible ideas!

Figure 19-9. Our Worst Possible Ideas for our question, "How Might We surface and actively discuss a range of ideas from different perspectives?"

With diverse cross-cultural teams, there is an extra dimension to this activity. What can be seen as a bad idea in one culture could actually be perceived as a good idea in another. In a previous role based in the United Kingdom, I remember being horrified when my American colleague suggested high-fives and a group hug at the end of the Sprint Review to celebrate the end of the Sprint. Having adopted British reserve from my time living in the country for 15 years, the idea made me deeply uncomfortable. For me it was the worst possible idea! For him, he thought it was a great way of motivating the team and recognizing the team's efforts. I think the rest of the team thought the same as me. The idea didn't catch on.

2. Crazy Eights

Loosened up and having discussed these "anti-solutions," we moved onto ideation for real. We used the Crazy Eights technique. This involved everyone individually sketching ideas to solve our How Might We questions. What is crazy about Crazy Eights is not the ideas this time, but instead it is the strict time in which participants have to do it in. The idea is that each person comes up with eight ideas in eight minutes. Yep, an idea a minute. This can allow creativity to emerge that might not otherwise come out without

Adopting Agile Across Borders | 379

such a constraint. And coming up with eight ideas in such a short space of time means participants think about alternatives and do not get stuck on one approach.

3. Solution Sketch

    Here each person takes what they consider to be their best idea and sketch it out again, adding more detail and refining the idea. One way to develop the idea is as a storyboard to fully tell the story of the How Might We.

    We dot voted on which Solution Sketches we wanted to take forward.

    To properly ground our ideas, our next task was to create our hypothesis statements.

    One of our hypothesis statements was:

    "We believe that by using diverging and converging techniques with the whole team, everyone's perspectives will be heard equally resulting in an increase of ideas and possible experiments."

Integrate

Prototyping and Validating

Using our hypotheses statements, we began to design our first experiments that would help us to better integrate. What emerged was the following:

- Using diverging and converging techniques in backlog refinement

- Creation of transparent profiles of each team member

- Making the Empathy Maps transparent at all times

- Building our first Team Charter with shared values and behaviors

In our retrospectives we inspected the results of our experiments. An important aspect of this inspection was looking at the data and results. It is easy to fall into the trap of only focusing on our emotional experiences and asking questions like "Did people feel like they were listened to more?", "Did

Chapter 19 | Unite and Move Forward

people feel that there was a more even contribution of ideas?" We started by reminding ourselves of our problem statement, How Might We question, and hypothesis, and asked ourselves a mixture of qualitative and quantitative questions such as:

- How many ideas did we generate?

- How many ideas did we reject?

- How many ideas did we decide to take forward?

- What happened to ideas that arose outside of the workshops?

- How long did it take for an item to go from idea until we committed to working on it?

- How long was spent in workshops and backlog refinement compared to previously?

- How often did people refer to the team member profiles?

- How often did people refer to the team member empathy maps?

- What examples do we have of people referring to a team member profile that resulted in better collaboration than what might have happened without it?

- What new knowledge about ourselves have we attained since the last Sprint?

This is by no means a perfect list, but it was a start.

We decided to keep the team member profiles and we updated them regularly. We did feel that they helped us to better empathize with each other and helped us on our journey as a team. The divergent and convergent approach to problem-solving techniques worked really well for us, and everyone said that they felt more involved in the process.

I do believe that the Design Thinking approach to map, bridge, and integrate our cultural diversity allowed us to take fuller advantage of the range of knowledge, perspectives, and skills in our team. Just like with everything in Agile teams, our journey to improvement never stops, and that includes working toward higher diversity and inclusion. Thought this was just a starting point, it has led to the development of some very exciting initiatives!

—Glaudia Califano

Conflict within teams is almost inevitable, but the risk of misunderstandings increases with greater diversity where people have not developed empathy for one another culturally. Lyssa Adkins for one has laid out some strategies for conflict management,[8] but she and others acknowledge that there is no silver bullet when it comes to resolving conflict. In fact, it is acknowledged that conflict can actually help a team. When facilitated and managed well, conflict can lead to a team exploring their problems more deeply, leading to a greater mutual understanding within the team and a higher degree of innovation. The important thing is to keep the objectives of the team at the forefront of the team's focus and to recognize and stop damaging personal conflict when it happens. Within any team or organization, there will always be some negative interactions, but the key to a healthy team is in having a greater ratio of positive interactions to negative ones.

Though we can achieve a lot in achieving diversity and inclusion within our teams, we will need support from other parts of the organization. The same principles of mapping, bridging, and integrating can be applied at an organization level as well.

Agile As a Culture Shift

The aim of our journey and of this book was to share stories of Agile adoption from around the world, to give a glimpse into what may be behind people's behaviors in different parts of the world, and to inspire the community to think about the impact that cultural factors have on Agile adoption. We hope that we have done that.

Adopting Agile methods requires a profound change of mindset for most teams and organizations that have come from a traditional "waterfall" background. Moving from these traditional ways of working to Agile is a culture shift in itself. Any culture shift is disruptive and hard for people, no matter the perceived simplicity of the implementation of the actual practices involved. This is the case whatever the national culture. The approach to contracts and procurement, for example, are areas that we found many are struggling with, though ways of doing so that embraces an Agile mindset are emerging.

---

[8]Adkins, L. (2010). *Coaching Agile Teams: A Companion for ScrumMasters, Agile Coaches, and Project Managers in Transition.* Addison-Wesley Professional. ISBN-13: 978-0-321-63770-3

Chapter 19 | Unite and Move Forward

The Emergence of Agile Contracts[9]

When it comes to supplier-client relationships, many common complaints like the adding or changing of scope, the availability of business people, or the use of the word "estimate" to somehow implicitly mean "promise" comes back to the conditions created at the very start of the relationship. How contracts are agreed can have consequences for the whole of an engagement.

During our travels, we spoke to many organizations and Agile practitioners on the subject of contracts. It turned out to be an area that many people were looking for explicit guidance on. We were often asked to give our own advice. With no silver bullet to hand, I instead want to share some of the ways that Agile thinkers and organizations that we met are approaching the subject of "Agile contracts."

By far, the most common starting point that we saw was the "Time and Materials" approach. Put simply, the supplier provides a fixed number of people for an agreed length of time. It is then up to the client what these people work on. This is a little closer to Agile thinking than traditional contracts where, rightly or wrongly "The Iron Triangle"[10] has been interpreted to fix scope, time, and budget. Though Time and Materials contracts do not require full requirements up front, the temptation can be to put more people on the project when it falls behind, despite how counterproductive this can be as summarized by Brook's law: "adding manpower to a late software project makes it later."[11]

From the supplier's side, Time and Materials manages the risk of the client changing directions and protecting themselves from the associated additional costs that change would incur. This does mean that the risk, control, and management responsibility is all placed on the client, while the supplier is secure in the knowledge that they will always get paid, whatever the outcome. This balance has never sat well with me; does it really embody the value of *customer collaboration over contract negotiation*? There must be another way.

We spoke to Martin Kearns, Scrum Alliance CST and one of the first Certified Coaches in the world. Martin is based in Australia where he gave a talk on "Contracts to Enable Agile Behavior" at the 1st Conference in 2016.[12] Martin

---

[9]Contribution based on the blogpost at www.redtangerine.org/2018/12/11/agile-contracts/

[10]Westland, J. (2018). *The Triple Constraint in Project Management: Time Scope & Cost*. Project Manager. www.projectmanager.com/blog/triple-constraint-project-management-time-scope-cost

[11]Brooks, F. (1975). *The mythical man-month and other essays on software engineering*. Addison-Wesley. ISBN-13: 978-0201006506

[12]Kearns, M. (2016). *Agile Contracts*. Slideshare. www.slideshare.net/MartinKearns2/1st-conf-agile-contracts

Adopting Agile Across Borders

said that Time and Materials is a good starting point. It gets agreement in place to run a few iterations, build trust, understand delivery capability, risks, and product viability. For him the "principles" – the desired outcomes – emerge and are not something that can be truly discovered at the start. Discovery workshops are great; however, the primary objective is to see behaviors, mindset, and to understand risks with project scope emerging later. Chief among the concerns is understanding the levels of client engagement and availability.

Those early iterations are run on the basis of a cap on Time and Materials and a realistic outcome. Through negotiation and discovery, what Martin terms "work principles" are evolved. This is a focus on the main variables of complexity and risk, with an escalation process driven by clearly visible metrics. An example of a work principle would be expectations around participation in meetings, with metrics of percentage of people attending that were supposed to, and percentage of those that remained for the entire meeting.

Subjects such as governance and constraints are defined, but at a high, overarching level. Progress is based on building a partnership, and Martin pushes the concept of "acts of reciprocity" where success is shared, but so too are set-backs. Clauses may be added which agree to both sides taking a share of the profits generated from the product. If deliveries are faster than expected, the savings are shared between supplier and client. If there is the need for a change in direction, suppliers are not expected to absorb such costs, but are expected to adapt to a change of plan, while the client accepts later delivery or dropped scope elsewhere.

I also spoke to Tushar Somaiya, an experienced Agile Coach currently based in Singapore with PALO IT. He has spoken and written[13] extensively on the subject of Agile contracts, and he talked me through some of the approaches that he has used.

Tushar's starting position is what he terms "The Master Contract Agreement." Here, only high-level terms are considered, such as the people that will be involved. There is no mention of scope nor timelines. Tied to this are one or more "Individual Statement of Objective"s (StO) written as user stories to be clear on what it is that the client wants to achieve. Implementation is not discussed at this stage. Instead, three months of funding, paid for in advance by the client, is started for a Proof of Concept based on breaking down the first StOs. At the end of this period, the client can decide to continue with the development, stop, or find another supplier – it is written into the Master Contract Agreement that the client owns all Intellectual Property rights allowing them to easily go elsewhere.

---

[13]Somaiya, T. (2012). *Contracts In Agile.* https://tusharsomaiya.com/2012/01/24/contracts-in-agile/

Chapter 19 | Unite and Move Forward

Should the client wish to continue, then a further list of epics are produced, and the team gives a first high-level estimate expressed as a range, for example, 8–10 months. This is little more than a guess, but it is a point to start from. The client and the team work together to divide the epics into those that are "must have" and "good to have," breaking them down into smaller stories as understanding grows or new ideas come up. A third classification of "cannot be delivered" serves to make visible scope that is completely unrealistic to achieve. The developing backlog is organized into a User Story Map.[14] User journeys based on personas[15] are defined to help define horizontal slices of functionality on the roadmap.

Both parties commit to a period, say six months, with a termination clause, for example, either side can terminate giving one-month notice. Tushar walked me through an example of how payments could be agreed. Every month the client pays a flat rate that is a majority of the ongoing client's running costs, irrespective of what is delivered. The content of each delivery is reviewed and after, say, three months, the client pays the outstanding running costs plus a weighted percentage depending on features that are delivered in the "must have" or "good to have" categories, for example, 20% and 10%, respectively. This method focuses suppliers on the most valuable features, and demands more money from the client for doing so. This encourages the client to think hard about pushing an item into the "must have" category. Without this clause, clients tend to label more items as "must have" and pressurize suppliers to deliver them.

Agile relationships should be a partnership, and welcome changing requirements for the client's competitiveness in the market. Tushar said that the contract should always include a clause for the allowance of supplier review and re-estimation at regular points without punishment, while clients should be allowed to change priorities or requirements.

Things get more complicated when multiple suppliers are involved. Tushar told me about some of the clauses that would be written into the Master Agreement to deal with this. All suppliers must keep the main code branch green and that it is their responsibility to ensure all test suites continue to pass after they have merged their own changes into the shared code base. However, the client has overall responsibility for coordinating and ensuring the right supplier takes responsibility for breakages – suppliers should not lose time or money chasing up issues caused by others. Key to success is identifying integration points and resolving dependencies as early as possible.

---

[14]Patton, J. *The New User Story Backlog is a Map.* jpattonassociates. www.jpattonassociates. com/the-new-backlog/

[15]Pichler, R. (2013). *10 Tips for Creating Agile Personas.* romanpichler. www.romanpichler. com/blog/10-tips-agile-personas/

Another example of handling contracts in Agile environments comes from Continuum, a software development company that we visited in Chile. Formal signed contracts are unavoidable with very large clients, including the state where their use is part of the client's pre-defined processes. For smaller clients, especially those that are located in the same region and thus share similar values, the contract is made up of a non-disclosure agreement and the work proposal. Considering a trait of the culture in this part of the world is long-term relationship building over short-term gain, Continuum's approach to contracts suggests they place more value in their reputation and building trust with their clients over agreeing formal terms in a traditional contract.

Written into the work proposal is the acknowledgement that the scope of the project is variable, regardless of the number of proposed Sprints, and the final implementation will depend on the prioritization made during the engagement. The document makes it clear in no uncertain terms that an Agile method is used and that there is an expectation that a client representative will be available for the teams. For example, a dedication to be available for 50% of the time during the initial stages of ideation and prioritization, with a significant amount of that time spent with Continuum's UX experts for initial designs. They aim to start development as soon as possible, with first Sprints happening in parallel to these workshops. Ongoing client availability is written into the agreement, for example, for one day equivalent per week.

The client's Product Owner gets flexibility in changing scope of work that has not started, while the team has flexibility in refining their estimates as they learn. The working agreement does not fix scope, only the agreed initial number of Sprints. Instead of defining scope, a clear objective is defined as part of the working agreement that is clear to all.

These are just some of the perspectives on the issue of Agile contracts that have emerged separately in different parts of the world. While there are differences in terminology and detail, it is interesting to note the commonalities in the approaches: explicit agreement of client involvement, accepting variability of scope, and building trust the goal ahead of agreeing formal contract wording. These principles certainly fit well with the value of *customer collaboration over contract negotiation*.

—David Spinks

The Lean-Agile Procurement Process[16]

"In the past we bought beautiful solutions... And then we needed to work out what to use them for."

---

[16]Contribution based on the blogpost at www.redtangerine.org/2019/04/02/lean-agile-procurement/

Chapter 19 | Unite and Move Forward

This line, or a similar variation, is one that many of us have heard uttered from the mouths of CEOs and CTOs in relation to procurement. Procurement has become an area which has become a specialization of its own, with individuals and sometimes whole departments dedicated to it. This is a reflection on a market that has dramatically changed with increasing complexity. There are ever-greater demands and time pressures, while there are more unexpected dependencies and uncertainties to deal with. This can translate into long delays and indecision, affecting a whole organization's agility.

I mused this over on a conference call with Mirko Kleiner. Among many other initiatives that include international speaking, Agile Enterprise Coaching and certified Scrum@Scale training, Mirko is one of, if not THE thought leader in Lean-Agile Procurement. Mirko began his career as a developer, and he says that coming across different cultures such as people from Russia and India in the distributed teams that he worked in was the best thing that could have happened to him. His cross-cultural interest and appreciation of how people in different parts of the world can learn from each other echoes our own.

Mirko found himself moving into Agile coaching and management positions and this included him getting involved in the pre-sales processes at the software engineering company that he was at. He was in uncomfortable and painful situations that were contradictory to the Agile thinking that was natural to him. The sales process involved agreeing scope, cost, and timelines up front. Decision making required detailed planning and took months to complete. The Development Teams were frustrated by having to give estimates based on what would turn out to be incomplete information to win the sale – lots of effort for no return. When sales were won, specifications would later be produced with escalating complexity and yet the team were still held to their original estimates. An Agile approach to contracts and a mindset of "just start" did not seem to be an option when working with the sorts of big corporations that Mirko was involved with at the time.

As an Agile Coach, Mirko was asked to help in procurement. He saw similar issues there. He looked at what was causing the most pain, and asked himself what was the minimum that needed to be done to make things better.

This led Mirko to come up with a thought experiment. "What if we have just 1 day to decide on a complex sourcing case?" he said. "Out of this powerful question 1 developed the Lean Procurement Canvas and Lean-Agile Procurement, a similar disruption for procurement as the Business Model Canvas and Lean Startup used to be for Business Development." The Lean Procurement Canvas is shown in Figure 19-10.

Adopting Agile Across Borders

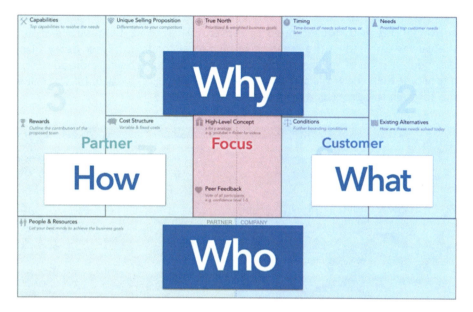

Figure 19-10. The Lean Procurement Canvas[17]

Mirko talked me through the main sections of the Lean Procurement Canvas. Defining the "why" is a starting point, the "True North" section used to define a prioritized list of business goals and desired outcomes that an initiative is aiming to achieve. The "what" section gets people thinking about the customer perspective, defining real customers through personas – these are real end customers, not internal stakeholders. It is important to define customer needs, required timings, constraints, and what are the existing or future alternatives available for them to solve their problem.

Next is the "how," a high-level definition of the required services that are needed. This is not about defining solutions. Included in this discussion are all options, including other suppliers and consequences if nothing is done. Costs and how rewards are distributed are also included. The "Unique Selling Proposition" section includes discussions on future propositions, including consideration for support and warranty. Traditionally, some vendors may offer SLA packages such as "Platinum Service," or "Gold Service," without it really being clear on what these actually mean. A discussion around the Lean Procurement Canvas allows the client to define what they want and then negotiate with vendors on a price to provide a service to meet these desires.

Finally, the "who" is discussed. How vendor and client need to work together to achieve success.

---

[17]The Lean Procurement Canvas. www.lean-agile-procurement.com/

Chapter 19 | Unite and Move Forward

Mirko told me that the Lean Procurement Canvas is just a tool to focus conversations. It is not intended to replace other tools. Discussions around the canvas can lead to the creation of high-level roadmaps, User Story Maps, the identification of value streams, key milestones, and their conditions. More important than the tools are the conversations that take place. Mirko walked me through the process that is outlined in Figure 19-11.

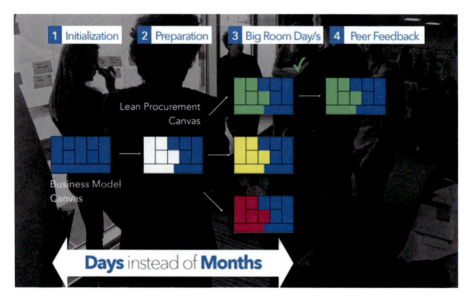

Figure 19-11. The Lean-Agile Procurement approach[18]

Initialization

The first step is to identify all of the people on the customer side that need to be involved with the vendor. The team must be empowered to make the procurement decisions while being given clearly defined boundaries; however, it is not just about identifying the decision-makers. People such as those that will need to work in partnership with the vendor and those that will be impacted should be included.

---

[18]*The Lean-Agile Procurement approach*. lean-agile-procurement.com. www.lean-agile-procurement.com/lean-agile-procurement-approach

Preparation

Based on the defined business goals, a first pass of filling in the Lean Procurement Canvas is done by this group in collaboration, with any supplementary material also being prepared. Then invitations are sent to potential vendor partners to take part in the "Big Room Day." The vendors are not given up-front information at this stage, instead they are asked to bring with them all of the people needed to deliver and their key decision-makers. These people are expected to have the right expertise and ready to answer any questions on the day.

Big Room Day(s)

All potential partners are either gathered together, or attend one-by-one. Sessions may run in parallel at the same time when multiple vendors attend a Big Room Day. Client and vendor co-develop the Lean Procurement Canvas and any appropriate additions such as User Story Maps and proof of concepts.

The Big Room day should include discussions such as agreeing responsibilities, warranty, intellectual property rights, etc. It allows for fast reactions. For example, in one session that Mirko was facilitating, a tricky issue regarding software licensing came up. Rather than compete with each other, the vendors in attendance were asked to come together to come up with a proposal for a way ahead.

Building relationships between client and vendor is as important as the content being produced. Both sides should get a feel for what it would be like working with each other. They need to build a mutual understanding, a trust in the other's competency, and a level of comfort working with one another.

Peer Feedback

The result of the Big Room Day should be a procurement decision and an Agile contract. This a working agreement between the client and the selected vendor, not a commitment to fixed scope and timescales. The process is focused on "Product" thinking, not "Project" thinking, with details of features of the product emerging through feedback cycles. The Lean Procurement Canvas is an evolving artifact like definitions of "Done" and Product Backlogs; they will change as more is learned. It becomes the key instrument for Agile partnership management.

In Mirko's experience, Big Room Days typically take two days, though he has experience of completing them in as little as five hours. Of great value, working software in the form of the proof of concept is often already available for review by the end. As the product development team are all together, they can in theory take the PoC and continue work on the product straight from the Big Room Day.

Chapter 19 | Unite and Move Forward

If there is indecision in which vendor is the best fit, and all are in agreement, there is nothing to stop work starting with more than one partner and a final decision made later – this is often cheaper and less disruptive than switching partners down the track. Vendors would be paid for their time all the way back to participation in the Big Room Day. It is a win-win situation for all; vendors get income for their efforts and are not left waiting for long periods for customer decisions on whether to engage with them.

Lean-Agile Procurement is a simple process but it is not easy. Mirko's main key to success is having the right people in the Big Room Day. This may include a broad range of people from customer representatives, operations, legal, governance, security, subject matter experts, and developers. It requires strong facilitation skills and people trained in running these sessions. Corporate politics can impede progress, in Mirko's experience one of the biggest barriers is for people to leave their silos and give up their traditional bases of power. He encourages use of tools such as Delegation Poker and Delegation Board[19] from Management 3.0 to help with this mind-shift. Mirko told me the story of a particular board member who wanted to retain the responsibility for all major decisions, yet refused to take the Product Owner role as he "wouldn't have enough time." Such scenarios are nothing new to many of us involved in Agile adoptions and limit the chances of success. Using the Lean-Agile Procurement approach is no different; without the right buy-in and commitment, it won't work.

People's availability is another common issue. The working agreements mentioned earlier would include clauses for availability and dedication to the initiative. Ideally, this should be around 80% availability, but as Mirko told me, a minimum of 40% is enough to at least get started. Anything less does not work.

Mirko showed me a diagram, shown in Figure 19-12, that represented a real-world implementation using Lean-Agile Procurement. Here, the typical lead time for procurement was six months; with Lean-Agile Procurement, this was reduced to five weeks.

---

[19]Delegation Poker and Delegation Board https://management30.com/practice/delegation-poker/

Adopting Agile Across Borders   391

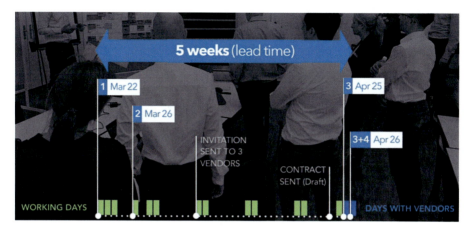

Figure 19-12. An example of improved lead time in the procurement process using a Lean-Agile Procurement approach

The green bars represent the active working days on the procurement. Imagine the reduction in lead time should people be fully dedicated! Mirko and I discussed how such analysis can spark a conversation on wholesale agility. Instead of having a conversation about implementing the mechanics of Scrum, we can talk about focus, limiting work in progress, increasing flow efficiency, and reducing wait times and overall lead times. In other words, talking about "being Agile" rather than "doing Agile." And this is in the context of spawning agility across the whole business ecosystem, not just at a team or organization level, but across the whole supply chain. These ideas are illustrated in Figure 19-13.

Chapter 19 | Unite and Move Forward

Figure 19-13. Spawning agility across the whole business ecosystem[20]

Mirko has seen Lean-Agile Procurement used to assess existing relationships as well as for procurement of new partnerships. He has seen its use make visible issues that may well have stayed hidden, for example continued use of suppliers that was completely unnecessary as services existed in-house. In partnership with CKW Group, Mirko's company Flowdays won the award for Best Procurement Consultancy project at the 2018 CIPS Supply Management Awards.[21] Phil Thomas, Head of Global Sourcing at Barclays is quoted as saying about Lean-Agile Procurement, "This is a game changer." Lean-Agile Procurement is already making waves beyond the Agile community.

But this is just the beginning. Mirko developed the Lean-Agile procurement process and the Lean Procurement Canvas out of a single thought experiment. Taking a Lean Startup approach, he has iteratively built it up using Build-Measure-Learn feedback cycles. It continues to evolve and has stayed open source and freely available for anybody to use.

---

[20] Kleiner, M. (2017). *One size doesn't fit it all – build your own maturity model for business agility.* flowdays.net. https://flowdays.net/en/blog-en/2017/6/11/one-size-doesnt-fit-it-all-build-your-own-maturity-model-for-business-agility

[21] Kleiner, M. (2018). *CKW & Flowdays win supply Management Award 2018 Europe.* lean-agile-procurement.com. www.lean-agile-procurement.com/blog-1/awards-2018

Adopting Agile Across Borders

Further into the future, Mirko envisages a world of organizations of "Teams-of-Teams" where companies are made up of fully empowered teams instead of functional departments. These teams are able to make all of their own decisions including procurement, and make them fast. It is an exciting glimpse into a possible future that Lean-Agile Procurement and other Agile methods can bring us.

—David Spinks

From our journey, our observations and the experiences that the global Agile community shared with us, we have seen that national cultural behaviors do affect workplace behaviors. These varying behaviors and people's innate values can be complementary, or a barrier to Agile adoption. However, we did not encounter issues anywhere that were not insurmountable given the right commitment, courage, focus, openness, and respect. And of course patience.

The adoption of Agile itself, when done well, will surface impediments, whether the root cause of these impediments are due to cultural behaviors, corporate culture, or organizational processes. But this is what Agile is really about: transparency, inspection, adaptation, and continuous improvement.

There are many stories of impediments being raised, tackled, and removed. New ideas being experimented with. New ways of working with one another that are emerging. All this is happening right now in Agile teams all around the world. Our journey and this book can barely scratch the surface of what is going on in the Agile movement today, but we are fortunate to have seen a glimpse of it in many places. The experiences of our journey and the stories in this book from some of those that we met have truly inspired us. They have left us with no doubt; Agile can work in any culture.

Index

A

Agile flywheel effect, 103, 104

Agile software development
    adoption, 19
    cultural behaviors/agile value, 18
    culture, 8–10
    experiences, 6–8
    Hofstede model, 12, 14
    Lewis model, 14–17
    practitioners, 20, 21
    principles, 4, 5
    stereotyping, 10, 11

Anglo-Persian Oil Company (APOC), 218

Argentina
    communication, 38
    conflict and uncertainty, 27
    culture, 30, 31
    environments, 35, 39
    foreign investment, 26
    history, 26
    leaders, 32
    local Agile community, 28
    people, 34
    10Pines, 33, 34
    population, 25
    practitioners, 29
    scale, 27
    self-organization, 37
    software industry, 29
    Spanish, 26
    vision, 36

Asia Pacific College (APC), 173

Astah community, 164

B

Bank Central Asia (BCA), 135

Black Economic Empowerment
    (BEE), 307

British coded-speech, 286

British Petroleum (BP), 218

British Raj, 106

Broad Based Black Economic
    Empowerment (BBBE), 307

C

Capitalism and Frederick Taylor's scientific
    management theory, 335

Chile
    accountant, 45–49
    agile community events, 43, 55
    Agile Consultant, 45
    communication style, 44
    Continuum's approach, 44
    definition, 41
    education system, 44
    history, 41
    retrospectives, 50–54
    trade, 42

© Glaudia Califano, David Spinks 2021
G. Califano and D. Spinks, *Adopting Agile Across Borders*,
https://doi.org/10.1007/978-1-4842-6948-0

Index

Colombia
  Agile inception, 64
  education sector, 58, 59
  Geniio, generating time/timely
       information, 69–71
  hardware retailer, 60–62
  history, 57, 58
  improved quality, internal
       client, 67
  increased collaboration/shared
       responsibility, 66, 67
  organizational structures, 60
  process improvements, 66
  reduced delivery times, contract
       completion, 67, 68
  scaling agile, EPM, 72, 74–77
  story map, 65
  supply chain, goods/services, 62, 63
Communication style, 44, 49, 119, 138, 178,
       229, 270, 301
Conformity, 123, 138, 148
Conscious Leaders, 204, 206
Cross-cultural communication, 365, 366
Cultural models, 355
CultureActive assessment, 372
Culture shift, Agile adoption
  emergency contracts, 382–385
  methods, 381

D

Design thinking process, 371
"Dirty War", 27
Diversity
  American organizations, 364
  broader spectrum, 368
  communication pattern, 365
  communication styles, 364
  demographics, 364
  design
       bridge, 377–379
       integrate, 379–381
       map, 369–373, 375, 376
  English communication
       pattern, 366, 367
  teams, 369
  visualizations, 365

E

East India Company (EIC), 105
**Economic Community of West African
       States (ECOWAS),** 322
Emerson's efficiency system, 341
Employee of the Month (EOM), 342

F

Filipinos, 177
Fun/Done/Learn retrospective (FDL), 159

G

Germany
  Agile managers
       contexts, 235, 236
       people, 236–238
       team members, 234, 235
  building consensus, 229
  cross cultural integration
       challenges, 242
       cooking, 244
       Portuguese, 245–247
       prerequisites, 244
       problems, 245
       workshop, 243
  definition, 225
  history, 225, 226
  knowledge and information, 229
  methods, 225
  Ordnung, 229
  organizations and culture, 228
  safe environment, 241
  Scrum master, building momentum,
       238–240
  streamlining, 230–233
  technology center, 227

H

Hofstede model, 12, 14, 18

I

India, 99
  Agile principles, 102
  culture, 109, 110
       hierarchical awareness, 110, 111

Index 397

individual recognition *vs.* team
recognition, 111, 112
issues, 114
relationships, 112
trust, 113, 114
geographical size, 109
history, 99
insights, 107
kingdoms, 100
trust
Agile mindset, 116
Agile Team, 115
Agile workshops, 117
feedback, 118
Indian National Congress (INC), 106
Indonesia, 121
Agile, 131, 132, 134
BCA, 135
book report, 124
communities/coaching, 132, 133
conformity, 123
cross-cultural awareness, 134
Dutch Guy building, 129–131
education system, 125
environment, 126, 127
financial service institute, 125
history, 121–123
mini-companies, 137
national motto, 137
personal retrospective, 126
punctuality, 123
Scrum training, 136
software industry, 127
spark self-learning, 126
suburban scene, 128
younger generations, 124
Iraq Petroleum Company (IPC), 218

J

Japan, 141
activities, 157
attitudes, 151
building community, 163, 164, 166
ceremonial protocol, 162
cross-cultural awareness, 163
culture, 157
FDL, 159, 161
history, 141–143

KDDI, 152–155
Mob Programming, 146–150
QA, 151
Scrum maturity, 159
Toyota Takaoka plant tour, 143–145
work setting, 158

K

Kanban System Design (KSD), 328

L

Lean-agile procurement process
Big Room Day, 389
coaching and management positions, 386
initialization, 388
Lean Procurement Canvas, 388
line, or a similar variation, 386
peer feedback, 389, 390, 392, 393
preparation, 389
Lewis model, 14, 18, 355

M

Masters in Information Technology (MIT), 174
Maurya Empire, 100
Mental model, 347, 350
Microsoft Azure Platform, 339
Migrant labor system, 315
Mini-companies, 137
Mob Programming, 146, 233
Mughal Empire, 105

N

Netherlands
Agile, 263
cRM system, 260
developer productivity, 259
emergency leaders, 252–257
experimentation, 265
history, 249–251
iconography, 249
management, 259, 260
Medan traffic, 263, 264
refinement session, 264
Scrum, 261, 262
Nexus framework, 74, 76

Index

O

Oral agreements, 120

P, Q

Pair-programming, 146

People's Action Party (PAP), 187

Philippines, 169
- Agile Teams, 180
- APC, 173, 175, 177
- communication style, 178, 179
- company structures, 179
- cultural behaviors, 181
- history, 170–172
- IT, 173

Poland
- Agile teams, 269
- art classes, 280, 281
- communication styles, 270
- gamification, 279
- history, 267–269
- icebreakers, 279
- one-way street, transparency, 271–276
- Polish culture, 270
- technology companies, 271
- West of East, 278

Professional Scrum Master I (PSM I), 136

R

Return on Investment (ROI), 193, 208, 349

S

Scrum Masters, 52, 62, 109, 118, 239, 258, 279, 311, 313

Sikhism, 100

Singapore
- Agile, 193, 194, 201
- Agile adoption, 190
- Agile coach, 212
- B2B company, 190
- bureaucratic system, 192
- communication, 193
- communism, 188, 189
- Conscious Leadership
  - awareness, 208
  - relationships, 207
  - self, 206
  - world view, 207
- consciousness, 198, 199, 203
- cultural component, 209
- education systems, 215
- hierarchy, 192
- history, 183, 184
- IT industry, 188
- KPI, 214
- leaders, 202, 203
- meritocratic approach, 185
- midlife crisis, 197
- organizational structures, 191
- PALO IT, 194–196
- PAP, 187
- salary transparency, 191
- SDG, 205, 206
- training, 192
- vision, 185

South Africa
- Afrikaners, 310
- Agile, 311, 312
- BEE, 308
- Black African majority, 310
- black females, 309
- Bback majority, 311
- cultural differences, 313, 314
- cultural traits, Agile adoption, 315–317
- GDP, 309
- history, 305–307
- IT industry, 308

Spanish colonization, 169

Sprint Planning, 64, 153, 186, 239, 260

Stacey Model, 339, 340

Statement of Objective (StO), 383

Sustainable Development (SDGs), 204

T

Taylorism
- Agile, 357
- automations, 336
- climate change, 357
- cultures, 358
- departments/hierarchies, 337–339
- global companies, 356
- industrial revolution, 336, 339
- learning culture, humans

Agile adoption, 354, 355
community, connection/passion, 353
cultural models, 356
David, inspiration, 344, 345
inspiration, 350
leadership, 352
learning iceberg, 346
mental models, 347, 348
organization, 352
reflections/awareness, 350
software, 353
team, 351, 352
organizational policies, 343, 344
organizations, 359
remote working, 360
self-organizing teams, 359
task/bonus system, 341–343
Toyota Production System, 340, 341
traditional management, 336
"Trucial States", 218
working practices, 337

U

United Arab Emirates
Agile, 221, 222
Communications technology, 219
effective teams, 220
European colonists, 217
leadership, 219
migration rates, 219
population, 217
Private sector employers, 220
revenues, 218
software engineer, 221

United Kingdom
act in competition, 286
British industry, 285
business, innovate/inspire, 293–299
Busting Silos, 291, 292
communication style, 301
eccentricities, 301
empirical approach, 287
history, 283, 284

negotiations and demands, 286
parliamentary system, 300
user-entered research, Afro Hair
problem, 288–290
Urbanization, 100
Uruguay
agile, 86
business context, 86
colonization, 79
economic instability, 80
history, 79
ownership
Agile community, 95, 96
context, 90
empowering teams, 93
reward system, 91
team together, 94
time for review, 92, 93
transparency, 91
project discovery, 81–86
project roadmap, 87–89
renewable energy, 81
stability and harmony, 80

V

Visual approach, 365, 366

W, X, Y, Z

West Africa
Agile adoption, 324
definitions, 323
history, 319–323
Learntor, 325–329
long-term planning, 330
long-term success, 324
Nigeria, 319
team members, 329
Women's place, 325
Women in Peacebuilding Network"
(WIPNET), 322
Women Peace and Security Network"
(WIPSEN), 322

Printed in the United States
by Baker & Taylor Publisher Services